Studies in Economic Transition

Series Editors
Jens Hölscher
The Business School
Bournemouth University
Bournemouth, Dorset, UK

Horst Tomann
Department of Economic Policy and Economic History
Freie Universitaet (FU) Berlin
Berlin, Germany

This series brings together theoretical and empirical studies on the transformation of economic systems and their economic development. The transition from planned to market economies is one of the main areas of applied theory because in this field the most dramatic examples of change and economic dynamics can be found. It is aimed to contribute to the understanding of specific major economic changes as well as to advance the theory of economic development. The implications of economic policy will be a major point of focus.

More information about this series at
http://www.palgrave.com/gp/series/14147

Ágnes Szunomár
Editor

Emerging-market Multinational Enterprises in East Central Europe

palgrave
macmillan

Editor
Ágnes Szunomár
Institute of World Economics
Centre for Economic and Regional Studies
Budapest, Hungary

Institute of International, Political, and Regional Sciences
Corvinus University of Budapest
Budapest, Hungary

ISSN 2662-6675 ISSN 2662-6683 (electronic)
Studies in Economic Transition
ISBN 978-3-030-55164-3 ISBN 978-3-030-55165-0 (eBook)
https://doi.org/10.1007/978-3-030-55165-0

This Palgrave Macmillan imprint is published by the registered company Springer Nature Switzerland AG.
The registered company address is: Gewerbestrasse 11, 6330 Cham, Switzerland

Preface

The change of East Central European (ECE) countries from centrally planned to market economies resulted in increasing inflows of foreign direct investment (FDI) to these transition countries. During the transition, the region went through radical economic changes, which had been largely induced by foreign capital. Foreign multinationals realized significant investment projects in ECE and established their own production networks. Investors, mainly from core European Union countries, were attracted by macroeconomic factors such as relatively low unit labour costs, market size, openness to trade and proximity. When it comes to institutional factors that influence inward FDI, the prospects of ECE countries' economic integration with the EU have already increased FDI inflows into the region.

Although the majority of investors arrived from Western Europe, the first phase of inward Asian FDI came also right after the transition, as Japanese and Korean companies indicated their willingness of investing in the ECE region already before the fall of the Iron Curtain. The second phase came after the New Millennium, when the Chinese government initiated the going global policy, which was aimed at encouraging domestic companies to become globally competitive, while Indian as well as other MNEs also made their first investment attempts in the ECE region already in the early 2000s.

Today, the rise of emerging-market MNEs is driven by the Asian economy, mainly China and India; however, this process is broader, incorporates a growing number of developing economies and is complemented by the growing share of emerging markets in world exports. In addition, emerging MNEs have become important players in several regions around the globe, ranging from the least developed countries of Africa through the developing markets in Latin America and Asia to the developed countries of the United States or the European Union, including East Central Europe. The ECE region is indeed a possible gateway to Europe for emerging MNEs. At the same time, the ECE region's appetite for investment is still significant, and emerging MNEs are offering an alternative source.

This volume brings together a collection of selected original studies conducted in the framework of the research project "Non-European Emerging-Market Multinational Enterprises in East Central Europe" supported by the National Research, Development and Innovation Office (NKFIH) of Hungary. Topics include the main theories of internationalization and foreign direct investment, the global patterns and recent trends of emerging MNEs as well as home and host country determinants behind the international expansion strategies of emerging companies. Besides its global focus, the volume maps out emerging countries' investment flows and types of involvement, and identifies the motivations of emerging MNEs' transactions in East Central Europe. Chapters present how pull determinants of emerging MNEs' investments differ from that of Western companies in terms of specific institutional and political factors that seem important for some of the emerging—especially Chinese—companies. This hypothesis echoes the call to combine macroeconomic and institutional factors for a better understanding of internationalization of companies.

This volume represents the first-ever attempt to systematically analyse emerging market multinationals' investment into European emerging countries. This type of investments, as we believe, differ from both emerging MNEs' investment into the core European countries and developed MNEs' investment into the emerging regions of Europe. An additional novelty of the research endeavour is that besides macroeconomic and institutional factors it incorporates political factors into the analysis which may also have an important role to play in attracting emerging, especially Chinese, companies to a certain region.

After this brief introduction to our research, the first section of the volume includes two chapters. Szunomár's chapter presents a review of the main scientific literature relating to the traditional and new theories of internationalization and foreign direct investment while Szanyi's chapter analyses the changing trends and patterns of foreign direct investments in East Central Europe. The following chapters—in two separate sections—examine several emerging country case studies by discussing the driving forces behind their international expansion strategies, focusing on these companies' global as well as European investments, with a special focus on the major host country determinants of East Central Europe, using various statistics as well as company interviews.

The second part of the volume focuses on Asian emerging MNEs and their activities in East Central Europe. The chapter by Szunomár examines the rise of Chinese multinationals, the role of the Chinese state in promoting the international expansion of Chinese companies as well as those factors that attracted Chinese MNEs into ECE countries. Gerőcs's study analyses Indian companies' experiences about going international with a particular focus on their investment strategy in ECE, building on macro statistical evidence and on a collection of qualitative data. Völgyi and Peragovics in their chapter offer a wider geographical focus concerning outward FDI of six emerging Asian countries—South Korea, Taiwan, Malaysia, Thailand, Indonesia and Vietnam—and their MNEs' activities in ECE region.

The third—and final—section of this volume deals with non-Asian emerging MNEs and analyses their presence in East Central Europe. Weiner presents the characteristics of Russian multinationals, with a special focus on domestic push and international pull factors that are equally important when examining the motives behind Russian outward FDI. Szigetvári discusses forms of Turkish outward FDI and the motivations of Turkish MNEs in his chapter, including those factors that drive Turkish companies into the ECE region. Ricz widens the geographical focus of this volume to the Latin American continent, by focusing on outward investment activities of the largest Latin American economy, Brazil. Last but not least, Kiss's chapter studies the internationalisation strategies of South African MNEs and the main driving forces from both the home and the ECE host country side.

As mentioned above, in order to gather corresponding data, the authors conducted face-to-face as well as online interviews with representatives of various emerging MNEs in the ECE region. Interviews were conducted anonymously in the form of semi-structured questionnaires. This approach was chosen as the topic of emerging FDI in European peripheries is new and has sparked academic interest only recently. Moreover, the available literature is rather limited and mostly based on secondary sources. In cases where interviews were not applicable, the authors often relied on other sources, such as the insights from business professionals, experts and academics from ECE countries.

In order to assess whether host or home country impact dominates in emerging MNEs' subsidiaries operating in ECE, the authors have compiled a set of questions (see the Annex). These questions were used to conduct interviews with the company representatives, mainly with top-level managers. The interviews were conducted by the authors between June 2017 and September 2019. Each interview lasted one to two hours, and all interviewees were guaranteed confidentiality. The answers were noted down by the respective authors in detail and were then analysed. Information from the company interviews was supplemented by data from the balance sheets of the subsidiaries. Since there are relatively few emerging MNEs in the ECE region, the number of interviews did not justify the use of qualitative data analysis software or to apply any coding techniques.

Throughout the research ECE is referred to as the five new EU member states which are also members of the OECD, namely, the Czech Republic, Hungary, Poland, the Slovak Republic and Slovenia. The Central and Eastern European (CEE) region is a broader term—comprising Albania, Bulgaria, Croatia, the Czech Republic, Hungary, Poland, Romania, the Slovak Republic, Slovenia, and the three Baltic States, Estonia, Latvia and Lithuania. Therefore, the book does not focus on the whole CEE region; however, in some cases the examples of the ECE countries will be supplemented with some of the CEE countries.

Since data in FDI recipient ECE (host) countries and emerging home countries show significant differences, the two data sets will usually be compared to point out the potential source of discrepancies in order to get a more complex and nuanced view of the stock and flow of investments. Besides home and host country statistics, international databases, especially that of the United Nations Conference on Trade and Development (UNCTAD) and Organisation for Economic Co-operation and Development (OECD), will be considered and compared.

Budapest, Hungary

Ágnes Szunomár

Acknowledgements

This book brings together a collection of selected original studies conducted in the framework of the research project "Non-European Emerging-Market Multinational Enterprises in East Central Europe" (K-120053) supported by the National Research, Development and Innovation Office (NKFIH) of Hungary between 1 December 2016 and 30 November 2021.

The editor would also like to acknowledge the support of the Bolyai János Fellowship of the Hungarian Academy of Sciences.

Contents

Notes on Contributors

Tamás Gerőcs is a political economist at the Institute of World Economics, Hungarian Academy of Sciences. He graduated from the Corvinus University of Budapest (BUC) in 2008. His major degree was International Relation; his minor was Investment and Network Analysis. Gerőcs is doing his PhD at SUNY Binghamton University. His research field of interest is semi-peripheries with a special regard for economic transformation in India and Hungary as well as theoretical questions in semi-peripheral dependent development with respect to external financial and trade dependencies.

Judit Kiss, D.Sc. is a research professor at the Institute of World Economics, Centre for Economic and Regional Studies, and a professor of International Economics and Development Studies at International Business School. She holds a BA in International Trade, an MA in International Relations, a PhD in Development Economics from the University of Economics (Budapest) and a doctorate in Sciences from the Hungarian Academy of Sciences. She was a visiting professor at Dar es Salaam University (Tanzania) between 1985 and 1989 and conducted field research in Botswana, China, India, Tanzania and Namibia. She has over 350 scientific publications in Hungarian and foreign languages, and has conducted consultancy and research for international organisations such as the EU, ILO, KPMG, UNCTAD, UNIDO, UNITAR and World Bank.

Tamás Peragovics is a PhD candidate at the Department of International Relations of Central European University, an external lecturer at the International Relations Department of ELTE University and a junior research fellow at the Institute of World Economics, Centre for Economic and Regional Studies. Peragovics holds two MAs in International Relations from ELTE University and CEU. His research focuses on China's relations with Central and Eastern European countries. His most recent article was published by the *European Journal of International Relations (EJIR)*.

Judit Ricz, Ph.D. is a research fellow at the Institute of World Economics, Centre for Economic and Regional Studies (IWE CERS), and an associate professor at the Department of World Economy at the Corvinus University of Budapest (DWE CUB). She has conducted various (domestic and international) research projects (at IWE CERS) and is active in teaching various courses (at IWE CUB) related to development economics and international political economy. Her research focuses on analysing different forms of state capitalism (mainly in Latin America, but also beyond) with the aim to formulate policy-relevant conclusions and lessons for other emerging and developing countries (including the Central Eastern European region). She is the author of one book and several other publications (peer-reviewed journals and book chapters) related to these topics (in both Hungarian and English), and speaker at numerous conferences (both domestic and international). Besides relying on a wide-ranging personal professional network, she is embedded in the extensive and long-standing research network of the IWE CERS combined with DWE CUB, which offers plenty of opportunities for synergies and feedback. She is fluent in English and Spanish.

Miklós Szanyi, D.Sc. is a professor at Szeged University, Faculty of Economics and Business Administration, Szeged, and a research adviser of the Institute of World Economics, Budapest. He graduated and received PhD from the Budapest University of Economics. He holds the title Doctor of Economics from the Hungarian Academy of Sciences. He carried out extensive research work on the East-Central European countries' transition process, foreign direct investments and multinational business conduct, innovation and technological progress. He is the author of over 200 scientific publications in Hungarian and foreign languages, three monographs and seven edited books. As a research expert he worked for various international organizations (the World Bank, OECD, UNCTAD).

Tamás Szigetvári, Ph.D. is an associate professor at the Institute of International Studies and Political Sciences of the Pázmány Péter Catholic University, Budapest, where he teaches courses in International economics, in Development economics and in EU trade policy. He is also a senior research fellow at the Institute of World Economics of the Centre for Economic and Regional Studies. His research activity focuses on economic developments in the EU outer periphery. He is an expert in the Executive Master in EU Studies program of CIFE. He holds his MSc in Economics and his PhD in International Relations from the Budapest University of Economic Studies (today Corvinus University of Budapest).

Ágnes Szunomár, Ph.D. is a senior research fellow at the Institute of World Economics, Centre for Economic and Regional Studies (IWE CERS), where she is the head of Research Group on Development Economics. She is also an associate professor at the Department of World Economy at the Corvinus University of Budapest (CUB). She studied International Relations at the Budapest College of Management and CUB and Politology at the Eötvös Loránd University's Faculty of Law and Political Sciences. She holds a PhD in Economics from CUB. She has been awarded with various scholarships (János Bolyai Research Scholarship by the Hungarian Academy of Sciences, Sasakawa Young Leaders Fellowship, teaching scholarships at CUB). Her research focuses on East Asia and China's foreign economic policy, including the relation between China and East Central Europe. She has also done research on emerging markets as well as on foreign direct investment issues and related policies in ECE countries. She led and participated in several international and Hungarian research projects. She has more than 90 scientific publications.

Katalin Völgyi, Ph.D. is a research fellow at the Institute of World Economics, Centre for Economic and Regional Studies in Budapest and a part-time assistant professor at Széchenyi István University in Győr, Hungary. Her main research field is economic integration and regionalism in East Asia. She defended her PhD dissertation at the Doctoral School of Regional and Economic Sciences of Széchenyi István University in 2014 and was awarded with a JSPS post-doctoral fellowship in 2015. She undertook a one-year research project on the East Asian economic integration and regionalism at Ritsumeikan University (BKC) in Japan. She won a research grant from the Toshiba International Foundation in 2014 as well as in 2017, which supported the publishing of her two textbooks:

one on Japan's economic development and the other one on the economic integration and regionalism in East Asia. In addition, she participated in several research projects financed by the International Visegrad Fund, the Hungarian Prime Minister's Office and the Hungarian Scientific Research Fund, most of them focused on East and Southeast Asia or these two regions' economic relations with CEE or Hungary.

Csaba Weiner, Ph.D. is a senior research fellow at the Institute of World Economics of the Centre for Economic and Regional Studies in Budapest, Hungary, which he joined in 2003 after graduating with his bachelor's degree in 2000 and master's degree in 2003, both in economics. His main areas of research interest are the energy sector in Central and Eastern Europe and the countries of the former Soviet Union; foreign direct investment in and from Russia; the Russian economy; and Russian–Hungarian relations. Weiner holds his PhD in Regional Sciences in 2011 after defending his doctoral thesis entitled "The Position of the Russian Gas Industry in the World Economy and Its Influence on International Cooperation". In 2016, his proposal on "Central and East European Energy Security Concepts" led to him being awarded the János Bolyai Research Scholarship by the Hungarian Academy of Sciences for the period 2016–2019. Supported by the New National Excellence Program of Hungary's Ministry of Human Capacities, Weiner was a Bolyai+ Teaching and Research Scholar at the Budapest Business School University of Applied Sciences during the 2018–2019 academic year. He has authored more than 70 publications and has been a speaker at some 70 conferences and workshops.

List of Figures

List of Tables

PART I

Introduction

CHAPTER 1

Theories of Internationalization and Foreign Direct Investment: How to Explain FDI from Emerging MNEs?

Ágnes Szunomár

1.1 Introduction

The rise of multinational enterprises (MNEs) from emerging markets is topical and important and poses a number of questions and challenges that require considerable attention in future from academia as well as business management. The recent takeovers of high-profile companies in developed or developing countries by emerging-market MNEs—such as Lenovo, Wanhua (China) and Hindalco (India)—as well as the greenfield or brownfield investments of emerging companies (Huawei, ZTE, Tata, etc.) show a new trend where new kinds of firms become major players globally. According to the World Investment Report, investments from

Á. Szunomár (✉)
Institute of World Economics, Centre for Economic and Regional Studies, Budapest, Hungary

Institute of International, Political, and Regional Sciences, Corvinus University of Budapest, Budapest, Hungary
e-mail: szunomar.agnes@krtk.mta.hu

Á. Szunomár (ed.), *Emerging-market Multinational Enterprises in East Central Europe*, Studies in Economic Transition,
https://doi.org/10.1007/978-3-030-55165-0_1

emerging markets reached a record level: based on the United Nations Conference on Trade and Development (UNCTAD) data, developing Asia now invests abroad more than any other region (UNCTAD 2013).

Majority of traditional theories explaining the different motivations for foreign direct investment (FDI) were born after World War II, in the 1960s and 1970s, when investments were typically flowed from developed countries to other developed or developing regions. Consequently, the rapid growth of FDI from emerging and developing countries in recent years—often directed at developed regions—has been a subject of numerous studies trying to account for special features of emerging-country MNEs' behaviour that is not captured by traditional theories.

Although emerging MNEs' FDI is not a completely new phenomenon it has been examined by scholars with a new momentum in the past one or two decades due to (1) the unprecedented size of the phenomenon; (2) the fact that developing Asia accounts for more than a quarter of all outward FDI and (3) the fact that this group of countries will soon be a net direct investor (UNCTAD 2015). The phenomenon itself is indeed existing since Japan and then later the Four Asian Tigers (Hong Kong, Singapore, South Korea and Taiwan) are all experiencing similar upward trend in terms of inward as well as outward FDI. These countries can be considered as predecessors of FDI from emerging countries today (such as BRICS—Brazil, Russia, India, China and South Africa). Consequently, we can differentiate between three waves of FDI (Andreosso-O'Callaghan 2016: 15): (1) FDI from emerging Europe and the United States after World War II; (2) FDI from Japan and then the Asian Tigers from the 1960s and 1970s and (3) FDI from BRICS countries after the turn of the millennium.

1.2 A Brief Overview of Traditional and New Theories

The theoretical framework of FDI, as well as the concept of internationalization, has evolved a lot in the past century. To briefly summarize the traditional theories of FDI, this section uses—and expands—the typology of Andreosso-O'Callaghan (2016: 16–17), where different theories can be labelled as micro-, meso- or macroeconomic levels. After these traditional theories the main findings of the Japanese school of FDI is also summarized briefly as it can be relevant in explaining, for example, Asian

FDI. The chapter then continues with those new theorists that consider traditional economic factors insufficient in explaining MNEs' FDI decisions and, as a result, develop new theoretical attempts to explain FDI decisions of emerging MNEs.

1.2.1 *Traditional Theories*

Macro-level theories include theories such as the capital market theory, the dynamic macroeconomic FDI theory or the exchange rate theory, economic geography theory, gravity as well as institutional approach and investment development path theory.

Capital market theory is one of the oldest theories of FDI (1960s) and states that FDI is determined by interest rates. However, it has to be added that when this theory was formulated, the flow of FDI was quite limited and some parts of it were indeed determined by interest rate differences. According to the dynamic macroeconomic FDI theory, FDI is a long-term function of MNE strategies, where the timing of the investment depends on the changes in the macroeconomic environment. FDI theory based on exchange rates considers FDI as a tool of exchange rate risk reduction, while that based on economic geography explores the factors influencing the creation of international production clusters, where innovation is the major determinant of FDI. Gravity approach to FDI states that the closer two countries are geographically, economically, culturally and so on—the higher will be the FDI flows between these countries. FDI theories based on institutional analysis explore the importance of the institutional framework on the FDI flows, where political stability is a key factor determining investments.

According to the investment development path (IDP) theory, which was originally introduced by Dunning in 1981 and refined later by himself and others (Dunning 1986, 1988, 1993, 1997; Dunning and Narula 1996; Duran and Úbeda 2001, 2005), FDI develops through a path that expresses a dynamic and intertemporal relationship between an economy's level of development, proxied by the Gross Domestic Product (GDP) or GDP per capita, and the country's net outward investment position, defined as the difference between outward direct investment stock and inward direct investment stock.

In the framework of the investment development path theory, Dunning also differentiated between five stages of development:

- Stage 1 is characterized by low incoming FDI, but foreign companies are beginning to discover the advantages of the country. In this phase there is no outgoing FDI since there are no specific advantages owned by the domestic forms.
- Stage 2 is characterized by growing incoming FDI due to the advantages of the country (such as low labour costs), while the standards of living are rising, which is drawing even more foreign companies to the country. Outgoing FDI is still rather low in this phase.
- In stage 3 incoming FDI is still strong, but its nature is changing due to rising wages. The outgoing FDI is taking off as domestic companies are getting stronger and develop their own competitive advantages.
- In stage 4 strong outgoing FDI seeks advantages—for example, low labour costs—abroad.
- In stage 5 investment decisions are based mainly on the strategies of multinational companies, and the flows of outgoing and incoming FDI come into an equilibrium.

At the meso level we find Raymond Vernon's product life cycle (PCM) model (Vernon 1966), which conceptualizes the role of the diverse stages of the product cycle in boosting the level of economic development among regional trading partners. Vernon's PCM theory was published at a time when the first traits of offshoring to developing (or lower wage) countries were experienced by the United States. Vernon differentiated between four stages of development of a new product:

1. domestic production—introduction phase,
2. export—growth phase,
3. export of capital—maturity phase and
4. foreign production—decline phase.

While the product matures, the market expands and economies of scale set in that drives the prices down, justifying exports to other countries. When production costs—especially labour cost—become a major component of total costs, production moves to lower labour cost countries. According to this theory, companies decide to invest abroad considering beneficial ownership and transaction cost as well as local conditions. As a result, FDI can be seen mostly in the phases of maturity and decline.

At the micro level (actually, at a rather mixed micro-macro level), Dunning's eclectic paradigm, also known as the OLI model, became the mainstream theoretical framework explaining FDI (Dunning 1992, 1998). This paradigm states that firms will venture abroad when they possess firm-specific advantages, that is ownership (O) and internalization (I) advantages, and when they can utilize location (L) advantages to benefit from the attractions these locations are endowed with. The OLI paradigm has changed a lot since it was first presented; ownership advantages, for example, have been divided into asset-based and transaction-based categories. "The asset-based ownership advantage is the exclusive or privileged possession of country-specific and firm-specific intangible and tangible assets, which gives the owner some proprietary advantage in the value-adding process of a particular product" while "the transaction-based ownership advantages reflect the ability of a corporation to coordinate, by administrative fiat, the separate but complementary activities better than other corporations of different ownership and the market" (Cuervo and Pheng 2003: 82). The transaction-based ownership advantage seems to be also very relevant for multinational companies from non-developed countries.

Different types of investment motivations attract different types of FDI, which Dunning (1992; Dunning and Lundan 2008) divided into four categories: market-seeking, resource-seeking, efficiency-seeking and strategic asset-seeking. The factors attracting market-seeking multinationals usually include market size, as reflected in GDP per capita and market growth (GDP growth). The main aim of a resource-seeking MNE is to acquire particular types of resources that are not available at home (such as natural resources and raw materials) or are available at a lower cost compared to the domestic market (such as unskilled labour). Investments aimed at seeking improved efficiency are determined by low labour costs, tax incentives and so on: localization advantages "comprise geographical and climate conditions, resource endowments, factor prices, transportation costs, as well as the degree of openness of a country and the presence of a business environment appropriate to ensure to a foreign firm a profitable activity" (Resmini 2005: 3). Finally, the companies interested in acquiring foreign (strategic) assets might be motivated by a common culture and language, as well as trade costs (Blonigen and Piger 2014; Hijzen et al. 2008). It should be emphasized that some FDI decisions may be based on a complex mix of factors (Resmini 2005: 3; Blonigen and Piger 2014). Much of the theoretical discussion is based on FDI outflows from developed countries, for which market-seeking and efficiency-seeking FDI are more prominent (Buckley et al. 2007; Leitão and Faustino 2010), while FDI from non-developed regions is motivated by an even more mixed composition of factors.

1.2.2 *The Japanese School of FDI*

In Asia, Japan was the first country to become an outward investor. Its catching-up strategy can be traced back to the Meiji Restoration that allowed the country to become the "lead goose" in Asia. This historical process inspired the Japanese school of FDI. Although it has often been left out from other theoretical overviews of FDI-related books or papers, this chapter plays special attention to this theory, as it can be especially relevant in explaining Asian FDI. In addition, interesting links can be found between the Japanese school's main ideas and the aforementioned product life cycle and/or investment development path theories.

In specific terms, the flying geese paradigm (FGP) is a view of Japanese scholars upon the technological development in Southeast Asia viewing Japan as a leading power. It was developed in the 1930s but gained wider popularity in the 1960s after its author Kaname Akamatsu (1962) published his ideas in the *Journal of Developing Economies*. According to the theory, the "lead goose" Japan provides support to East Asian industrialization through FDI. This catching-up experience was emulated by others and Japan's model was followed by the Four Asian Tigers, including South Korea and Taiwan, and later by China. Akamatsu stated that "these countries, advanced and less advanced, do not necessarily go forward at the same speed in their development of a wild-geese-flying pattern, nor do they always make gradual progress, but they are at times dormant and at other times make leaping advances" (Akamatsu 1962: 18). However, when building up the theory, Akamatsu did not really explain the motivation or driving force behind a country's upgrade. Kojima (1960) made an attempt to do so and explained the driving force to be the accumulation of capital, that is the Heckscher-Ohlin factor. In a later article he also mentioned "the Ricardian advantage by learning-by-doing and economies of scale" as the potential driving force (Kumagai 2008: 8).

At the turn of the millennium, the FGP model was reformulated by Kojima (2000) and Ozawa (2001). In his article Kojima (2000) reviewed several empirical studies that tried to verify the FGP, while Ozawa (2001) analysed the relationship among FDI, competitiveness and economic development based on the ideas of Michael Porter. Ozawa identified three main phases of development as he analysed the waves of FDI inflow and outflow from a country. These are factor-driven, investment-driven and innovation-driven phases of development.

- In the phase of economic growth the country is underdeveloped and targeted by foreign companies wanting to use its potential advantages (especially low labour costs). In this stage there is almost no outgoing FDI.
- In the second phase the country attracts market-seeking inward FDI and intermediate goods industries from developed countries. In this phase, new FDI is drawn by the growing internal markets and by the growing standards of living. This development generates outward FDI to less-developed countries in labour-intensive and resource-based industries.
- In the third phase of economic growth the competitiveness of the country is based on innovation, while the incoming and outgoing FDI are motivated by market factors and technological factors.

Nowadays, the FGP is generally used to "depict the sequential development of a group of countries, and the concept is sometimes thought to be obsolete" (Kumagai 2008: 17).

1.2.3 *New Theoretical Attempts*

As mentioned above, although Asian FDI is not a new phenomenon what is different today is the scale and pace at which it has evolved since the early 2000s, in particular, since China launched its "go global" strategy (2000) and started to invest more and more globally. Nevertheless, traditional theories as well as economic factors seem to be insufficient in explaining FDI decisions of emerging (Asian as well as non-Asian) MNEs.

In the last decade international economics and business researchers acknowledged the importance of institutional factors in influencing the behaviour of MNEs (e.g., Tihanyi et al. 2012). According to North (1990: 3), institutions are the "rules of the game" which are "the humanly devised constraints that shape human interactions". Institutions serve to reduce uncertainties related with transactions and minimize transaction costs (North 1990). Similarly, Meyer and Nguyen (2005: 67) argue that informal constraints are "much less transparent and, therefore, a source of uncertainty". In response to such observations, Dunning and Lundan (2008) extended the OLI model with the institution-based location advantages, which explain that institutions developed at home and host economies shape the geographical scope and organizational effectiveness of MNEs.

To catch the special features of emerging MNEs' behaviour, Mathews extended the OLI paradigm with the linking, leverage and learning framework (LLL), which explains the rapid international expansion of companies from Asia Pacific (Mathews 2006). Here *linking* means partnerships or joint ventures that latecomers form with foreign companies in order to minimize risks involved with internationalization as well as to acquire "resources that are otherwise not available" (Mathews 2006: 19). Latecomers when forming links with incumbents also analyse how the resources can be *leveraged*. They look for resources that can be easily imitated, transferred or substituted. Finally, repeated processes of linking and leveraging allow latecomers to *learn* and conduct international operations more effectively (Mathews 2006: 20).

Although emerging-market MNEs from various emerging countries differ in many respects, to some extent they share common characteristics. Barnard (2010), for example, writes about the lack of strong firm capabilities among MNEs from South Africa and Taiwan. Due to the geographical, cultural and institutional distance between the home and host countries, emerging companies—like all other MNEs—suffer from the "liability of foreignness" (Kostova and Zaheer 1999; Hymer 1976), while they also suffer from—as Amendolagine and Rabellotti (2017) call it—the "liability of emergingness", which is related to their emerging-market origin, reducing their legitimacy in advanced markets (Madhok and Keyhani 2012; Ramachandran and Pant 2010).

When it comes to the "special" role of the home country, that is the role of the state, Kalotay and Sulstarova (2010) highlight that Russian MNEs' investments are also influenced by home-country policies. Similarly, Anwar and Mughal (2014) argue that Russian outward FDI follows the eclectic paradigm to a certain extent, but home-country factors also play a significant role. Kalotay (2010) divides these home-country advantages into home-country-based competitive advantages, business environment advantages, development strategy advantages and state involvement advantages. Peng (2012) reports that Chinese MNEs are characterized by three relatively unique aspects: (1) the significant role played by home-country governments as an institutional force, (2) the absence of significantly superior technological and managerial resources and (3) the rapid adoption of (often high-profile) acquisitions as a primary mode of entry.

Surprisingly, with the exception of China, there is no specific going global strategy in the majority of emerging countries. While China's FDI expansion is driven by state-owned enterprises, Russian outward expansion is mainly driven by private companies (Skolkovo 2009); state support for Russian multinationals is quite weak due to the lack of developed policy instruments. On comparing the Chinese and Brazilian outward FDI strategies, Ricz and Szunomár (2019) concluded that Chinese outward FDI strategy has taken a much more aggressive stance to promote Chinese companies abroad, while that of its Brazilian counterpart was a rather a defensive one. Brazilian industrial policies were focusing on already existing dynamic comparative advantages, as they preferred to support industries that were already highly competitive internationally and did not promote further structural changes in the domestic economy. In contrast, the Chinese government has promoted and guided outward FDI with the main aim of acquiring assets that were scarce in the country or considered to be crucial for further development of the domestic economy.

The motivations of developed-country MNEs are often different from those of emerging countries. For example, Hanemann (2013) points out commercial reasons behind most Chinese investments: (1) the acquisition of rich-world brands and technology to increase competitiveness and (2) money-saving by moving higher value-added activities to countries where regulatory frameworks are more developed. In the case of emerging MNEs, the primary drivers of internationalization are not only industry-driven processes, such as circumventing transportation costs, trade barriers and intangible asset-seeking, as Dunning and Lundan (2008) or even Ramamurti and Singh (2009) demonstrated, but also more firm-specific characteristics (Feenstra 1998). For example, in the case of Indian MNEs, the most important characteristic in this regard is access and usage of modern technology (Ramamurti 2012). Similarly, the main driver for other emerging MNEs to specialize in global value chains (GVCs) is to get access to state of the art technology which can help develop capacities in their home base.

Gubbi et al. (2010) find that Indian MNEs are fond of undertaking acquisitions overseas. Since 2002 a marked shift in corporate attitude towards global markets took place in Brazil, too, but "multi-latinas" have emerged throughout Latin America (Casanova and Kassum 2013). While some emerging-market MNEs focus on neighbouring regions, others target the global market, including the countries of the developed world. According to Gubbi and Sular (2015) Turkish firms, for example, seem to be using the European countries to (1) present themselves as a European Union company, (2) make use of special features of these countries to expand their businesses within and to other countries and (3) make use of the favourable tax treatment policies available to foreign investors.

GVCs have increased the interdependencies between trade and FDI, while participation in GVCs has allowed emerging countries to specialize on the global market. Some of the emerging countries'—especially China's and India's—development has already been GVC-driven in the past decades; consequently, it might have influenced their outward FDI flows. Martínez-Galán and Fontoura (2018) made a study on OECD as well as emerging countries and found that a country's degree of GVC participation has positively contributed to bilateral FDI transactions. Carill-Caccia and Pavlova (2018) also found that foreign takeovers, in terms of both the number of projects and their value, are mostly driven by FDI supporting exports and to a certain extent vertical FDI.

1.3 Driving Forces and Location Choices Behind the International Expansion Strategy of Emerging MNEs: Push and Pull Factors

Various factors determine the direction and intensity of MNEs' FDI flows. While there are important factors on the firm level such as—among others—size, performance and industry (Terpstra and Yu 1988; Nachum and Zaheer 2005), country-level characteristics may play an even more important role when it comes to emerging MNEs (Schüler-Zhou et al. 2012), especially those with autocratic, authoritarian regimes. As highlighted by Dunning (1998), at the country level, both home- and host-country characteristics determine the location decisions of MNEs. As result, in this book we concentrate on exploring the country-level driving forces of outward FDI that can be grouped into push and pull factors (or home-country and host-country determinants, respectively) to differentiate between the factors that drive investment out of the home country and those that attract investments into another (host) country.

Push factors—or home-country factors—are those factors that drive (push) investment to other countries. Several types of push factors contribute to the internationalization of companies from developing countries. Masron and Shahbudin (2008) differentiated between institutional and structural push factors. Structural push factors—such as GDP, export-orientedness, interest rates, stock returns and exchange rate volatility—are related to the home country's domestic economy and market. Institutional push factors are related to the distance between home and host countries—such as cultural proximity, which can be measured by the size of the home-country diaspora in the host country—and government policies, including proactive and interventionist strategies to promote the international expansion of MNEs, specific incentives, taxes, country and industry recommendations, and the role of actors and their interplay (see also Peng 2012; Voss et al. 2009; Luo et al. 2010; Schüler-Zhou et al. 2012).

Host-country determinants—or pull factors—are those characteristics of the host-country markets that attract FDI towards them. Pull factors—just like push factors—can be grouped into institutional and structural factors. Structural pull factors include access to markets, low factor costs and new opportunities for asset-seeking companies, such as acquiring already well-known brands, valuable know-how, knowledge as well as distribution networks and channels and company-level relations. Institutional factors include international and regional investment and trade agreements, host-government policies (creation of tax free zones, offering reduced tax, etc.), institutions such as government-related investment promotion agencies (IPAs) as well as institutional stability (IPR protection, product safety standards), privatization opportunities, the possibility to participate in the host country's public procurement processes and the role of local home-country diaspora (Makino et al. 2002; Buckley et al. 2007; Schüler-Zhou et al. 2012).

When analysing the impact of institutional characteristics—such as forms of privatization, capital market development, state of laws and country risk—on East Central European (ECE) countries, the studies show varying results. According to Bevan and Estrin (2004: 777), institutional aspects were not a significant factor in investment decisions of foreign firms. Carstensen and Toubal (2004) argue that these aspects could explain the uneven distribution of FDI across Central and Eastern European countries. Fabry and Zeghni (2010) point out that in transition countries, FDI agglomeration may rather be explained by institutional weaknesses—such as poor infrastructure, the lack of developed subcontractor networks and an unfavourable business environment—than by positive externalities resulting from linkages, such as spillovers, clusters and networks. Based on a study of 19 Latin American and 25 Eastern European countries in the period 1989–2004, Campos and Kinoshita (2008) found that structural reforms, especially financial reforms and privatization, had a strong positive impact on FDI inflows.

The example of extra-EU foreign investors in ECE is presented in a study by Kawai (2006), who analysed motivations and location determinants of Japanese MNEs. The author found that in 2004 Japanese investment in ECE was low when compared with European counterparts and 90% of it was located in the Czech Republic, Hungary and Poland (Kawai 2006: 6). Japanese MNEs' investment in ECE was motivated by relatively low labour and land costs and well-educated labour force necessary in manufacturing sectors while access to rich EU markets has also played a role.

1.4 The Book's objectives

The rise of emerging-market multinationals is a new and dynamic process, while their approach towards host economies is relatively unique compared to more developed MNEs. In this chapter we have made an attempt to summarize the existing theories of internationalization and FDI, presenting the traditional theories, the Japanese school of FDI and some of the new theoretical avenues as well as the push and pull factors behind the international expansion strategy of multinationals.

Theories are indeed numerous; however, the majority of traditional theories do not really capture the motivations behind emerging countries' investments since these theories were designed to explain capital movements from developed countries to developing—or other developed—regions. New theories—or extended/re-invented old theories—often refer to the "specialties" the emerging countries possess, such as the essential function of home-country governments in promoting outward investment, the significance of institutions in influencing emerging MNEs' behaviour and the outstanding role devoted to learning from others' experiences.

Emerging countries share several common features but they also differ in many respects: their economic as well as political development is divergent and so is their current political system (democracy, autocracy or something in between) and the mechanisms of economic coordination (market, bureaucratic, ethic or forced). Consequently, their motivations for and characteristics of outward investments often vary considerably. As a result, the scientific literature—including this volume—shall not undertake to write on the subject in a generalized manner but uses case studies and/or a comparative approach instead.

This volume will focus on emerging MNEs' strategies, operation and challenges in East Central Europe by discussing their differences from the traditional theories as well as from other types of MNEs in the ECE region. In order to contribute to the expanding literature on such topics, several yet open questions have to be answered. What are the driving forces behind the international expansion strategy of emerging MNEs? How important is the ECE region in their localization strategies? What are the global patterns and recent trends of inward FDI flows to the ECE region? What factors seem to determine FDI location in the ECE region: how do macroeconomic and institutional factors affect inward FDI from emerging as well as developed MNEs? What ECE countries and what types of sectors receive the majority of emerging companies' investments? How do emerging MNEs influence the host ECE region: do they generate, for example, locational advantages through their own activities? What policy measures could be implemented to attract FDI from emerging regions and to help the companies to accommodate to the ECE region?

All these questions shall be explored in the following pages.

References

Akamatsu, K. (1962). A Historical Pattern of Economic Growth in Developing Countries. *The Developing Economics, 1*(1), 3–25.

Amendolagine, V., & Rabellotti, R. (2017). Chinese Foreign Direct Investments in the European Union. In J. Drahokoupil (Ed.), *Chinese Investment in Europe: Corporate Strategies and Labour Relations* (pp. 99–120). Brussels: ETUI.

Andreosso-O'Callaghan, B. (2016). Emerging Asian Economies and MNCs Strategies A Review of the Literature. In Taylor & B. Andreosso-O'Callaghan (Eds.), *Emerging Asian Economies and MNCs Strategies.* (Chap. 8, pp. 15–35). Cheltenham: Edward Elgar.

Anwar, A., & Mughal, M. Y. (2014). *Why Do Russian Firms Invest Abroad? A Firm Level Analysis.* MPRA Paper, No. 58178. Munich Personal RePEc Archive. Retrieved from https://mpra.ub.uni muenchen.de/58178/1/MPRA_paper_58178.pdf

Barnard, H. (2010). Overcoming the Liability of Foreignness Without Strong Firm Capabilities: The Value of Market-based Resources. *Journal of International Management, 16*, 165–176.

Bevan, A. A., & Estrin, S. (2004). The Determinants of Foreign Direct Investment Into European Transition Economies. *Journal of Comparative Economics, 32*(4), 775–787.

Blonigen, B. A., & Piger, J. (2014). Determinants of Foreign Direct Investment. *Canadian Journal of Economics, 47*(3), 775–812.

Buckley, P. J., Clegg, J., Cross, A. R., Liu, X., Voss, H., & Zheng, P. (2007). The Determinants of Chinese Outward Foreign Direct Investment. *Journal of International Business Studies, 38*(4), 499–518.

Campos, N. F., & Kinoshita, Y. (2008). *Foreign Direct Investment and Structural Reforms: Evidence from Eastern Europe and Latin America*. IMF Working Paper 08/26.

Carill-Caccia, F., & Pavlova, E. (2018). *Foreign Direct Investment & Trade: A Global Value Chains Analysis*. European Trade Study Group (ETSG) Papers, No. 276. Retrieved March 7, 2020, from https://www.etsg.org/ETSG2018/papers/276.pdf

Carstensen, K., & Toubal, F. (2004). Foreign Direct Investment in Central and Eastern European Countries: A Dynamic Panel Analysis. *Journal of Comparative Economics, 32*(1), 3–22.

Casanova, L., & Kassum, J. (2013). *Brazilian Emerging Multinationals: In Search of a Second Wind*. INSEAD Working Paper No. 2013/68/ST, May.

Cuervo, J. C., & Pheng, L. S. (2003). Ownership Advantages/Disadvantages of Singapore Transnational Construction Corporations. *Construction Management and Economics, 21*, 81–89.

Dunning, J. H. (1981). Explaining the International Direct Investment Position of Countries: Towards a Dynamic and Development Approach. *Weltwirtschaftliches Archiv, 117*, 30–64.

Dunning, J. H. (1986). The Investment Development Cycle Revisited. *Weltwirtschaftliches Archiv, 122*, 667–677.

Dunning, J. H. (1988). The Eclectic Paradigm of International Production: A Restatement and Some Possible Extensions. *Journal of International Business Studies, 19*(1), 1–31.

Dunning, J. H. (1992). *Multinational Enterprises and the Global Economy*. Wokingham, UK: Addison-Wesley Publishers Ltd.

Dunning, J. H. (1993). *Multinational Enterprises and the Global Economy*. Reading, MA: Addison-Wesley Publishing.

Dunning, J. H. (1997). *Alliance Capitalism and Global Business*. London and New York: Routledge.

Dunning, J. H. (1998). Location and the Multinational Enterprise: A Neglected Factor? *Journal of International Business Studies, 29*(1), 45–66.

Dunning, J. H., & Lundan, S. M. (2008). Institutions and the OLI Paradigm of the Multinational Enterprise. *Asia Pacific Journal of Management, 25*, 573–593.

Dunning, J. H., & Narula, R. (1996). The Investment Development Path Revisited: Some Emerging Issues. In J. H. Dunning & R. Narula (Eds.), *Foreign Direct Investment and Governments: Catalysts for Economic Restructuring*. London and New York: Routledge.

Duran, J. J., & Úbeda, F. (2001). The Investment Development Path: A New Empirical Approach and Some Theoretical Issues. *Transnational Corporations, 10*(2), 1–34.

Duran, J. J., & Úbeda, F. (2005). The Investment Development Path of Newly Developed Countries. *International Journal of the Economics of Business, 12*(1), 123–137.

Fabry, N., & Zeghni, S. (2010). Inward FDI in Seven Transitional Countries of South-Eastern Europe: A Quest of Institution-based Attractiveness. *Eastern Journal of European Studies, 1*(2), 77–91.

Feenstra, R. C. (1998). Integration of Trade and Disintegration of Production in the Global Economy. *Journal of Economic Perspectives, 12*(4), 31–50.

Gubbi, S. R., Aulakh, P. S., Ray, S., Sarkar, M. B., & Chittoor, R. (2010). Do International Acquisitions by Emerging-Economy Firms Create Shareholder Value? The Case of Indian Firms. *Journal of International Business Studies, 41*, 397–418.

Gubbi, S. R., & Sular, S. A. (2015). Why Do the Turkish Firms Invest in Mainland Europe? In L. Tihanyi, E. R. Banalieva, T. M. Devinney, & T. Pedersen (Eds.), *Emerging Economies and Multinational Enterprises* (Advances in International Management, Volume 28) (pp. 441–470). Emerald Group Publishing Limited.

Hanemann, T. (2013, January 1). The EU-China Investment Relationship: From a One-Way to a Two Way Street. *New Europe Online*. Retrieved August 17, 2017, from http://www.neurope.eu/kn/article/eu-china-investment-relationship-one-way-two-way-street

Hijzen, A., Görg, H., & Manchin, M. (2008). Cross-Border Mergers and Acquisitions and the Role of Trade Costs. *European Economic Review, 52*(5), 849–866.

Hymer, S. H. (1976). *The International Operations of National Firms: A Study of Direct Foreign Investment*. Cambridge, MA: MIT Press.

Kalotay, K. (2010). The Future of Russian Outward Foreign Direct Investment and the Eclectic Paradigm: What Changes after the Crisis of 2008–2009? *Competitio, 9*(1), 31–54.

Kalotay, K., & Sulstarova, A. (2010). Modeling Russian Outward FDI. *Journal of International Management, 16*, 131–142.

Kawai, N. (2006). The Nature of Japanese Foreign Direct Investment in Eastern Central Europe. *Japan aktuell—Journal of Current Japanese Affairs, 5*, 3–41.

Kojima, K. (1960). Capital Accumulation and the Course of Industrialisation, with Special Reference to Japan. *The Economic Journal, LXX*, 757–768.

Kojima, K. (2000). The "Flying Geese" Model of Asian Economic Development: Origin, Theoretical Extensions, and Regional Policy Implications. *Journal of Asian Economics, 11*, 375–401.
Kostova, T., & Zaheer, S. (1999). Organizational Legitimacy Under Conditions of Complexity: The Case of the Multinational Enterprise. *Academy of Management Review, 24*(1), 64–81.
Kumagai, S. (2008). *A Journey Through the Secret History of the Flying Geese Model.* IDE Discussion Paper No. 158. Retrieved April 6, 2020, from https://www.ide.go.jp/English/Publish/Download/Dp/158.html
Leitão, N. C., & Faustino, H. C. (2010). Portuguese Foreign Direct Investments Inflows: An Empirical Investigation. *International Research Journal of Finance and Economics, 38*, 190–197.
Luo, Y., Xue, Q., & Han, B. (2010). How Emerging Market Governments Promote Outward FDI: Experience from China. *Journal of World Business, 45*(1), 68–79.
Madhok, A., & Keyhani, M. (2012). Acquisitions as Entrepreneurship: Asymmetries, Opportunities, and the Internationalization of Multinationals from Emerging Economies. *Global Strategy Journal, 2*(1), 26–40.
Makino, S., Lau, C.-M., & Yeh, R.-S. (2002). Asset-Exploitation Versus Asset-Seeking: Implications for Location Choice of Foreign Direct Investment from Newly Industrialized Economies. *Journal of International Business Studies, 33*(3), 403–421.
Martínez-Galán, E., & Fontoura, M. P. (2018). Global Value Chains and Inward Foreign Direct Investment in the 2000s. *The World Economy, 42*(1), 175–196.
Masron, T. A., & Shahbudin, A. S. Md. (2008). 'Push Factors' of Outward FDI: Evidence from Malaysia and Thailand. Manuscript, Universiti of Sains, Malaysia. Retrieved May 4, 2010, from http://www.wbiconpro.com/468B-Arifin.pdf
Mathews, J. A. (2006). Dragon Multinationals: New Players in 21st Century Globalization. *Asia Pacific Journal of Management, 23*, 5–27.
Meyer, K. E., & Nguyen, H. V. (2005). Foreign Investment Strategies and Sub-national Institutions in Emerging Markets: Evidence from Vietnam. *Journal of Management Studies, 42*(1), 63–93.
Nachum, L., & Zaheer, S. (2005). The Persistence of Distance? The Impact of Technology on MNE. Motivations for Foreign Investment. *Strategic Management Journal, 26*(8), 747–768.
North, D. (1990). *Institutions, Institutional Change and Economic Performance.* Cambridge: Cambridge University Press.
Ozawa, T. (2001). The "Hidden" Side of the "Flying-Geese" Catch-Up Model: Japan's Dirigiste Institutional Setup and a Deepening Financial Morass. *Journal of Asian Economics, 12*, 471–491.
Peng, M. W. (2012). The Global Strategy of Emerging Multinationals from China. *Global Strategy Journal, 2*, 97–107.

Ramachandran, J., & Pant, A. (2010). The Liabilities of Origin: An Emerging Economy Perspective on the Costs of Doing Business Abroad. In T. Devinney, T. Pedersen, & L. Tihanyi (Eds.), *The Past, Present and Future of International Business and Management* (pp. 231–265). New York: Emerald Group Publishing.

Ramamurti, R. (2012). What is Really Different About Emerging Market Multinationals? *Global Strategy Journal, 2*(1), 41–47.

Ramamurti, R., & Singh, J. V. (2009). Indian Multinationals: Generic Internationalization Strategies. In R. Ramamurti & J. V. Singh (Eds.), *Emerging Multinationals in Emerging Markets* (pp. 110–166). Cambridge: Cambridge University Press.

Resmini, L. (2005). *FDI, Industry Location and Regional Development in New Member States and Candidate Countries: A Policy Perspective.* Workpackage No. 4. The Impact of European Integration and Enlargement on Regional Structural Change and Cohesion, EURECO, 5th Framework Programme, European Commission.

Ricz, J., & Szunomár, Á. (2019). Driving Forces Behind the International Expansion Strategies of Non-European EMNEs—A Comparative Analysis of the Chinese and Brazilian Cases. *KÖZ-GAZDASÁG, 14*(3), 168–189.

Schüler-Zhou, Y., Schüller, M., & Brod, M. (2012). Push and Pull Factors for Chinese OFDI in Europe. In I. Alon, M. Fetscherin, & P. Gugler (Eds.), *Chinese International Investments.* London: Palgrave Macmillan.

Skolkovo. (2009). Global Expansion of Emerging Multinationals: Post-Crisis Adjustment. *SIEMS Monthly Briefing*, May. Skolkovo Institute for Emerging Market Studies. Retrieved from http://www.skolkovo.ru/images/stories/book/SIEMS_Monthly_Briefing_2009-05_eng.pdf

Terpstra, V., & Yu, C. M. (1988). Determinants of Foreign Investment of US Advertising Agencies. *Journal of International Business Studies, 19*, 33–46.

Tihanyi, L., Devinney, T. M., & Pedersen, T. (2012). *Institutional Theory in International Business and Management* (Advances in International Management, Vol. 25). Bingley: Emerald Group Publishing Ltd.

UNCTAD. (2013). *World Investment Report—Global Value Chains: Investment and Trade for Development.* New York and Geneva: United Nations.

UNCTAD. (2015). *World Investment Report—Reforming International Investment Governance.* New York and Geneva: United Nations.

Vernon, R. (1966). International Investment and International Trade in the Product Cycle. *Quarterly Journal of Economics, 80*, 190–207.

Voss, H., Buckley, P. J., & Cross, A. R. (2009). An Assessment of the Effects of Institutional Change on Chinese Outward Direct Investment Activity. In I. Alon, J. Chang, M. Fetscherin, C. Lattemann, & J. McIntyre (Eds.), *China Rules—Globalization and Political Transformation* (pp. 135–165). London: Palgrave Macmillan UK.

CHAPTER 2

Changing Trends of Foreign Direct Investments in East Central Europe

Miklós Szanyi

2.1 Introduction: Different Worlds

The 1980s and 1990s witnessed fundamental changes in world economy and politics. The economic and political frames of the post-Second World War international status quo changed dramatically. On the one hand, a new technological paradigm started to evolve during the early 1970s that greatly enhanced the multifaceted globalization process. Consequently, new economic branches evolved, new organizational and institutional solutions of doing business were invented, and the scope of economic activity spread to global magnitudes. This is the time of the development of a new type of international production cooperation system: the global value chain (GVC). The new pattern meant the breakup of the production system and the factory-level specialization of components rather than complete final products, the typical labor division pattern of the previous epoch. The spatial dimensions of the new cooperation system also spread to global dimensions. The first attempts of component-based international

M. Szanyi (✉)
Institute of World Economics, Centre for Economic and Regional Studies, Budapest, Hungary

Á. Szunomár (ed.), *Emerging-market Multinational Enterprises in East Central Europe*, Studies in Economic Transition,
https://doi.org/10.1007/978-3-030-55165-0_2

production systems were tested during the early 1970s in the automotive industry (Volkswagen investments in Brazil and Mexico to serve local and US markets with main components delivered from Germany). They were soon followed by Japanese automotive investments in the USA and Britain.

The use of new digital technologies in production (CAD-CAM), communication systems (satellite transmission) and data processing enabled huge manufacturing and trade companies as well as financial institutions to split their activities and move the elements of the value chains also internationally (hence the term "global value chain"—GVC). This was a fundamentally new approach of doing business, which was of course also expressed in corporate strategic thinking. Instead of vertically integrated conglomerates big businesses started to concentrate efforts on "core competences", the types of activities that provided the most competitive advantage (Prahalad and Hamel 1990). Additional activities were outsourced to strategic partners or simply purchased from the markets. The spread of component-level international specialization was also enhanced by the overall liberalization process of economic activities but most importantly trade in the frames of GATT/World Trade Organization. Also, the establishment of regional cooperation organizations and the deepening of the integration process in Europe contributed to the required stability and security of global business conduct. Complicated international transactions required also political stability that was enhanced internationally mainly by policies pursued by the USA. While the concept of exporting democracy is frequently criticized today, it successfully completed its main aim, the provision of "home conditions" for (not only US-based) global business. In fact, this type of criticism does not query the efficiency of the system but rather its failure of providing sufficient opportunities of sustainable development in less developed regions of the global economy (Szentes 2005). Global business has developed its network-based GVCs through foreign direct investments (FDI).

East Central Europe (ECE) belonged to the Soviet-controlled region of Europe. Its political and economic development took shape in the Soviet system. The totalitarian political regime was coupled with omnipotent high-level bureaucratic coordination in the economy. The bureaucratic control favored industrial concentration, the establishment of large vertically integrated companies. Another important micro-level difference of the system against most market economies was the treatment of innovations. Due to its uncertainty innovation posed rather a threat to planning bureaucrats than any kind of opportunity. Engineering and research capacities were used to "innovate around" already existing technical solutions of the West. Innovation and also the efficiency of the more simple production activity were hampered by the lack of appropriate incentives to work better. Hence, most companies of the Soviet bloc were clumsy, oversized, poorly performing units. They also lacked modern knowledge of management and marketing, since there was no need for these activities in the system of central planning. The obvious differences between Soviet-type state-owned enterprises (SOEs) and multinational businesses made the type of close cooperation spreading in GVCs technically impossible. But, of course, such cooperation was not desired by the commanders of the centrally planned economies either. State control over all kinds of international economic contacts effectively blocked such undesirable attempts if there were any.

Countries of the Soviet bloc tried to develop self-supplying economies, first relying on their own rather small capacities, later in the framework of the international cooperation system of the socialist countries (Council for Mutual Economic Assistance—COMECON). The international cooperation mechanism was also bureaucratically controlled. In this system the Soviet economy effectively subsidized the other smaller countries through rather favorable terms of trade in the multilateral trade. Access to relatively cheap energy and raw materials also contributed to the serious endogenous systemic problem of the ECE countries—the existence of "soft budget constrains" (Kornai 1980). The first world economy shock of the ECE countries also came from this direction in the form of increasing oil prices. During the late 1970s and the 1980s the Soviets could not keep pace with the advancing technological development of the West, which also threatened the political bloc's military capability. The announcement of the Strategic Defense Initiative by the Reagan government targeted a major technology-driven jump to new levels of the arms race. Due to the serious rigidity of the Soviet economy the new rounds of armament required reallocating resources from civilian consumption and from the subsidization of the ECE allies. Hence, for ECE countries the epoch of cheap energy ended. In Hungary and Poland this and some other more internally driven processes launched serious economic crisis.

From the viewpoint of this chapter it is important to mention that socialist ECE countries were not uniform. Most importantly, Poland and Hungary experimented with some reforms especially in the sphere of the economy. These reforms could not unfold to the degree that could change the fundamental logic of the central planning system. Nevertheless, they helped accumulating some experience with the non-socialist world economy. The Soviets also supported this partial opening to the West since they hoped to get access to new technologies (restricted by the Western technology embargo, the COCOM) through the bridges. Developing new contacts in some ECE countries became politically and economically interesting also for the West. Politically it could mean more Western influence in the region. This was manifested by, for example, President George Bush's visit to Poland and Hungary in 1989 and the Budapest visit of the US foreign affairs minister Cyrus Vance in 1978. But it also meant potential new business opportunities, the reforms continued and business conditions became more favorable. It was in this period that the first foreign investments were carried out in ECE countries by some global companies. Due to the regulations of the time (similar to more recent regulations in China), only joint ventures could be established. The volume of investments remained relatively small and the cooperation activity was restricted to license production and trade representation.

2.2 FDI in the Process of ECE Transition

The political and economic transformation of the ECE countries started in 1989. The countries were not uniform. Poland and Hungary deviated quite significantly from the Soviet masterpiece both politically (more libertarian governments, travel opportunities to the West) and economically (economic reforms aimed at the introduction of certain elements of the traditional market economic institutional systems). Nevertheless, their reforms could not reach significant impact and the general problems of central planning remained in place (lack of incentives, initiatives and efficiency, rigid structure, high level of energy consumption and waste, general slowdown of technological development, etc.). The development level was somewhat higher in Poland, Czechia and Hungary than in Bulgaria or Romania; nevertheless, neither of these countries could continue catching up with the developed countries. Szanyi and Szabó (2020) calculated that especially after the oil shocks of the 1970s all ECE countries' development gap increased rather quickly. Despite of the Inherited historically higher development level and reform attempts these countries could not achieved convergence. The collapse of the Soviet-type economy in the ECE region caused very serious losses in economic output and employment. The process continued during the transition process in the form of the "transformational crisis" (Kornai 1993).

Transition from central planning to market economy posed huge workload of legislative tasks for governments and adjustment tasks for economic agents. The ECE countries' ways in mastering these tasks had not been uniform. Roland (2000) summarizes practices in the main task areas. Most important differences occurred in the speed and sequencing of the changes. Since both Poland and Hungary accumulated significant external debt, these countries were forced to act more quickly. The Polish government's "big bang" approach, the shock therapy, produced remarkable results in a number of fields, most importantly in the stabilization of macroeconomic processes. In Hungary liberalization was a bit more gradual; nevertheless, the government could scale back on subsidies for SOEs only with the usage of a "supply-side shock therapy" (Szanyi 2002). This meant a ban on bailing out debt-ridden SOEs and the introduction of a series of laws that enforced economic agents (both creditors and debtors) to engage in significant reorganization of activities in the frames of a new and rather harsh bankruptcy law. Other countries did not take measures in the shock therapy manner. The Czech government, for example, devalued the currency by 60% in order to support the cost competitiveness of Czech firms. This measure could effectively postpone SOEs' adjustment and modernization until the late 1990s when the impact of devaluation ceased to exist due to more significant domestic inflation. Other countries like Romania and Bulgaria simply drifted in the current and seemed to be less deliberate or thought through in their transformation process.

The four Visegrad countries (Poland, Czechia, Slovakia and Hungary, V4) had always been relatively more developed than the Balkan countries (Romania, Bulgaria, Serbia), and also their transition process seemed to be more consequent and quicker. Due to this difference, they were treated as forerunners. With regard to FDI the most important element of the transition policy mix was privatization. The first major investments were carried out as privatization acquisitions. First Hungary opened up the "treasure box". Due to its reform heritage Hungarian governments were especially keen on enhancing the adjustment process in the economy. The experience with various incentives for SOEs did not pay off during the 1980s and most SOEs remained entangled in the paternalistic relationship with the state. The essence of the "ownership reform" envisaged already in 1987 was the transformation of state ownership to a private one: large-scale privatization (Antal et al. 1987). Few years later, during the early 1990s Hungarian governments were rather quick to launch major privatization programs. Most of these aimed for the auction sale of SOEs to the highest bidder. Additionally management buy-outs (MBOs) were also promoted, mainly in medium- and smaller sized SOEs. Since the transition heritage did not include larger scale capital reserves in SOEs or among the population, tenders were regularly won by multinational companies. The first true FDI deals were conducted in 1990. The Hungarian government preferred the sales method because it badly needed the cash revenues to maintain solvency.

Unlike Hungary, all other transition economies were rather slow to sell the "family silver" to foreigners. They preferred different privatization methods. In Poland the strong influence of the Solidarity movement forced the governments to shape privatization transactions with due regard to social consensus among the stakeholders. This meant detailed preparations and negotiations of each transaction. Also, some of the emblematic companies of the Solidarity movement, for example, the Gdansk Shipyard, had to be exempted from the privatization process. In Czechia the ideologically less determined and rather pragmatic Klaus government used the privatization program to gain social support. A large part of the state property was simply distributed among citizens in the country's voucher privatization schemes. This privatization method seemed to be especially quick, and politicians had high hopes that the gifted ownership rights will generate genuine new bourgeoisie in the citizenry. But the method turned out to be a failure. Citizens sold their coupons to investment funds and did not care much about becoming part of the asset owner class. Moreover, the funds that collected and utilized the coupons for acquiring ownership rights in the SOEs were established by major state-owned banks. Thus, as a result of the voucher privatization schemes there was a mere transformation of the form of state ownership, but hardly any company's ownership became private (Mertlik 1997). Later, by the end of the 1990s other countries also launched privatization sales campaigns and much of the state property was sold to foreign owners.

The other main form of FDI during the 1990s was genuine new investments (greenfield investments). In Hungary and Poland the first large-scale greenfield FDI projects were launched during the mid-1990s, when the economy was stabilized and also a generous investment incentive system was introduced. In Hungary the incentives included not only tax holidays (corporate income tax) but also very advantageous regulations of special tax- and customs-free processing zones. Investors could establish such zones on their own provided they erected a fence and hired a customs officer for the facility. Many multinational firms established processing units in the zones. Later during the EU accession negotiations these regulations had to be abandoned and also the tax holidays converted to regular European support tools. Nevertheless, the good ten years of existence enhanced FDI flows to Hungary, making the country a primary destination of investments during the 1990s. In this period other countries either paid little attention to capital attraction or had just established their promotion network, including investment promotion agencies. Nevertheless, they caught up quickly in this regard, and by the 2000s the attraction capacity of the ECE countries did not vary much anymore (Antalóczy et al. 2011). Competition for the major investment projects had become rather fierce among the ECE countries. The generous cash subsidies, infrastructure development support and other advantages queried the net benefits of some investment projects. A kind of race to the bottom had evolved (for data see Tables 2.2, 2.3 and 2.4 and Fig. 2.2).

The role of FDI in the ECE transition process was manifold. As mentioned earlier, multinational firms participated in the privatization process to varying degrees in all ECE countries. Thus, they became important players in ownership changes. In Hungary, the preference on FDI in privatization was explained also by the restructuring and modernization needs of the economic units. Money was needed for new investments and technologies. Also, the use of modern management and marketing practices and knowledge contributed to the massive inflow of technological and management knowledge to the country. These circumstances were also considered and fairly big hopes were attributed to the spillover effects. That is, this knowledge should have spilled down to domestic business units as well (Szanyi 2003). The empirical evidence on spillover effects is rather mixed (Görg and Greenaway 2004). Various reasons may explain the fairly weak externalities (Iwasaki et al. 2012). Most important is perhaps the fact that many important facilities of the multinational businesses remained isolated in the host ECE economies. Their activity was not designed to incorporate much of local supplies but rather to perform simple processing. Another fairly negative feature has been the spatial duality of multinational and home businesses. FDI has not spread evenly in the ECE countries. Capital cities and very few other industrial centers attracted the lion's share of investments (Antalóczy and Sass, 2005; Szanyi 2018).

Nevertheless, despite substantial differences in transition policies the ECE countries became strongly integrated in multinational corporate networks. This means that the evolving new global labor division pattern had incorporated much of the ECE economy. Production sites of the region became regular parts of GVCs. However, fairly few local companies were capable of developing their own GVCs and incorporating foreign (possibly not ECE) sites in their networks. Poland was more successful in this regard, but in all other countries home-born multinationals are rather exceptional. This lack of ECE multinationals poses a very important difference when compared with other even relatively less developed countries of the EU. ECE countries' integration in the global economy is rather one sided, asymmetric. Nölke and Vliegenthart (2009), therefore, called the ECE development model "dependent market economy (DME)".

2.3 FDI and GDP in Figures

Both GDP growth and FDI stock accumulation showed significant parallels in the ECE countries. Nevertheless, the timing of changes in the trends was not exactly the same in all countries; moreover, the dynamics of the development also showed important differences. Figure 2.1 shows the GDP development pattern of five ECE countries. As is seen, the trendlines show considerable similarity over time, most importantly in crisis periods. Clearly seen is the impact of the transformational crisis in the first half of the 1990s. However, it is also obvious that the depth and duration of the crisis was not uniform. Bulgaria and Romania, for example, could reach the 1990 level of the GDP only in 2003 while Hungary and Czechia were already there by 1994 (see also data in Table 2.1). Nevertheless, Czechia's

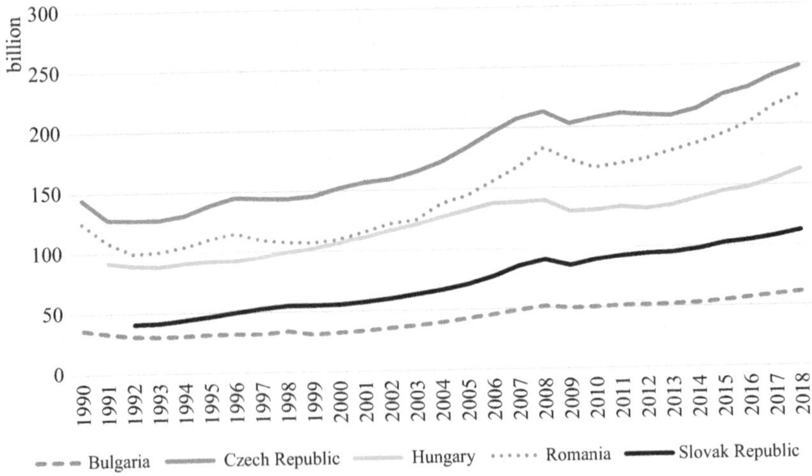

Fig. 2.1 GDP in some selected ECE countries, 1990–2018, billion USD (Source: World Bank)

Table 2.1 GDP in the ECE countries (constant 2010 billion USD)

	1990	*1992*	*1994*	*1996*	*1998*	*2000*	*2002*	*2004*	*2006*	*2008*	*2010*	*2012*	*2014*	*2016*	*2018*
Bulgaria	36	31	31	32	33.7	32.3	35.5	39.8	45.5	51.8	50.6	51.6	52.8	56.8	60.8
Croatia				41.9	45.6	46.7	50.8	55.9	61.2	65.5	59.8	58.3	57.9	61.4	65
Czechia	41	35	48	67	66.5	61.6	81.9	119	155.5	235.7	207.5	207.3	207.8	195.1	245.2
Hungary		89	91	92.3	99.2	107	117	127	137.8	139.6	131.1	131.6	139.8	148.3	162.6
Poland				268	298	326	337	367	403.2	449.9	479.3	511.5	535.8	573.4	632.7
Romania	125	99	105	116	108	110	122	138	156.2	183.1	166.2	173.1	185.3	201.7	224.6
Serbia				24.6	27	25.6	28.8	32.8	38	42.7	41.8	42.4	42.9	45.1	48.1
Slovakia		40	44	49.9	55	55.6	60	66.7	77.1	90.2	90.2	94.5	97.8	104.7	112.2
Slovenia	31	27	29	31.1	33.7	36.8	39.4	42.3	46.4	51.4	48.2	47.3	48.1	50.7	55.3

Source: World Bank

transformational crisis shows a W-shaped curve with a second slack period in 1998–2000. War-torn Serbia's economic growth was delayed. Differences in the levels of GDP can be explained by both the size differences and the development level differences of the countries. If we compare Hungary and Czechia, both countries have roughly ten million inhabitants. The higher Czech GDP curve shows higher development level. If we compare Hungary to Romania (19.5 million inhabitants) the almost parallel trends during the 1990s until the mid-2000s mean significantly lower level of Romania's development (possibly very sluggish economic performance or both). This situation changed from the second half of the 2000s, with Hungarian performance slowing and Romanian accelerating. In 2018 the per capita GDP of Romania increased to the same level as that of Hungary.

Seen from an overall perspective the development pattern of the ECE countries can be phased as follows. After 1990 several years of economic decline occurred (except in Poland, where the economy had already been badly demolished prior to the political transition). This period lasted in the V4 countries until the mid-1990s (with a second downturn during the late 1990s in Czechia). The recession lasted much longer in the Balkan countries, in most cases well beyond 2000. During the 2000s the ECE region witnessed very quick development. One of the main messages of this chapter is that the exceptionally robust economic development was largely based on a significant increase in FDI and especially their new output and the massive presence of de novo multinational affiliates in the region. This process is illustrated by the trendlines of Fig. 2.2 and the data of Table 2.2.

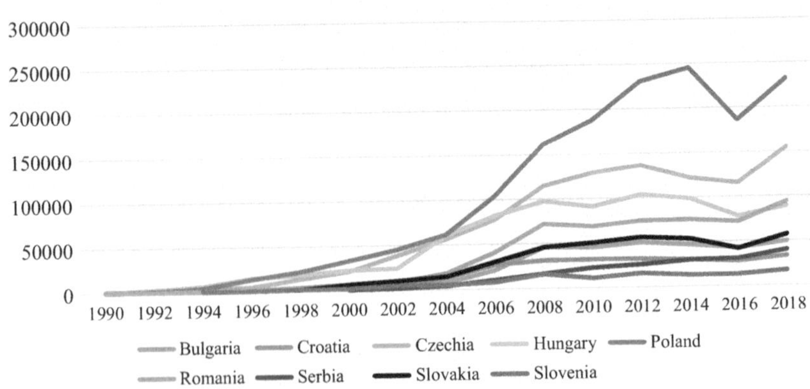

Fig. 2.2 Inward FDI stock in ECE, USD million (Source: UNCTAD)

Table 2.2 Inward stock of FDI, USD million, 1990–2018

	1990	*1992*	*1994*	*1996*	*1998*	*2000*	*2002*	*2004*	*2006*	*2008*	*2010*	*2012*	*2014*	*2016*	*2018*
Bulgaria	112	102	457	502	1352	2704	3889	7569	20,707	46,011	44,970	49,871	465,39	42,165	49,276
Croatia	n.a.			568	2365	2664	6029	12,989	26,812	31,061	31,517	31,609	29,761	27,645	32,884
Czechia	1363	2167	3542	5300	13,457	21,644	38,450	56,415	77,460	114,369	128,504	136,442	121,530	115,204	155,024
Hungary	570	2944	6804	15,009	18,255	22,870	24,416	60,328	81,760	97,397[a]	90,845	103,567	98,360	77,721	88,736
Poland	109	1289	4404	13,724	21,722	33,477	[illegible]	61,427	103,616	161,406	187,602	230,604	245,161	185,903	231,848
Romania	0	117	861	1595	4250	6953	8786	18,009	41,001	71,864	68,699	74,171	74,732	71,804	94,021
Serbia[b]	n.a.				n.a.	1017	1959	3947	10,094	16,387	22,299	25,451	29,564	30,345	39,833
Slovakia	282		474	735	2062	6970	10,225	14,501	30,327	45,933	50,328	55,816	53,216	41,615	57,109
Slovenia	1643		295	689	2359	2389	5074	4962	7452	15,782	10,667	15,526	12,743	12,731	16,809

Source: UNCTAD

[a]Due to data provision error instead of the 2008 value we use 2007 data in the case of Hungary.

[b]Up until 2004 Serbia and Montenegro were together.

The 2008 crisis heralded the end of the quick growth of FDI and GDP alike in the ECE countries (with the partial exception of Poland). The global financial crisis decimated FDI flows globally. Some authors predict a general slowdown of the globalization process (Witt 2019) because of similar declines in the rate of growth of world trade and the slowing down of the liberalization process. GDP production returned back to the pre-crisis levels by 2014 in most ECE countries, but only by 2018 in the case of Czechia and Slovenia. Poland was hit by the crisis much less and could preserve economic growth throughout the period. As is seen in the data of Table 2.2 the FDI stock declined during this period in most ECE countries. The primary explanation of the time had been that many multinational firms transferred profits and financial assets back to the parent companies from their ECE affiliates in order to cover losses suffered in their home countries (Sass and Szalavetz 2014). While this argument certainly holds, literature on FDI measurement highlighted a number of important factors that make international FDI statistics increasingly unreliable (Antalóczy and Sass 2015; Kalotay 2012). This indicates that both extraordinary increases and declines in the stock data may be caused by huge one-off transactions that distort the statistics. Since the phenomenon may possibly lastingly influence FDI statistics, it is necessary to explain it in a nutshell.

There are multiple problems with FDI statistics, especially after the 2008 crisis. The main problem is that the Balance of Payment-based information source of national FDI data providers does not distinguish capital flows according to the purpose of the capital transfer. FDI should mean significant and lasting control over corporate assets of non-residents in a country. During the 2000s even prior to the crisis, capital transfers that served other purposes (mainly tax optimization and capital round-tripping) started to increase. Also, special financial holding affiliates appeared in some countries with especially advantageous tax regulations (besides classic tax havens, also countries like Ireland, Netherlands, Luxemburg, Hong Kong, Hungary). These "special purpose entities" (SPEs) are usually small in size with few employees, carry out no meaningful production or service activity but conduct large-scale financial transfers. These are not meant to be classic FDI with lasting control over locally disposed assets. Nevertheless, since they are conducted as intra-firm transactions, that is, not with the mediation of the financial sector, their turnover is registered as FDI flows. Capital flows with similar purpose may occur also without SPE intermediation between mother headquarters and affiliates. Both of these happened on mass scale in the case of Hungary. The National Bank of Hungary made extensive efforts to separate the non-FDI-like capital flows from the BoP accounts. Antalóczy and Sass (2015) calculated that the cumulative amount of these two types of transfers caused very significant impacts. For example, in 2008 the total amount of FDI inflow was almost 50 billion euros, but without transfers to SPEs only 4.2 billion euros and net from direct cash flows only 3.1 billion euros (ibid., p. 16).

This phenomenon does not affect all ECE countries to the same degree. Very low tax rates in Hungary obviously attracted corporate revenues to be taxed advantageously in the country. However, other ECE countries may also have had similar statistical problems with more limited impact. The data in Table 2.2 seems to provide some evidence for this. FDI stock started to accelerate especially quickly after the 2008 crisis in both Poland and Czechia. These countries do not filter the BoP data of FDI (Hunya 2014). Thus, it is likely that the large differences that were observed between the Hungarian data and these two countries' figures are at least partially caused by non-FDI-like capital flows. Therefore, a rather careful treatment of comparative data is suggested especially for the last 10–15 years. The more so since many other sources of smaller scale distortion were also detected. Consequently, the FDI analysis may demonstrate mainly long-term tendencies and cannot be nuanced without risking significant errors.

2.4 ECE Countries in the Global Labor Division

We continue the analysis of the main trends of GDP development and FDI with the impacts of the foreign-owned sector in the host economies. First and most importantly we need to determine if the ECE countries possess such large-scale FDI stock that controls complete sectors, maybe the whole national economy. This would then imply that the premises of the DME model are present. In Table 2.3 FDI stock is compared with GDP in order to measure the relative size of FDI penetration. The data indicates that during the first decade of the transition process Czechia (mainly through the privatization of Skoda Auto and related businesses) and Hungary (more general opening to FDI) were the main host countries of FDI. By the year 2000 Czechia's FDI stock reached 38.9% of the GDP, while Hungary's stock was 48.6%. Poland is the largest economy in the ECE region. Due to its size and also because of the country's vigorous local business development the level of FDI did not increase to the same

Table 2.3 Inward FDI stock as percentage of GDP

	1990	*1992*	*1994*	*1996*	*1998*	*2000*	*2002*	*2004*	*2006*	*2008*	*2010*	*2012*	*2014*	*2016*	*2018*
Bulgaria	0.5		0.6	4.5	12.3	21.5	24	31.7	65.8	92.2	90	92.6	82.5	79.2	75.4
Croatia				5	13.1	19.1	28.4	39.1	63.5	44.9	52.7	55.9	51.7	53.5	53.9
Czechia	n.a.		9.9	13.6	26.1	38.9	54.8	52.7	54.8	52.7	62.3	65.7	58.7	59	63.3
Hungary[a]	1.6		16	33.2	33.2	48.6	38.2	60.7	73	70.5	69.5	81.3	69.5	60.9	56.3
Poland	0.2		5.3	9.7	15.1	20.5	23.9	25.4	30.6	30.7	39.2	46.2	45	39.4	39.6
Romania			1.8	4.1	10.4	18.8	20.5	25.2	33.6	36.7	41.6	43.3	37.5	38.3	39.2
Serbia[b]					n.a.	16.3	20.4	16.4	32	32.7	53.1	58.9	63	74.6	78.7
Slovakia	n.a.		3.2	5.8	12.1	23.4	43.2	35.3	55	48.4	55.8	59.6	52.5	46.4	53.8
Slovenia	n.a.		2.2	10.8	14.5	15.1	23.1	15.1	20	29	22.3	32.9	25.4	28.2	31.1

Source: 1990–2008 UNCTAD; 2010–2018 own calculations based on UNCTAD and World Bank data

[a]Due to data provision error instead of the 2008 value we use 2007 data.

[b]Up until 2004 Serbia and Montenegro were together.

extent as in the other V4 countries. The Balkan countries started FDI attraction much later mainly due to the wars attached to the dissolution of former Yugoslavia. Later, both Serbia and Croatia developed effective investment attraction institutions and caught up with the V4 in terms of relative FDI importance. We must add, however, that the Serbian economy is still rather weak. As seen in the data of Table 2.1 the level of GDP hardly doubled from its very low level of 1996. In that year GDP production was extremely low in the country due to the war conditions of the previous years and the extensive war damages caused by allied air raids. Thus, despite the relative importance of FDI, the Serbian economy still has not recovered.

More or less similar is the picture in Bulgaria, the least-developed country of the ECE region (Bitzenis 2003). Bulgarian industrial production was based on heavy industry that lost ground after the transition. Since the stabilization of the economy lasted very long, investment climate was very unfavorable. Moreover this country lies farther than any other from the main investor core European countries. Both of these factors strongly thwarted FDI inflows. Unlike Poland, Bulgaria was not capable of launching economic progress based on local business, mainly due to systemic weaknesses: high level of corruption and organized crime (Krastev 2002). The relatively high level of FDI that developed during the 2000s means mainly FDI dominance in trade and financial services, not so much manufacturing activity.

In the case of Romania we see genuine local business development and effective FDI impact combined during the 2000s. Romania seems to have overcome similar difficulties of weak institutional background that Bulgaria faced, which thwarted FDI and overall economic development of the country during the 1990s. With the use of the "European anchor" after the country's EU accession in 2007 several of these weaknesses were put under control (Racovita 2011). Although the situation is still far from perfect and there are serious threats of withdrawal, strong social institutions could effectively block many efforts of political parties to increase systemic corruption. Slovenia's relatively low level of FDI penetration can be explained by the country's governments' deliberate policies that omitted opening toward multinational companies. This could be explained by the relatively strong industrial fundamentals of the country, which already possessed own multinational companies in a number of economic branches at the beginning of the transition process. Therefore, the modernization and restructuring needs did not seem so urgent, compared to other ECE countries.

The data in Table 2.3 also shows that the FDI penetration process in ECE has slowed down especially after the 2008 crisis. One potential explanation is of course the overall deceleration of FDI in the world economy, especially on the side of highly developed countries' multinational companies (Hunya and Schwarzhappel 2018). This tendency was reinforced even further by the slowing down of the liberalization process in the world economy and the most current return of outright protectionism in world trade. However, we can see from the data that FDI decelerated even before the 2008 crisis in those ECE countries with the highest level of penetration. This fact can be interpreted as a sign of saturation of these economies. And indeed, the presence of the majority of the largest multinational companies in the region makes new companies' genuine investments less likely over time. Antalóczy and Sass (2015) reported that already by the end of the 1990s 76 out of the 100 largest non-financial multinational companies of the world had been present in Hungary. Genuine new investments were made afterward mainly by those firms that grew up to global size since then. They were mostly multinationals from emerging market economies, Chinese, Indian and Russian firms, and high tech, mainly internet-based, service providers that appeared on the global markets during the 2000s.

ECE economies showed signs of investment saturation already at a relatively low-level engagement in the multinational firms' GVCs. In this sense Nölke and Vliegenthart's (2009) conclusion was right concerning the asymmetric interdependence of the ECE countries on the DME model. The "manufacturing work bench of Europe" was occupied by the large multinationals coming mainly from core Europe, but also from overseas (mainly automotive and electronics investments). Especially telling is the fact that the banking sector and financial intermediation in general, as well as wholesale and retail trade, have been dominated by multinational firms in virtually all ECE countries. In some extreme country cases these investments were the single most important ones, validating the DME model's most striking criticism: FDI stock does not enable host economies' overall modernization process. The dominance of multinational firms in the banking sector of the ECE countries is shown by the data of Table 2.4.

The exaggerations concerning the potential positive development impacts of FDI in the ECE region became visible during the early 2000s. First the inflow of new capital investments decelerated, then big fluctuations in the in- and outflows appeared. Moreover, domestic business has

Table 2.4 Foreign and government ownership in banking sector (%)

	Foreign-owned banks					*State-owned banks*			
	1995	*2000*	*2008*	*2010*	*2013*	*1995*	*2000*	*2008*	*2010*
Bulgaria	8	74	84	81	66	70	18	2	3
Croatia	10	48	91	89	90	71	21	4	4
Hungary	22	75	85	83	59	61	6	3	4
Poland	4	48	67	62	76	80	34	17	22
Romania	0	28	88	84	81	89	56	6	8
Slovakia	9	71	96	94	83	84	15	1	1
Slovenia	7	13	31	28	26	48	26	51	51

Source: Cull et al. (2018)

been rather ambivalent concerning the impacts of the DME model on their business opportunities. Thus, ample disappointment concerning both macro- and micro-level impacts evolved over time. The positive BoP impact of FDI inflows in balancing trade deficit disappeared. Although this process was fully counterbalanced by increasing trade surplus of manufacturing multinationals in the countries where significant investments were made in automotive and electronics industries, increasing profit transfers back to the mother companies also limited the BoP balancing impact. In countries with no significant manufacturing investments the multinational retail chains' sourcing policy and other factors preferring large-scale product imports continuously created trade deficits. In the simplistic language of political populism that started to flourish in several ECE countries, profit transfers were also regarded as hostile behavior of multinational firms. Thus, political criticism on the FDI-led development model strengthened (Szanyi 2016a) and became an important issue of political campaigns.

Some ECE observers interpreted the turn in the treatment of FDI as a new phase in local business and political elites' struggle for power (Drahokupil 2008; Schoenman 2014; Naczyk 2014). The FDI-led development model was supported by reformist local economic and political forces, the "comprador elite" (Drahokupil 2008). This elite was called comprador because it served multinational firms' interests and followed the advice of the international advising community during the early phase of the transition process. This cooperation was rewarded with high-level positions in business and government, and the persons in question frequently revolved among the various business and political positions. This situation has been queried by another political and business elite that emphasized economic patriotism, preference of local business over multinationals. The phenomenon has not been restricted to ECE but has been global (Clift and Woll 2012); nevertheless, in some ECE countries the concept became overwhelming, offering fundamental changes in the economic models of these countries (most importantly Hungary and Poland).

The clash of liberalism and protectionism is as old as modern economic thinking. The turn toward economic patriotism could be interpreted as a new round in this debate. However, the actual implementation of protectionist measures in Hungary and Poland is not in conformance with the original principles of economic patriotism (nationalism). What we see is not a temporary curtailment of competition on selected markets in order to enhance all national capital owners' opportunities. Instead, many of the measures are not meant to be temporary; moreover, they are selective with regard to national capital owners. They aim at not just the curtailment of competition but putting it off entirely in favor of political clients. The economic policy steps are complemented by the deliberate destruction of economic, political and social control institutions to make the applied selective measures irreversible (Szanyi 2019a). The elimination of competition on various local markets deteriorates the quality and efficiency of economic activity and will ultimately lead to declining economic performance.

The sustainability of the new "patriotic" economic model is rather questionable, since it is not competitive with global business. Due to obvious demonstration effects in the affected societies the political sustainability could also be queried. There is need for adequate level of social and government income in order to maintain a necessary minimum level of consumption. Two sources of income are applicable. The ECE region is part of the EU, and up till now transfers from structural funds and the agricultural fund helped keep the economies afloat. The other source is the often-blamed multinational business sector. Since local capital owners' activity is concentrated on less complex economic activities (mainly trade and construction) it is possible to maintain fair relationships with selected multinational firms without hurting the national business elite's (political clients) interests. Automotive and electronics industries are such complex businesses where little national interest is at stake. However, they are robust in terms of production, turnover, exports and employment. These sectors are the most viable parts of the ECE economies, even if they work on rather low levels of the related GVCs, as described earlier. Thus, the "patriotic" economic model is keen on providing good investment opportunities for selected multinational firms (Szanyi 2019). In this way it does very little in pushing this economic segment to upgrade activities and overcome the low value capture trap in the ECE countries (Szalavetz 2017). The DME model is reinforced even further, though in a slightly different variation. If this is the case or whether the newly applied policy can alter the status of disadvantageous asymmetric interdependence depends most importantly on the development of home-grown multinational business.

Theoreticians of global FDI flows envisaged the overall modernization of the host economies through spillover effects. The FDI development path model of Dunning and Narula (1996), for example, suggested a linear development pattern. Countries first receive FDI and learn the know-how of doing business. Then they become capital exporters, provided their overall economic development reaches a phase when excessive capital searches for investment opportunities abroad. The theory seems to have some flaws. For one, quite obviously, not all ECE countries have been successful in attracting FDI. Moreover, some emerging market economies started exporting capital not because their overall development level surpassed a theoretical threshold level of knowledge generation or development (Kalotay and Sulstarova 2010). Skyrocketing Chinese FDI cannot be explained by the FDI development path model either. High hopes concerning the spillovers were also exaggerated (Görg and Greenaway 2004). By the 2000s, as is seen in the figures, even the extensive development impacts of FDI accumulation have been exhausted (Szanyi 2017). The integration to global production networks is also thought to bring much harm and not only good (Gál and Schmidt 2017; Szalavetz 2017), suggesting that the development potential of FDI is limited. Nevertheless, it is important to analyze outward FDI (OFDI) trends as well, since they can potentially limit the asymmetry of interdependence in ECE countries even if we cannot take as granted that this process would automatically happen as suggested by the theory. Table 2.5 provides the necessary data.

The 2012 and 2014 peaks of the Polish OFDI are most probably caused by the distorting capital flows (SPEs) that were mentioned in the previous section. Despite this, it is clear that Poland, Czechia and Hungary are responsible for the lion's share of ECE's OFDI. It seems that these three countries could successfully integrate in the world economy also as donor countries. And yes, if we search for some proof in company case studies we

Table 2.5 FDI outward stock, USD million

	1990	*1992*	*1994*	*1996*	*1998*	*2000*	*2002*	*2004*	*2006*	*2008*	*2010*	*2012*	*2014*	*2016*	*2018*
Bulgaria	124			0	35	67	125	n.a.	343	1248	2583	1867	2195	2114	2712
Croatia	n.a.			n.a.	730	760	1064	2426	2407	3635	4443	4506	5444	4963	6634
Czechia	n.a.		108	323	661	738	1496	3061	5058	9913	14,923	15,176	19,041	18,644	34,759
Hungary	159		95	494	1286	1280	4641	4472	12,693	14,179	22,314	34,741	39,641	25,029	29,019
Poland	95		202	295	841	268	1280	2661	10,705	21,814	16,407	57,525	65,217	24,790	28,510
Romania	66		37	40	119	136	155	301	278	912	2327	1417	696	910	745
Serbia	n.a.			n.a.	n.a.	n.a.	n.a.	n.a.	n.a.	n.a.	1960	2204	2819	3031	3805
Slovakia	0			79	326	555	409	618	1282	1901	3457	4413	2975	2651	3689
Slovenia	560			6	435	772	1066	2450	3942	8650	8147	7796	6193	5739	6749

Source: UNCTAD

can easily find Czech CEZ, Polish PKN Orlen and Hungary's OTP or Gedeon Richter. A proper analysis of these major investors proved that although they have majority foreign ownership (they are listed companies) the management of these firms is by and large under the control of local managers. Hence, they can be treated as "home multinationals". However, an equally important part of the V4 OFDI is controlled by other nations' multinationals. The "indirect OFDI" means investments that are carried out by the ECE affiliates of more developed countries' multinational companies (Kalotay and Sass 2010). Rugraff (2010) sees this more typical for Czechia and Hungary, but in the case of Poland local multinationals are the main OFDI players. In these cases the investment decisions are taken in the foreign headquarters. In many cases the investment transaction is also financed by sources extended from the headquarters (e.g., in the form of intra-company loan). If we also consider these circumstances the seemingly significant OFDI portfolio of the V4 countries is much less impressive. Sass (2017) evaluated as marginal the impact of V4 multinational companies on the home economy. They are too few and too small yet.

2.5 Potential Future Scenarios

The current status of ECE countries in the process and level of their integration into global business varies. Some laggards like Romania or Serbia still show dynamic and increasing engagement through new FDI projects. Others rely more on the expansion of local business (Poland, Slovenia). Yet, a rather general phenomenon is the exhaustion of the FDI-led development model, at least its dominant version of the 1990s and early 2000s. The problem is not only that many multinational affiliates work isolated and strongly integrated in strictly designed international cooperation systems of the GVC, having no physical contact to local firms to deliver any kind of externalities (spillovers). The situation is worse than that. Even those affiliates that are entangled in the development of local supplier networks deliver only limited spillovers. They are not becoming primary players of innovative local business clusters. The design of affiliates' activity range is usually specialized on low value added segments of the GVC. The income-generating potential does not increase even in case there is upgrading in the activity of the affiliates or the local suppliers (Szanyi 2017). Szalavetz (2017) called this situation "the low value capture trap" of GVC activities in ECE countries. The limited scope of activities and limited incomes do not allow local business and local workforce to improve and learn. There is a built-in lever in multinational affiliates' activity that reinforces ECE countries' role as assemblers of the GVCs very much in line with the DME model. The lack of further development opportunities in this economic segment threatens ECE countries with locking in in the middle-income trap.

Growth of real GDP started to accelerate around 2014 in most ECE countries. This revival of the region was based most importantly on cash transfers from the structural funds of the EU. Calculations with Hungarian data showed that the transfers were responsible for at least 4% GDP growth annually. If we discount this from the actual growth figure negative growth rate appears in most years of the last EU budgetary period (2014–2020). Poland, Hungary and Czechia have been the most successful recipients of the transfers measured in terms of per capita amounts. The growth-enhancing effects of the EU contributions were strongest in these economies. The usage of the money included two main areas: infrastructure (linear travel infrastructure, renovations of public estates, health care) and agriculture. From the overall economy's viewpoint agriculture is much less important than services or manufacturing (employment, income generation, exports, etc.) with the exception of Poland. Agricultural subsidies financed mainly the incomes of agricultural producers. Some of this money could have been spent on consumption, thus stimulating other economic branches. Other parts were used for rural development projects. Bulk of the cohesion funds was spent on rural development as well. Unfortunately, these development programs have only very limited longitudinal impact and do not strengthen future growth potentials. Therefore, the transfers usually have only a one-off growth impact and do not help overcoming the dangers of the middle-income trap. Hence, the question remains regarding the drivers of future progress toward an "innovation based development phase" (álá WEF's Global Competitiveness Report) or the sustainable and inclusive development pattern envisaged by the EU.

Sass (2017) looked for alternative development engines in the V4 countries. She found a revival of SOEs in many ECE countries, especially if we observe both direct and indirect state control (special voting rights and governance solutions—see Baltowski and Kozarzewski (2016) for the example of Poland). There is ample evidence that V4 countries' governments lastingly strengthened their direct economic influence through state ownership after the 2008 crisis (Szanyi 2016). SOEs can potentially become drivers of economic development. The more so since many SOEs in the developed countries work profit-oriented, similarly to regular business units. Whether ECE SOEs will do so or not in the long run cannot be evaluated yet. There is also the potential weakness that this development path is bound to increase moral hazard (Szanyi 2017). Nonetheless from the viewpoint of FDI and multinational business conduct SOEs can be of primary importance in the future. Because of their sheer size and robust background provided by states they may become primary players in their markets. For example, the high-level FDI dependence of the Hungarian financial sector (over 80% of turnover in 2012) was cut back by deliberate policies of the Hungarian government to less than 30% by 2018. Some of the multinational banks were purchased by the government, while others were forced out of the market through measures of regulatory capture. The newly acquired banks were usually reprivatized to Hungarian capital owners (Mihályi 2015; Szanyi 2017). Locally owned big business is concentrated in the V4 countries. Within local big business SOEs play outstanding role, genuine private firms of this size category are present in significant numbers only in Czechia and Poland (Sass 2017).

We can observe changes in the perception of multinational business in the ECE region. The slowing down of economic progress based on the FDI-led economic model, increasing dependency and the rather disadvantageous changes in the institutional frames of global business conduct were realized by the ECE governments. FDI attraction remained an important policy target; however, some governments applied investment incentives on selective basis and differentiated among "good" and "bad" investments. Hungary and Poland continued the support of manufacturing investments but made efforts to limit the strong multinational influence in trade, financial services and the media (Sass 2017; Szanyi 2019). Since 2010 the Hungarian government has signed strategic cooperation agreements with many of the largest and most important multinational companies. In exchange for further fiscal support the government would like to see more corporate activity in R&D, education and the development of local supplier networks. As regards attraction policies OECD's FDI Regulatory Restrictiveness indices show that advantageous investment conditions remained in place in the ECE countries. Most flexible is Czechia, but Hungary also offers good investment climate in spite of the populist anti-globalist rhetoric of the government since 2010 (Éltető and Antalóczy 2017). Poland has always been the least allowing country (Sass 2017).

To sum up we can expect that the ECE region will continuously rely on the primary role of multinational business. The governments will use investment attraction policies more selectively. There will be further efforts to strengthen the locally owned companies to access multinational companies' GVCs. Also, more intensive direct state intervention will occur in specific markets, including an increasing role for SOEs. The support of local big business and bourgeoisie will be another main target of economic policies. This should counterbalance the asymmetric dependence on global business and provide new impetus for economic progress. Nevertheless, the application of selective policy tools always increases moral hazard. The emergence of unhealthy collusion of business and politics is more likely in countries where political and social control over governments is weak. The Polish and Hungarian governments effectively rolled back the institutions of social control in the recent past, thus increasing the risk of moral hazard (Szanyi 2019a). The lack of effective social and political control on business-polity relationships can deteriorate economic performance since competition, the main driver of efficiency and progress, is often curtailed. The evolving cronyism can undercut the potential positive economic impacts of less dependence on multinational business. This scenario would not allow overcoming the middle-income trap.

References

Antal, L., Bokros, L., Csillag, I., Lengyel, L., & Matolcsy, G. (1987). Fordulat és Reform 1987. (Turn and Reform, 1987). *Medvetánc, 2*, 5–47.

Antalóczy, K., & Sass, M. (2005). A külföldi működőtőke-befektetések regionális elhelyezkedése és gazdasági hatásai Magyarországon. Regional Distribution of Foreign Direct Investments and Their Economic Impacts in Hungary. *Közgazdasági Szemle, 52*(4), 494–520.

Antalóczy, K., & Sass, M. (2015). Through Glass Darkly. The Content of Statistical Data on Foreign Direct Investment. *Külgazdaság*, English Language Special Issue.

Antalóczy, K., Sass, M., & Szanyi, M. (2011). Policies for Attracting Foreign Direct Investment and Enhancing Its Spillovers to Indigenous Firms: The Case of Hungary. In E. Rugraff & M. W. Hansen (Eds.), *Multinational Corporations and Local Firms in Emerging Economies* (pp. 181–210). Amsterdam University Press.

Baltowski, M., & Kozarzewski, P. (2016). Formal and Real Ownership Structure of the Polish Economy: State-Owned Versus State-Controlled Enterprises. *Post-Communist Economies, 28*, 3.

Bitzenis, A. (2003). What Was Behind the Delay in the Bulgarian Privatization Process? *Emerging Markets Finance and Trade, 39*(5), 58–82.

Clift, B., & Woll, C. (2012). Economic Patriotism: Reinventing Control Over Open Markets. *Journal of European Public Policy, 19*(3), 307–323.

Cull, R., Peria, M., & Verrier, J. (2018). *Bank Ownership. Trends and Implications.* Policy Research Working Paper No. 8297, Washington, DC: The World Bank.

Drahokupil, J. (2008). Who Won the Contest for a New Property Class Structural Transformation of Elites in the Visegrád Four Region. *Journal for East European Management Studies, 13*(4), 360–377.

Dunning, J., & Narula, R. (1996). The Investment Development Path Revisited: Some Emerging Issues. In J. H. Dunning & R. Narula (Eds.), *Foreign Direct Investment and Governments.* London: Routledge.

Éltető, A.- Antalóczy, K. (2017): FDI Promotion of the Visegrád Countries in the Era of Global Value Chains. Institute of World Economics of HAS, Working Paper No. 229. Budapest.

Gál, Z., & Schmidt, A. (2017). Geoeconomics in Central and Eastern Europe. In M. Munoz (Ed.), *Advances in Geoeconomics.* London: Routledge.

Görg, H., & Greenaway, D. (2004). Much Ado About Nothing? Do Domestic Firms Really Benefit from Foreign Direct Investment? *The World Bank Research Observer, 19*(2), 171–197.

Hunya, G. (2014). *Hit by Deleveraging.* WIIW FDI Report. Vienna: Central-, East- and Southeast Europe.

Hunya, G., & Schwarzhappel, M. (2018). *FDI in Central, East and Southeast Europe: Declines Due to Disinvestment.* WIIW FDI Report, 2018. Vienna: WIIW.

Iwasaki, I., Csizmadia, P., Illésy, M., Makó, C., & Szanyi, M. (2012). The Nested Variable Model of FDI Spillover Effects. Estimation Using Hungarian Panel Data. *International Economic Journal, 26*(4), 673–709.

Kalotay, K. (2012). Does It Matter Who Invests in Your Country? *Columbia FDI Perspectives*, No. 66, April 30.

Kalotay, K., & Sass, M. (2010). Outward FDI from Hungary and Its Policy Context. *Columbia FDI Profiles*, June 24.

Kalotay, K., & Sulstarova, A. (2010). Modelling Russian Outward FDI. *Journal of International Management, 16*(2), 131–142.

Kornai, J. (1980). *Economics of Shortage.* North-Holland.

Kornai, J. (1993). *Transformational Recession: A General Phenomenon Examined Through the Example of Hungary's Development.* Discussion Paper Series. Harvard Institute of Economic Research, Harvard University.

Krastev, I. (2002). The Balkans: Democracy Without Choices. *Journal of Democracy, 13*(3), 39–53.

Mertlik, P. (1997). Czech Privatization: From Public Ownership to Public Ownership in Five Years. In B. Blaszczyk & R. Woodward (Eds.), *Privatization in Post-Communist Countries.* Warsaw: CASE.

Mihályi, P. (2015). *A privatizált vagyon visszaállamosítása Magyarországon* 2010–2014 (Re-nationalization of Privatised Property in Hungary 2010–2014). Institute of Economics, Centre for Economic and Regional Studies, Hungarian Academy of Sciences, Discussion Paper, MTDP 2015/7.

Naczyk, M. (2014). Budapest in Warsaw: Central European Business Elites and the Rise of Economic Patriotism Since the Crisis. *Sciences Po Paris*, July 15. Retrieved from http://papers.ssrn.com/sol3/papers.cfm?abstract_id=2550496.

Nölke, A., & Vliegenthart, A. (2009). Enlarging the Varieties of Capitalism: The Emergence of Dependent Market Economies in East Central Europe. *World Politics, 61*(4), 670–702.

Prahalad, C. K., & Hamel, G. (1990). The Core Competence of the Corporation. *Harvard Business Review, 33*(3), 79–91.

Racovita, M. (2011). Europeanization and Effective Democracy in Romania and Bulgaria. *Romanian Journal of Political Sciences, 11*, 1.

Roland, G. (2000). *Transition and Economics, Politics, Markets and Firms*. Cambridge, MA; London: MIT Press.

Rugraff, E. (2010). Strengths and Weaknesses of the Outward FDI Paths of the Central European Countries. *Post-Communist Economies, 22*(1), 1–17.

Sass, M. (2017). Is a Live Dog Better Than a Dead Lion?: Seeking Alternative Growth Engines in the Visegrad Countries. In G. Bela & D. Jan (Eds.), *Condemned to Be Left Behind? Can Central and Eastern Europe Emerge from Its Low-Wage Model?* (pp. 47–79). Brussels, Belgium: European Trade Union Institute (ETUI).

Sass, M., & Szalavetz, A. (2014). Crisis-Related Changes in the Specialization of Advanced Economies in Global Value Chains. *Competition and Change, 18*(1), 54–69.

Schoenman, R. (2014). *Networks and Institutions in Europe's Emerging Markets*. Cambridge University Press.

Szalavetz, A. (2017). Upgrading and Value Capture in Global Value Chains in Hungary: More Complex Than What the Smile Curve Suggests. In B. Szent-Iványi (Ed.), *Foreign Direct Investment in Central and Eastern Europe: Post-crisis Perspectives* (pp. 127–150). Basingstoke: Palgrave.

Szanyi, M. (2002). *Bankruptcy Regulations, Policy Credibility and Asset Transfers in Hungary*. Institute for World Economics Working Paper No. 130. Budapest: Institute for World Economics of the Hungarian Academy of Science.

Szanyi, M. (2003). *An FDI-Based Development Model for Hungary – New Challenges?* Institute for World Economics Working Paper No. 141. Budapest: Institute for World Economics of the Hungarian Academy of Science.

Szanyi, M. (2016). The Reversal of the Privatisation Logic in Central European Transition Economies: An Essay. *Acta Oeconomica, 66*(1), 33–55.

Szanyi, M. (2016a). *The FDI-Led Development Model Revisited? The Case of Hungary*. Working Paper No. 220. Budapest: Institute of World Economics, CERS, HAS.

Szanyi, M. (2017). Impacts of the Crisis on the FDI-Led Development Model in Hungary: Emergence of Economic Patriotism or Shift from the Competition State to Patronage. In P. Havlik & I. Iwasaki (Eds.), *Economics of European Crises and Emerging Markets* (pp. 149–170). Springer.

Szanyi, M. (2018). Regional Inequalities and Foreign Direct Investments. The Case of Hungary. In S. Fadda & P. Tridico (Eds.), *Inequality and Uneven Development in the Post-Crisis World* (pp. 145–166). Routledge.

Szanyi, M. (2019). The Emergence of Patronage State in Central Europe: The Case of FDI-Related Policies in Hungary Since 2010. In T. Gerőcs & M. Szanyi (Eds.), *Market Liberalism and Economic Patriotism in Capitalist World-Systems*. Springer International Publishing.

Szanyi, M. (2019a). The Emergence of Patronage and Changing Forms of Rent Seeking in East Central Europe. *Post-Communist Economies*. https://doi.org/10.1080/14631377.2019.1693738.

Szanyi, M., & Szabó, G. (2020). Defining the Long-Term Development Trends of Countries in East-Central Europe in the Context of Political Cycles. *International Journal of Public Administration*.

Szentes, T. (ed.) (2005–6). *Fejlődés, versenyképesség, globalizáció* [Development, Competitiveness, Globalization]. Budapest: Akadémiai Kiadó.

Witt, M. (2019). De-globalization: Theories, Predictions, and Opportunities for International Business Research. *Journal of International Business Studies, 50*, 1053–1077.

PART II

Emerging Multinationals from Asia

CHAPTER 3

Home and Host Country Determinants of Chinese Multinational Enterprises' Investments into East Central Europe

Ágnes Szunomár

3.1 Introduction

Chinese outward foreign direct investment (FDI) has increased in the past decades; however, in the last one and a half decades this process has accelerated significantly. In 2012, China became the world's third largest investor—up from sixth in 2011—behind the US and Japan and it still holds its position with 129.8 billion USD in 2018. In the meantime, the stock of Chinese outward FDI has reached 1938 billion USD according to the United Nations Conference on Trade and Development (UNCTAD) data. As a result, Chinese multinational enterprises (MNEs) are not only the largest overseas investors among developing countries but are a top

Á. Szunomár (✉)
Institute of World Economics, Centre for Economic and Regional Studies, Budapest, Hungary

Institute of International, Political, and Regional Sciences, Corvinus University of Budapest, Budapest, Hungary
e-mail: szunomar.agnes@krtk.mta.hu

Á. Szunomár (ed.), *Emerging-market Multinational Enterprises in East Central Europe*, Studies in Economic Transition,
https://doi.org/10.1007/978-3-030-55165-0_3

global investor with continuing growth potential. Several factors fuelled this shift, including the Chinese government's wish for globally competitive Chinese firms or the possibility that outward FDI can contribute to the country's development via multiple channels, such as through (1) investments in natural resources exploration, (2) export of domestic technologies, products, equipment and labour, (3) technological upgrading and (4) increasing competitiveness by promoting brands and by building global networks of sales, supply and production (Sauvant and Chen 2014: 141–142; Luo et al. 2010: 76; Caseiro and Masiero 2014: 248).

Although traditionally Chinese outward FDI is directed towards the countries of the developing world, Chinese investments into the developed world, including Europe, increased significantly in the past decade. While the resource-rich regions remained important for Chinese companies, they started to become increasingly interested in acquiring European firms after the global economic and financial crisis of 2008. The main reason behind the shift towards such an entry mode is that through European firms Chinese companies can have access to important technologies, successful brands and new distribution channels (Clegg and Voss 2012: 16–19). As a result, Europe has emerged as one of the top destinations for Chinese investments. According to Rhodium Group's statistics, annual FDI flows in the 28 EU economies has grown from 700 million EUR in 2008 to 30 billion EUR in 2017, which represents a quarter of the total Chinese FDI outflows that year.

Nevertheless, Chinese approach towards Europe is far from being unified since China follows different motives and uses different approaches when dealing with different countries or regions of Europe (Szunomár 2017): the access to successful brands, high technology and know-how motivates China when entering Western European markets, investments in the green energy industry and sustainability brings Chinese companies to Nordic countries, and greenfield investments (manufacturing), acquisitions and recently also infrastructural projects pulls them to Central and Eastern Europe (CEE), including also the non-EU member Western Balkan countries.

In recent years Chinese companies have increasingly targeted CEE countries, with East Central Europe (ECE)—the Czech Republic, Hungary, Poland, the Slovak Republic and Slovenia—among the most popular destinations. Compared with the Chinese economic presence in the developed world or even in Europe, China's economic impact on the ECE countries is still relatively small but it has accelerated significantly in the past decade. This development is quite a new phenomenon but not an unexpected one. On the one hand, the transformation of the global economy and the restructuring of China's economy are responsible for growing Chinese interest in the developed world, including Europe. On the other hand, ECE countries have also become more open to Chinese business opportunities, especially after the global economic and financial crisis of 2008, with the intention of decreasing their economic dependency on Western (European) markets.

In line with the above, the aim of this chapter is to map out the main characteristics of Chinese investment flows, types of involvement, and to identify the home and host country determinants of Chinese FDI within the ECE region, with a focus on structural/macroeconomic, institutional and political pull factors. According to our hypothesis, pull determinants of Chinese investments in the ECE region differ from those of Western companies in terms of specific institutional and political factors that seem important for Chinese companies. This hypothesis echoes the call to combine macroeconomic and institutional factors for a better understanding of internationalization of companies (Dunning and Lundan 2008). The novelty of this chapter is that—besides macroeconomic and institutional factors—it incorporates political factors that may also have an important role to play in attracting emerging, especially Chinese, companies to a certain region.

In order to assess the role and importance of outward FDI from China towards the ECE region, it must be evaluated within a global context, taking into account its geographical, as well as sectoral, distribution and major push as well as pull factors. Therefore, this chapter first describes the driving forces behind the international expansion strategies of Chinese MNEs by presenting the historical evolution and main characteristics of outward FDI as well as the major push drivers and public policies. Next, it examines the changing patterns of Chinese outward FDI in the ECE region by showing the major trends, patterns and available data. It then discusses the main trends, patterns and Chinese investors' potential motivations when choosing a specific ECE destination for their placements, which is followed by the author's conclusions.

As the topic of Chinese FDI in European peripheries is new and has started to draw academic attention only recently and the available literature is rather limited and based mostly on secondary sources, the author conducted personal as well as online interviews with representatives of various Chinese companies in the ECE region. Personal interviews were conducted at four companies; where personal interviews were not applicable (three companies), the author used other sources, such as former employees of different Chinese companies that have invested in ECE, business professionals, experts and academics from ECE countries. The interviews were conducted anonymously by the author between May 2017 and September 2019 and all interviewees were guaranteed confidentiality. Each interview lasted from one to two hours. The author used semi-structured questionnaires; that is she drew up a questionnaire and structured the interview based on some basic questions concerning the background of investment, motivations before the investment and the significance of the same factors later, a few years after the investment took place. Several more questions arose based on the original questions and the responses to them; therefore, the structure of each interview was unique. The answers were noted down by the author in detail and were then analysed. Later, information from the company interviews was supplemented by data from the balance sheets of the subsidiaries.

The author will usually take into account FDI by mainland Chinese firms (where the ultimate parent company is Chinese), unless marked explicitly that due to data shortage or for other purposes they deviate from this definition. Since international statistics or national data in FDI recipient ECE countries and Chinese data show significant differences, these datasets will be compared to point out the potential source of discrepancies in order to get a more complex and nuanced view of the stock and flow of investments. Statistics from the Ministry of Commerce of the People's Republic of China (MOFCOM), UNCTAD and Organisation for Economic Co-operation and Development (OECD) will be considered and sometimes compared.

3.2 Driving Forces Behind the International Expansion Strategies of Chinese MNEs

From the late 1970s, in hand with the so-called "Open Door" policy reforms, the Chinese government encouraged investments abroad to integrate the country with the global economy, although the only entities allowed to invest abroad were state-owned enterprises (SOEs). The total investment of these first years was not significant and concentrated on the neighbouring countries, mainly Hong Kong. The regulations were liberalized after 1985 and a wider range of enterprises—including private firms—were permitted to invest abroad. After Deng Xiaoping's famous journey to

South China in 1992, overseas investment increased dramatically; Chinese companies established overseas divisions almost all over the world, concentrated mainly in natural resources. Nevertheless, according to UNCTAD statistics, Chinese outward FDI averaged only 453 million USD per year between 1982 and 1989 and 2.3 billion USD between 1990 and 1999.

In 2000, before joining the World Trade Organization (WTO), the Chinese government initiated the so-called going global or "zou chu qu" policy, which was aimed at encouraging domestic state-owned as well as private companies to become globally competitive. It introduced new policies to induce firms to engage in overseas activities in specific industries, notably in trade-related activities. In 2001 this encouragement was integrated and formalized within the tenth five-year plan, which also echoed the importance of the "Go Global" policy (Buckley et al. 2007). This policy shift was part of the continuing reform and liberalization of the Chinese economy and also reflected the Chinese government's desire to create internationally competitive and well-known companies and brands. Both the 11th and 12th five-year plans stressed again the importance of promoting and expanding outward FDI, which became one of the main elements of China's new development strategy.

Chinese outward FDI has steadily increased in the last decade (see Figs. 3.1 and 3.2), particularly after 2008, due to the above-mentioned

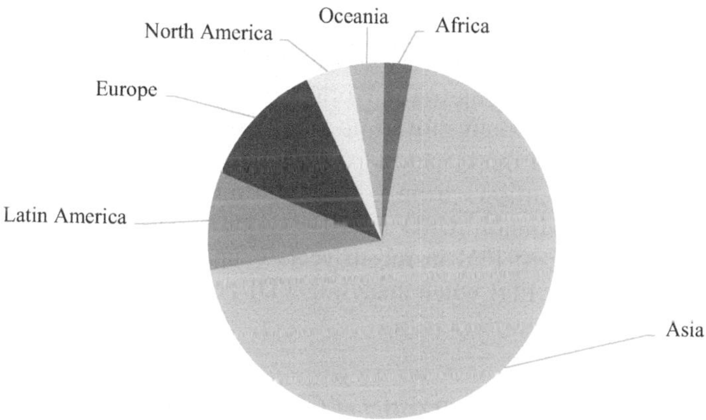

Fig. 3.1 Geographical distribution of China's outward FDI stock, 2017. (Data source: MOFCOM/NBS, PRC)

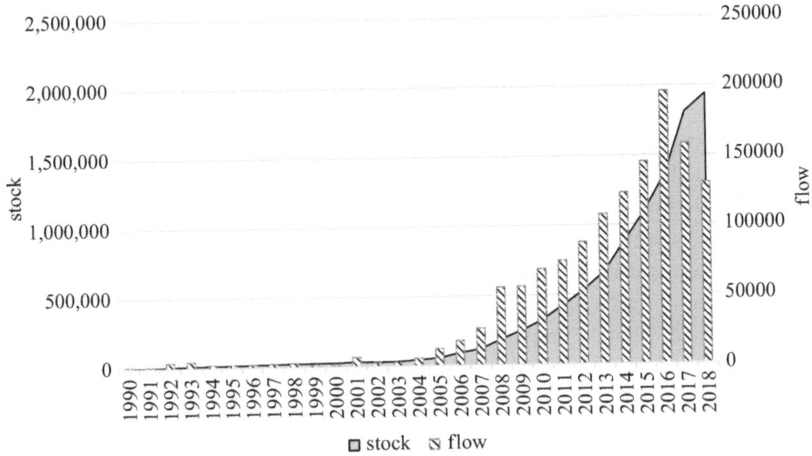

Fig. 3.2 Chinese global outward FDI stock and flow, annual, million USD. (Data source: UNCTAD)

policy shift and the global economic and financial crisis. The crisis brought more overseas opportunities to Chinese companies to raise their share in the world economy as the number of ailing or financially distressed firms has increased. While outward FDI from the developed world decreased in several countries because of the recent global financial crisis, there was a greater increase in Chinese outward investments: between 2007 and 2011, outward FDI from developed countries dropped by 32 per cent, while China's grew by 189 per cent (He and Wang 2014: 4; UNCTAD 2013). As a consequence, according to the World Investment Report 2013, in the rankings of top investors, it moved up from the sixth to the third largest investor in 2012, after the US and Japan—and the largest among developing countries—as outflows from China continued to grow, reaching a record level of 84 billion USD in 2012. Thanks largely to this rapid increase of its outward FDI in recent years China also became the most promising source of FDI when analysing FDI prospects by home region (UNCTAD 2013: 21).

3.2.1 *Characteristics of Chinese FDI Globally*

As has been already mentioned in the introduction, traditionally Chinese outward FDI is directed towards the developing world, especially Asia;

however, Chinese investments into the developed world have increased significantly in the past decade. The EU, for instance, received 0.4 billion USD investment flow from China in 2003, 6.3 billion USD in 2009—with an annual growth rate of 57 per cent, which was far above the growth rate of Chinese outward FDI globally—and 35 billion in 2016 (Clegg and Voss 2012; Hanemann and Huotari 2017: 4). While the resource-rich regions remained important for Chinese companies, they started to become more and more interested in acquiring European firms after the financial and economic crisis. The main reason for this is that through these firms Chinese companies can have access to important technologies, successful brands and new distribution channels, while the value of these firms has fallen too due to the global financial crisis (Clegg and Voss 2012: 16–19).

This increase is impressive by all means; however, according to Chinese statistics, China still accounts for less than ten per cent of the total FDI inflows into the EU and the US. Nevertheless, during the examination of the actual final destination of Chinese outward FDI, Wang (2013) found that as a result of round-tripping investments—when the investment is placed in offshore financial centres only to flow it back in the form of inward FDI to China to benefit from fiscal incentives designed for foreign investors—developed countries receive more Chinese investments than developing economies: according to his project level data analysis, 60 per cent of Chinese outward FDI went to developed economies like Australia, Hong Kong, the US, Germany and Canada.

As Fig. 3.2 shows outward FDI has started to gain momentum in the new millennium. The year of the global economic and financial crisis, 2008, provided a tremendous impetus to Chinese outward FDI, while 2015 was the first year when Chinese outward FDI exceeded inward FDI. However, following this rapid growth, China's global outward FDI has started to decline from 2017 onwards, as a result of Beijing's administrative control to limit capital outflows. This control has been maintained in 2018 (and 2019) too; consequently, outward FDI flows declined further. Besides the already mentioned administrative control, the Chinese state also "pressured highly leveraged firms to sell off overseas assets; and it reduced liquidity in the financial system amidst a broader clean-up of the financial sector, thus drying out financing channels for overseas investments" (Hanemann et al. 2019: 8). Another potential reason for these declining outflows could be that more and more countries have continuing reservations about Chinese companies' investments, including national security concerns that result in, for example, the implementation of foreign investment screening mechanisms in many developed countries.

Several experts believe that Chinese outward FDI could be greater if host countries were more hospitable. According to He and Wang (2014: 4–5), there are several reasons for this: (1) SOEs are the dominant players in Chinese outward FDI and they are often viewed as a threat for market competition as they are supported by the Chinese government; (2) foreign companies often complain that Chinese companies may displace local companies from the market as they take technology, resources and jobs away and (3) there are fears about Chinese companies' willingness to adapt to local environment, labour practices and competition. Although the above-mentioned problems indeed exist, they are often overestimated as Chinese companies are willing to accommodate to the international rules of investment as well as to the local environment (Sass et al. 2019).

According to Scissors (2014: 5), however, if the concern is about national security, the role of Chinese ownership status is overblown as Chinese rule of law is weak, which means that a privately owned company has to face as much pressure and constraint as its state-owned competitor. Nevertheless, it is worth differentiating between the two types of SOEs: locally administered SOEs (LSOEs) and centrally administered SOEs (CSOEs). Most of the LSOEs operate in the manufacturing sector and they are facing competition from both private companies and other LSOEs, while CSOEs are smaller in number but more powerful as they operate in monopolized industries such as finance, energy and telecommunication (He and Wang 2014: 5–6). Although the share of private firms is growing, SOEs still account for the majority—more than two-thirds—of total Chinese outbound investments. However, the range of investors is broader; next to state-owned and private actors it includes China's sovereign wealth fund and firms with mixed ownership structure. The role of SOEs seems to be declining in the past few years, although the government will continue to emphasize their importance as it relies on the revenue, job creation and provision of welfare provided by the SOEs (He and Wang 2014: 11–12).

Regarding the entry mode of Chinese outward investments globally, greenfield FDI continues to be important, but there is a trend towards more mergers and acquisitions (M&As) and joint venture projects overseas. Overall, greenfield investments of Chinese companies outpace M&As in numerical terms; however, greenfield investments are smaller in value in total as these include the establishment of numerous trade representative offices.

As Clegg and Voss note (2012: 19), the industry-by-country distribution of Chinese outward FDI is difficult to determine from Chinese statistics. However, based on their findings, it can be stated that Chinese investments in the mining industry are taking place mainly in institutionally weak and unstable countries with large amounts of natural resources and that these investments are normally carried out by SOEs. Investments in manufacturing usually take place in large markets with low factor costs, while Chinese companies seek technologies, brands, distribution channels and other strategic assets in institutionally developed and stable economies.

Generally speaking, Chinese outward FDI is characterized by natural resource-seeking, market-seeking (see Buckley et al. 2007) and recently also strategic asset-seeking motives (see Di Minin et al. 2012; Zhang et al. 2012); however, motivations differ between regions. In developed economies Chinese investment is less dominated by natural resource-seeking or trade-related motives but more concerned with the wide range of objectives, including market-, efficiency- and strategic assets-seeking motives. In the case of developed countries, Chinese SOEs usually have the majority of deal value but non-state firms make the greater share of deals (Rosen and Hanemann 2009). In addition to greenfield investments and joint ventures, China's M&A activity in developed countries has recently gained momentum and continues an upward trend since more and more Chinese firms are interested in buying overseas brands to strengthen their own.

3.2.2 *Push Factors and Public Policies Behind Chinese Outward FDI*

As mentioned in Chap. 1 of this book, driving forces of outward FDI can be grouped into push and pull factors (or home country and host country determinants, respectively) to differentiate between the factors that drive investment out of the home country and those that attract investments into another (host) country. When it comes to push factors, we can differentiate between institutional and structural types. While structural push factors are related to the home country's domestic economy and market, institutional push factors are related to the distance between the home and host countries—such as cultural proximity, which can be measured by the size of the Chinese diaspora in the host country—and government policies.

China's rise is often compared to the post-war "Asian Miracle" of its neighbours. When we analyse the internationalization processes of Japanese, Korean and Chinese companies there are indeed several common features and similarities. Nevertheless, one of the main common characteristics of these three nations is the creation and support of the so-called national champions, that is, domestically based companies that have become leading competitors in the global market. In fact, during their developmental period, both the Japanese and Korean governments provided strong state financial support to their companies to protect and promote them as well as to strengthen them against international competition. China has followed them later in subsidizing domestic industries and supporting their overseas activities, for example, in the form of government funding for outward FDI.

Irwin and Gallagher (2014) found that—unlike Japan or Korea—China's market entry has more to do with developing project expertise and supporting exports than it does with tariff-hopping or outsourcing industries fading on the mainland. They identified two major reasons for China's high (31%) ratio of outward FDI lending to total outward FDI. "First, China has a greater incentive to give outward FDI loans than Japan or Korea ever did because its borrowers are state-owned so it can more easily dictate how they use the money. Second, China has a greater capacity to give outward FDI loans because it has significantly higher savings and foreign exchange reserves than Japan and Korea, both today and especially during equivalent developmental stages" (Irwin and Gallagher 2014: 22–23). Peng (2012) reports that Chinese MNEs are characterized by three relatively unique aspects: (1) the significant role played by home country governments as an institutional force, (2) the absence of significantly superior technological and managerial resources and (3) the rapid adoption of (often high-profile) acquisitions as a primary mode of entry.

According to the "Go Global" strategy, Chinese companies should evolve into globally competitive firms; however, Chinese companies go abroad for varieties of reasons. The most frequently emphasized motivation is the need for natural resources, mainly energy and raw materials, in order to secure China's further development (resource-seeking motivation). Mutatis mutandis, they also invest to expand their market or diversify internationally (market-seeking motivation). Nevertheless, services such as shipping and insurance are also significant factors for outward FDI for Chinese companies if they export large volumes overseas (Davies 2013: 736). Moreover, despite China's huge labour supply, some companies move their production to cheaper destinations (efficiency-seeking motivation), for example, Southeast Asia. Recently, China's major companies are also looking for well-known global brands or distribution channels and management skills, while another important reason for investing abroad is technology acquisition (strategic asset-seeking motivation). Scissors (2014: 4) points out that clearer property rights—compared to the domestic conditions—are also very attractive to Chinese investors, while Morrison (2013) highlights an additional factor, that is, China's accumulation of foreign exchange reserves: instead of the relatively safe but low-yielding assets such as US treasury securities, the Chinese government wants to diversify and seeks more profitable returns.

In China, initially, only large SOEs from the natural resource sector were supported to invest abroad to overcome the resource scarcity of the Chinese economy. Later on, to help small and medium-sized enterprises (SMEs) develop their international markets, a government regulation on capital support for SMEs was introduced in 2000, at the very beginning of the "going global" policy. In contrast, the promotion of outward FDI by privately owned companies was only approved in February 2006.

However, the government's "paternalism" over outward investments has not ended with the liberalization steps listed above. Through the approval process for outward FDI projects and access to foreign exchange and preferential loans, the government can exert direct influence on the growth and patterns of outward investments. The MOFCOM requested that companies invest in countries that

1. have a close relationship with China,
2. exhibit complementarities to the Chinese economy,
3. are important trading partners of China,
4. have signed investment and taxation agreements with China and
5. are part of an important economic region in the global economy (MOFCOM 2004).

The desired geographical and industry direction of Chinese companies' investment has been governed by the so-called "Catalogue of Industries for Guiding Foreign Investment". The Catalogue has usually been issued by the National Development and Reform Commission and the MOFCOM. Initially, in the early 2000s, there were 67 recommended countries and 7 recommended industries for Chinese outward FDI. The country recommendations included 26 Asian countries (three in Central

Asia), 13 African countries, 12 European countries (10 of them in the EU, old member states + Czech Republic, Hungary and Poland), 11 countries in North and South America and 5 countries in Oceania.

The Catalogue retains the classification of industries based on those that are encouraged, restricted or prohibited. For manufacturing, the most recommended industries are usually electric machines and consumer electronics, while for services, trade and distribution were suggested most often. In the highly technologically developed EU member countries, France, Germany, the UK and Sweden, investment in R&D was advocated as well. Rather surprisingly, investment in IT services was recommended in the "new" EU member countries.

China is indeed paradigmatic for state control of major corporations. However, in opposition to older versions of state capitalism and developmental states, there is neither a classical top-down control nor a "single-guiding enterprise model" such as the South Korean Chaebol or Japanese Keiretsu system. We can distinguish between different views on the characteristics of Chinese state control. One possible opinion is Nölke et al.'s (2015) state-permeated market economy, where mechanisms of loyalty and trust between members of state-business coalitions are based on informal personal relations. Witt and Redding (2013) consider the Chinese system as a system combining predatory elements with personal relations, while the Chinese themselves are emphasizing the advantages of the strong but effective government that provides internal as well as external stability.

We also support the idea that China forms a unique model on its own, which can be characterized by a sustained—or even never-ending—transition from socialism to capitalism. In China, there are new forms of profit-oriented and competition-driven state-controlled enterprises, such as China Mobile, that have emerged recently, while there are several private firms and public-private hybrids, such as Huawei, Lenovo or Geely, that have also been able to become successful companies on the Chinese market as well as globally (Nölke et al. 2015). These days, such non-state—but politically supported—national firms are considered—and treated—as "national champions" by state managers: they are or were protected from competition and granted different types of state support, including, for example, export subsidies (Naughton 2007; Ten Brink 2013). With some exceptions—such as the IT sector, which is deeply integrated into global production networks—most industries are dominated by national (state-controlled, hybrid and private) capital and not by foreign multinationals (Nölke et al. 2015).

3.3 Chinese Outward FDI in ECE

Although various Chinese companies have been operating in Europe since the early 2000s, they are still facing challenges. Due to the geographical, cultural and institutional distance between the home and host countries, Chinese companies—like all other MNEs—suffer from the "liability of foreignness" (Kostova and Zaheer 1999; Hymer 1976), while they also suffer from—as Amendolagine and Rabellotti (2017) call it—the "liability of emergingness", which is related to their emerging market origin, reducing their legitimacy in advanced markets (Madhok and Keyhani 2012; Ramachandran and Pant 2010). The case of Chinese information and communications technology (ICT) companies such as Huawei is even more complex: in addition to these above-mentioned challenges, they also have to face national security concerns raised by most of the European states (Muralidhaara and Faheem 2019).

Chinese FDI flows to Europe, more specifically to the EU, peaked in 2016 when Chinese companies invested 37 billion EUR in the EU. It was a 77 per cent increase from the previous year (Hanemann and Huotari 2017: 4). From 2017 onwards, as Chinese global outward FDI has dropped, Chinese FDI transactions in the EU have also declined: in 2018 Chinese companies invested 17.3 billion EUR based on MERICS's report (Hanemann et al. 2019). However, this report also outlines the fact (p. 9) that Chinese outward FDI flows in 2018 would have been significantly higher if transactions connected to the acquisitions of stakes below 10 per cent would have been added to them.[1] The report mentions (on p. 9) the 7.3 billion EUR acquisition of a 9.7 per cent stake in Daimler in February 2018 as an example for recent acquisitions of stakes right below that threshold.

Figure 3.3 presents those EU countries (+ the UK) that host more than one billion USD Chinese FDI stock.[2] Majority of the top destinations are Western, Northern and Southern European countries with only one ECE country—Hungary—on the list of the top 12. Germany, France and Sweden—the top three destinations—together host more Chinese investment than the remaining nine countries combined. Chinese FDI stock in

[1] The ten per cent threshold is traditionally required for a transaction to qualify as FDI. Transactions that fall under the ten per cent threshold are usually qualified as portfolio investments and are not included in majority of the FDI datasets.

[2] The non-EU member Switzerland hosts the biggest amount of Chinese FDI stock in Europe. In 2018 it reached 18,084 million USD according to OECD Statistics.

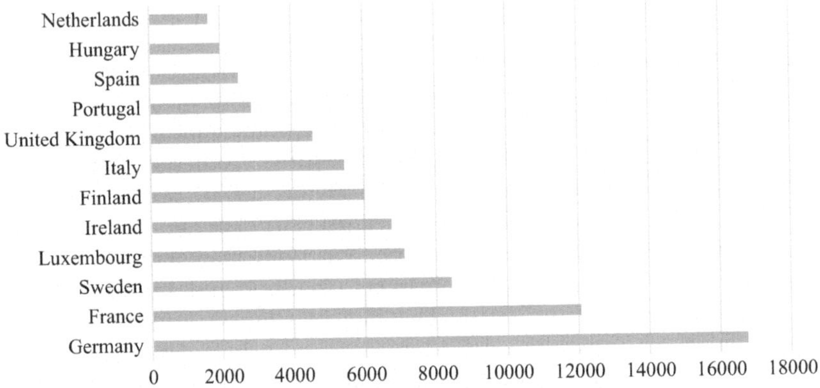

Fig. 3.3 Top 12 EU destinations for Chinese outward FDI (FDI stock, 2018, million USD). (Data source: OECD)

the ten new CEE member states—in those CEE countries that joined the EU in 2004 and 2007[3]—is relatively modest when compared to that in the core EU countries. The ten new member states together host a bit less than 5000 million USD Chinese FDI stock, which represents a bit more than six per cent of the total Chinese investment stock in the EU. Annual FDI flows are characterized by rather hectic movements and often related to one or two transactions per year. In 2018, Luxembourg, Sweden and Italy were the major receivers of Chinese MNEs' transactions; in 2017, it was Sweden, the UK and Portugal.

In the past years Chinese companies gained foothold in a wide range of industries in Europe. According to MERICS-Rhodium Group calculations (Hanemann et al. 2019), in 2018 the top sectors included automotive, financial and business services, ICT and health and biotech; in 2017 the most popular sectors were transport, utilities and infrastructure, ICT and real estate. The share of SOEs in total Chinese investment in Europe had started to decline between 2010 and 2012 (to 80–90 per cent); reached the lowest peak in 2016 (36 per cent); increased again in 2017 as a result of some major transactions of SOEs as well as the already mentioned capital controls that affected manly the private companies; and decreased again (to 41 per cent) in 2018 (Hanemann et al. 2019: 13–14).

[3]Czech Republic, Estonia, Hungary, Latvia, Lithuania, Poland, Slovakia and Slovenia joined in 2004 and Bulgaria and Romania in 2007.

3.3.1 Characteristics and Major Trends of Chinese Outward FDI in ECE

The transition of CEE—including ECE—countries from centrally planned to market economies resulted in increasing inflows of FDI to these countries. During the transition, the region went through radical economic changes which had been largely induced by foreign capital. Foreign MNEs realized significant investment projects in this region and established their own production networks. Although the majority of investors arrived from Western Europe, the first phase of inward Asian FDI also occurred right after the transition: Japanese and Korean companies indicated their willingness to invest in the ECE region even before the fall of the iron curtain. Their investments took place during the first years of the democratic transition. The second phase came in the new millennium, when the Chinese government initiated the "Go Global" policy, which was aimed at encouraging domestic companies to become globally competitive. Therefore Europe—including European peripheries—also became a target region for Chinese FDI (see Szunomár 2017).

Although China considers the CEE region as a bloc (this is one of the reasons for creating the 16 +1 initiative, which is a joint platform for the 16 CEE countries—now 17, including Greece—and China), some countries seem to be more popular investment destinations than others. CEE countries host Chinese FDI to varying degrees: the four Visegrád countries, Czechia, Hungary, Poland and Slovakia, take more than 75 per cent of the total Chinese outward FDI to the broader CEE region, while the other CEE countries—despite slight increases in many cases—have not received significant amounts of Chinese FDI flows so far.[4] The reason behind this representation is twofold. On the one hand, Chinese companies prefer EU member states. As Chinese companies are often targeting EU markets with their products, they prefer to establish or purchase company sites in the EU member states to avoid trade barriers such as tariffs

[4] Countries in the Balkans have not received so far big amounts of FDI from China, despite some of them being EU members and others potential candidates. Romania, Serbia, Greece and Bulgaria are the major recipients in the Balkan region; they host 80 per cent of the Chinese FDI stock in the Balkans (still, it is just one quarter of the Chinese FDI stock in the Visegrád region). Based on Chinese statistics, countries such as Albania and Bosnia and Herzegovina seem not to attract any significant Chinese FDI at all (both data are below 10 million USD), while North Macedonia, Montenegro, Slovenia and Croatia also host less than 100 million USD Chinese FDI stock.

and non-tariff barriers (e.g. quotas or embargoes) in market access. On the other hand, China tries to play safe. It targets with FDI CEE countries that have already attracted investments from elsewhere, for example, the US, Japan or Western Europe, Germany, in particular.

The selected five ECE countries account for a major share of the population (around 66 million) and economic output (more than 1000 billion USD according to the World Bank) of CEE. Moreover, all of the five countries have strengthened their relations with China in recent years. Among ECE countries, Hungary, Czechia and Poland have received the bulk of Chinese investment in recent years, while Slovakia and Slovenia lag a little behind due to their small size and lack of efficient transport infrastructure. Besides stock and flow amounts, comparison of the data of the ECE countries shows that in per-capita terms, too, Hungary is the most important host country for Chinese FDI as it has more FDI per capita than the other four.

As can be seen from Fig. 3.4, Chinese outward investment stock in the five ECE countries has steadily increased in the last one and a half decades, particularly after 2004 and 2008: after the countries' accession to the EU and the economic and financial crisis, respectively. According to Chinese statistics, there was a real rapid increase from 9.6 million USD in 2004 to 673 million USD in 2010. By 2017, the amount of Chinese investments had further increased and reached 1009 million USD according to the data published by the MOFCOM.

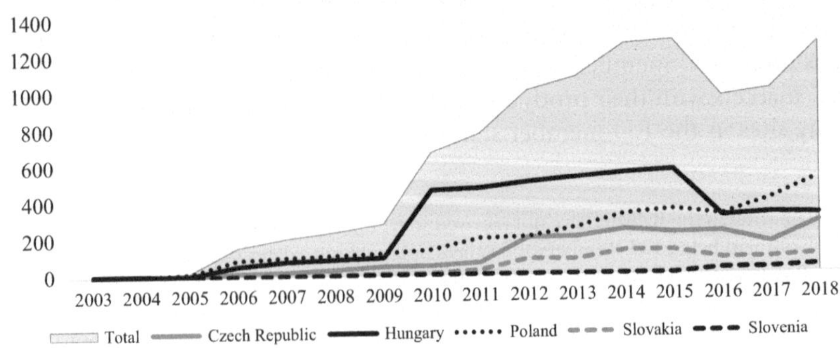

Fig. 3.4 Chinese FDI stock in ECE countries, Chinese statistics, million USD, 2003–2018. (Data source: MOFCOM)

At this point, it is important to note that MOFCOM statistics are adequate to show the main trends of Chinese outward FDI stocks and flows; however, apart from this, they prove to be a less reliable data source as they do not show the Chinese investments that have flowed to a country through a foreign country, company or subsidiary. To identify the home country of the foreign investor who ultimately controls the investments in the host country, the new International Monetary Fund (IMF) guidelines recommend compiling inward investment positions according to the Ultimate Investing Country (UIC) principle. Therefore we decided to use the database of the OECD as it tracks back data to the ultimate parent companies (see Fig. 3.5). When comparing the two datasets—MOFCOM and OECD—we find huge discrepancies that justify the assumption that Chinese companies are indeed using intermediary companies when investing in Europe, including in ECE countries. It also confirms that Chinese FDI is much more significant in the ECE region—especially in Czechia, Hungary and Poland—than previously thought.

Based on OECD statistics, FDI flows are relatively hectic (see Fig. 3.6), which probably means that FDI flows from China are connected to one or two big business deals per year. Disinvestments are less characteristic for the majority of the analysed countries; however, one big disinvestment indeed took place in Czechia in 2018, which is probably the result of the financial problems of one particular Chinese company, CEFC China Energy, a major Chinese company that invested in Czechia.

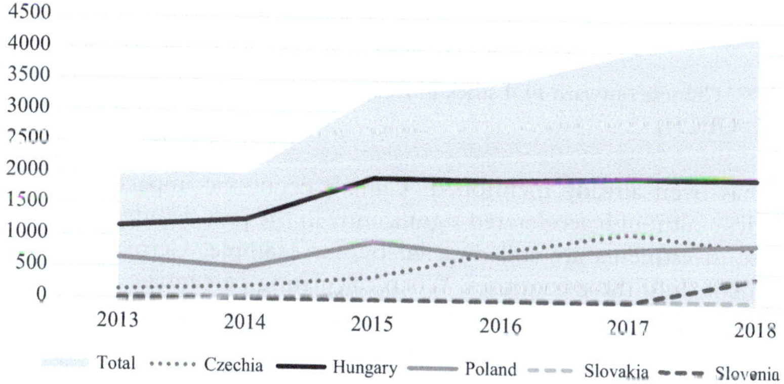

Fig. 3.5 Chinese FDI stock in ECE countries, OECD statistics, million USD, 2013–2018. (Data source: OECD)

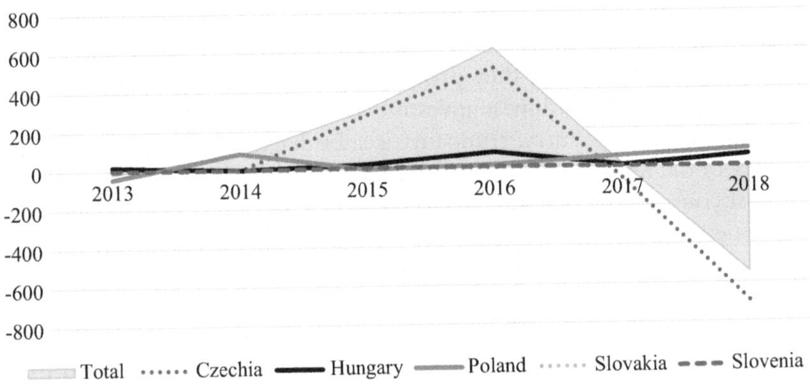

Fig. 3.6 Chinese FDI flow to ECE countries, million USD, 2013–2018. (Data source: OECD)

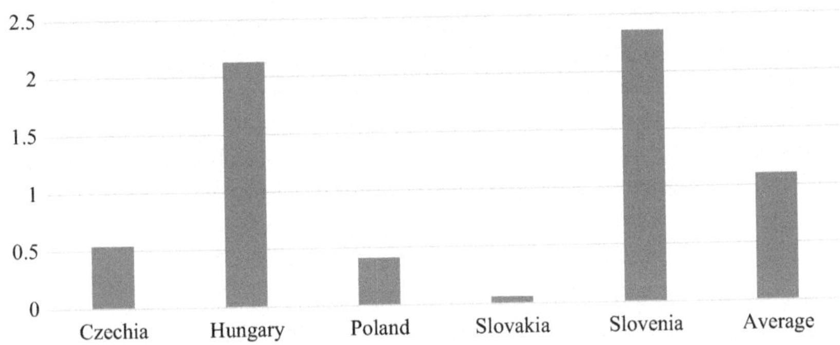

Fig. 3.7 Chinese outward FDI stock in ECE as a percentage of total FDI, 2018. (Source: OECD)

As has been already mentioned, China's economic impact on ECE countries—although accelerated significantly in the past decade—is small; Chinese investments are still dwarfed by, for example, German MNEs' investments into these countries. When calculating percentage shares, we found that Chinese FDI stocks are around 1 per cent of the total inward FDI stocks in ECE countries (see Fig. 3.7). As a result, China's share of the total FDI in ECE is still far from being decisive: it is below 1 per cent for Czechia, Slovakia and Poland and below 2.5 per cent for Hungary and Slovenia. It is worth mentioning that in ECE countries, (Western)

European investors are still responsible for more than 70 per cent of the total FDI stocks, while among non-European investors, companies from the US, Japan and South Korea are typically more important players than those from China.

3.3.2 *Changing Patterns of Chinese MNEs' Activities in ECE*

As presented in Table 3.1, Chinese investors typically target secondary and tertiary sectors of the selected five ECE countries. Initially, Chinese investment flowed mostly into manufacturing (assembly), but over time, services have attracted more and more investment as well. For example, in Hungary and Poland there are branches of the Bank of China and the Industrial and Commercial Bank of China as well as offices of some of the largest law firms in China, such as Yingke Law Firm (established in Hungary in 2010 and in Poland in 2012) and Dacheng Law Offices (established in Poland in 2011 and in Hungary in 2012). The main Chinese investors targeting these five countries are primarily interested in telecommunication, electronics, the chemical industry and transportation.

The main entry modes of and sectors targeted by Chinese investment are similar in all ECE countries, despite being more diverse in the more popular target countries (Hungary and Poland). With regard to certain sectors, such as tourism, Chinese companies have preferred to target Slovenia.

Although the main entry mode used to be greenfield in the first years after Chinese companies had discovered the ECE region, M&As became more frequent later on, especially after the global economic and financial crisis of 2008. However, ECE countries—unlike countries in, for example, Western Europe—are not offering too many M&A opportunities since the number of successful, globally competitive companies are lower in the region. The low number of such acquirable companies is one of the potential reasons for the lack of new investments in these countries in recent years. On the one hand, Chinese companies have been increasingly motivated by gaining access to brands and new technologies and by discovering market niches that they can fill on European markets in the past decade. On the other hand, new Chinese greenfield projects have been targeting less developed regions (of Europe) with low factor costs. The ECE region lies somewhere in between: it has just a few good M&A deals while it is a less attractive destination for greenfield projects when

Table 3.1 Characteristics of major Chinese investment in the ECE region

	Hungary	*Poland*	*Czechia*	*Slovakia*	*Slovenia*
Entry mode	Greenfield/ brownfield, M&A, joint ventures	Greenfield and M&A	Greenfield and M&A	Greenfield and M&A	M&A and greenfield
Main sectors	Chemical, IT/ ICT, electronics, wholesale and retail, automotive, banking, hotels and catering, logistics, real estate	IT/ICT, electronics, heavy machinery, publishing and printing, real estate, municipal waste processing	Electronics, IT/ICT, transport equipment, automotive, shipping, engineering, food, media, plate-making	automotive industry, IT/ ICT	Chemical, automotive, airport construction/ airplane production industry, electronics/ high technology, IT/ICT
Most important Chinese companies	Wanhua, Huawei, ZTE, Lenovo, Sevenstar Electronics, BYD Electronics, ZMJ, Comlink, Yanfeng, China-CEE Fund	Liu Gong Machinery, Huawei, ZTE, Haoneng Packaging, Shanxi Yuncheng Plate-making Group, Sino Frontier Properties Ltd., China Everbright International Ltd.	Shanxi Yuncheng, Changhong, SaarGummi, Noark, Huawei, ZTE, Shanghai Maling, COSCO, YAPP, CEFC, Buzuluk Komarov, China CNR	SaarGummi, ZVL Auto, Inalfa Roof Systems, Mesnac, Lenovo, Huawei	Zhejiang Jinke Culture Industry, Elaphe, Sino-Pipistrel Asia Pacific, TAM Durabus, Fotona, Arctur, Acies Bio, Chiho Tiande Group, China-CEE Fund, Huawei

Source: Own compilation

compared to countries, for example, in the Balkans. Nevertheless, the ECE region's position as a manufacturing or logistic base is still important for the Chinese MNEs—due to EU membership of these countries and the resulting "Made in EU" label on products assembled here—as will be explained in more detail in Chap. 4.

The Amadeus database, which provides information for public and private companies across Europe, lists 413 companies with Chinese ultimate owner in the five ECE countries: 230 in Czechia, 14 in Hungary, 61 in Poland, 103 in Slovakia and 5 Slovenia. More than half (243) of those 413 companies are located in the respective capitals of the five ECE countries, but the majority of the other companies are also operating in bigger cities of the analysed countries or in smaller cities near the capitals.

It has to be emphasized though that the number of companies listed by the Amadeus database does not really reflect the amount of Chinese FDI stock in these countries since—as mentioned above—Hungary hosts the majority of Chinese FDI—almost two billion USD—in the region, followed by Poland and Czechia. There are three potential reasons for this phenomenon. First, this database—as many other similar databases—seems to be incomplete as it does not include all of the Chinese companies that have invested in the ECE countries. For example, in the Hungarian case, for some reason, even some of the most significant investors are not listed by the Amadeus database: Huawei, which has its logistic centre as well as parts of its assembly activity in Hungary; BYD, which produces electronic buses in Northern Hungary; and Joyson, which develops and manufactures automotive safety systems in the eastern part of the country, just to mention a few. Second, majority of the numerous companies that are listed by Amadeus in, for example, Czechia or Slovakia are small wholesale or retail companies or firms operating restaurants or mobile food service activities. They employ a few people, and their assets as well as turnover are not very significant. Third, Hungary also hosts a lot of Chinese wholesale and retail companies, as well as restaurants, but those are operated by local Chinese nationals, that is, by Chinese people that arrived in the country in the late 1980s or the early 1990s when there were no visa requirements between the two countries. As a result, these companies do not appear in the Amadeus database. According to the company information database of Opten Ltd Hungary,[5] there were 1117 companies registered in Hungary with Chinese ownership in 2019.

3.4 Host Country Determinants of Chinese Outward FDI in the ECE Region

Chinese MNEs' motivations are often different from those of developed countries. For example, as Hanemann (2013) points out, there are commercial reasons behind most investments: (1) the acquisition of well-known brands or (high-)technology to increase competitiveness and (2) money-saving by moving towards higher value-added activities in countries where regulatory frameworks are more developed.

As mentioned already, host country determinants—or pull factors—are those characteristics of the host country markets that can help attract MNEs' investment. Pull factors—just like push factors—can be grouped into institutional and structural factors. We can further categorize institutional factors by dividing them into two levels: the supranational level and the national level. Both levels are important elements in the location decisions of Chinese companies investing in the five ECE countries (see McCaleb and Szunomár 2017). Based on the literature mentioned in the Chap. 1 as well as based on interviews conducted with company representatives and experts, in the case of Chinese MNEs, the main structural and institutional pull factors are presented in Table 3.2.

3.4.1 ECE Countries' Structural and Institutional Pull Factors for Chinese MNEs

When searching for possible pull factors that could make ECE countries a favourable investment destination for Chinese investors, the labour market is to be considered as one of the most important elements: a skilled labour force is available in sectors for which Chinese interest is growing, with labour costs being lower than the EU average. However, there are differences within the broader CEE region as well; unit labour costs are usually cheaper in Bulgaria and Romania than in the five ECE countries. Corporate taxes can also play a role in the decision of Chinese companies to invest in the region. Nevertheless, the differences in labour costs and

[5] https://www.opten.hu/kozlemenyek/egyre-tobb-a-tisztan-hazai-erdekeltsegu-milliardos-ceg-magyarorszagon.

Table 3.2 Major characteristics of analysed Chinese companies in the ECE region

Structural/macroeconomic pull factors	*Institutional pull factors*	
	Supranational	*National*
Market access	International and regional investment and trade agreements, free trade agreements	Host government policies (including strategic partnership agreements between the government and certain companies)
Low factor costs (resources, materials, labour)	Advanced institutional setting; institutional stability (such as IPR protection)	Tax incentives, special economic zones
Qualification of labour force	European production and services standards (such as product safety standards)	"Golden visa" programmes (residence visa for a certain amount of investment)
Various opportunities for asset-seeking companies: brands, know-how, knowledge, networks, distribution channels, access to global value chains, etc.	Chance for participation at EU level public procurement processes	Institutions such as banks, government-related investment promotion agencies (IPAs)
Company-level relations		Possibility for more acquisitions through privatization opportunities
The high level of technology		Home country diaspora in the host country

Source: Own compilation based on reviewed literature and company interviews

corporate taxes within the broader CEE region do not really seem to influence Chinese investors. After all, there is more investment from China in ECE countries (especially in Czechia, Hungary and Poland) than in Romania or Bulgaria, where labour costs and taxes are lower. This can be explained by the theory of agglomeration as outward FDI in ECE countries is the highest in the region (see McCaleb and Szunomár 2017).

Although the above-mentioned efficiency-seeking motives play a role, the main type of Chinese FDI in ECE countries is definitely market-seeking investment: by entering these markets, Chinese companies have access to the whole EU market; moreover, they might also be attracted by free trade agreements between the EU and third countries, such as Canada, and the EU neighbouring country policies as they claim that their ECE subsidiaries are to sell products in the ECE host countries, the EU and Northern American or even global markets (see Wiśniewski 2012: 121). For example, the subsidiary of Nuctech (a security scanning equipment manufacturer) in Poland also sells to Turkey; the subsidiary of Guangxi LiuGong Machinery in Poland targets the EU, North American and Commonwealth of Independent States (CIS) markets, while Huawei's logistic centre in Hungary supplies over 50 countries located in Europe and North Africa.

Based on the interview results, Chinese companies wanted to operate in ECE due to their already existing businesses in Western Europe and to strengthen their presence in the wider European market. In addition, there are also cases of Chinese companies following their customers to the ECE region, as in the case of Victory Technology (supplier to Philips, LG and TPV) or Dalian Talent Poland (supplier of candles to IKEA) (see McCaleb and Szunomár 2017: 125). Moreover, through their ECE subsidiaries, Chinese firms can participate in public procurements and access EU funds. As a case in point, Nuctech established its subsidiary in Poland in 2004, initially targeting mainly Western European markets, before focusing more on the ECE (CEE) region, which benefits from different EU funds. Recently, Chinese firms have also become interested in investing in the food industry as a result of the growing awareness about food safety standards and certificates. They are interested in exporting agricultural products which meet EU safety certificates to China where food safety causes problems. These factors lead us to the institutional host country determinants of the ECE region (Table 3.3).

As for supranational institutional factors, we can state that the change in the ECE countries' institutional setting due to their economic integration into the EU has been the most important driver of Chinese outward FDI in the region, especially in the manufacturing sector. EU membership of ECE countries allowed Chinese investors to avoid trade barriers, and ECE countries could serve as an assembly base for Chinese companies. Moreover, not only actual EU membership but also the prospects of EU membership attracted Chinese investors to the region: thus, some companies made their first investments even before 2004, that is, in the early 2000s. New investments arrived in the year of accession, too. The second "wave" of Chinese FDI in CEE dates back to the global economic and financial crisis, when financially distressed companies all over Europe, including ECE, were often acquired by Chinese companies.

Table 3.3 Major characteristics of analysed Chinese companies in the ECE region

Location	*Year of investment*	*Company type*	*Industry*	*Entry mode*	*Employees direct (indirect)*	*Pull factors*
Central Hungary	2004/2008	Private	Telecommunications	Greenfield	330 (over 2500)	Macroeconomic, institutional (supranational, national)
Mazovian (north-eastern) region of Poland	2007	Private	Telecommunications	Greenfield	425	Macroeconomic, institutional (supranational, national)
Northern Hungary	2011	SOE	chemical	M&A	Over 2500	Macroeconomic, institutional (supranational)
Central Hungary	2010	Private	Printer manufacturing, imaging technology	M&A (acquisition of a company that had a Hungarian subsidiary)	372	Macroeconomic, institutional (supranational)
Northern Hungary	2017	SOE	Automotive	Greenfield	n.a.	Macroeconomic, institutional (supranational, national)
Mazovian (north-eastern) region of Poland	2010	SOE	Industrial machinery	Greenfield	77	Macroeconomic, institutional (supranational, national)

(*continued*)

Table 3.3 (continued)

Location	*Year of investment*	*Company type*	*Industry*	*Entry mode*	*Employees direct (indirect)*	*Pull factors*
Malopolska (southern) region of Poland	2009	Private	Other miscellaneous manufacturing	Greenfield	n.a.	Macroeconomic, institutional (supranational, national)

Source: Own compilation based on interview results and data from the Amadeus database

This table contains the list of companies where the author either managed to conduct interviews on investment motivations or collected information on them from secondary sources.

Another aspect of EU membership that has induced Chinese investment in the five ECE countries was institutional stability (including, e.g., the protection of property rights). This was important for early investors from Japan and Korea and was one of the drivers of FDI by Chinese firms, given the unstable institutional, economic and political environment in their home country. These findings are in line with those of Clegg and Voss (2012: 101), who argue that Chinese outward FDI in the EU shows "an institutional arbitrage strategy" as "Chinese firms invest in localities that offer clearer, more transparent and stable institutional environments. Such environments, like the EU, might lack the rapid economic growth recorded in China, but they offer greater planning and property rights security, as well as dedicated professional services that can support business development".

National-level institutional factors include, for example, strategic agreements, tax incentives and privatization opportunities. The significance of such factors has begun to increase only recently as the majority of ECE countries—with the exception of Hungary—neglected relations with China in the early 2000s, starting to focus on the potentials of this relationship only since the aftermath of the global financial crisis of 2008. Based on our observations as well as responses from interviewees, Chinese companies indeed appreciate business agreements that are supported by the respective host country government. Thus, the high-level strategic agreements with foreign companies investing in Hungary offered by the Hungarian government could have also spurred Chinese investment in the region. Moreover, personal (political) contacts between representatives of the respective host country government and Chinese companies also proved to be important when choosing a host country in the ECE region.

Based on the available literature, companies interested in acquiring foreign assets might be motivated by a common culture and language as well as trade costs (see Blonigen and Piger 2014; Hijzen et al. 2008). We also found that in the case of Chinese MNEs' motives in the ECE region, a significant role is devoted to other less quantifiable aspects, such as the size and feedback of Chinese ethnic minority in the host country, investment incentives and subsidies, possibilities of acquiring visa and permanent residence permit, and the quality of political relations and government's willingness to cooperate. A clear example for that is the stock of Chinese investment in Hungary, which is the highest in the ECE region (as well as in the broader CEE region).

Hungary is a country where the combination of traditional economic factors and institutional factors seems to play an important role in attracting Chinese investors. The country has historically had good political relations with China, established earlier than by other ECE countries. From 2003 onwards, the Hungarian government has intensified bilateral relations to attract Chinese FDI. Moreover, Hungary is the only country in the region that has introduced special incentives for foreign investors from outside the EU, that is, a "golden visa" programme which enables investors to acquire a residence visa in exchange for investing a certain amount of money. Moreover, Hungary has the largest Chinese diaspora in the region, which is an acknowledged attracting factor for Chinese FDI in the extant scientific literature—in other words, a relational asset that constitutes an ownership advantage for Chinese firms when they invest in countries with a significant Chinese population (see Buckley et al. 2007). An example for this is Hisense's explanation of the decision to invest in Hungary which, besides traditional economic factors, was motivated by "good diplomatic, economic, trade and educational relations with China; big Chinese population; Chinese trade and commercial networks, associations already formed" (see CIEGA 2007).

3.4.2 *The Role of Political Relations in Attracting Chinese FDI to the ECE Region: Friendship Factor?*

In addition to the above-mentioned supranational- and national-level institutional pull factors, political relations between China and the respective ECE countries also seem to have influenced Chinese MNEs' investment decisions. Those countries that have acted in favour of China, supported Chinese global and regional initiatives and/or welcomed and fostered Chinese MNEs' investments typically host—or have hosted during the period of rather friendly ties—more Chinese FDI stock than those ECE countries that remained neutral over the opportunity to host Chinese FDI and/or where the political leaderships have a rather negative stance on China.

Hungary, for example, seems to be politically committed to China. In fact, Hungary was among the first countries to establish diplomatic relations with China (3 October 1949); since then, diplomatic gestures have been made and confidence-building measures taken from time to time. For instance, Hungary was the first European country to sign a memorandum of understanding with China on promoting the Silk Road Economic

Belt and the Maritime Silk Road during the visit of China's foreign minister Wang Yi to Budapest in June 2015. The Hungarian government was also very keen on promoting the Budapest-Belgrade railway, a long-negotiated soon to be started construction project under the Belt and Road umbrella. When signing the construction agreement in 2014, Prime Minister Viktor Orbán called it the most important moment for the cooperation between the EU and China (see Keszthelyi 2014). Supporting China's infrastructural endeavour is, however, not the only field where Hungary excelled in exams. In 2016, Hungary (and Greece) prevented the EU from backing a court ruling against China's expansive territorial claims in the South China Sea (see *The Economist* 2018), while in 2018, Hungary's ambassador to the EU was alone in not signing a report criticizing the Chinese One Belt, One Road (OBOR) initiative for benefitting Chinese companies and Chinese interests and for undermining principles of free trade through its lack of transparency in procurement (see Sweet 2018). In addition, as mentioned in the section above, it provided incentives for Chinese MNEs that have invested in the country. It has to be mentioned, though, that in the past few years the amount of Chinese FDI stock has been very slightly increasing in Hungary. The potential reason for that is China now focuses on infrastructure projects in the EU and the already mentioned Budapest-Belgrade railway project—if successfully implemented—would be a good base for reference when applying for other projects within the EU.

Starting from a rather cold and critical stance, Czechia's relationship with China changed a few years ago. Since then, similar political factors—compared to the Hungarian case—have been observed in Czech-Chinese relations: after Czech "political sympathy" emerged, inflows of Chinese FDI to Czechia started to increase. As a case in point, the Czech president Milos Zeman—who was the only high-level European politician visiting Chinese celebrations of the end of World War II in 2015—declared that he wants his country to be China's "unsinkable aircraft-carrier" in Europe (see *The Economist* 2018). Zeman also had a Chinese adviser on China, coming directly from a Chinese company with a controversial background. Moreover, as a potential result of the improving political relations, the Chinese company CEFC recently invested sizeable amounts—1.5 billion EUR—in Czechia. It has to be added, however, that this company is now under investigation by Chinese authorities for "suspicion of violation of laws" (see Lopatka and Aizhu 2018). As a result, Czech-Chinese relations have been cooling off again, and new Chinese FDI flows have not arrived since then; moreover, disinvestment has taken place in 2017 (see Figs. 3.5 and 3.6)

Slovakia can be currently perceived as one of the most pro-Western states in the region, particularly in terms of its relatively pro-EU stances, especially when compared with other Visegrád countries. As a result, Slovakia was more ignorant towards China during the past years, although it supported 16(17) + 1 and Belt and Road initiatives but with less enthusiasm and rather chose a "wait and see" approach. Similarly, Slovenian-Chinese relations have not received high priority on the political level, not even in the country's foreign policy orientation. Besides, the former (2004–2008; 2012–2016) as well as current (2020–) prime minister, Janez Jansa, has a rather negative stance on China: previously (while in opposition) he met the Dalai Lama and travelled to Taiwan at the invitation of the government of the Republic of China. Consequently, Chinese investment into both Slovakia and Slovenia has relatively insignificant when compared to Chinese MNEs' investments in the other three ECE countries.

Poland used to be more enthusiastic about the potentials of its economic relationship with China. Recently, however, the country has taken a more critical—or even cautious—stance. For Poland, high trade deficits represent the biggest problem with regard to the country's bilateral ties with China: Poland imports from China goods to a value of some 12 times that of Poland's exports to China, with the deficit reaching 20 billion EUR according to Eurostat. Potential security risks of Chinese investments caused the Polish government to reconsider its rather positive approach towards China and to use firm rhetoric about trade deficits as a serious political problem. This reconsideration was signalled, for example, by the cancellation of a tender in February 2018 for a land in Łódź where a transhipment hub was to be built and in which a Polish-Chinese company expressed interest. Another example was a government adviser's statement in connection with the Central Communication Port, a current flagship project of the Polish government, saying that Chinese (party) financing in return for control over the investment would be rejected (see Szczudlik 2017). As a probable result of this, investment flows are stagnating in the past one or two years. Poland is, however, too big a market for China to completely turn back on it; therefore it is possible that Chinese MNEs will be more persistent there.

3.5 Conclusions

The rise of Chinese multinationals is a new and dynamic process, while their approach towards their host economies is relatively unique compared to more developed MNEs. This chapter presented the main features of Chinese outward FDI globally, focusing both on push and pull factors behind the international expansion strategies of Chinese MNEs.

As presented in the above sections, initially the Chinese government had promoted outward FDI mainly to secure access to natural resources, while later market-seeking and efficiency-seeking motivations started to become important too. More recently the desire to acquire new technologies and managerial experience also came to the fore. The Chinese government has promoted and guided outward FDI with the main aim of acquiring assets that were scarce in the country or considered as crucial for further development of the domestic economy. With this objective it has mainly focused on the dynamic comparative advantages available in the host countries. Chinese MNEs' motivations for investment, however, vary from host country to host country: Chinese outward FDI in emerging or developing countries is characterized more by resource-seeking motives, while Chinese companies in the developed world are rather focusing on buying themselves into global brands or distribution channels, getting acquainted with local management skills and technology. Regarding modes of entry, investments shifted from greenfield projects to M&As, which represent currently around two-thirds of all Chinese outward FDI in value. This shift is driven by the financial crisis; however, it also seems to be a new trend of Chinese FDI to the developed world, while greenfield investment remains significant in the developing world. Outward FDI has also become more diversified in the past years: from mining and manufacturing it turned towards high technology, infrastructure and heavy industry, and lately to the tertiary sector, business services and finance but also health care, media and entertainment.

On the home country side, the Chinese government has pursued both proactive and interventionist strategies at the same time to promote the international expansion of Chinese companies in various sectors. This feature— that is, the prominent role of the state in initiating and intervening in corporate capital outflows—seems to be a distinctive element in the behaviour of Chinese MNEs when compared to multinational corporations of developed countries. These national champion companies were either state-owned or state-backed private firms that have benefitted from government subsidies and for a shorter or longer period of time were protected from—domestic as well as foreign—competition.

Asia continues to be the largest recipient of total Chinese outward FDI, accounting for nearly three-quarters, followed by the EU, Australia, the US, Russia and Japan. The numbers might be misleading though due to round-tripping investments. According to project-level analysis, 60 per cent of Chinese outward FDI is aimed at developed economies. As for Chinese MNEs' FDI to the EU, Chinese investors have preferred "old European" investment destinations not only because of market size but also because of well-established and sound economic relations with these countries.

The decline in Chinese outward FDI flows is relatively significant in the past few years; however, Chinese companies are still spreading and expanding in Europe, which often results in scrutiny and caution in some of the European countries as well as on the EU level. Chinese greenfield investments and acquisitions are perceived—especially but not exclusively by Western European governments—to threaten the competitiveness, strength and unity of Europe, both economically and politically. However, in Eastern and Southern Europe, where China is engaging within the so-called 16(17) + 1 framework, some of the countries rather welcome than fear Chinese FDI transactions.

Chinese investment in ECE countries constitutes a small share in China's total FDI stock, even if compared to Chinese total FDI stock in Europe, and is quite a new phenomenon. Nevertheless, Chinese FDI in the ECE region is on the rise and may increase further due to recent developments between China and certain countries of the region, especially Hungary. The analysis of the motivations behind Chinese outward FDI in ECE shows that Chinese MNEs mostly search for markets. ECE countries' EU membership allows them to treat the region as a "back door" to the affluent EU markets; moreover, Chinese investors are attracted by the relatively low labour costs, skilled workforce and market potential. It is characteristic that their investment patterns in terms of country location resemble that of the world's total FDI in the region.

As demonstrated in the analysis above, macroeconomic or structural factors do not fully explain the decisions behind Chinese FDI in the broader CEE region, including ECE countries. For example, Hungary, Czechia and Poland, the three largest recipients of Chinese investment in CEE, are not the most attractive locations either in terms of cutting costs or when searching for potential markets in the broader CEE region. This indicates that institutions may be crucial for Chinese companies when deciding on investment locations. In order to map out the real significance of such institutional factors, these were divided into two levels: the supranational level and the national level. Supranational institutional factors that attract Chinese companies to the ECE region are linked to the EU membership (economic integration) of ECE countries, especially to the institutional stability provided by the EU. Country- or national-level institutional factors that impact location choice within ECE seem to be privatization opportunities, investment incentives, such as tax incentives, special economic zones, "golden visas" or resident permits in exchange for a given amount of investment, and the size of the Chinese ethnic population in the host country.

Although we could not find clear evidence for causal links between the level of political relations and the amount of Chinese investment in ECE countries, good political relations between the respective host country and China seem to play an important role in attracting investment from Chinese state-owned as well as private companies. Examples are (1) Hungary's good political relations with and strong political commitment to China, while hosting the biggest stock of Chinese FDI in the ECE and the broader CEE region; (2) the positive political shift in Czech-Chinese relations that induced increasing amounts of Chinese FDI in Czechia; (3) stagnating stock of FDI in Poland as a result of a more critical stance on China and (4) the parallel between the lack of real interest to host Chinese MNEs from Slovakia and Slovenia and the low levels of Chinese FDI stock in these countries.

In order to investigate the topic in far more detail and find clear evidence on the existence of a political factor—or a "friendship factor"—among pull factors for Chinese FDI in the ECE region, a further possible step could be firm-level in-depth interviews with the officials of the most important Chinese companies that have invested in the ECE region, as well as personal interviews with government officials and business organizations in these countries.

References

Amendolagine, V., & Rabellotti, R. (2017). Chinese Foreign Direct Investments in the European Union. In J. Drahokoupil (Ed.), *Chinese Investment in Europe: Corporate Strategies and Labour Relations* (pp. 99–120). Brussels: ETUI.

Blonigen, B. A., & Piger, J. (2014). Determinants of Foreign Direct Investment. *Canadian Journal of Economics, 47*(3), 775–812.

Buckley, P. J., Clegg, L. J., Cross, A. R., Liu, X., Voss, H., & Zheng, P. (2007). The Determinants of Chinese Outward Foreign Direct Investment. *Journal of International Business Studies, 38*(4), 499–518.

Caseiro, L., & Masiero, G. (2014). OFDI Promotion Policies in Emerging Economies: The Brazilian and Chinese Strategies. *Critical Perspectives on International Business, 10*(4), 237–255.

CIEGA. (2007). Investing in Europe. A Hands-on Guide. Retrieved November 4, 2016, from http://www.e-pages.dk/southdenmark/2/72.

Clegg, J., & Voss, H. (2012). Chinese Overseas Direct Investment in the European Union. Retrieved August 17, 2017, from http://www.chathamhouse.org/sites/default/files/public/Research/Asia/0912ecran_cleggvoss.pdf.

Davies, K. (2013). China Investment Policy: An Update. OECD Working Papers on International Investment. 2013/01. OECD Publishing. Retrieved August 17, 2017, from https://doi.org/10.1787/5k469l1hmvbt-en.

Di Minin, A., Zhang, J. Y., & Gammeltoft, P. (2012). Chinese Foreign Direct Investment in R&D in Europe: A New Model of R&D Internationalization? *European Management Journal, 30*, 189–203.

Dunning, J., & Lundan, S. M. (2008). Institutions and the OLI Paradigm of the Multinational Enterprise. *Asia Pacific Journal of Management, 25*(4), 573–593.

Hanemann, T. (2013, January 27). The EU-China Investment Relationship: From a One-way to a Two-way street. *New Europe Online*. Retrieved August 17, 2017, from http://www.neurope.eu/kn/article/eu-china-investment-relationship-one-way-two-way-street.

Hanemann, T., & Huotari, M. (2017). Record Flows and Growing Imbalances – Chinese Investment in Europe in 2016. MERICS Papers on China, No 3. Retrieved October 15, 2017, from https://www.merics.org/fileadmin/user_upload/downloads/MPOC/COUTWARDFDI_2017/MPOC_03_Update_COUTWARD FDI_Web.pdf.

Hanemann, T., Huotari, M., & Kratz, A. (2019). *Chinese FDI in Europe: 2018 Trends and Impact of New Screening Policies*. Rhodium Group (RHG) and the Mercator Institute for China Studies (MERICS). Retrieved from https://www.merics.org/en/papers-on-china/chinese-fdi-in-europe-2018.

He, F., & Wang, B. (2014). Chinese Interests in the Global Investment Regime. *China Economic Journal, 7*(1): 4–20. Retrieved October 15, 2017, from https://doi.org/10.1080/17538963.2013.874067.

Hijzen, A., Görg, H., & Manchin, M. (2008). Cross-Border Mergers and Acquisitions and the Role of Trade Costs. *European Economic Review, 52*(5), 849–866.

Hymer, S. H. (1976). *The International Operations of National Firms: A Study of Direct Foreign Investment*. Cambridge, MA: MIT Press.

Irwin, A., & Gallagher, K. P. (2014). *Exporting National Champions: China's Outward FDI Finance in Comparative Perspective*. GEGI Working Paper, Boston University, June 2014, Paper 6. Retrieved from http://www.bu.edu/pardee-school/files/2014/11/Exporting-National-Champions-Working-Paper.pdf.

Keszthelyi, C. (2014). Belgrade-Budapest Rail Construction Agreement Signed. *Budapest Business Journal*, December 17.

Kostova, T., & Zaheer, S. (1999). Organizational Legitimacy Under Conditions of Complexity: The Case of the Multinational Enterprise. *Academy of Management Review, 24*(1), 64–81.

Lopatka, J., & Aizhu, C. (2018). CEFC China's Chairman to Step Down; CITIC in Talks to Buy Stake in Unit. *Reuters*, March 20. Retrieved November 28, 2018, from https://www.reuters.com/article/us-china-cefc-czech/cefc-chinas-chairman-to-step-down-citic-in-talks-to-buy-stake-in-unit-idUSKBN1GW0HB.

Luo, Y., Xue, Q., & Han, B. (2010). How Emerging Market Governments Promote Outward FDI: Experience from China. *Journal of World Business, 45*(1), 68–79.

Madhok, A., & Keyhani, M. (2012). Acquisitions as Entrepreneurship: Asymmetries, Opportunities, and the Internationalization of Multinationals from Emerging Economies. *Global Strategy Journal, 2*(1), 26–40.

McCaleb, A., & Szunomár, A. (2017). Chinese Foreign Direct Investment in Central and Eastern Europe: An Institutional Perspective. In J. Drahokoupil (Ed.), *Chinese Investment in Europe: Corporate Strategies and Labour Relations* (pp. 121–140). Brussels: ETUI.

MOFCOM (2004): Foreign Trade Law of The People's Republic of China. Available at: http://english.mofcom.gov.cn/aarticle/policyrelease/internationalpolicy/200705/20070504715845.html.

Morrison, W. M. (2013). China's Economic Conditions. CRS Report for Congress. Retrieved August 15, 2017, from http://www.au.af.mil/au/awc/awcgate/crs/rl33534.pdf.

Muralidhaara, G. V., & Faheem, H. (2019). Huawei's Quest for Global Markets. In China Europe International Business School (Ed.), *China-Focused Cases*. Singapore: Springer.

Naughton, B. (2007). *The Chinese Economy: Transitions and Growth*. Cambridge: MIT Press.

Nölke A., Ten Brink T., Claar S., May C. (2015): Domestic structures, foreign economic policies and global economic order: Implications from the rise of large emerging economies. *European Journal of International Relations* 2015, Vol. 21(3) 538–567

Peng, M. W. (2012). The Global Strategy of Emerging Multinationals from China. *Global Strategy Journal, 2*, 97–107.

Ramachandran, J., & Pant, A. (2010). The Liabilities of Origin: An Emerging Economy Perspective on the Costs of Doing Business Abroad. In T. Devinney, T. Pedersen, & L. Tihanyi (Eds.), *The Past, Present and Future of International Business and Management* (pp. 231–265). New York: Emerald Group Publishing.

Rosen, D. H., & Hanemann, T. (2009). China's Changing Outbound Foreign Direct Investment Profile: Drivers and Policy Implications. Policy Brief – Peterson Institute for International Economics, PB09-14. Retrieved August 15, 2017, from http://www.iie.com/publications/pb/pb09-14.pdf.

Sass, M., Szunomár, Á., Gubik, A., Kiran, S., & Ozsvald, É. (2019). Employee Relations at Asian Subsidiaries in Hungary: Do Home Or Host Country Factors Dominate? *Intersections: East European Journal of Society and Politics, 5*(3), 23–48.

Sauvant, K. P., & Chen, V. Z. (2014). China's Regulatory Framework for Outward Foreign Direct Investment. *China Economic Journal, 7*(1), 141–163.

Scissors, D. (2014). *China's Economic Reform Plan Will Probably Fail.* Washington, DC: AEI. Retrieved August 15, 2017, from https://www.aei.org/wp-content/uploads/2014/02/-chinas-economic-reform_130747310260.pdf.

Sweet, R. (2018). EU Criticises China's 'Silk Road', and Proposes Its Own Alternative. *Global Construction Review*, May 9. Retrieved November 28, 2018. from http://www.globalconstructionreview.com/trends/eu-criticises-chinas-silk-road-and-proposes-its-ow/.

Szczudlik, J. (2017). Poland's Measured Approach to Chinese Investments. In J. Seaman, M. Huotari, & M. Otero-Iglesias (Eds.), *Chinese Investment in Europe – A Country-Level Approach.* ETNC Report, December.

Szunomár, Á. (2017). *Driving Forces Behind the International Expansion Strategies of Chinese MNEs.* IWE Working Paper 237.

Ten Brink, T. (2013). *Chinas Kapitalismus. Entstehung, Verlauf, Paradoxien / China's Capitalism: Emergence, Trajectory, Paradoxes.* Frankfurt; New York: Campus.

The Economist. (2018). China Has Designs on Europe. Here Is How Europe Should Respond. Print Edition of 4 October, 2018.

UNCTAD. (2013). *Global Value Chains: Investment and Trade for Development.* United

Wang, B. (2013). A Misread Official Data: The True Pattern of Chinese ODI. *International Economic Review* (GuoJi Jing Ji Ping Lun) 2013/1, pp. 61–74.

Wiśniewski, P. A. (2012). Aktywność w Polsce przedsiębiorstw pochodzących z Chin [Activity of Chinese Companies in Poland]. *Zeszyty Naukowe, 34.* Kolegium Gospodarki Światowej, SGH, Warszawa.

Witt, M. A., & Redding, G. (2013). Asian Business Systems: Institutional Comparison, Clusters and Implications for Varieties of Capitalism and Business Systems Theory. *Socio-Economic Review, 11*(2), 265–300.

Zhang, Y., Duysters, G., & Filippov, S. (2012). Chinese Firms Entering Europe: Internationalization Through Acquisitions and Strategic Alliances. *Journal of Science and Technology Policy in China, 3*(2), 102–123.

CHAPTER 4

Indian Companies' Global Aspirations in East Central Europe

Tamás Gerőcs

4.1 Introduction

The majority of discussion about companies' internationalization is theorized upon western experiences (cf. Dunning 1988; Nölke and May 2019). A vast empirical evidence suggests that companies from the Global South, particularly from the BRICS countries (Brazil, Russia, India, China and South Africa), are exercising an increasing geopolitical power in international relations. Their experience of going international, however, has remained conceptually underexplored. In this chapter I will elaborate on the Indian companies' experiences about going international with a particular focus on their investment strategy in East Central Europe (ECE). The chapter builds on macro statistical evidence from the Hungarian Statistical Office, Reserve Bank of India (RBI) and Eurostat, plus on a collection of qualitative data that was gathered after conducting interviews with some of the largest Indian companies operating in the region. After the introduction, the first two sections of the chapter contain a theoretical

T. Gerőcs (✉)
Institute of World Economics, Centre for Economic and Regional Studies, Budapest, Hungary

Á. Szunomár (ed.), *Emerging-market Multinational Enterprises in East Central Europe*, Studies in Economic Transition,
https://doi.org/10.1007/978-3-030-55165-0_4

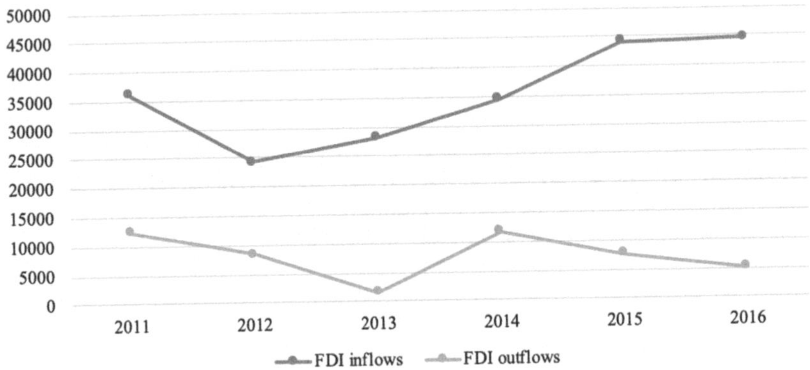

Fig. 4.1 FDI inflows and outflows to and from India in million USD. (Source: Author's own compilation based on UNCTADStat [https://unctadstat.unctad.org/EN/])

discussion on Indian companies' global aspiration, while the last two sections provide empirical evidence on their activity in the European Union, comparing western and ECE characteristics (Fig. 4.1).

Multinational companies from the BRICS countries have become key drivers of increases in foreign direct investment (FDI) globally, accounting for 62% of total developing country outward foreign direct investment (OFDI) stock in 2016—with China alone accounting for 36% (Kuzminska-Haberla 2012; Perea and Stephenson 2018: 114). Between 2000 and 2015, developing countries quadrupled their share in total global FDI stocks, increasing from 4% to over 15%, equal to approximately USD 3000 billion by 2015. One reason for the spectacular rise is that OFDI can enhance their capacity for innovation and extended trade relations (Hattari and Rajan 2010; Exim Bank 2014) (Fig. 4.2).

Indian companies used to be laggards among large BRICS investors. In the late 1980s the dominant share of Indian OFDI still targeted the Global South, but since the 2000s we see a gradual rise in advanced economies, such as western Europe and the ECE region (Pradhan and Singh 2009; Pradhan and Aggarwal 2011; Pradhan 2017). This phenomenon shows the emergence of the Indian "global contender" multinationals, whose history have been characterized by the elimination of economic protectionism and the concomitant liberalization of the Indian economy (Venkata Ratnam 1998, 2006; Pradhan 2004; Panagariya 2004; Athukorala

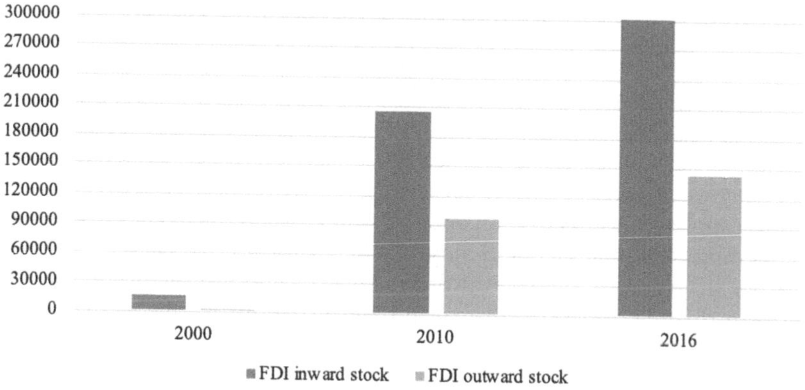

Fig. 4.2 Inward and outward stocks of FDI in India in million USD. (Source: Author's own compilation based on UNCTADStat [https://unctadstat.unctad.org/EN/])

2009). Given the fact that Indian firms contributed to overseas investments since the late 1960s and have witnessed a number of key structural amendments[1] in the country's industrial policy agenda that have considerably influenced their investment behaviour, Indian companies' experience offers one of the most insightful case studies to assess the changes in the global landscape of foreign direct investment.

From the beginning of the 2000s until the end of 2016, the total amount of India's foreign direct investment was roughly estimated at USD 255.4 billion (Gerőcs 2018a). While the magnitude of OFDI has risen remarkably over the last decade, a thorough analysis of the change of the character of investments, including the transformation of the sectoral composition and the geographical characteristics, such as both home and host country attributions, is still needed for understanding Indian multinationals' global aspirations.

[1] The three pillars of economic reforms in 1991 have been the cornerstone of economic policy and foreign exchange regulations, for example, the central bank's liberalization in relation to balance of payment activities. As a result of the liberalization, Indian firms have been seeking joint venture partnership with foreign companies. The transformation for overseas investment was further supported by administrative relaxation of the foreign exchange control, particularly as the FERA was replaced by the FEMA in 2000 (Gerőcs 2017, 2018).

4.2 Motivations for Internationalization

We apply Ramamurti and Singh's (2009) categorization for the various internationalization strategies that Indian companies follow. They introduced four generic categories, each of which reflects a particular strategy in a particular area, making differences in the companies' profiles, for example, their sectoral, size-wise or age composition. None of these categories apply to western companies in more stable financial conditions. According to Ramamurti and Singh (2009) Indian firms need to develop further from these categories if they want to achieve firm-specific advantages in the world market (Fleury and Fleury 2011).

The first category is called the "local optimizer". Firms in this category optimize production processes for the local Indian market where they are based. These companies have their competitive advantage in those special technological adaptations which fit well to the demands of other developing economies, for example, in terms of factor prices or the availability of labour (Pradhan and Singh 2011). Internationalization of local optimizers often targets other developing countries. The dominant industry in this category is manufacturing, especially auto-part production. The second category is called the "low-cost partner", whose core competences are in the area of management and corporate governance in general. Their operational skills and project management enable them to become global suppliers of large western multinationals in cutting-edge industries. Technological standards and technology-intensive specialization are the most significant ingredient in their internationalizations' success stories. Therefore, these companies rely heavily on both the qualified workforce in India and the Indian diaspora in western countries. This category consists of firms mostly in the pharmaceutical industry and service sectors, especially software and IT business providers who managed to specialize in Business Process Outsourcing (BPO) from western companies in the early 2000s. Both pharmaceuticals and IT companies are able to take advantages of the large pool of highly qualified Indian workforce at their own disposal and the high-profile institutions at home. Both IT and pharma companies are in the forefront of industrial conglomerates since the 1990s (Venkata Ratnam 2006).

The third category is called "global consolidator". These enterprises developed their competences in standardized production such as steel, textile or manufacturing. These companies were usually pioneering in their internationalization processes; some of them started overseas investments as early as the 1960s to overcome protectionist barriers at home. As their first attempt of internationalization during the period of import substitution industrialization (ISI) (in the 1960s and 1970s), firms pursued horizontal acquisitions in South-East Asian companies (Agarwala et al. 2004; Nayyar 2008). At a later stage in development these firms aimed at vertical integration in global value chains that helped them better access to western markets (Gereffi et al. 2005; Gereffi 2014). These supplier companies specialized in what proved to be unviable in the west due to intensified competition, crisis of overproduction and the relatively high level of production costs compared to the squeezed profit potential in their home markets. Global consolidators took over these positions by their ability for financial consolidation and cost reduction (Nayak 2011). Finally, the fourth category is called "global first mover". These companies are pioneering in combining state-of-the-art technologies with low-cost manufacturing. They are already on the technological frontiers in some of the most progressive industries where competition with western corporations are fierce. These are global innovators in engineering industries; one example is the Indian wind power alternative energy industry.

Using Dunning's (1988) categories for understanding investment strategies as a more generalized pattern, market-seeking strategies are still the most important among Indian firms; 51% of the respondents indicated market access as the main driver for overseas investment, while asset seeking (only 15%) and resource seeking (13%) were behind the decision—according to a survey conducted by the Federation of Indian Chambers of Commerce and Industry (FICCI 2006; Gerőcs 2018a: 20).[2]

Consequently, industrial composition reflects a shift from originally market-seeking to asset-seeking strategies (Kumar 2008). Manufacturing suppliers specialized in intermediate technologies in relatively low-tech industries. Their main competitive advantage was the ability of absorbing, assimilating and adapting foreign technologies to their local labour-abundant production systems. As many of the scholars on the subject of Indian multinationals agree, the comparative advantage of the largest Indian companies has dramatically changed from low level of technological capabilities and labour-intensive production to middle-ranked knowledge-based, technologically driven investment strategies aiming at advanced economies

[2] Interestingly in the post crises survey 22% of the respondents mentioned efficiency seeking as a main objective of overseas investment which reflected upon the rising competition from other developing countries with low production costs on the global stage.

(Gerőcs 2018b; Nölke et al. 2018). The shift has been largely driven by sectors, such as IT, pharmaceuticals, steel and ore, plus automotive. "Global contenders"[3] require sophisticated management practices and high level of technical expertise which they can acquire through FDI in countries which exhibit high-quality infrastructure or whose economies are embedded and connected to large-scale production systems where state-of-the-art technology is not only accessible but transferable to the periphery of the system.

However, when we examine internationalization from a more global perspective not all the stories of Indian companies become immediate successes of technological uplifting. These are often part of global processes in which counteracting world-economic forces simultaneously shape companies' fate. When we take these economic forces into account, the picture becomes more complicated. It is not only the decision of the particular management or the industrial policy that the state initiated, but many other world-economic aspects matter for the decision of the investing enterprises (Venkata Ratnam 2006; Gopinath 2007). In the following section we will gain a more thorough insight into the structure of the world economy from this more complex perspective.

4.3 Indian Investment in Global Outlook

More recent studies suggested that the primary drivers of internationalization are not only industry-driven processes, such as circumventing transportation costs, trade barriers or intangible asset-seeking, as Dunning et al. (2008) or even Ramamurti and Singh (2009) demonstrated, but more firm-specific characteristics (Feenstra 1998). The most important characteristic in this regard is Indian companies' access and usage of modern technology (Ramamurti 2012). The main driver for Indian multinationals to specialize in global value chains is to get access to state-of-the-art technology which can help them develop capacities in their home base.

Narayanan and Bhat (2011) has provided empirical evidence that there is a strong correlation between the level of productivity and the degree of internationalization among Indian companies. Their model comprises of a three-scale productivity scheme in which high-productivity companies—having both foreign and home-based R&D activities—have the most incentives to invest abroad. Companies in the middle-ranked productivity

[3] Global contender: see description in Boston Consulting Group's (2018) "Global Challengers Report".

range tend to prefer exporting over investment into foreign locations, whereas low-productivity firms still depend on domestic sales and, in many cases, rely on state subsidies or protectionist market policies (cf. Topalova and Khandelwal 2011; Thomas and Narayanan 2017: 8). In the following section we analyse those factors which Pradhan (2004) emphasized as the crucial firm-specific determinants for Indian companies when they enter foreign, mostly advanced, markets to specialize in the local production system. These factors are the (1) imported technology, (2) export-intensity, (3) size and age of the supplier company, and (4) the sectoral composition of global contenders.

4.3.1 Technology Import

We can get a better insight into the structural transformation that has been characterizing global contenders from India, when focusing on their productivity improvements, the evolution of which is one of the strongest determinants for international FDI activity—according to Narayanan and Bhat (2011). In terms of OFDI's firm-specific objectives, Indian enterprises do not only intend to increase market share by acquiring intangible assets, but specific asset- and efficiency-seeking FDI targets technologically intensive production systems with new technologies, skills and marketing networks. These acquisitions concentrate in Europe from where technology import usually originates (Milelli 2007). Technology import is a crucial determinant; it is also related to the capacity of the foreign subsidiary to transfer acquired or embedded technology back to the parent company. We distinguish between two types of technology import in relation to Indian companies' internationalization experience. One is "embedded technology" in the form of capital goods, where we find a very strong correlation and complementary effect between Indian companies' trade and investment activities (Katrak 1990). Capital goods can be the product of foreign investments—especially if the production is part of an integrated value chain system—or they can be subject to international commerce (Sauvant and Pradhan 2010). The other form of technology import is when the company purchases know-how-related services, such as licenses for which the purchaser company is required to pay fees and royalties. In order to be able to reduce costs, Indian enterprises usually prefer to access cutting-edge technologies through trade and investment.

4.3.2 *Export Intensity*

Export intensity is another important determinant for Indian companies' overseas operations. Trade experience, for example, does matter for companies' foreign investment decisions because this experience creates knowledge about the destination which trade had previously destined. Export experience from the past typically helps to learn about local supplier networks, consumer preferences or any institutional mechanism important for trade, production and distribution. The common denominators for Indian companies investing in a foreign location are the following: an advantageous and stable (at least predictable) fiscal regime, favourable inter-governmental treaties with India covering bilateral trade and investment agreements as well as a comprehensive economic partnership with the Indian government. On top of that, low-tax regimes, including the avoidance of double-taxation standards, can also play a crucial role. As a more recent prerequisite global contenders prefer to have access to international financial markets (Pradhan 2017: 54).

4.3.3 *Firms' Size and Age*

The average size and age of firms concerned with internationalization is another widely discussed area (Chaudhry et al. 2018; Pradhan 2017: 62). It seems obvious that the bigger the given company is, the higher its chances for internationalization. Similarly, the older and more experienced the firm in concern is, the more likely that it can take the risk for overseas expansion, because of the previously gained experience in trade.

This presumption could apply to Indian companies in the period prior to the 2000s, but more recent studies show a rather mixed picture, which does not contradict the hypothesis above, but provides a more nuanced understanding of the working of these determinants (Ramamurti 2012). As for the size of Indian companies in concern, it is valid to say that large Indian firms are the biggest foreign investors. In fact, their share among investor groups rose from 64.4% in 1989 to 83.6% by 2015 (Pradhan 2017). Simultaneously, the role of small- and medium-sized enterprises (SMEs) in this realm is increasing too (cf. Pradhan and Das 2013). Their number has climbed recently in areas, such as IT and BPO service providers (ibid.). The net worth of their projects is, however, much smaller on average; therefore, their share among the investor groups is still miniscule of their larger competitor, at around 2%. They are usually small suppliers of large Indian chains, following their partners in internationalization. When the larger partner decides to shift operation overseas they also have to follow suit; otherwise, they risk losing out from the cooperation (Narayanan and Bhat 2011).

The age of the company is another variable indicating Indian companies' internationalization strategy. Approximately 50% of new foreign investments have been made by Indian companies operating for 20 years or less (Chaudhry et al. 2018; Pradhan 2017). Furthermore, 15.4% of the investment has been made by firms in the range of 20–30 years, while 10.8% of investments have been made by 30- to 40-year-old investor firms. Pradhan (2017) shows that past experience in investment or in trade is the strongest determinant for expansion, because international experience is a cumulative and transferable process. However, recent statistics show that the average age for companies before foreign market entry has also dramatically fallen in the last few years. An increasing number of Indian enterprises internationalize quicker than their ancestors would have in the past. The decrease of the average age for internationalization is mostly attributable to the increasing number of IT companies and other service sector participants. Many of these companies have the first experience with foreign investment while they are still in the phase of start-ups. This is especially true of Indian IT start-ups active in the Silicon Valley, or in other logistic centres in the west (e.g. in the UK or in Germany).

4.3.4 *The Ownership Structure of the Foreign Affiliates*

The ownership structure of Indian companies' foreign affiliates has been shifting since the 1980s—a process reflecting broader changes in the economy. Approximately 65% of the foreign subsidiaries of Indian companies comprised of joint ventures (JV) with minority stakes of the parent company in the 1980s (cf. Kumar 2008). In 2010–2015, fully owned subsidiaries (FOSs) of Indian companies accounted for 69% of the total OFDI approvals (Pradhan 2017: 58).

The preference of Indian firms to acquire FOSs in foreign affiliates could be attributed to the economic liberalization in India and to the protection of R&D centres in the host economies (Pradhan 2017). It is also worthwhile to mention that while Indian enterprises have increasingly tried to penetrate developed markets through mergers and acquisitions (M&As), greenfield investments are still the most popular mode of entry in key developing countries, mostly in South-East Asia (Nayyar 2008;

Khan 2012; Gerőcs 2017). This is probably due to the fact that markets in developed countries are well established and usually do not encourage greenfield investments from foreign investors. This spectacular shift in property relations reflects upon Indian companies' broader structural changes. Parent companies' decisions of ownership are influenced by the host country's regulatory framework. Before the 1990s, the majority of Indian OFDI went to Eastern Africa and South-East Asia, where foreign investment was permitted only in the form of joint ventures—to the benefit of the host economy (Perea and Stephenson 2018). Indian enterprises possessed modest technological advantage compared to western competitors and did not have enough experience in cross-border business operations; therefore, JVs reduced risks in developing countries with unstable business environments.[4]

Although restrictions on full ownership have been gradually relaxed in many developing countries, a reverse process can be observed in the developed economies, particularly in the EU.[5] The latter is lamented by some commentators (see, e.g. Emmott et al. 2018) as the first steps in a potential trade war, between the likes of the US, EU and China. Despite restrictive tendencies, advanced countries still convey a liberal approach to foreign trade and investment (Kohli 2005). This has benefitted Indian companies since the 1990s, because they have been able to shift from JV in developing markets to a strongly preferred FOS ownership structure in developed markets, such as that of the EU and the US (RBI 2016). FOS allows affected Indian companies to protect the modes of their productivity increases, underpinned by developed countries' patent systems. Furthermore, parent firms can use the existing patent system to legally purchase and upgrade their existing technological capacity. Despite the opportunity, Indian firms still prefer to avoid this mode of acquiring technology, due to the high transaction costs associated with it (Charlie 2012; Ramamurti 2012). On the other hand, a secure and reliable patent system remains attractive for Indian companies when choosing a country to invest.

FOSs currently account for the dominant share of Indian foreign investments, highlighting differences between developing and developed

[4] Governments in developing countries can still maintain capital account restrictions, requiring, for example, technology transfer from foreign investors through joint ventures in order to help these investments get embedded in the local economy.

[5] Political distresses in Europe, particularly in the southern member states and in the UK after the Brexit, could mean, however, that negotiation of a key bilateral agreement between India and the EU remained unsettled (Charlie 2012; Perea and Stephenson 2018).

economies in terms of transactions. In developed economies, over 80% of Indian investments were through FOSs before 2015, but slightly declining since then. The latest data from 2017 shows that the share dropped to 61%, which is largely due to some politically sensitive technological acquisitions in which the host country's government insisted on technology-sharing in the form of joint venture to avoid technological espionage (Nayyar 2008; Ramamurti 2012). Property transfers are double-edged swords; they can serve the interests of the investing company, but the host government can also enforce special restrictions if it intends to protect domestic technological monopolies.

Despite the suspension of the bilateral trade agreement, Indian companies' risk appetite to invest in European assets actually grew substantially, thanks to which the annual bilateral trade in goods and services amounted to over EUR 100 billion since 2012, and the EU became India's second largest trading partner. We see a distinct shift of Indian investments in favour of Europe at the expense of the US within developed countries. Europe had a share of 52% in 1989 but by 2015 over 76% of Indian foreign investments in developed countries targeted the European Union.

This spectacular geographical shift has been driven by Indian IT and ICT companies' internationalization processes. But pharmaceutical, automotive and steel companies also contributed to the global dynamism (Pradhan 2017).

4.3.5 *Sectoral Advantages in Advanced Markets*

After the economic liberalization of the 1990s the sectoral composition of Indian OFDI has dramatically changed (Fig. 4.3). During the ISI period foreign investments were traditionally dominated by large manufacturing companies in energy and textile industries (Panagariya 2004; Kumar 2008; Rajan and Yanamandra 2015). This was in line with the protectionist tendencies of import substitution industrialization (ISI) during that period. Large business conglomerates in manufacturing and extractive industries used low level of technology and labour-intensive production when they followed their market-seeking strategy. These investments were compelled to take minority stakes in joint ventures by both the recipient and sending regulatory authorities.

Since the 2000s, OFDI has become more and more diversified as investments spread widely across economic sectors. The share of primary sector OFDI was estimated at 19% and 6% of approved foreign

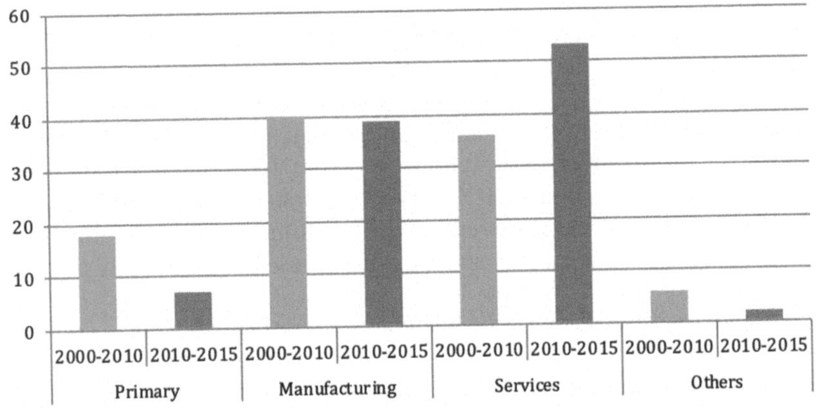

Fig. 4.3 Sectoral composition of Indian OFDI 2000–2010 and 2010–2015. (Source: Author's own compilation based on data from Reserve Bank of India and Indian Investment Centre [also cited in Chaudhry et al. 2018: 19])

investments in 2010 and 2015, respectively (Pradhan 2017). Manufacturing captured 40% and 39% of India's overall approved OFDI in between 2010 and 2015 respectively while the service sector accounted for 35% and 53% in the same period. In 2010 service sector became the leading force in OFDI, overtaking the position of manufacturing for the first time. Manufacturing still accounted for 40% of total Indian OFDI in 2009 because companies from the industry have also risen to take advantage of their global presence. Complex, technologically advanced companies dealing with pharmaceuticals, medicinal chemicals and forestry products, metal and ore products, coke and refined petroleum products, and so on have all emerged as important global contenders between 2010 and 2015.

This new trend might also be attributed to the liberal economic environment in India which helped the technologically intensive industries to strengthen competitiveness and also supported cross-border activities to boost their overseas export. Meanwhile manufacturing had overtaken services in terms of approved investments in 2000 and 2010, and service sector rebounded to become the leading OFDI sector in 2010 and 2015. In contrast to manufacturing, service sector enjoys majority ownership and companies follow asset-seeking strategy and rely more on mergers and acquisitions (than greenfield investments) in advanced economies (Nayyar 2008) (Fig. 4.4).

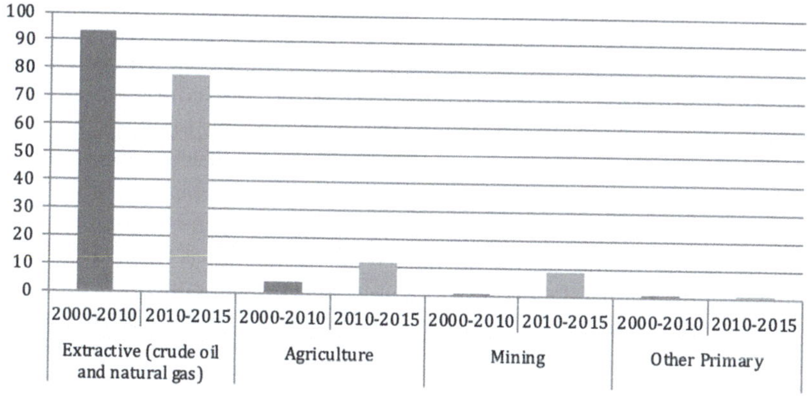

Fig. 4.4 Indian OFDI breakdown within primary sector. (Source: Author's own compilation based on data from Reserve Bank of India and Indian Investment Centre [also cited in Chaudhry et al. 2018: 20])

4.3.6 *Fragmented Company Productivity and R&D Intensity*

Indian companies' technology-seeking strategy is strongly related to the last important determinant for their internationalization process which is acquiring research and development (R&D) activity. As it has been proven by Topalova and Khandelwal (2011) R&D intensity has a positive relationship with foreign investment activity at the overall level of the firm, but the effect is not evenly distributed between the parent company and its affiliates. It is important to note that R&D opportunities have probably been one of the most important factors for Indian companies to seek operations in advanced economies and to diversify away from their home market. Their global aspiration is to access knowledge and competences which could compensate for competitive weaknesses and help reduce their latecomer disadvantage on the global level (Mathews 2002; Taylor 2017). Foreign subsidiaries have to accomplish knowledge transfer to enhance product development in home-based R&D centres. There is a strong positive correlation between subsidiaries' activity in foreign R&D clusters and the company's overall productivity gains (De Beule and Somers 2017). As a consequence, global contenders can achieve productivity improvement by entering foreign research clusters and linking up with other companies or institutional settings. This demonstrates how Indian companies attempt to get embedded in productions networks where knowledge is transferred.

4.4 Host Country Factors

De Beule and Somers (2017) highlight a very important attribution for Indian investments in relation to the level of the host country's technological development. There is often a technological gap between the host and the home economies, which needs to be bridged when technology-seeking investment is located. Otherwise, the local affiliate in the host country may face knowledge-transfer disruptions and limitations in embeddedness-related operation. Such a technological gap decisively influences the choice for the investment location. Host countries' technological development can influence investment decisions in multiple forms. For instance, what type of investment is the most appropriate: greenfield or brownfield; should investments target high-end industrial clusters or find intermediate technological transmitters? Indian companies may prefer R&D activity in other developing or transition economies, because they can actually reduce their gap by this way (Kumar and Aggarwal 2005). Those countries which host a large amount of FDI from advanced multinationals may be the best choices because Indian firms can still get access to the specific knowledge and competence they search for. As a selection criterion, the host economy has to exhibit the type of technology in the particular industry which is the concern for Indian investors. Indian companies are usually competitive in low- and medium-tech segments, which make them more inclined to locate their technology-seeking investments to economies that are specialized in middle-end technologies and medium-tech manufacturing. These should be close to India's level of development (Amighini et al. 2013).

Now we turn to the specificities of these host country determinants. The most important host country factors are measured by Pradhan (2004) and summarized in the following list:

- Large and sophisticated local market
- Local labour costs
- Intellectual property rights and patent law
- Technological and scientific strength
- Availability of skilled workforce
- Institutional settings, technological clusters including university and corporate R&D hubs

What matters the most for technology-seeking investment is to integrate into the host economy's production system where it can get access to local knowledge and competence which it can transfer to the parent company (Pradhan and Singh 2009). Given that India has had no such similar "embedded" home-based R&D infrastructure as advanced countries usually do, internationalization of Indian R&D might result in the substitution of domestic R&D operations.

This observation applies to investments in the European Union which trade block contains many of the important host country attributions that attract Indian FDI—and which involves the classical features elaborated by Dunning et al. (2008). The EU also consists of very heterogeneous economic structures of both advanced (western and partly southern) and transitional (eastern and partly southern) member states (Milelli 2007). This makes Indian companies' choices of the investment location very complex and dynamic in time. We need to ask the question, why certain Indian firms prefer ECE destination over western or southern countries in their strategic locational choice. According to Amighini et al. (2015) if technological gaps between the home country and the host country are too big, firms may not possess adequate absorptive capacity to exploit knowledge and competence that might be in abundance in the host economy. In order to bridge the technological gap, firms from developing countries may prefer R&D investments in other developing or transitional countries where they can better exploit even the most advanced technologies if those are available amid local presence of mature western multinationals (Chase-Dunn et al. 2000). Any limitations on firm-level and economy-wide absorptive capacity in host countries may disrupt OFDI's home effects. When undertaking OFDI decisions, the firm's absorptive capacity is a key to determining the appropriate match with targeted knowledge and technology. Absorptive capacity can influence the home effects of OFDI in two different ways. First, firms distant from cutting-edge technology may benefit most from spillover effects as they are starting from a low technological base (Girma et al. 2008). Counterarguments suggest that these firms may not have the capacity to make the best application of acquired technologies (Narula 2004). Rather, as Narula (2004) argues, firms closest to the technology frontier are placed the best to adopt cutting-edge technologies available through OFDI.

At some point, the investor firm should have sufficient absorptive capacity to invest in acquiring knowledge at the frontier. Companies therefore begin their investment in targeted countries where the technological gap is smaller and from where they can gradually upgrade their operation to advanced destinations, with better technological endowments (Pradhan and Singh 2009). Evidence from India suggests that, when the knowledge gap between firms is too great, interactions between firms are less likely to lead to knowledge transfer or spillovers because firms are unable to absorb the capacity (Humphrey and Memedovic 2003; Amighini et al. 2015). Using OFDI to target highly sophisticated knowledge so as to leapfrog to the knowledge frontier may therefore not be an effective strategy until Indian firms first improve absorptive capacity. Different levels of development may thus call for different OFDI strategy in acquisition and innovation (Nayyar 2008).

As Amighini et al. (2015) have also demonstrated, Indian multinationals are more competitive in low- to medium-technological segments which makes them less attracted to countries with very high level of technological endowments. In these economies Indian companies have better chance to exploit inward FDI from western multinationals and to link it to their home country R&D base (home effect) as an alternative way to access and transfer specific knowledge to their own technological system. Indian manufacturing companies therefore prefer to locate into countries that have specialized themselves in middle-end technologies, for example, medium-tech manufacturing which is not distant from their own technological capabilities.

As we will see, ECE is one of the most ideal locational choices for fostering such investment strategy because the region exhibits geographical proximity to western markets (most advanced technology), that is, allows investing companies to follow their market-seeking and technological-seeking strategies. On the other hand, the vertical specialization of these countries in lower- and middle-tech segments of manufacturing value chains makes them functionally closer to the technological adaptability for Indian companies. The latter fact helps to make technological adaptation and embeddedness in the home environment easier for Indian companies; thus, the reverse flow from overseas subsidiaries to the Indian parent is more encouraged.[6] Host market R&D intensity therefore seems to be one of the key elements in determining overseas investment in Europe where the ECE region serves as a gateway to enter.

[6] In the auto and chemical and pharmaceuticals industries, evidence reveals that OFDI firms generate reverse technology spillovers to domestic firms that did not invest abroad (Nair et al. 2015).

4.5 Indian Investment in Europe

Three types of motivation inspired Indian companies to invest in Europe, the most important among which was the access to affluent markets with strong purchasing power. In addition, clear and strict patent laws made it possible for Indian companies to purchase technological licenses that they could adopt to their production systems in the home economy.[7] Advanced infrastructure with a large pool of highly skilled workforce was another important element behind the motivation to relocate capacities to Europe (Milelli 2007). Furthermore, since the end of the world-economic crises in 2008, the diversification of Indian investments in the European Union has risen mostly because of the share of Central and Eastern Europe grew substantially. The ECE region does not belong to the category of advanced markets according to the world investment reports; hence, some of the investment characteristics differ from western European markets.

The EU is, however, still secondary compared to the US, despite the fact that Indian investment grew almost ten times between 2000 and 2014 in Europe. Since 2011 the growth rate has slowed down to 5–6% per year (2012–2014), which is in line with similar global trends. See the sectoral breakdown of Indian investments in Europe in Table 4.1.

Indian companies invested in Europe between 2000 and 2016 an estimated 60–80 billion USD out of their total stock of foreign assets which stood at 255.4 billion USD in 2016. It is difficult to give a precise

Table 4.1 Indian investments in Europe in sectoral breakdown

Sector	*Value (million USD)*	*Percentage*
Manufacturing	128.9	36.8
Finance, insurance, real estate	100.1	28.6
Transport, storage, communication	65.15	18.6
Agriculture, mining, hunting, forestry	34.6	9.9
Wholesale, retail trade, restaurants, hotel	8.9	2.6
Community, social and personal services	8.04	2.3
Construction	1.13	0.32
Electricity, gas, water	3	0.87

Source: Reserve Bank of India database (also cited in Roman et al. 2014: 1669)

[7] A well-known example is Tata Steel's Corus acquisition with which it obtained 60-odd patents. Tata Steel had not possessed any patent prior to the transaction.

evaluation on the stock of Indian FDI in Europe because of two things. First, offshore activity of companies which is similar to western multinationals' practices is rampant, although less widespread than in other BRICS countries. Second, in terms of investment trends in Europe, Eurostat provides data on country breakdown only until 2012. After 2012 we have to rely on major companies' annual reports and a different dataset provided by the Reserve Bank of India (RBI). Despite the methodological differences in the statistics, the estimation of 60–80 billion USD is a fairly good proxy for Indian capital in Europe.

4.5.1 *Western Europe*

The UK is the largest host economy in the EU which attracts Indian investors. Besides the historical legacies, such as the common language, and the large number of Indian expatriates, the legal systems in both countries are very similar. As a result, the UK and India are top investors in each other economies. India is the fifth largest investor in the UK but there has been a steady decline of the country's share in Indian OFDI because of the rise of other European countries, most spectacularly Germany.[8] In 2010 UK's share fell from 47% of all Indian OFDI in Europe to 36% by 2013 whereas Germany grew to the second place with a an estimated 15 billion USD investment from India (see Fig. 4.5).

Comparing Indian investments in Germany and in the UK we observe different characteristics. Investments in the UK are much more diverse both in terms of scale and scope. These cover as wide range of industries as IT, chemicals, steel, finance, automotive, logistics, media and retail. What is peculiar about the composition of Indian investments is that both large acquisitions such as the Infosys relocation from the US and the Corus transaction by Tata Steel coexist with sporadic minor transactions usually conducted by diaspora networks in areas from media, finance and retail services. By 2016 Indian companies invested approximately 30 billion USD in the UK. Large Indian companies such as Tata Tea, Corus and Jaguar employed approximately 90,000 people in that country at the time.

[8] It is worth to note that the third largest destination of Indian investments in Europe is the Netherlands with approximately 18% of the total Indian OFDI. The Netherlands serves as a logistical hub for European transportation and it is also regarded as a tax haven by international investors. Therefore it is difficult to estimate the real size and value of investments in the country as some of the registered projects are transferred elsewhere.

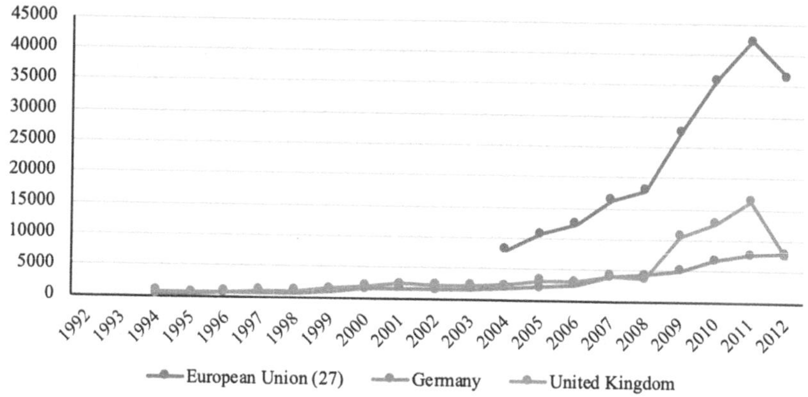

Fig. 4.5 Stock of Indian direct investment in the EU (million euro). (Source: Author's own compilation based on Eurostat [https://ec.europa.eu/eurostat])

In contrast, Germany host a smaller number of Indian companies (between 200 and 300 entities as of 2016), 73% of which were in manufacturing and software service industries. One of the most characteristic features of the German economy which attracts a lot of foreign investment is the fact that a large number of small- and medium-sized companies especially in manufacturing are the backbone of the German innovation system. This network of manufacturing firms, sometimes family-owned SMEs, draws resemblances to the structure of the Indian economy.[9] Unit labour cost is another interesting factor in Germany, because taking the high level of productivity into account, labour costs are comparably lower than in other advanced economies. Therefore technology-seeking investors can have better access to the most advanced technology they need in the German production systems (not necessarily only in Germany, as we will see). These investments concentrate in machinery building, machine tools, automotive spare parts and telecommunication. Germany's other advantage is that it provides a strategic location for investors with robust infrastructure and advanced logistics system connecting Benelux, Scandinavian and ECE regions. German companies are spread across Europe, having built the largest and most widespread production networks in manufacturing across the European Union. Besides the advanced infrastructure, Germany hosts the world's top technical universities

[9] On the internationalization of Indian SMEs.

(Charlie 2012: 35). This has become a great advantage when Indian companies target R&D clusters near universities or close to important clients' headquarters. This is a form of climbing up on the technological ladder, and similarly to Chinese endeavours there has been precedent for Indian companies to acquire highly protected patents[10] (on China, see Szunomár's chapter in this book).

4.5.2 *Central and Eastern Europe*

Transition economies such as the ECE countries carry a mixture of advanced (IT services, pharmaceutical) and developing economies' (low-tech manufacturing, extractive industries) investment portfolios. Indian "low-cost partner" and "global consolidator" companies use these locations neither for their domestic market purposes, nor for any strategic asset purchasing strategies, but typically for accessing western markets and high-end technologies through gradual specialization. Similar to other foreign investors, ECE countries serve as a gateway for foreign investors who seek entrance to the EU. See the rise of Indian investments in ECE countries in Fig. 4.6.

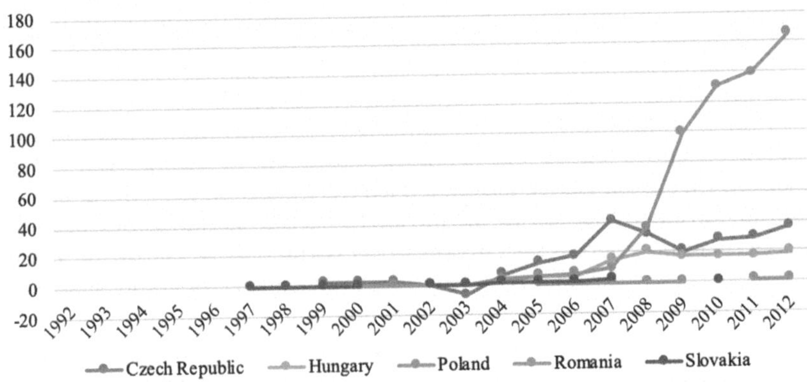

Fig. 4.6 Stock of Indian direct investment in ECE (million euro). (Source: Author's own compilation based on Eurostat [https://ec.europa.eu/eurostat])

[10] One notable example is the pharmaceutical industry in which Piramal Healthcare purchased Bayer's molecular imaging R&D portfolio in 2012.

Furthermore, Indian "low-cost partner" and "global consolidator" or in some instances even "global first mover" companies might also want to combine their operations with more advanced production systems from Germany.[11]

According to the survey which we conducted amongst the largest Indian companies which had operation in Hungary,[12] their investment targeted Hungary as a small and peripheral economy before they proceeded to enter large and advanced markets. The reason is that some of the Indian firms found it difficult to compete in larger, more competitive markets far away, lacking the networks and experience of developed country firms. In our research we found that Indian investors usually expand into larger and more complex European markets after first successfully expanding in smaller, lower- or middle-income nearby economies in Central, Eastern and South-Eastern Europe. In the following a more detailed analysis of the ECE characteristics that attract investment from India is done. We continue to use Pradhan's (2017) categorization combined with our own empirical findings through the interviews we conducted.

4.5.2.1 *Access to Advanced Market*

As mentioned before, one of the most important comparative advantages of the Central and Eastern European region in attracting foreign investment is its geographical proximity to the world's largest and most sophisticated market inside the European Union. ECE countries serve as a good entrance to the more advanced western European market (Liu and Dicken 2006). Not only countries in the region are geographically close to western markets but ECE economies are part of the German production systems, and therefore they are capable of providing the necessary infrastructure and skilled workforce for servicing important tasks, particularly in manufacturing. Secondly, these countries are part of the European Union's single market scheme and therefore setting up facilities in their

[11] A good example is the automotive industry which had been one of the strongest economic drivers in ECE countries to be integrated into western, mostly German, production networks. Indian automotive suppliers are increasingly becoming global consolidators also in automotive production networks.

[12] The survey was distributed in the form of a questionnaire amongst the largest Indian companies in Hungary. The research was part of the "Non-European emerging-market multinational enterprises in East Central Europe" agenda. The findings are not representative due to the size differences of the respective companies. The largest respondent set up its first branch in Budapest in 2001; since then it employs 2400 people.

home base provides them with the possibility of legally accessing goods, services, patent rights and most favourable treatments in the European Single Market. Since 2004 when these countries joined the EU they adopted legal schemes including regulation on taxation, labour code, intellectual property rights (IPR) and patent laws when they incorporated *acqui communitaire* into their national legislature. The gateway metaphor means that investment in their local economies could help to overcome administrative and tariff barriers in the European Single Market.[13]

The domestic market size of ECE countries would probably not be attractive enough for Indian investors, given the fact that the region is politically highly fragmented, and the average purchasing power is hardly exceeding 60% of their western counterparts, but as a legal and geographical gateway, they seem to be able to provide the most attractive legal and economic environment for Indian firms seeking entrance to Europe. The gateway function has been appreciated by Indian firms for another reason (Gerőcs 2017). After the global economic crisis, both the southern periphery of Europe and even western economies were challenged by fiscal deterioration and skyrocketing debt. In comparison to the old EU member states ECE countries provided much sounder fiscal position, lower debt levels and predictable and stable monetary environment which—according to Pradhan (2017)—Indian companies value high as they are more exposed to external financial environment than their western counterparts.

4.5.2.2 *Intellectual Property Rights and Patent Law*

Multi- and bilateral agreements are guarantees for securing a stable patent system and protecting intellectual property rights. These agreements are regulated under the supervision of the WTO in which India became a member in 1995. As Pradhan (2017) highlighted, Indian investors seeking market and efficiency improvements tend to prefer locations with highly sophisticated and developed secure patent system. The regulation of intellectual property rights and patent laws is not limited to state

[13] Some of the forms in which ECE countries promote investment opportunities as a gateway to the protected European market—for example, through low and flat corporate and income taxes—also resemble Ireland's similar experience with US capital in the early 1990s. As Ireland was able to serve US capital with investment-friendly regulation when US capital sought to enter the newly forming European Single Market, in a similar vein Central and Eastern European countries follow the pattern of peripheral FDI attraction targeting capital from BRICS countries.

legislation in Europe but European authorities; for example, European Commission's competition agency oversees the national legislation of the member states (Varju and Papp 2019). Therefore, negotiations and agreement of IPR and patent law are between European Commission on the one hand and the Indian government on the other. National authorities have a highly limited scope in this regard. The advantage of the EU membership is that the strict regulation and the sophisticated laws apply in the ECE region as well; hence Indian companies can enjoy protection similar to advanced western economies. Disadvantage is that there has been a stalemate in the forming of a new bilateral trade and investment agreement between the EU and India since 2007 which can have a negative effect on ECE's investment strategy. Despite all of this, national governments tend to fabricate their own bilateral agreements with the Indian government in which certain regulations are shared and mutually discussed.[14]

4.5.2.3 *Institutional Settings, Technological Clusters and R&D Hubs*

In addition to the mutual economic agreements, Indian investors may also want to target host economies with "weaker" institutional quality (Perea and Stephenson 2018). Indian OFDI is less discouraged by flexible institutional environment in host countries; in fact smaller technological or institutional gap between the home and the host economies might help develop absorptive capacity, which is an important transmission mechanism for transferring knowledge and capacity to the parent company. However, technological capacities, high prestigious universities and innovation clusters are important factors as they provide infrastructural links to larger western technological hubs.[15] As our interview, for example, with

[14] Good example is Hungary which represented itself in a ministerial visit in October 2013 in Mumbai and Delhi. Hungarian prime minister was joined by approximately 100 businessmen and several business forums were held between Hungarian and Indian corporate representatives. Government representatives held meetings in the meantime, and Hungary was able to strengthen its comprehensive relationship with the Indian government by the visit which also resulted in a bilateral agreement. As further result, the two countries' investment agencies, Invest India and the Hungarian Investment Promotion Agency (HIPA) concluded a three-year cooperation agreement to help Indian investors' orientation in the country (Gerőcs 2013, 2018b).

[15] A good example is Infopark Budapest, which hosts university facilities from two major technological and economic universities. One of the largest Indian investments in ECE, the Tata Consultancy Services' (TCS) regional headquarter has been placed in Infopark Budapest, Hungary. TCS underlined the fact that there was no inter-governmental agree-

the Tata Consultancy Services showed, the European market not only is important for widening the economies of scale of the company's business model, but can serve to diversify the product variety for their western clients. In short, the regional centre can help to enhance TCS' technological economies of scope as well.[16]

4.5.2.4 ECE Comparative Advantage

Another important factor for Indian capital to invest in ECE is the fact that the region has a highly advanced and integrated infrastructural and logistical system which is part of the German production network-system. The geographical and legal proximity to western markets in combination with highly developed infrastructure and the availability of sophisticated and skilled workforce makes the region especially appealing for manufacturing companies seeking efficiency in large advanced markets. Moreover, it is not only the geography and advancement in labour conditions but the relatively low prices also make ECE an attractive option for Indian companies in Europe. The relative prices in ECE are much below the average of the western markets not just because of the cheap labour force but also due to the low flat tax regimes[17] and lower transport costs. Moreover, the education system in many of the countries in our concern prioritizes vocational schools from which trainees can be employed by companies up to several years below the minimal wage and contracted by the partnering school. This model was emulated after the German vocational training system. It provides a large amount of relatively skilled and semi-skilled,

ment at the time when the management decided to set up the regional headquarter in Budapest; however, the Hungarian Investment Promotion Agency (HIPA) and its predecessor institutions proved to be "extremely" helpful in the procedure. TCS typically hires fresh graduates who advanced their studies in IT and business in Hungary. They also tend to rely on diaspora workforce (interview).

[16] TCS responded that the main reason for the locational choice was the cultural and geographical proximity to their clients, Hungary's NATO and EU membership, the available good pool of talents, cost efficiency, good and stabile business environment, and geographical and political stability. The Budapest HQ sustains a very close relation with the Indian Center (interview). See also: company report (Tata Consultancy Services 2016).

[17] Take the example of Hungary, where the centrally regulated flat corporate tax rate is only 9%. Due to the fact that the state subsidizes investing companies with various non-fiscal means—as direct tax subsidizes are prohibited in the EU—the estimated effective corporate tax rate in Hungary is around 7.2%. As media investigation showed the 30 largest multinationals in Hungary, among which there is no Indian company so far, pay an average estimated 3.6% effective corporate tax rate due to very favourable one-off subsidies (Bucsky 2018).

young and trainable workforce for industrial companies in areas such as automotive manufacturing, or electronic and pharmaceutical companies.

ECE economies' large qualified workforce is already employed and trained by western companies in their own established production systems. Indian "global contender" companies might also want to link their own capacities to the European production system. A good example is the automotive industry which had been one of the strongest economic drivers in ECE countries to be integrated into western, mostly German, production networks. As a consequence, Indian companies are motivated to increase their presence in ECE where German auto manufacturers are the most active. In Hungary for instance 8 out of the 17 registered companies with Indian (full or majority) ownership active in the country brought greenfield investments in manufacturing. The largest example so far has been Apollo Tyres' investment in 2014. Six of these companies are active in the automotive industry. Five companies are in IT or BPO services, two in chemical or pharmaceutical industries and two companies in the food processing industry. Other positive examples from the automotive industry can be found in Tata Motors' relocation in Nitra, Slovakia, where the new Jaguar Land Rover production plant has been opened and in Hungary where a new engineering office[18] has been put in operation to serve Tata's suppliers located in the EU. In short, favourable labour legislation, education, and low and competitive tax regimes combined with the availability of large, cheap and skilled workforce with advanced infrastructure and geographical proximity, plus legal integration to the world's largest protected market with the strongest purchasing power make many of the ECE countries appealing gateway choices for Indian companies that seek entrance to the EU.

4.5.2.5 *Technology- and Asset-Seeking Investments in the Region*

In terms of the asset-seeking investment strategy, there has been a gradual increase in the ECE region in industries like IT or financial services. As a prime example, TCS moved its regional headquarter in Budapest,

[18] According to Tata Group's statement the new Jaguar Land Rover engineering office in Budapest will be a small R&D centre for developing Jaguar Land Rover's electronic vehicles. The office will employ "Assisted and Automated Driving Vehicle Based Validation Engineer" and "Assisted and Automated Driving Data Analysis Engineer". Similar so-called Supplier Technical Engineering offices are already operating in the UK, Ireland, North America and China. Source: https://media.jaguarlandrover.com/news/2018/11/jaguar-land-rover-confirms-technical-engineering-office-hungary.

Hungary, while Infosys provides services to western clients from Brno, Czechia, and Wipro opened parallel bureaus in Budapest, and Bucharest in Romania. These transactions are examples for technology-intensive investments that target host economies with strong embeddedness in western production and service networks but which countries simultaneously exhibit closer technological ties with India than with advanced economies. The local absorptive capacity helps to relocate technological-intensive businesses but it helps technology transfer back and forth. IT companies' preference of ECE for their regional activity is one of the convincing examples of the type of technology-seeking investment and the specificities this region can offer for Indian companies. These services are also positioned typically in the middle segments in the value chain hierarchy, specializing in IT support to larger western firms. The region has become so attractive and popular for this type of IT and BPO companies that since the economic crises in 2009 some of the older operations from western Europe have been relocated to ECE for financial reasons but also because of the narrower technological gap.

Other than the technology-seeking strategy, resource-seeking investments in ECE targets the primary sector, most typically energy and mining, although some of these projects are regarded as failures due to what Lall (1982, 1983) defined as wrong choice of the partner by the investor firm.[19] Resource-seeking investments in the primary sector are, however, very rare in the region and usually happen only in the Balkans or the post-Soviet region. Indian companies are typically following a technology-seeking investment strategy in the ECE region. These investments target the middle-rank of the regional value chains, and are made in automotive and chemical (pharma) industries. Besides manufacturing, IT service companies are also very active in the region. The strategic target, as mentioned above, is to link up with western production systems and gain technological advancement that can be reverse-transferred to the parent company (Gerőcs 2018a).

[19] One notable example is Gujarat Heavy Chemicals (GHCL) which purchased 65% of Romanian soda ash firm SC Upsom in 2005. Soon after the acquisition the natural gas price which is crucial for the production at GHCL was substantially increased by the state monopoly Romgas which made the project unprofitable. The other large acquisition was made by ArcelorMittal which purchased Sidex Galati, a steel company in Galati, Romania, in 2001 (Roman et al. 2014).

4.6 Final Remarks

Developing countries' share in global investment has been steadily rising since the 2000s. Multinational companies from the BRICS countries are the key drivers of this increase, amongst which Indian companies have spectacularly caught up in the last decade. The driving force for Indian companies to internationalize is to improve their competitiveness by accessing advanced technologies which they can build into their home-based production systems. As empirical evidence showed, foreign investment can increase potential for technological uplifting which has been one of the main reasons for Indian companies' internationalization since the 2000s. However, limited absorptive capacity in the home economy, vis-à-vis trading partner in the region, can be an obstacle for enhanced home effects of R&D-related investments; therefore, there is no guarantee that technology investment improves the overall productivity of the company. Still, about two-thirds of Indian OFDI went to developed western countries, mostly notably to the EU, including Central and Eastern Europe, while the remaining third was placed in fellow developing countries. As for Indian OFDI entering ECE these are becoming increasingly technology- and asset-seeking investments, as the region is well embedded in Germany's production networks by hosting key manufacturing activities as lower-cost locations. The most important regional networks which Indian companies targeted are automotive, pharmaceutical, IT and BPO services. Companies in IT services for instance serve global clients from their regional headquarters, such as centres in Budapest (TCS), Brno (Infosys) and Bucharest (Wipro). From these locations Indian multinationals are better able to access state-of-the-art technologies which they can transfer back to their parent company. ECE also serves as an entrance to the European Single Market. Many Indian companies relocate operations first here to gain experience in the European Single Market, but at a later stage when they obtained adequate knowledge and experience they might move forward to the core of the European market, using ECE as a gateway. As a concluding remark we might highlight the core of our finding that companies from developing countries might use their investment strategy in other developing or transitional economics—that are located close to advanced markets—as a catch-up strategy to access technology, increase domestic capacity, upgrade production processes, boost competitiveness and augment managerial experience and access financial markets for their global aspirations.

References

Agarwala, R., Kumar, N., & Riboud, M. (Eds.). (2004). *Reforms, Labour Markets and Social Security in India*. Oxford: Oxford University Press.

Amighini, A. A., Rabellotti, R., & Sanfilippo, M. (2013). Do Chinese State-Owned and Private Enterprises Differ in Their Internationalization Strategies? *China Economic Review, 27*, 312–325.

Amighini, A., Cozza, C., Giuliani, E., Rabellotti, R., & Scalera, V. G. (2015). Multinational Enterprises from Emerging Economies: What Theories Suggest, What Evidence Shows. A Literature Review. *Economia e Politica Industriale, 42*(3), 343–370.

Athukorala, P.-C. (2009). Outward Foreign Direct Investment from India. *Asian Development Review, 26*(2), 125–153.

Boston Consulting Group. (2018). "Global Challengers," Chapter Two: Meet the Challengers. Retrieved from https://www.bcg.com/de-de/publications/2018/global-challengers-2018.aspx.

Bucsky, P. (2018, November 9). Hungary Is One of the Biggest Losers of Multinationals' Transferpricing. *g7.hu magazine*. Retrieved from https://g7.hu/allam/20181109/magyarorszag-az-egyik-legnagyobb-vesztese-a-multik-transzferar-trukkjeinek/.

Charlie, A. (2012). 'Indian Companies in the European Union, Reigniting Economic Growth', Europe India Chamber of Commerce (EICC), Brussels.

Chase-Dunn, C., Yukio Kawano, Y., & Brewer, D. B. (2000). Trade Globalization Since 1795: Waves of Integration in the World-System. *American Sociological Review, 65*(1). Looking Forward, Looking Back: Continuity and Change at the Turn of the Millenium (February 2000), pp. 77–95.

Chaudhry et al. (2018). *Deconstructing Indian Overseas Foreign Direct Investments, Historical & Contemporary Trends*. Oxfam Discussion Papers.

De Beule, F., & Somers, D. (2017). The Impact of International R&D on Home-Country R&D for Indian Multinationals. *Transnational Corporations, 24*(1), 27–55.

Dunning, J. H. (1988). The Eclectic Paradigm of International Production: A Restatement and Some Possible Extensions. *Journal of International Business Studies, 19*(1), 1–25.

Dunning, J. H., Kim, C. S., & Park, D. H. (2008). Old Wine in New bottles: A Comparison of Emerging-Market TNCs Today and Developed-Country TNCs Thirty Years Ago. In K. P. Sauvant (Ed.), *The Rise of Transnational Corporations from Emerging Markets: Threat Or Opportunity?* (pp. 158–178). Cheltenham, UK: Edward Elgar Publishing.

Emmott, B., Gros, D., Jin, K., & Roach, S. S. (2018). Trumps Trade War. In: Project Syndicate. Retrieved from https://www.project-syndicate.org/bigpicture/trump-s-trade-war.

EXIM Bank. (2014). *Outward Direct Investment from India: Trends, Objectives, and Policy Perspectives.* Mumbai: EXIM Bank.

Feenstra, R. C. (1998). Integration of Trade and Disintegration of Production in the Global Economy. *Journal of Economic Perspectives, 12*(4), 31–50.

FICCI (Federation of Indian Chambers of Commerce and Industry). (2006). *India Inc.'s Acquisitions Abroad.* New Delhi.

Fleury, A., & Fleury, M. T. A. (2011). The Internationalization of Indian firms. In A. Fleury & M. T. A. Fleury (Eds.), *Brazilian Multinationals Competences for Internationalization* (pp. 366–380). Cambridge University Press.

Gereffi, G. (2014). Global Value Chains in a Post-Washington Consensus World. *Review of International Political Economy, 21*(1), 9–37.

Gereffi, G., Humphrey, J., & Sturgeon, T. (2005). The Governance of Global Value Chains. *Review of International Political Economy, 12*(1), 78–104.

Gerőcs, T. (2013). A magyar cégek nagy fantáziát látnak Indiában ("Hungarian Companies See the Potential in India"). *Napi Gazdaság.* Retrieved from https://www.napi.hu/belfold/a_magyar_cegek_nagy_fantaziat_latnak_indiaban.567807.html.

Gerőcs, T. (2017, October). *Internationalization of Indian Multinational Enterprises Motivations, Strategies and Regulation from the Experience of Indian Investments: A Focus on Europe.* Centre for Economic and Regional Studies HAS Institute of World Economics, Working Paper Nr. 234 (2017), 1–40.

Gerőcs, T. (2018a). Indian Companies' Technological Investments in the EU with a Special Focus on Central and Eastern Europe'. *Institute of World Economics, Hungarian Academy of Sciences, Working, 248*, 1–57.

Gerőcs, T. (2018b). India világgazdasági integrációja ("India's World Economic Integration"). In J. Kiss (Ed.), *Stratégiaváltás a világgazdaságban (Strategical Change in the World Economy)* (pp. 143–178). Akadémiai Kiadó.

Girma, S., Gorg, H., & Pisu, M. (2008). Exporting, Linkages and Productivity Spillovers from Foreign Direct Investment. *Canadian Journal of Economics, 41*(1), 320–340.

Gopinath, S. (2007). *Overseas Investments by Indian Companies – Evolution of Policy and Trends.* Mumbai: RBI.

Hattari, R., & Rajan, R. S. (2010). India as a Source of Outward Foreign Direct Investment. *Oxford Development Studies, 38*(4), 497–518.

Humphrey, J., & Memedovic, O. (2003). *The Global Automotive Industry Value Chain: What Prospects for Upgrading by Developing Countries.* Vienna: United Nations Industrial Development Organization.

Katrak, H. (1990). Imports of Technology and the Technological Effort of Indian Enterprises. *World Development, 18*(3), 371–381.

Khan, H. (2012). *Outward Indian FDI: Recent Trends and Emerging Issues.* RBI. Bombay Chamber of Commerce and Industry, 2/3/2012.

Kohli, R. (2005). *Liberalizing Capital Flows: India's Experiences and Policy Issues.* Oxford: Oxford University Press.

Kumar, N. (2008). Internationalization of Indian Enterprises: Patterns, Strategies, Ownership Advantages, and Implications. *Asian Economic Policy Review, Japan Center for Economic Research, 3*(2), 242–261.

Kumar, N., & Aggarwal, A. (2005). Liberalization, Outward Orientation and In-house R&D Activity of Multinational and Local Firms: A Quantitative Exploration for Indian Manufacturing. *Research Policy, 34*, 441–460.

Kuzminska-Haberla, A. (2012). *The Promotion of Outward Foreign Direct Investment – Solutions from Emerging Economies.* Working Paper, Institute of International Business, University of Gdansk No. 31, Poland.

Lall, S. (1982). The Emergence of Third World Multinationals: Indian Joint Ventures Overseas. *World Development, 10*(2), 127–146.

Lall, S. (1983). Multinationals from India. In S. Lall (Ed.), *The New Multinationals: The Spread of Third World Enterprises* (pp. 21–87). New York: John Wiley and Sons.

Liu, W., & Dicken, P. (2006). Transnational Corporation's and "Obligated Emneddedness": Foreign Direct Investment in China's Automobile Industry. *Environment and Planning A, 38*(7), 1229–1247.

Mathews, J. A. (2002). Competitive Advantages of the Latecomer Firm: A Resource-Based Account of Industrial Catch-Up Strategies. *Asia Pacific Journal of Management, 19*(4), 467–488.

Milelli, C. (2007). *Outward Expansion by Indian Firms: The European Route.* Working Paper 2007–25, Paris EconomiX.

Nair, S. R., Demirbag, M., & Mellahi, K. (2015). Reverse Knowledge Transfer from Overseas Acquisitions: A Survey of Indian MNEs. *Management International Review, 55*(2), 277–301.

Narayanan, K., & Bhat, S. (2011). Technology Sourcing and Outward FDI: A Study of IT Industry in India. *Technovation, 31*(4), 177–184.

Narula, R. (2004). *Understanding Absorptive Capacity in an 'Innovation System' Context: Consequences for Economic and Employment Growth.* MERIT-Infonomics Research Memorandum Series 3, Maastricht.

Nayak, K. J. R. A. (2011). *Indian Multinationals. The Dynamics of Explosive Growth in a Developing Country Context.* Palgrave Macmillan.

Nayyar, D. (2008). The Internationalization of Firms from India: Investment, Mergers and Acquisitions. *Oxford Development Studies, 36*(1), 111–131.

Nölke, A., & May, C. (2019). Liberal Versus Organised Capitalism: A Historical-Comparative Perspective. In T. Gerőcs & M. Szanyi (Eds.), *Market Liberalism and Economic Patriotism in the Capitalist World-Systems* (pp. 21–42). Palgrave.

Nölke, A., May, C., Mertend, D., & Schedelik, M. (2018). Challenges for the Stability of State-Permeated Capitalism in Large Emerging Countries: The Cases of Brazil and India. In Paper Prepared for the 25th IPSA World Congress of Political Science July 21–25, 2018, Brisbane, Australia. Retrieved from https://www.researchgate.net/publication/260416776_The_Rise_of_Large_Emerging_Economies_Is_a_State_Capitalist_Consensus_Replacing_the_Washington_Consensus.

Panagariya, A. (2004). *India in the 1980s and 1990s: A Triumph of Reforms*. IMF Working Paper WP/04/43. International Monetary Fund.

Perea, J. R., & Stephenson, M. (2018). Outward FDI from Developing Countries, Chapter 4. Global Investment Competitiveness Report 2017/2018, pp. 101–134.

Pradhan, J. P. (2004). The Determinants of Outward Foreign Direct Investment: A Firm-Level Analysis of Indian Manufacturing. *Oxford Development Studies, 32*(4), 619–639.

Pradhan, J. P. (2017). Indian Outward FDI: A Review of Recent Developments. *Transnational Corporations (UNCTAD), 24*(2), 43–70.

Pradhan, J. P., & Aggarwal, R. (2011). On the Globalness of Emerging Multinationals: A Study of Indian MNEs. *Economia e politica industriale – Journal of Industrial and Business Economics, 38*(1), 163–180.

Pradhan, J. P., & Das, K. (2013). Exporting by Indian Small and Medium Enterprises: Role of Regional Technological Knowledge, Agglomeration and Foreign Direct Investment. *Innovation and Development, 3*, 239–257.

Pradhan, J. P., & Singh, N. (2009). Outward FDI and Knowledge Flows: A Study of the Indian Automotive Sector. *International Journal of Institutions and Economies, 1*(1), 155–186.

Pradhan, J. P., & Singh, N. (2011). Business Group Affiliation and Location of Indian Firms' Foreign Acquisitions. *Journal of International Commerce, Economics and Policy, 2*(1), 19–41.

Rajan, R. S., & Yanamandra, V. (2015). *Managing the Macroeconomy. Monetary and Exchange Rate Issues in India*. Basingstoke: Palgrave Macmillan.

Ramamurti, R. (2012). What Is Really Different About Emerging Market Multinationals? *Global Strategy Journal, 2*(1), 41–47.

Ramamurti, R., & Singh, J. V. (2009). Indian Multinationals: Generic Internationalization Strategies. In R. Ramamurti & J. V. Singh (Eds.), *Emerging Multinationals in Emerging Markets* (pp. 110–166). Cambridge: Cambridge University Press

RBI. (2016). Master Direction – Direct Investment by Residents in Joint Venture (JV) / Wholly Owned Subsidiary (WOS) Abroad, RBI/FED/2015-16/10.

Roman, T., Manolica, A., & Maha, L.-G. (2014). The Dynamics of Indian FDI in Europe and Its Impact on Romanian–Indian Relations. *Current Science, 107*(10), 1666–1672.

Sauvant, K. P., & Pradhan, J. P. (2010). Introduction: The Rise of Indian Multinational Enterprises: Revisiting Key Issues. In K. P. Sauvant & J. P. Pradhan (Eds.), *The Rise of Indian Multinationals: Perspectives on Indian Outward Foreign Direct Investment* (pp. 1–24). New York: Palgrave Macmillan.

Tata Consultancy Services. (2016). Company Disclose, "kiegészítő melléklet" e-beszámoló. Retrieved August 20, 2017.

Taylor, H. (2017). Uncovering the Institutional Foundations of Specialization Patterns in the Indian Pharmaceutical Industry. *Transnational Corporations, 24*(1), 57–79.

Thomas, R., & Narayanan, K. (2017). Determinants Outward Foreign Direct Investment: A Study of Indian Manufacturing Firms. *Transnational Corporations, 24*(1), 9–26.

Topalova, P., & Khandelwal, A. (2011). Trade Liberalization and Firm Productivity: The Case of India. *Review of Economics and Statistics, 93*(3), 995–1009.

Varju, M., & Papp, M. (2019). Member State Economic Patriotism and EU Law: Legitimate Regulatory Control Through Proportionality? In T. Gerőcs & M. Szanyi (Eds.), *Market Liberalism and Economic Patriotism in the Capitalist World-Systems* (pp. 127–151). Palgrave.

Venkata Ratnam, C. S. (1998). Economic Liberalization and the Transformation of Industrial Relations Policies in India. In A. J. Venkata Ratnam & A. Verma (Eds.), *Challenge of Change: Industrial Relations in Indian Industry*. Mumbai: Allied Publishers Limited.

Venkata Ratnam, C. S. (2006). *Industrial Relations*. Delhi: Oxford University Press.

CHAPTER 5

Outward Foreign Direct Investments from South Korea, Taiwan, and ASEAN in the V4 Countries

Katalin Völgyi and Tamás Peragovics

5.1 Introduction

This chapter focuses on outward FDI of six emerging Asian countries (South Korea, Taiwan, Malaysia, Thailand, Indonesia, and Vietnam) in V4 countries, namely, Hungary, Poland, Slovakia, and the Czech Republic. Of the six Asian countries, South Korea and Taiwan belong to the top 20 home countries of FDI in the world in terms of their annual FDI outflows. Thailand and Malaysia also occasionally appear in this category. In comparison to the four countries aforementioned, Indonesia and Vietnam are less relevant investors on the global level.

In the first section of our study, we investigate the general trends of outward foreign direct investments from the six Asian countries according to size and geographical/sectoral distribution, with special emphasis on

K. Völgyi (✉) • T. Peragovics
Institute of World Economics, Centre for Economic and Regional Studies, Budapest, Hungary
e-mail: volgyi.katalin@krtk.mta.hu

Á. Szunomár (ed.), *Emerging-market Multinational Enterprises in East Central Europe*, Studies in Economic Transition,
https://doi.org/10.1007/978-3-030-55165-0_5

push factors. In terms of outward FDI stock, South Korea is the largest investor followed by Taiwan, Thailand, Malaysia, Indonesia, and Vietnam. Concerning the geographical distribution of outward FDI, every country shows an Asian bias of various degrees. The targeted sectors of their investments have a wide range. We identify several push factors incentivizing outward FDI from these countries such as rising production costs (wages, land prices), diminishing supply of domestic resources, saturated domestic market, avoiding trade barriers and securing advanced technology for economic upgrading, and government policy promoting outward FDI. The latter often reinforces the aforementioned Asian bias of outward FDI.

In the second section of our study, we focus on the investment activities pursued by companies of the six Asian countries in the EU, with special emphasis on V4 countries. South Korea is one of the most important non-European FDI source countries for the V4. Of the six Asian countries, the second largest investor is Taiwan. The four ASEAN countries analysed have only sporadic or no investments in the V4. Companies originated from the six Asian countries have been operating in several manufacturing and services sectors of the V4, for example, automotive, electronics, food, chemical industry, logistics, finance, real estate, construction, warehousing and storage, IT services, wholesale and retail trade, accommodation, and catering. By closing the second section, we pay special attention to the main pull factors with which V4 countries attract Asian investments in the automotive and electronics sectors, which are the most preferred ones for them. Our research is mainly based on company data provided by AMADEUS, and information collected from company interviews,[1] the websites of companies, investment promotion agencies, embassies, ministries, and relevant media. We have found evidence for market-seeking and efficiency-seeking motivations for these investments. Main pull factors of the V4 are the following: free access to the EU market (EU membership since 2004), relatively low-cost production base, skilled labour, government incentives, and relatively developed infrastructure, anti-dumping measure of the EU, and presence of large home-country purchasers of components manufacturers.

We end the chapter with some concluding thoughts.

[1] In 2019, one Malaysian and two South Korean companies answered our interview questions via email.

5.2 Foreign Direct Investments of South Korea, Taiwan, and Selected ASEAN Countries

5.2.1 *Outward Foreign Direct Investments from Developing Asia in a Global Context*

In 2006, the UNCTAD World Investment Report chose outward FDI from developing and transition economies as its core topic which signalled the emerging role of developing and transition economies in global outward foreign direct investments. Most of these economies are located in developing Asia. In 2014, the share of developing Asia in total FDI outflows reached 31.7%, becoming the largest source of global outward foreign direct investments and eclipsing North America and Europe. In 2018, its share in global FDI outflows reached 40% and developing Asia was the second largest source of foreign direct investments behind Europe. In this section, we focus on the outward FDI of six countries of emerging Asia: South Korea, Taiwan, Malaysia, Thailand, Indonesia, and Vietnam.

While South Korea and Taiwan have been among the top 20 home economies of FDI for several years, Thailand and Malaysia also occasionally appear in this category. In 2018, the UNCTAD list of top 20 FDI home countries featured South Korea and Taiwan at the 9th and 17th places, respectively. (Thailand was ranked 18th.) As for the 2018 list of top 100 non-financial multinational enterprises (MNEs) ranked by foreign assets, two made it from emerging Asia: one from South Korea (Samsung) and the other from Taiwan (Hon Hai Precision Industries). Nevertheless, almost one fifth of the top 100 non-financial MNEs from developing and transition economies ranked by foreign assets came from South Korea, Taiwan, Malaysia, or Thailand in 2017. What explains South Korea's and Taiwan's exceptional performance is that they belong to the first-tier newly industrialized countries in Asia. Accordingly, their economic development took off sooner than the ASEAN countries. South Korea and Taiwan are also net FDI source countries, meaning that their outward FDI stock is larger than their inward FDI stock. The four ASEAN countries are still net FDI recipients. Although Malaysia is close to becoming a net FDI source country, its outward FDI stock exceeded inward FDI stock in two consecutive years, in 2015 and 2016.

5.2.2 *Size and Geographical/Sectoral Distribution of Outward Foreign Direct Investments from South Korea, Taiwan, and Selected ASEAN Countries*

Of the six Asian countries, South Korea is the largest investor. Its outward FDI stock amounted to 387.6 billion US dollars in 2018 (Fig. 5.1). South Korea is followed by Taiwan (339.7 billion USD), Thailand (121.4 billion USD), Malaysia (118.9 billion USD), Indonesia (72.3 billion USD), and Vietnam (10.7 billion USD).[2]

5.2.2.1 South Korea

Until the late 1980s, FDI flows in and out of South Korea were modest because of capital controls and an overall restrictive FDI regime. The South Korean government started relaxing regulations in the 1980s. A marked change took place in 1987, which was made necessary by a surplus balance of payments, the rise of domestic input prices, and the upward revaluation of won, the South Korean currency. Following the initial easing of the FDI regime, FDI flows substantially increased, with outflows exceeding inflows. The increase came to a halt during the 1997–98 economic crisis, and inflows briefly exceeded outflows. This reversal occurred because the more liberal FDI regime, in part demanded by the IMF, attracted "fire-sale FDI", while the overseas operations of South Korean

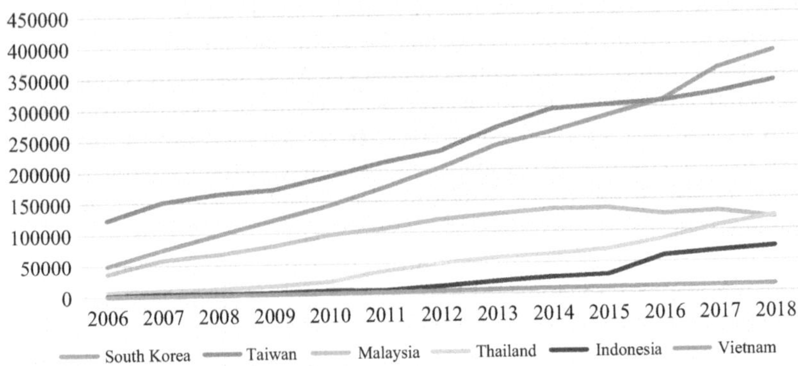

Fig. 5.1 Global outward FDI stock from the six Asian countries (million US dollars). (Source: UNCTADSTAT)

[2] Source of data: UNCTADSTAT.

companies were curtailed by the domestic financial crisis. Full-fledged market opening for both inflows and outflows took place only after the 1997–98 economic crisis (Sa-Kong and Koh 2010, p. 29). This led to increasing FDI outflows in 2000 at a pace that exceeded inflows (Hill and Jongwanich 2011, p. 7). The result of this overall success story is that South Korea has today become one of the top FDI home countries not just among emerging economies, but also globally.

Based on the data of the Export-Import Bank of Korea (Eximbank), 40.7% of the cumulative amount of outward foreign direct investments (between 1980 and 2016) went to Asia. North America and Europe came in second and third, hosting 25% and 16%, respectively. Of all the countries welcoming South Korean outward FDI, the USA is the largest recipient (22.5%). China is the second largest recipient (16%), attracting as much FDI as the European region did.

A sectoral analysis reveals that one third of investments were concentrated in the manufacturing sector (e.g. electronic equipment and components, electric equipment, motor vehicle, petrochemical, and metal products). Other South Korean investments went to mining and extraction (16.8%), service industry, wholesale and retail trade (11.5%), finance and insurance (11.2%), and real estate (9.6%). Two other key insights shown by the data are that the manufacturing sector's share in outward FDI has been decreasing in the period analysed (1987–2016), and that the mining and extraction sector's share experienced a sudden surge after 2008.

While the bulk of South Korean outward foreign direct investments is related to chaebols (family-founded conglomerates), SMEs have been internationalizing their activities since the 1980s. A small part of outward FDI is related to individual investors. As for state-owned enterprises, such as Korean National Oil Corporation, Korea Resources Corporation, Korea Electric Power Corporation, and Korea Gas Corporation, they also secure raw materials and energy needed for the South Korean economy through overseas investments.

5.2.2.2 *Taiwan*

Under pressure from rising domestic input prices and an appreciating national currency, Taiwan, like South Korea, started to liberalize its FDI regime in 1987 to support FDI outflows. As a result, the late 1980s saw a significant increase in the amount of annual FDI outflows and inflows. Except for 2006, annual FDI outflows have exceeded inflows to Taiwan. Similar to South Korea, Taiwan has become one of the top FDI home countries, not only among emerging economies, but also on the global level.

According to the data[3] provided by the Investment Commission of the Ministry of Economic Affairs, Taiwanese outward direct investments show a more significant Asian concentration than Koreans do. Of all of Taiwan's outward FDI, 77% went to Asia in the 1952–2016 period. Quite unsurprisingly, this geographical bias is mainly due to Taiwanese investments in Mainland China, which attracted 59% of the total. Due to its appeal as a tax haven, the second largest host region of Taiwanese outward FDI is Latin America. In comparison, the North American and European region hosts a mere 5.4% and 2.7%, respectively, of Taiwanese outward FDI.

The sectoral distribution of outward FDI shows the dominance of the manufacturing sector, with 60.6% of Taiwanese investments focusing on electronic components, computers, electrical equipment, basic metal, and chemical products. Sectors such as finance and insurance (18%) and wholesale and retail trade (9.3%) are also highly sought after by Taiwanese companies.

Among the Taiwanese businesses investing abroad are SMEs, large companies (e.g. OEM/ODM in electronics, computers, such as Foxconn, Quanta Computer), and conglomerates (e.g. Formosa Plastics). There is also evidence of overseas direct investments made by Taiwanese state-owned companies, such as China Steel, petroleum refiner CPC, shipbuilder CSBC, Taiwan Sugar, and Taiwan Salt Industrial Corp. (Hsu 2017).

5.2.2.3 *Malaysia*

Malaysia began investing abroad in the mid-1970s, though inward FDI flows continued to significantly outpace outward FDI. Since then, Malaysia grew out to be one of the most significant investors, second only to Singapore among the ASEAN members. The value of FDI outflows from Malaysia jumped in the 1990s, and consistently surpassed inflows between 2007 and 2015. Malaysia's outward FDI stock reached 136.9 billion US dollars in 2015 and exceeded inward FDI stock in both 2015 and 2016. By 2018, however, it registered a decrease to 118.9 billion US dollars.

In terms of sectoral composition, Malaysia's outward FDI stock (2015) is concentrated in the service sector (60%), underscoring the growing regionalization of Malaysian companies in finance, insurance, property development and infrastructure, information and communication, retail

[3] Cumulative amount of approved outward FDI between 1952 and 2016.

trade, and utilities subsectors (e.g. power generation). Sizeable investments are also made in the mining (24%) and agriculture sectors (8%) (Central Bank of Malaysia 2017), while the manufacturing sector accounts for only 6%. In terms of geographical distribution, there is a clear preference for countries of Southeast Asia and the Asia Pacific. The bulk of Malaysian outward FDI is channelled into regional economies like Singapore (16%), Indonesia (10%), India (3%), Hong Kong (3%), and Thailand (2%), as well as advanced economies like Canada (9%) and Australia (5%). Another chunk of investments is found in offshore financial centres (14%), such as Labuan, only to be redirected to other locations (Central Bank of Malaysia 2017). In the balance of payments statistics of 2015, the UK, Germany, and the Netherlands are the only European destinations specified, together hosting no more than 6% of total outward Malaysian FDI stock.

Initially, outward foreign direct investments were undertaken primarily by government-linked companies (GLCs) mainly in the oil and gas and agriculture sectors (MITI Malaysia 2017). By contrast, private companies including SMEs have recently become active overseas investors. Nevertheless, the bulk of outward FDI is still related to GLCs such as Petronas, Sime Darby, or CIBM.

5.2.2.4 Thailand, Indonesia, and Vietnam

In addition to Singapore and Malaysia, three other countries in the ASEAN region—Thailand, Indonesia, and Vietnam—have recently emerged to become new investors. Thailand's outward FDI stock has been increasing sharply since 2007. While outward FDI stock is still considerably lower than inward FDI stock, Thailand is an important investor, especially in its home region. According to the UNCTAD data, the outward FDI stock of Thailand grew from 8.3 billion US dollars to 121.4 billion US dollars between 2007 and 2018, surpassing the outward FDI stock of Malaysia.

Statistics based on the report of the Stock Exchange of Thailand show that 192 Thai listed companies had outward FDI stock at the end of 2015. Seventy-nine per cent of them have direct investments in ASEAN member countries, with CLMV[4] countries being preferred targets of Thai outward FDI. While 59% of Thai listed companies have investments in CLMV countries, 41%, 21%, and 19% of Thai listed companies have made direct investments in East Asia, North America, and Europe, respectively. The sectoral distribution of Thai outward foreign direct investments between 2006 and 2015 shows the dominance of mining, energy and utilities, with

[4] CLMV stands for Cambodia, Laos, Myanmar and Vietnam

a 55% share.[5] Other important target sectors are industrials (16%), agro and food industry (13%), and property and construction (8%) (Stock Exchange of Thailand 2016).[6]

Like Thailand, Indonesia started to promote inward FDI in the 1970s to enhance its economic development. With the exception of the 1998–2004 period, annual FDI inflows have exceeded FDI outflows (Sambodo 2017, p. 130). In 2018, according to UNCTAD statistics, the inward FDI stock of Indonesia reached 226.3 billion US dollars. Although its outward FDI stock grew rapidly from 1 billion US dollars in 2006 to 72.3 billion US dollars in 2018, it amounts to only 32% of its inward FDI stock and also falls behind Malaysia's and Thailand's outward FDI stock. According to Carney and Dieleman (2011, p. 1), the relatively low level of Indonesian outward foreign direct investments may be explained by two factors. On the one hand, official statistics are often not too reliable, which means that the outward FDI of Indonesian business groups is underreported.[7] On the other hand, outward FDI may be genuinely low, "(i) mpeded by a combination of institutional and firm-level factors that arrest the internationalization of all but the largest firms". Both may account for the absence of Indonesian companies among the world's top non-financial 100 MNEs from developing and transition economies. Bank Indonesia, which publishes the official data on FDI, reports only on inward FDI in details (e.g. sectoral distribution, country of origin, form of investment). According to the latest (2012) bilateral data gathered by UNCTAD, the bulk of Indonesia's outward FDI stock concentrated in China (38.4%) and Singapore (35%), while 82% of the total was outplaced across Asia. The United States and the EU hosted only 2.5% and 14.6%, respectively, of Indonesian outward FDI stock.

Like their Thai and Indonesian counterparts, Vietnamese companies are emerging investors from Southeast Asia. Their investments started to

[5] This is calculated on the basis of accumulated net value of outward FDI between 2006 and 2015.

[6] Industrials: automotive, industrial materials and machinery, paper and printing materials, petrochemicals and chemicals, packaging, steel; agro and food industry: agricultural business, food and beverage; property and construction: construction materials, construction services, property fund and real estate investment trust, property development.

[7] The owners of most of the largest business groups are of Chinese descent. For them, the incentive to hide investments is high, "(b)ecause outward direct investments carry the stigma of disloyalty to Indonesia, and is often portrayed negatively in the Indonesian press" (Carney and Dieleman 2011, p. 7).

increase in recent years. According to UNCTAD statistics, the outward FDI stock of Vietnam (10.7 billion USD, 2018) is much lower than that of Thailand or Indonesia. The data of the General Statistics Office of Vietnam show that Vietnamese companies mainly invest in the following five sectors: mining and quarrying (45.3%), agriculture, forestry and fishing (15.8%), utilities (11.3%), information and communication (9.3%), and arts, entertainment, and recreation (5.9%). The bulk of the total registered outward foreign direct investments from Vietnam is to be found in two countries, Laos (25.1%) and Cambodia (17.6%), with ASEAN hosting more than half of all registered outward FDI from Vietnam. Russia (12.9%), Venezuela (9.2%), and Peru (6.8%) also feature prominently among the most important destinations for Vietnamese FDI. The United States and Germany, the only EU country in the list, account for only a small share of the total Vietnamese outward foreign direct investments, with 2.8% and 0.5%, respectively.

Outward FDI from Thailand, Indonesia, and Vietnam have been made by state-owned enterprises, GLCs, private conglomerates, large companies, and SMEs. In the case of Indonesia, we have already mentioned the dominance of business groups owned by ethnic Chinese in outward foreign direct investments. Salim, Lippo, Sinar Mas, Gudand Garam, and Bakrie are representative examples of them. The Indonesian government encourages the outward FDI of state-owned enterprises such as Aneka Tambang, Semen Indonesia, and Bank Negara Indonesia. In the case of Thailand, FDI outflows are led by large private firms, such as Banpu, Siam Cement Group, Charoen Pokphand Group (ethnic Chinese owner), and Thai Beverages as well as GLCs such as PTT, Thai Airways International, and Electricity Generating Authority of Thailand (Sermcheep 2017, p. 16). Banpu was the only Thai company listed among the world's top 100 non-financial MNEs from developing and transition economies ranked by foreign assets in 2017. As for Vietnam, the recent surge of outward FDI was mostly conducted by state-owned enterprises such as Song Da, Petrovietnam, Viettel, and Vietnam Rubber. As a large private company, HAGL has made several investments in the agriculture and real estate sectors of neighbouring countries (ASEAN Secretariat and UNCTAD 2016, p. 31). SMEs from Thailand, Indonesia, and Vietnam have recently started to expand their activities in the ASEAN region.

5.2.3 Motivations and Push Factors for Outward Foreign Direct Investments from South Korea, Taiwan, and Selected ASEAN Countries

There are several push factors, which have incentivized the outward FDI of the six Asian countries, such as rising production costs (wages, land prices), saturated domestic market, diminishing supply of domestic resources, avoiding trade barriers and securing advanced technology for economic upgrading, and government policy promoting outward FDI.

In the case of South Korea, in the 1980s and 1990s, rising domestic wages started to drive domestic companies (especially small and medium sized) to invest or relocate labour-intensive manufacturing first in Southeast Asia and then in China. These efficiency-seeking investments in Asia were export oriented and often combined with the aim of gaining access to third countries (e.g. the United States) through preferential trade access. The reasons explaining the jump in outward foreign direct investments from Taiwan in the 1990s are similar to the case of South Korea. Rising labour costs and the appreciation of the Taiwanese dollar started to drive Taiwanese companies (first SMEs and then large companies) to relocate their production to Southeast Asia and later to China to maintain their export competitiveness. In other words, the objective was to create export platform in low-cost locations to supply developed markets such as the United States. In comparison to the sectoral and geographical patterns of South Korean outward FDI, Taiwanese investments show a more significant bias towards Asia and the manufacturing sector. Common culture and history, along with the presence of ethnic Chinese business communities in Southeast Asia, significantly contributed to the internationalization (regionalization) of Taiwanese companies. Rising labour costs, combined with the shortage of industrial space and increasing concerns about the environment, also pushed large Taiwanese companies of heavy and chemical industry to invest abroad and seek markets primarily in (Southeast) Asia (Tolentino 2000). Because of the rising labour costs, Malaysian manufacturing companies also started to invest in neighbouring countries like Cambodia, Laos, Vietnam, and China in the 1990s (Ariff and Lopez 2007, p. 24). The increase of domestic wages is one of the main reasons behind the recent jump in investments of Thai, Indonesian, and Vietnamese companies in extractive industry and agriculture. According to Cheewatrakoolpong and Boonprakaikawe (2015,

p. 125), Thai labour-intensive manufacturing companies also invest abroad due to labour shortage and increasing wages at home.

In the case of every country, besides rising wages, a saturated domestic market or, in other words, market-seeking motives can be emphasized as well. In the 1990s, South Korean and Taiwanese FDI started to migrate to North America or Europe in order to gain markets and avoid trade barriers. Doing so also allowed this kind of FDI to penetrate important trading blocs like NAFTA and the EU. And over time, China has become more and more attractive not only for efficiency-seeking FDI but also for market-seeking FDI from South Korea and Taiwan because of its huge consumer market (Chung 2007, p. 69; Hsu 2014). According to Yean et al. (2015), a limited or saturated domestic market and a diminishing supply of natural resources are the most important push factors behind outward FDI from Malaysia. Malaysian companies are thus investing abroad to obtain new markets for achieving economies of scale and higher potential returns. In other ASEAN countries, market-seeking motive is more prevalent in the case of SMEs (ASEAN Secretariat and UNCTAD 2016, p. 109), which can be a result of high competition in the domestic market.

A diminishing supply of resources mainly drives outward FDI from the four ASEAN countries in extractive industry and agriculture. In the case of Malaysia, as oil fields and arable lands are becoming a scarcity, Petronas and plantation companies invest abroad to seek resources elsewhere. A high share of outward FDI from Thailand, Indonesia, and Vietnam is related to companies in extractive industry or agriculture, with businesses investing abroad primarily to secure access to natural resources such as arable land. An example in this regard is Vietnam Rubber's investment in Laos and Cambodia (ASEAN Secretariat 2012, p. 85). In the case of South Korea, natural resource–seeking outward foreign direct investments have been made since the 1960s. Because of the lack of domestic natural resources, this type of investments has been supported by the South Korean government even in the period of a generally restrictive outward FDI policy (Nicolas et al. 2013, p. 29).

Besides the market-seeking motive, in the 1990s, South Korean and Taiwanese companies started to invest in developed countries to acquire strategic assets (e.g. advanced technology), to support their domestic industrial upgrading. This kind of motive has been shown by Malaysian companies since the 2000s, as well.

Finally, we have to highlight the role of government policy in promoting outward FDI. South Korea had a restrictive government policy that hindered outward FDI in the past. Since 1987, regulations in this area underwent a gradual relaxation over time. In 2005, the government launched a campaign for actively promoting outward FDI, which significantly contributed to the increase of outward FDI afterwards. Oh and Mah (2017, p. 260) call this post-2005 promotion plan a driving engine of outward FDI, "(i)n which the limit on the amount of investments was relaxed, better insurance policies were provided and increased financial support became available for investors". The South Korean government is engaged in the provision of four types of outward FDI services: financial support (e.g. loans provided by the Korea Eximbank, of up to 90% of the invested capital abroad to small and medium enterprises), taxation (e.g. avoidance of double taxation), overseas investment services (e.g. insurance provided by the Korea Export Insurance Corporation against war and civil disturbance, expropriation, inconvertibility, and the threat of contract risks related to new overseas investments), and institutional services (e.g. information provided by several institutions [Korea Eximbank, Ministry of Strategy and Finance, International Management Institute]; the latter one especially helps small and medium enterprises) (Kim and Rhee 2009, pp. 132–133).

Similar to South Korea, Taiwan began easing FDI regulations in 1987; most conditionalities were removed and capital controls relaxed only after the Asian financial crisis of 1997–98. Since 1994, the Taiwanese government has announced four times the so-called Go South policy to promote outward FDI in (Southeast) Asia. The repetition of this policy goal signalled the Taiwanese government's intention to reduce or at least limit the country's economic dependence on Mainland China. (Political and security considerations have also played an important role in the introduction of "Go South" policy.) The latest iteration of the "Go South" policy was launched in 2016, targeting Southeast Asia (ASEAN) and South Asia (mainly India) to benefit from a growing market of the middle class in these countries, as well as to react to Indian Prime Minister Modi's "Make in India" scheme that aims to turn India into a global manufacturing hub (Churchman 2016).

As in the case of South Korea and Taiwan, the Malaysian government also played a key role in promoting outward FDI. Since the beginning of the 1990s, the central bank of Malaysia gradually relaxed capital outflow regulations. Tax exemptions and incentives have likewise incentivized companies to invest abroad. One illustration of this preferential treatment is that all foreign income by Malaysian companies has been fully exempted from tax since 1995. In 2003, another incentive was introduced to encourage Malaysian companies to acquire foreign-owned high-tech firms from abroad (MASSA News, June 2005; cited in Ariff and Lopez 2007, p. 21). The EXIM Bank of Malaysia supports outward investors with various financial instruments like overseas investment insurance, overseas project financing facility, and guarantee facility (OECD 2013, pp. 128–129). At the beginning of the 1990s, the Mahathir government greatly promoted South-South co-operation in its foreign policy, which covered investment and technology co-operation. Two organizations, Malaysian South-South Association (MASSA) and Malaysian South South Cooperation Berhad (MASSCORP), were established. MASSA is a non-profit business association, with members from the Malaysian business sector. Its main purpose is to promote trade and investments with emerging markets. MASSCORP is a public limited company incorporated in 1992. A consortium of 86 Malaysian shareholders, its members are corporate leaders in their respective fields of business. The organization's objectives are to initiate and promote joint ventures between Malaysian entrepreneurs and Southern investors, to undertake the privatization of enterprises in South countries, and to support the transfer of Malaysian expertise and capital to South countries.

As for the role of government policy, the Thai government started its outward FDI promotion only in 2013. Cheewatrakoolpong and Boonprakaikawe (2015, p. 140) suggest that this late launch of a promotion policy explains the difference between outward FDI performance in Thailand and Malaysia prior to 2013. Thailand's measures to support outward FDI can be divided into four categories: investment protection, fiscal measures (e.g. double taxation agreement), financial measures (e.g. long-term loan), information provision, and facilitation (e.g. the establishment of Thai Overseas Investment Information Centre [providing overseas market information] and Thai Overseas Investment Development Centre [training for Thai investors]) (Kaewsang 2014). According to the Board of Investment of Thailand, the prioritized sectors for Thailand's outward FDI consist of textile and garment, food and agricultural industry, and automotive parts and components. The first-tier destination countries are Cambodia, Myanmar, Laos, Vietnam, and Indonesia (Kaewsang 2015).

As for Vietnam, though the government has no clear mechanism to promote outward FDI, it does not restrict domestic investors from taking their capital abroad. The majority of companies engaged in overseas investments are large state-owned enterprises that enjoy strong government-backed financial resources. In Indonesia, the Investment Coordination Board (BKPM) functions as an investment promotion agency and facilitates outward FDI. It has a designated division to provide information about investment opportunities in and policies of other countries, offering consultation services to interested clients. Overall, the Indonesian government neither restricts nor explicitly incentivizes outward FDI (US State Department's Office of Investment Affairs 2017).

5.3 Outward Foreign Direct Investments from South Korea, Taiwan, and Selected ASEAN Countries in Visegrád Countries

5.3.1 Outward Foreign Direct Investment from the Six Asian Countries in the EU

The geographical distribution of the total outward FDI from the six Asian emerging countries shows that Asia is the most preferred regional destination, while the EU attracts only a small portion. The national FDI statistics available in the six countries differ in a number of ways, which makes their use somewhat problematic. They are created with different methodologies that analyse various time periods. The geographical distribution is also diverse, while time series data are often missing. Therefore, we decided to use Eurostat statistics to render the six Asian countries' FDI in the EU (CEE) comparable. As these statistics are also not without certain deficiencies, we use them with some reservations.[8]

Among the six Asian countries, South Korea, Taiwan, and, to a lesser extent, Malaysia and Thailand are important investors in terms of global outward FDI. Nevertheless, these four countries accounted for only 0.76% of extra-EU28 inward FDI stock (6441 billion euros) in the EU in 2017. The FDI stock of Indonesia and Vietnam in the EU is barely visible (Table 5.1).

5.3.1.1 South Korea

South Korea is the biggest investor in the EU. South Korean companies started to increase their investments in the EU at the beginning of the

[8] Missing data or unpublished data.

Table 5.1 Outward FDI stock of the six Asian countries in EU28 and V4 (2017, million euros)

	EU28	*Hungary*	*Poland*	*Slovakia*	*Czech Republic*
South Korea	27,849	1658	946	2948	2714
Taiwan	3729	40	26	15	236
Malaysia	14,518	12	(-)0.3	64	21
Thailand	1868	10	29	3	26
Indonesia	552	0.6	(-)0.1	0	0
Vietnam	117	(-)1.2	(-)0.2	91	2

Source: Eurostat

1990s. Big conglomerates, or chaebols, such as Samsung, LG, Daewoo, and Hyundai led this initial upsurge of Korean FDI in the EU. South Korean companies invested heavily in Germany, the Netherlands, and the UK, and also in CEE countries such as Poland, the Czech Republic, and Hungary. South Korean companies also participated in the privatization of state-owned enterprises in the CEE region. For example, Daewoo actively invested in the automotive industry of Poland, the Czech Republic, and Romania (van Hoesel 1999, p. 113). The objective for South Korean companies was to have access to an important consumer market and to overcome protectionist pressures and to acquire strategic assets (e.g. advanced technology), to take advantage from low labour costs in the CEE region and use it as a production platform for the European market. This motivation also explains the different sectoral preferences with which South Korean investments came to the EU and the CEE region. In the 1990s, CEE countries attracted mostly manufacturing FDI from South Korea, while in EU member states, outward FDI from South Korea in the retail and whole sale trade outpaced or was equal to manufacturing FDI from South Korea (Hwang 2003, p. 37).

According to Eurostat statistics, South Korean outward FDI stock in the EU showed an increasing trend between 2000 and 2017, with the exception of 2008 and 2011. In 2017, the top seven EU destination countries of South Korean outward FDI included four Western European and three CEE countries. Germany, the Netherlands, Ireland, and the UK host 60% of the total outward FDI stock from South Korea. Slovakia, the Czech Republic, and Hungary account for 26%. Interestingly, South Korean FDI stock in Slovakia and the Czech Republic combined outpaces that of the UK.

As for sectoral distribution, 94.6% of South Korean outward FDI stock in the EU was concentrated in the manufacturing (31.5%) and services sectors (63.1%). The bulk of South Korean outward FDI stock in Slovakia, the Czech Republic, and Hungary is in the manufacturing sector like electronics, metal and machinery, and automotive sector. Most of the South Korean outward FDI stock in Germany, the Netherlands, Ireland, and the UK is concentrated in the services sector such as wholesale and retail trade of motor vehicles, motorcycles, as well as finance and insurance. According to data from the Korea Eximbank, South Korean companies in the EU heavily invested in finance and insurance, real estate and leasing, science and technology services, and mining besides traditionally preferred sectors such as manufacturing and wholesale and retail trade (EEAS 2015, p. 14).

5.3.1.2 *Malaysia*

Malaysia has the second largest outward FDI stock in the EU, which registered a 20-fold increase between 2000 and 2015. According to Eurostat statistics, Malaysia's outward FDI stock grew significantly in 2015 after heavy investments in the Netherlands. In 2017, however, the stock slightly contracted. Malaysian outward FDI stock is geographically much more concentrated than the South Korean one, with the Netherlands alone accounting for 87% of the total. Taking into consideration Luxembourg and Germany, these three countries host 97% of Malaysian FDI. In 2017, V4 countries represented only a small fragment (0.7%) of the Malaysia's total outward FDI stock.

The bulk of Malaysian outward FDI in the EU is concentrated in the services sector, which follows the general sectoral pattern of global outward FDI stock of Malaysia. In the old EU15 countries, Malaysian FDI took the form of acquisitions and, to a lesser extent, the setting up of high-end R&D facilities (Agenzia ICE 2013, p. 3) to gain access to new markets, to strategic assets (technology, brand and marketing capabilities, etc.), and in some cases to natural resources (in mining and agriculture/resource-based manufacturing sector). The old EU15 countries drew investments from Malaysian companies in sectors like finance, telecommunication, property development, transport, construction, manufacturing, mining, energy, and plantation/resource-based manufacturing. For instance, Sime Darby, Petronas, and CIMB have investments in various sectors in different EU15 countries. At the same time, the footprint of Malaysian companies in the CEE region, including the V4 countries, is severely limited. An important exception is plastics manufacturer Triplus, which established a small factory in Slovakia in 2001. The location provides cheap labour combined with proximity to the EU market (Agenzia ICE 2013, p. 10).

5.3.1.3 Taiwan

Taiwanese FDI stock in the EU amounts only to approximately one fourth of Malaysian FDI stock. While the Netherlands accounted for 63% of total Taiwanese FDI stock in 2017, its distribution among other member countries was more balanced than in the case of Malaysia. V4 countries hosted 8.5% of total Taiwanese FDI stock in the EU. In general, Taiwanese companies have a strong Asian (and American) bias, leaving Europe as a somewhat neglected and untapped region for Taiwanese capital. Not only was this true in the 1990s, the Eurostat data on Taiwanese outward FDI stock in the EU between 2000 and 2017 do not reveal any unambiguous trend of change, either positive or negative.

On a country-by-county basis, Taiwanese companies have displayed growing interest towards the V4 countries after 2004. But because of the deficient data of Eurostat (by country and year) we have to handle FDI trends of Taiwan with caveat. According to the research of EIAS (which is based on AMADEUS dataset) (EIAS 2014, pp. 13–15), most of the 1100 Taiwanese companies located in Europe were concentrated in Germany, the Netherlands, and the UK. The presence of Taiwanese companies is also relevant in V4 countries.

In terms of sectoral distribution, Taiwanese companies in the EU are active primarily in the services sector (e.g. finance and insurance, professional and scientific services, wholesale and retail trade, ICT) and the manufacturing sector (e.g. computers, electronic and optical products; motor vehicle and parts; electrical equipment manufacturing). Taiwanese firms invest in Europe to gain access to technology, knowledge, distribution channels, and the European market and for competitive advantage (EIAS 2014, p. 14). Similar to their Korean counterparts, Taiwanese companies invested in the manufacturing sector in the V4 countries, thus benefitting from lower labour costs and proximity to the EU market. V4 countries are attractive locations for corporate subsidiaries and OEM/ODM manufacturing sites as well.

5.3.1.4 Other ASEAN Investors (Thailand, Indonesia, and Vietnam)

Singapore and, to a lesser extent, Malaysia account for the lion's share of ASEAN's outward FDI stock in the EU. As Thailand, Indonesia, and

Vietnam are considered to be newcomers to the EU's investment market, their investments have not been studied adequately so far. According to Eurostat, outward FDI from Indonesia and Vietnam is low and sporadic, with presence only in certain countries. The bulk of Thai outward FDI in the EU is concentrated in the Netherlands and Luxembourg. The preferred sector is the steel, chemical, and food and beverage industries. Most of the Thai investments in the EU are undertaken by the following companies: Charoen Pokphand Group, Thai Beverages, PTT, and other companies, for example, Sahaviraya Steel, Indorama Ventures, Singha (Sroithong 2014). The three countries' sectoral preference in the V4 countries will be discussed on a case-by-case basis in the next section.

5.3.2 *Outward Foreign Direct Investment from the Six Asian Countries in Hungary, Slovakia, Poland, and the Czech Republic*

As mentioned above, outward FDI from the six Asian countries shows a clear Asian bias, which is supported in many cases by governmental policy. Foreign direct investments in Slovakia, Hungary, Poland, and the Czech Republic mainly originate in the EU. The V4 are deeply integrated into the global value chains (GVCs). South Korea is nevertheless one of the most important non-European FDI source countries for the V4. According to Eurostat, South Korea has by far the largest FDI stock in V4 countries. While the second largest investor is Taiwan, the four ASEAN countries analysed have only sporadic or no presence whatsoever in the V4 countries.

Due to incomplete and insufficient data, the exact number of companies from the six Asian countries operating in the V4 countries is difficult to come by. The estimation used below is based primarily on company data provided by AMADEUS. Additional information was collected from company interviews, company websites and acquired from investment promotion agencies, embassies, ministries, and relevant media sources (Table 5.2).

Sectoral distribution shows that companies from the six Asian countries operating in the V4 countries have targeted the manufacturing and services sectors. South Korean manufacturing companies are mainly present in the automotive and electronics industry. There are two South Korean car assembly factories in V4 countries: the Kia plant in Zilina (Slovakia) and the Hyundai plant in Nosovice (Czech Republic). Many car parts manufacturers, often suppliers of the two car factories, are active in the

Table 5.2 Estimated number of companies from the six Asian economies in V4 countries

Asian country	*Number of companies*
South Korea	430
Taiwan	100
Vietnam	70
Malaysia	30
Thailand	30
Indonesia	10

Source: Data based on AMADEUS database and authors' calculation

automotive subsectors like plastics and chemical industry, electrical engineering, mechanical engineering, composite materials, iron and steel industry, and textile industry. The same logic underpins the presence of South Korean companies in the electronics industry. Samsung Electronics has plants in every V4 country surrounded by a number of South Korean suppliers. In sum, we can say the backbone of South Korean investments in the V4 is presented by chaebols (Samsung, LG, Hyundai/Kia) and their suppliers. Other South Korean companies are also engaged in different service industries such as logistics, finance, real estate, construction, warehousing and storage, IT services, wholesale (e.g. motor vehicle parts, household appliances), tour operator activities, accommodation, and catering.

Taiwanese companies in V4 countries' manufacturing sector are dominantly ICT-related OEM/ODM manufacturers such as Wistron,[9] Foxconn,[10] Compal,[11] and Darfon[12] or components manufacturers such as Eson,[13] AU Optronics,[14] and Ferroxcube.[15] There are two Taiwanese

[9] Wistron produces desktop computers, servers, and LCD monitors/TVs in the Czech Republic.

[10] Foxconn produces LCD TVs for Sony in Slovakia; computers and workstations for home and businesses for HP and Cisco in the Czech Republic; and desktop computers, servers, storages, and telecommunication devices for Huawei in Hungary.

[11] Compal produces computers and peripheral equipment in Poland.

[12] Darfon produces computers and peripheral equipment in the Czech Republic.

[13] Eson produces metal frames and stands for LCD TVs of Sony in Slovakia.

[14] AU Optronics produces LCD module for TVs in Slovakia and solar module in the Czech Republic.

[15] Ferroxcube produces electronic components and boards in Poland.

bicycle factories: Giant in Hungary and Ideal in Poland. In the services sectors, Taiwanese companies operate in repair and the wholesale of computers and computer peripheral equipment, customer services, real estate, catering, and ICT services. Several Taiwanese companies with manufacturing or service bases in V4 countries belong to the big league of Taiwanese companies. Many of them can be found among Taiwan's top 20 non-financial outward investors (Kuo and Kao 2011, p. 2).

According to AMADEUS, of the four ASEAN countries, Vietnam has the largest number of companies in the V4 countries, even though its FDI stock in the region is smallest. This is no contradiction since most of the Vietnamese companies are smaller wholesale or retail companies. Large state-owned companies, which account for bulk of Vietnam's outward FDI, are absent from the V4 (except Vinamilk). Malaysia, Thailand, and Indonesia have a limited number of companies present in the V4. But similar to Vietnam, large state-owned/government-linked or private companies or conglomerates of Malaysia and Indonesia are absent from the V4. In the case of Thailand, petrochemical company Indorama Ventures and food companies Thai Union Group and Thai President Foods are worth to be mentioned as large private companies operating in the V4. ASEAN companies are nonetheless active in several industries of the V4 such as electronics (HIT Electronics[16] in Poland), petrochemicals (Indorama Ventures in Poland), food (Vinamilk, Thai Union in Poland; Thai President Foods in Hungary), chemical/automotive (Indorama Ventures[17] in Slovakia and the Czech Republic), wholesale and retail (Vakomtek in Poland), IT services (FPT Software in Slovakia), property development (Kwasa Europe SARL in Poland), and catering (restaurants).

In the final part of this chapter, we discuss more thoroughly the automotive and electronics sectors, the industries in which the most representative companies from the six Asian countries operate in the V4. Our objective is to assess the main motivations and pull factors for these companies.

[16] We consider HIT Electronics as an Indonesian company because it was established in Indonesia, although its owner originates from South Korea.

[17] We consider Indorama Ventures as a Thai company because it was established in Thailand, although its owner originates from India.

5.3.3 *Motivations and Pull Factors for South Korean, Taiwanese, and ASEAN MNEs in V4 Countries*

5.3.3.1 *Automotive Sector*

In the 1990s, the V4 countries began to open up their economies to foreign direct investments, which brought industrial restructuring, modernization, and economic development. For these countries, "(t)he automotive industry was at the forefront of their FDI-driven development strategy in which foreign transnational corporations took over the CEE automotive industry through heavy capital investment, restructuring it and incorporating it into European and global production networks in the 1990s and 2000s" (Pavlínek 2015, p. 209). Daewoo Motors was a forerunner of South Korean motor vehicle manufacturers investing in V4 countries. In 1995, it purchased state-owned FSO and FSC plants in Warsaw and Lublin, Poland, to assemble its own brands and manufacture commercial vehicles. In 1998, Daewoo Motors (with Austrian Steyr) bought a 50.2% stake in Avia truck manufacturer in the Czech Republic. During the 1997–98 Asian financial crisis Daewoo Group collapsed and sold their automotive investments in Poland and the Czech Republic. The second wave of South Korean carmakers in the V4 countries is represented by greenfield investments of Hyundai and Kia, which opened their first factories in Europe. Kia plant in Zilina, Slovakia, started to operate in 2006. Near this plant, but on the other side of the border in Nosovice, the Czech Republic, Hyundai plant began to produce cars in 2008. Kia and Hyundai invested in the CEE because they wanted to fulfil the increasing demand of the EU market from a low-cost production base (market- and efficiency-seeking motivation). Their decision was also significantly influenced by the EU membership of V4 countries since 2004 which means free access to the regional market (institutional factor). Beyond these factors, skilled labour, government incentives, and relatively developed infrastructure influenced the investment decision of South Korean investors (Dore 2004; Doležalová and Dailida 2016, pp. 77–79). South Korean car manufacturers have attracted their domestic suppliers (which are often their own subsidiaries at the same time) representing different automotive subsectors to V4 countries (market-seeking motivation). The following are the most important ones that are often present in two or three V4 countries: Mobis (axle and control panel, brake systems), Yura (cable harnesses), Hanon Systems (air conditioning), Sungwoo Hightech (metal body parts), Sejong (exhaust systems), Seoyon E-HWA (plastic interior parts), Dymos (car seats), Donghee (suspension and fuel tanks), and Hysco (steel products). The company interviews made with two South Korean automotive companies reinforced this main pull factor for components manufacturer companies, namely, the presence of their main domestic purchasers in V4 countries. South Korean car and car components manufacturers have become integrated into the automotive cluster of V4 countries (CEE region), where several Western European, American, and Japanese car and car components producers have been operating. According to the company interviews, the presence of automotive supply chains in V4 countries and the industrial tradition of V4 countries in the automotive sector are also important pull factors for South Korean companies.

Of the other five Asian countries, Taiwan, Malaysia, and Thailand have outward foreign direct investments in the automotive industry, but these are rare in V4 countries, so we cannot speak about trends. It may be worth highlighting—for example—the strategic asset-seeking investments of Thai Indorama Ventures in the automotive subsector of petrochemicals in Slovakia and the Czech Republic. In 2018, Indorama Ventures, a global petrochemicals producer, acquired Europe's largest producer of tyre cord fabrics, Kordárna Plus, with two production sites (in the Czech Republic and Slovakia) located in the European Tire Industry Hub to expand their global footprint in high-value-added tyre cord segment. This deal was preceded by three other acquisitions (PHP, Performance Fibers, Glanzstoff) of Indorama Ventures. In 2017, the Czech subsidiary of Glanzstoff (Glanzstoff Bohemia) also became part of Indorama Ventures.

5.3.3.2 Electronics Sector

Besides the automotive industry, the consumer electronics sector of V4 countries is very attractive for MNEs, among others, South Korean and Taiwanese companies. Samsung and LG (surrounded by several suppliers) from South Korea are operating in every V4 country with manufacturing and/or service activities. Taiwanese foreign direct investments in V4 countries are vigorously concentrated in consumer electronics (EIAS 2015, p. 70). Some of these Taiwanese OEM/ODM companies and components manufacturers (mentioned above) are also often present in more than one V4 country.

The first South Korean investors started to appear in the V4 countries' consumer electronics sector in the 1990s. For example, the first South Korean investor in V4 countries' consumer electronics sector was Samsung Electronics, which created a joint venture with Hungarian Orion TV producer in Jászfényszaru, Hungary, in 1989. In 1990, Samsung Electronics became the sole owner of the factory which has been expanded and the technology of its products continuously developed since then. In 1998, Samsung Electronics relocated its TV production from England to Hungary. In 1996, Samsung Electronics opened its sales office in Warsaw, Poland. In 1992, LG Electronics (formerly Goldstar) established its first sales office (and regional headquarter in CEE) in Budapest. In 1999, LG Electronics opened its first factory in Mlawa, Poland, while relocating its TV production from England (Kim and Kim 2006, p. 217). In 1994, Daewoo Electronics opened a factory of TV sets in Pruszkow, Poland, which was operating till 2009. South Korean early comers in the V4 electronics industry were looking for a low-cost production base for fulfilling European demand (Radosevic 2004, p. 162) (market- and efficiency-seeking motivation).

In the case of Taiwan, foreign direct investments started to flow very slowly into V4 countries. In the mid-1990s, the Taiwanese government proposed to establish Taiwanese industrial zones in Pilsen, the Czech Republic, and in Lodz, Poland, but ultimately these industrial zones have not been realized (Tubilewicz 2007, p. 68). Foreign direct investments of Taiwanese electronics companies began to increase in the V4 countries only in the late 1990s and early 2000s. V4 countries' upcoming accession (2004) to the EU played a significant role in the jump of Taiwanese as well as Korean investments in the V4 consumer electronics sector. V4 countries providing trade barrier–free access to the whole European market and relatively low-cost production base became more attractive for market-seeking and efficiency-seeking investors. Anti-dumping tariffs imposed by the EU on goods originating from Asian countries (television sets, refrigerators, bicycles, polyethylene terephthalate [PET]) constituted an additional incentive for establishing plants within the EU (Kaliszuk 2016, p. 63). Besides the access to the EU market and low labour costs, government incentives and adequate quality of infrastructure also underpinned the growing interest of South Korean and Taiwanese investors in V4 countries.

As we mentioned before, Samsung Electronics has been present in Hungary since the beginning of the 1990s. Its main activity is assembly of TV sets, which first started with colour TV sets and gradually (in line with technological development) has moved towards LED and OLED TV sets. The upsurge of foreign direct investments after 2000 has brought new Samsung investments to V4 countries. In 2000, Samsung

Electro-Mechanics was established as a new subsidiary in Szigetszentmiklós, Hungary, to produce electronic parts of TV sets. Now it only deals with packaging and trading services. In 2002, cathode-ray tube and plasma display panel factory Samsung SDI Magyarország was opened in Göd, Hungary, which closed in 2014 when demand for plasma TVs fell off. In 2017, the factory was reopened and expanded to produce batteries of electric cars for the European market.

Samsung Electronics opened its second TV factory in Galanta, Slovakia, in 2002. It moved its production of its factory in Barcelona to Galanta (efficiency-seeking motivation). In 2008, a new factory, Samsung Electronics LCD, began the production of LC panels (key component for LCD TV sets) in Voderady, Slovakia. The largest part of the production at Samsung Electronics LCD is delivered Galanta factory and Foxconn factory in Nitra, Slovakia (SARIO, 2011, p. 15). Samsung Electronics' subsidiaries belong to the most important electro-technical companies in Slovakia. But in 2018, Samsung Electronics announced that it would consolidate the production of its Slovakian factories and close one of them to enhance efficiency.

In Poland, Samsung opened an R&D Institute in Warsaw in 2000 to respond to the needs of the European market while increasing the number of manufacturing facilities in V4 countries. "The institute developed at a very fast pace and claims to be the biggest and fastest-growing modern technology R&D centres in CEE region. The institute expanded geographically in Poland, opened a branch in 2011 in Poznan and two others in 2013 in Lodz and Cracow" (Magasházi et al. 2015, p. 171). Samsung Electronics has not established any TV factories in Poland but it acquired Polish Amica factory (in Wronki) in 2009 to attain a leading position in the European home appliance market (market-seeking motivation). By considering anti-dumping duty imposed on Korean refrigerators (LG, Daewoo Electronics) in 2006, the acquisition of Amica factory was also a preventive move (Kaliszuk 2016, p. 64). Besides the opportunity for increase of European sales, other pull factors such as Amica's advanced technology, qualified staff (strategic asset-seeking motivation), and strategic location also played a significant role in the acquisition.

In the Czech Republic, Samsung Electronics does not have any manufacturing facilities. Its sales and business development subsidiary, Samsung Electronics Czech and Slovak, was established in Prague in 2005.

Besides Samsung it is worth mentioning the other significant electronic company of South Korea, LG Electronics, which has had a strong presence in Poland among V4 countries, where it has been operating several LG subsidiaries. LG opened its TV assembly plant in Mlawa in 1999, which was expanded with a new plant in 2006. Similar to Samsung Electronics, the technological development of TV sets has been continuous at LG factories. In 2006, LG opened its new LCD TV factory in Wroclaw and it also started to produce refrigerators (and washing machines) at this new factory to avoid anti-dumping measures (LCD TVs, refrigerators) imposed by the EU. In Wroclaw, it created LG's Poland Cluster with the establishment of further subsidiaries to fulfil the growing European demand. LG Innotek was established in 2006 to produce inverters and power modules; LG Display (formerly LG. Philips Display) was launched in 2005 to produce LCD modules; LG Chem was opened in 2005 to produce polarizers. This production cluster serves as the main European production hub of LG and employs more than 10,000 employees (including those of supplier companies) (Dudáš 2015, p. 126).

Samsung and LG are important players in the consumer electronics sector of V4 countries. They have attracted further South Korean component manufacturers (market-seeking motivation). Just to mention a few of them: *Samsung*: Dong Jin Precision (2003, Slovakia), Nuritech SK (2004, Slovakia), Seong Ji (2005, Slovakia, 2009, Hungary), Hansol Technics Europe (2007, Slovakia), Fine DNC (2007, Slovakia), Jin Young G&T (2009, Slovakia), Sangjin Micron (2012, Hungary); *LG*: Heesung Electronics (2005, Poland), Dong Yan Electronics (2004, Poland), Dongseo (2006, Poland), Starion (2006, Poland), Ssang Geum (2005, Poland).

Taiwanese electronic companies prefer to settle down in the Czech Republic, but there are some companies which are present in more than one V4 country such as Foxconn, AU Optronics, Asus, and Acer. Foxconn created its first subsidiary in Pardubice, the Czech Republic, in 2000, which is its regional headquarter for Europe, the Middle East, and Africa. Foxconn's second Czech plant was opened in Kutna Hora in 2008. Foxconn has become the second largest exporter of the Czech Republic. In Hungary, Foxconn has been present—through its subsidiaries (PCE Paragon, FIH Europe)—since 2004. It opened its first factory in Komárom next to its main purchaser, mobile phone manufacturer Nokia. For a certain period, it was operating three other factories in Székesfehérvár, Pécs, and Debrecen. The last one of these factories was closed in Székesfehérvár in 2014, and the production of this factory was moved to Komárom plant. It also lost its main customer, Nokia, when it moved out in 2012. Now the only plant of Foxconn in Hungary produces computers, servers, and telecommunication equipment (for Huawei). In Slovakia, Foxconn bought 90% of Sony's LCD module factory in Nitra in 2010. "Sony has entered a new strategic alliance with Foxconn for the production of LCD TVs for the European region" (Schröter 2010). Acer and Asus have been running sales/customer service and repair activities in every V4 country. In the Czech Republic, AU Optronics launched a solar module factory in 2010 to fulfil the needs of European customers through local production in an atmosphere of growing EU antidumping measures (Olson 2012). AU Optronics opened its second European factory in Trencin, Slovakia, in 2011 to produce LCD modules for TV makers nearby (market-seeking motivation).

In the case of ASEAN countries, we found only some companies that invested in V4 countries' consumer electronics sector. For example, HIT Electronics from Indonesia established its first European factory in Poland in 2006, which is a supplier for LG's factory in Mlawa. We suppose that HIT Electronics followed the strategy of other suppliers and opened a factory near the European plant of its main purchaser, LG. Another ASEAN company example is LED indoor and outdoor lightening manufacturer Ligman from Thailand. Ligman established a plant in Prestanov, the Czech Republic, which is used as a platform to the company's expansion in the European market (market-seeking motivation). The Malaysian company, which we interviewed, was invited by its main home purchaser (a Japanese company) in Malaysia to invest in one of the V4 countries, where this purchaser also had been operating a factory. The Malaysian company, which produces plastic injection parts for home appliances, audio/video equipment, and automobiles, has primarily had a market-seeking motive similar to South Korean suppliers of LG and Samsung. Other pull factors, such as the strategic location and EU membership of the host country and low-cost unskilled and skilled labour, were mentioned in the company interview.

Finally, we can highlight those foreign direct investments that are related to services provided to manufacturing companies. For example, Nepco operates waste management for Samsung factories in Hungary and Slovakia. Hyundai Glovis provides logistics services for Hyundai factory in the Czech Republic and Kia factory in Slovakia. These companies followed their purchasers to gain new markets (market-seeking motivation).

5.4 Conclusions

Emerging Asia has become a significant source of FDI in global terms. In our study, we focused on outward foreign direct investments from six Asian countries (South Korea, Taiwan, Malaysia, Thailand, Indonesia, and Vietnam) in the V4. The main aim of our study was to determine the motivations and pull factors for these investments. First, we prepared a general overview on global outward FDI from South Korea, Taiwan, and the four ASEAN countries. On the basis of this overview, we concluded that the geographical distribution of outward FDI from the six Asian countries varies but generally supports an Asian bias, which is often underpinned by governmental policy. Therefore, the EU is clearly not the primary regional destination for outward FDI from the six Asian countries.

In numbers, South Korea, Taiwan, Malaysia, and Thailand accounted for only 0.76% of extra-EU28 inward FDI stock (6441 billion euros) in the EU in 2017. As for Indonesia and Vietnam, their FDI stock in the EU is sporadic and barely visible. In spite of the low share of South Korea in extra-EU28 inward FDI in the EU, it is one of the most important non-European FDI source countries for the V4. Of the six Asian countries, Taiwan is the second largest investor. Foreign direct investments from the four ASEAN countries are very small or missing in the V4.

Companies originated from the six Asian countries have been operating in several manufacturing and services sectors of the V4 countries. The automotive and electronics industry is the most preferred sector. Having analysed the motivations and pull factors for the investments of those Asian companies (mainly South Korean and Taiwanese) operating in these two sectors, we conclude the following. Since 2000, there has been an upsurge of investments from South Korea in the automotive industry and from South Korea and Taiwan in the electronics industry of V4 countries. We have found evidence for market-seeking and efficiency-seeking motivations for these investments. Main pull factors of the V4 are the following: free access to the EU market (EU membership since 2004), relatively low-cost production base, skilled labour, government incentives, and relatively developed infrastructure. In addition, we have to highlight the fact that many components manufacturers have followed their customers investing in the V4 countries or, in other words, the presence of large manufacturing companies, such as LG Electronics, Samsung Electronics, Kia, and Hyundai, is also a significant pull factor. And finally, in the case of the electronics industry, we have to mention the anti-dumping measures of the EU which have motivated several Asian companies to invest and produce in the EU.

References

Agenzia ICE. (2013). Malaysia: An Overview of Malaysian Outward Foreign Direct Investment, January 2013. Retrieved from http://www.ice.gov.it/paesi/asia/malaysia/upload/173/Malaysia%20OFDI%20review-Oct12.pdf.

Ariff, M., & Lopez, G. (2007). Outward Foreign Direct Investment: The Malaysian Experience. Paper Presented at the International Workshop on Intra-Asian FDI Flows: Magnitude, Trends, Prospects and Policy Implications, New Delhi, India, 25–26 April, 2007. Retrieved from http://icrier.org/pdf/Mohamed%20Ariff%20and%20Greg%20Lopez.pdf.

ASEAN Secretariat. (2012). *ASEAN Investment Report 2012: The Changing FDI Landscape*. Jakarta: ASEAN Secretariat.

ASEAN Secretariat and UNCTAD. (2016). *ASEAN Investment Report 2016: Foreign Direct Investment and MSME Linkages*. Jakarta: ASEAN Secretariat.

Carney, M., & Dieleman, M. (2011). Indonesia's Missing Multinationals: Business Groups and Outward Direct Investment. *Bulletin of Indonesian Economic Studies, 47*(1), 105–126.

Central Bank of Malaysia. (2017). Annual Report 2016. Retrieved from http://www.bnm.gov.my/files/publication/ar/en/2016/ar2016_book.pdf.

Cheewatrakoolpong, K., & Boonprakaikawe, J. (2015). Factors Influencing Outward FDI: A Case Study of Thailand in Comparison with Singapore and Malaysia. *Southeast Asian Journal of Economics, 3*(2), 123–141.

Chung, Y. I. (2007). *South Korea in the Fast Lane: Economic Development and Capital Formation*. New York: Oxford University Press.

Churchman, K. (2016). Taiwan Pivots Away from China, Towards the South: Tsai and the DPP See More Promise in ASEAN, July 7, 2016. Retrieved from http://nationalinterest.org/feature/taiwan-pivots-away-china-towards-the-south-16879.

Doležalová, E., & Dailida, Y. (2016). *Foreign Direct Investments in the Czech Automotive Industry: A Case Study of Hyundai Motor Company*. Norwegian School of Economics, Bergen. Retrieved from https://brage.bibsys.no/xmlui/handle/11250/2403794.

Dore, C. (2004). Plant Background. Kia Press. Retrieved from https://press.kia.com/content/dam/kiapress/EU/download-files/Corporate/1087657378-slovakia-Plant-Background.doc.

Dudáš, T. (2015). Korean Investments in V4 Countries: Past, Present and Trends for the Future. In M. Grešš & M. Grančay (Eds.), *Mutual Relations Between the Republic of Korea and V4 Countries in Trade and Investment: Conference Proceedings – International Scientific Conference and Workshop* (pp. 120–129). Bratislava: Vydavatelstvo Ekonóm.

EEAS. (2015). European Union – South Korea: Trade and Investment Relations, Edition 2015. Retrieved from http://eeas.europa.eu/archives/delegations/south_korea/documents/news/2016/2014_factfile_final.pdf.

EIAS. (2014). Taiwan's Outward Foreign Direct Investment (OFDI) into the European Union and Its Member States – Quantitative Research, EIAS Report October 2014. Retrieved from http://www.eias.org/wp-content/uploads/2016/03/Taiwan_2014_Quantitative2.pdf.

EIAS. (2015, September). A Survey on 10 Leading Taiwanese Enterprises Investing in the EU and Its Member States. Retrieved from http://www.eias.org/wp-content/uploads/2016/02/A-Survey-on-10-Leading-Taiwanese-Enterprises-Investing-in-the-EU-and-its-Member-States.pdf.

Hill, H., & Jongwanich, J. (2011). Asia Rising: Emerging East Asian Economies as Foreign Investors, Australian National University, Working Papers in Trade and Development, No. 2011/7. Retrieved from https://acde.crawford.anu.edu.au/sites/default/files/publication/acde_crawford_anu_edu_au/2016-12/wp_econ_2011_07_hill_jongwanich.pdf.

van Hoesel, R. (1999). *New Multinational Enterprises from Korea and Taiwan.* New York and London: Routledge.

Hsu, K. (2014). AEC 2015: Taiwan Industry Response. Retrieved from http://www.aseancenter.org.tw/upload/files/20141029_1-2.pdf.

Hsu, C. (2017). New Southbound Policy: 'Southbound' Plan Forging Connectivity in the Region. *Taipei Times*, June 10. Retrieved from http://www.taipeitimes.com/News/taiwan/print/2017/06/10/2003672284.

Hwang, K. S. (2003). *Why Do Korean Firms Invest in the EU? Evidence from FDI in the Peripheral Regions.* EI Working Paper, No. 5. Retrieved from http://www.lse.ac.uk/europeanInstitute/LEQS%20Discussion%20Paper%20Series/EIWP2003-05.pdf.

Kaewsang, C. (2014). Investment Opportunities in AEC, Presentation at Making AEC Working for SMEs, Thailand Development Research Institute, Bangkok, March 28, 2014. Retrieved from http://tdri.or.th/wp-content/uploads/2014/03/TDRI-forum_Chokedee_BOI.pdf.

Kaewsang, C. (2015). Thai Overseas Investment Promotion. Retrieved from http://www.bangkokbank.com/BangkokBankThai/Documents/Site%20Documents/AEC/ThaiOverseasInvestmentPromotion.pdf.

Kaliszuk, E. (2016). Chinese and South Korean Investment in Poland: A Comparative Study. *Transnational Corporations Review, 8*(1), 60–78.

Kim, D. J., & Kim, Y. C. (2006). *Newly Industrializing Economies and International Competitiveness: Market Power and Korean Electronics Multinationals.* Basingstoke and New York: Palgrave Macmillan.

Kim, J. M., & Rhee, D. K. (2009). Trends and Determinants of South Korean Outward Foreign Direct Investments. *Copenhagen Journal of Asian Studies, 27*(1), 126–154.

Kuo, A., & Kao, M. S. (2011). Leading Multinationals from Taiwan Increase Their Foreign Assets Despite the Global Crisis. Retrieved from http://ccsi.columbia.edu/files/2013/11/Taiwan_2011.pdf.

Magasházi, A., Szijártó, N., & Tétényi, A. (2015). Integrated in Global Value Chains by Korea-V4 Participation. In M. Grešš & M. Grančay (Eds.), *Mutual Relations Between the Republic of Korea and V4 Countries in Trade and Investment: Conference Proceedings – International Scientific Conference and Workshop* (pp. 156–177). Bratislava: Vydavatelstvo Ekonóm.

MITI Malaysia. (2017). Malaysia International Trade and Industry Report 2016. Retrieved from http://www.miti.gov.my/miti/resources/MITI%20Report/MITI_REPORT_2016.pdf.

Nicolas, F., Thomsen, S., & Bang, M. (2013). *Lessons from Investment Policy Reform in Korea*. OECD Working Papers on International Investment, No. 2. Retrieved from https://www.oecd.org/daf/inv/investment-policy/WP-2013_2.pdf.

OECD. (2013). *OECD Investment Policy Reviews: Malaysia 2013*. OECD Publishing. https://doi.org/10.1787/9789264194588-en.

Oh, J. H., & Mah, J. S. (2017). The Patterns of Korean Foreign Direct Investments in Vietnam. *Open Journal of Business and Management, 5*(2), 253–271.

Olson, S. (2012). AUO Starts EU Project with Solar Module Factory Located in Czech Republic. Retrieved from https://www.pv-tech.org/news/auo_starts_eu_project_with_solar_module_factory_located_in_czech_republic.

Pavlínek, P. (2015). Foreign Direct Investment and the Development of the Automotive Industry in Central and Eastern Europe. In B. Galgóczi, J. Drahokoupli, & M. Bernaciak (Eds.), *Foreign Investment in Eastern and Southern Europe After 2008. Still a Lever of Growth?* (pp. 209–255). Brussels: European Trade Union Institute.

Radosevic, S. (2004). La industria electrónica en los países de Europa Central y Oriental: Una nueva localización de la producción global. *Información Comercial Española, ICE: Revista de economía, 818*, 151–164.

Sa-Kong, I., & Koh, Y. (Eds.). (2010). *The Korean Economy: Six Decades of Growth and Development*. Seoul: Korea Development Institute.

Sambodo, M. T. (2017). Indonesia's Outward Foreign Direct Investment. In C. Lee & S. Sermcheep (Eds.), *Outward Foreign Direct Investment* (pp. 128–151). Singapore: ASEAN, ISEAS – Yusof Ishak Institute.

SARIO. (2011). Electrical Engineering Industry. Retrieved from http://www.sario.sk/sites/default/files/content/files/electrotechnical_industry.pdf.

Schröter, A. (2010). Foxconn to Buy 90% of Sony's Slovakian LCD Facility. Retrieved from https://evertiq.com/news/16589.

Sermcheep, S. (2017). The Rise of Outward Foreign Direct Investment from ASEAN. In C. Lee & S. Sermcheep (Eds.), *Outward Foreign Direct Investment* (pp. 5–29). Singapore: ASEAN, ISEAS – Yusof Ishak Institute.

Sroithong, A. (2014). BOI's Thai Overseas Investment Promotion. Retrieved from http://www2.thaieurope.net/wp-content/uploads/2014/04/14_BOI.pdf.

Stock Exchange of Thailand. (2016). 2015 Outward Foreign Direct Investment of Thai Listed Firms, Research Paper 1/2016. Retrieved from https://www.set.or.th/dat/vdoArticle/attachFile/AttachFile_1471343804482.pdf.

Tolentino, P. E. (2000). *Multinational Corporations: Emergence and Evolution*. London and New York: Routledge.

Tubilewicz, C. (2007). *Taiwan and Post-communist Europe: Shopping for Allies*. Abingdon and New York: Routledge.

US State Department's Office of Investment Affairs. (2017). Investment Climate Statement. Retrieved from https://www.export.gov/apex/article2?id=Vietnam-1-Openness-to-Restrictions-Upon-Foreign-Investment.

Yean, T. S., Nee, T. Y., & Yi, A. K. J. (2015). Outward Foreign Direct Investment from Malaysia. *Journal of Southeast Asian Economies, 32*(3), 358–374.

PART III

Non-Asian Emerging Multinationals

CHAPTER 6

Russian Multinational Direct Investment in East Central European Countries

Csaba Weiner

6.1 Introduction

6.1.1 The Historical Context of Russian OFDI and Multinationals

Russian multinationals play a very active role in outward foreign direct investment (OFDI). With the exception of 2015, Russia has since 2002 been among the top 20 countries in the world with the largest OFDI stock[1] (UNCTAD FDI database n.d.).

The history of Russian OFDI dates back to the nineteenth century and covers six main periods. According to Liuhto and Majuri (2014: 211) these include the following: (1) OFDI before the socialist era; (2) the stagnation of OFDI after the Russian Revolution of 1917; (3) the gradual growth of the foreign activities of red multinationals in the period from

[1] Similarly, the acronym for inward foreign direct investment is IFDI.

C. Weiner (✉)
Institute of World Economics, Centre for Economic and Regional Studies, Budapest, Hungary
e-mail: weiner.csaba@krtk.mta.hu

Á. Szunomár (ed.), *Emerging-market Multinational Enterprises in East Central Europe*, Studies in Economic Transition,
https://doi.org/10.1007/978-3-030-55165-0_6

the end of the 1960s until the dissolution of the Soviet Union in 1991; (4) the emergence of the first real Russian multinationals in 1992–1996; (5) the golden era of Russian multinationals between 1997 and 2008; and (6) the survival or withdrawal of Russian multinationals during and after the global financial meltdown, the Ukrainian conflict and the most recent 2014–2016 crisis (Kari Liuhto, email communication, 27 January 2020). In contrast, Kuznetsov believes that the golden ages began not in 1997, but only sometime in 2002/2003, and marks the ongoing period as 'adaptation to new reality' (Alexey Kuznetsov, email communication, 12 February 2020).

The actual state of the economy and the changing role of the Russian state have been reflected in Russia's OFDI data. Since the dissolution of the Soviet Union, four crises have shaken the Russian economy: (1) the transformational recession of 1992–1996; (2) the currency, fiscal, debt and banking crisis in 1998; (3) the global financial crisis of 2008–2009; and (4) the crisis of 2014–2016, caused by low oil prices and Western sanctions against Russia over its actions in Ukraine.

Since the early 1990s, the political and economic systems have undergone substantial changes in Russia. The main dividing line was the targeted campaign launched against the Yukos oil company in 2003. State–business relations have changed significantly since that time. Following a largely liberal capitalist system, the state has substantially expanded its role in the economy, and thus an etatist period began (Vasileva 2014). The crises of 2008–2009 and 2014–2016 have not contributed to a further such significant increase in the role of the Russian state. During Boris Yeltsin's presidency (1991–1999), the Russian state actively contributed to the creation of large private monopolies, giving birth to future multinationals (Kalotay 2008: 98).

In the 1990s, Russian OFDI did exist but it could mostly be regarded as capital flight from an unstable environment to offshore paradises and tax havens (Filippov 2008: 6–8). Due to negative domestic push factors, this kind of OFDI, called an 'exodus' by Vahtra and Liuhto (2004), has appeared from time to time relating to the crisis periods. This is also closely associated with the phenomenon of 'round-tripping' (i.e., FDI leaving the country and returning). The opposite of exodus is 'expansion', which is driven by either international pull[2] or positive domestic push factors.

[2] For international pull factors, we do not use either positive or negative attributes, as we believe that they are positive in themselves.

According to the data collected by the Central Bank of Russia (CBR), FDI outflows from Russia received a big boost first in 2003 and then in 2006 (Table 6.1). In 2008, they hit a new record high. In the 2000s, the marked rise in international energy and commodity prices led to spectacular developments in resource-based sectors in Russia, encouraging Russian companies to venture abroad (Filippov 2008: 7). The growth of Russian assets abroad has largely been driven by cross-border mergers and acquisitions (Kuznetsov 2013: 7).

The effects of the global financial crisis began to be felt as of the third quarter of 2008 onwards, followed by a significant decline in 2009. Russian metal giants suffered the consequences of the downturn more than Russian oil and gas companies (Kuznetsov 2010a: 12). However, in 2013, Russian FDI outflows stood at a new record level. This impetus was broken when the Russian crisis began in 2014. Russian multinationals have faced constraints in international financial markets. Sanctions against Russian banks financing Russian multinationals came to represent a big threat to Russian OFDI (UNCTAD 2015: 69). Consequently, the year 2015 saw a drastic reduction in Russian FDI flows—in both directions. Moreover, a new Russian anti-offshore law took effect in January 2015, aiming to prevent the cash drain from Russia to offshore centres, the use of cross-border tax evasion schemes and, thus, to reduce round-tripping investment (UNCTAD 2016: 7, 94). However, as during the 2008–2009 crisis, significant acquisitions still took place in 2014–2016 (UNCTAD 2016: 62; 2017: 68). In 2017 and 2018, higher Russian FDI outflows were again reported, but these changes are dependent on whether the asset/liability principle or the directional principle is applied to measure them.

The list of the top 15 Russian non-financial multinationals ranked by foreign assets in 2017 shows that out of these, only six were state-controlled (UNCTAD 2019: 58–59). Russia's leading multinationals have a concentrated ownership structure, with either government supremacy or oligarchic dominance (Liuhto 2016: 260).

6.1.2 *The Size and Geographical Distribution of Russian OFDI*

For a long time, both the Central Bank of Russia and the Russian Federal State Statistics Service (Rosstat) provided official data on Russian OFDI. However, since 2014, only CBR data have been available. A common feature of these FDI statistics is that they are organised on the basis

Table 6.1 FDI outflows from, and inflows into, Russia, according to the CBR, 1994–2018 (millions of dollars)

	1994	*1995*	*1996*	*1997*	*1998*	*1999*	*2000*	*2001*	*2002*	*2003*	*2004*	*2005*	*2006*	*2007*
Asset/liability principle														
Outflows	281	606	923	3184	1210	2195	**3179**	2541	**3533**	**9724**	13,782	**17,880**	29,993	44,801
Inflows	690	2066	2579	4865	2761	3286	2678	2847	3474	7929	15,403	15,508	37,595	55,874
Directional principle														
Outflows	–	–	–	3184	1210	2195	**3152**	2502	**3484**	**9550**	13,663	**16,747**	29,840	43,849
Inflows	–	–	–	4865	2761	3286	2651	2808	3425	7755	15,284	14,375	37,442	54,922

	2008	*2009*	*2010*	*2011*	*2012*	*2013*	*2014*	*2015*	*2016*	*2017*	*2018*
Asset/liability principle											
Outflows	55,663	**43,281**	**52,616**	**66,851**	48,822	**86,507**	**57,082**	**22,085**	22,314	**36,757**	**31,377**
Inflows	74,783	36,583	43,168	55,084	50,588	69,219	22,031	6853	32,539	28,557	8785
Directional principle											
Outflows	56,735	**34,450**	**41,116**	**48,635**	28,423	**70,685**	**64,203**	**27,090**	26,951	**34,153**	**35,820**
Inflows	75,856	27,752	31,668	36,868	30,188	53,397	29,152	11,858	37,176	25,954	13,228

Source: Own compilation based on CBR (2020a, 2020b)

Note: Bold cells indicate years when FDI outflows exceeded FDI inflows

– Not available

of the immediate host and investing country, and not according to the ultimate host and investing country. This is particularly problematic as certain third countries, largely de jure or de facto tax havens and offshore centres, play a significant role in intermediating Russian FDI. At a later stage, FDI is trans-shipped to the final target country or round-tripped back to Russia (Kalotay et al. 2014: 6).

According to the CBR based on the directional principle, at the end of 2018, Russia's OFDI stock was USD 344 billion (Table 6.2). Yet, because of round-tripping, both inward and outward FDI are overestimated (Kuznetsov 2017: 78–79). Foreign assets of the top 15 Russian non-financial multinationals reached USD 105.1 billion at the end of 2017 (UNCTAD 2019: 59).

The economic crisis of 2014–2016, the depreciating Russian currency, the 2015 Russian anti-offshore law, various amendments to the tax code and the 2018 creation of inner offshore zones have caused changes in round-tripping and trans-shipping, reflected in IFDI and OFDI stock and flow data relating to intermediary countries, particularly those of Cyprus and the British Virgin Islands (Table 6.3) (UNCTAD 2016: 60; 2019: 56).

The bulk of Russia's OFDI stock is in developed countries (UNCTAD 2016: 12). The most important destinations for Russian OFDI are Europe and the United States (UNCTAD 2015: 69). These observations are based on CBR data.

CBR data show most of Russia's OFDI stock is in Cyprus and the Netherlands, two developed EU countries. However, OFDI stock in the British Virgin Islands, a developing Caribbean economy, statistically part of Latin America and the Caribbean (like the Bahamas and the Cayman Islands), has recently substantially decreased. The role of Latin America and the Caribbean is still very much overstated (Kuznetsov 2017: 79).

By definition, Cyprus and the Netherlands are neither tax havens nor offshore jurisdictions, but in reality, many EU countries—including, for example, Luxembourg—should be historically included into these categories. Moreover, the United Kingdom, Ireland, Austria and Switzerland are also leading 'conduit countries' (Bulatov et al. 2016: 400).[3]

Relying on official statistics, UNCTAD (2017: 68) claims Russian firms have targeted emerging markets moderately. According to these statistics, CIS countries have attracted only minor Russian OFDI, mainly

[3] In contrast, based on the directional principle, Russian FDI stock in Luxembourg and Ireland is negative (CBR 2019c).

Table 6.2 OFDI stock from, and IFDI stock in, Russia, according to the UNCTAD and CBR, end of period, 1993–2018 (millions of dollars)

	1993	*1994*	*1995*	*1996*	*1997*	*1998*	*1999*	*2000*	*2001*	*2002*	*2003*	*2004*	*2005*
UNCTAD													
OFDI	**2301**	2588	3346	4390	7633	8866	9553	19,211	43,254	61,248	89,522	105,773	139,241
IFDI	183	3280	5601	8145	13,612	12,912	18,303	29,738	50,544	68,847	94,511	120,201	178,635

	2006	*2007*	*2008*	*2009*	*2010*	*2011*	*2012*	*2013*	*2014*	*2015*	*2016*	*2017*	*2018*
CBR (asset/liability principle)													
OFDI	–	–	–	298,357	361,121	361,750	409,567	479,501	**411,270**	**367,593**	418,034	468,567	433,587
IFDI	–	–	–	377,447	488,993	454,949	514,926	565,654	371,491	347,690	477,670	529,644	498,989
CBR (directional principle)													
OFDI	–	–	–	–	–	–	–	385,321	**329,818**	**282,651**	334,275	380,047	344,318
IFDI	–	–	–	–	–	–	–	471,474	290,039	262,748	393,910	441,123	409,720
UNCTAD[a]													
OFDI	232,881	363,481	197,273	288,289	336,355	315,742	332,834	385,322	**329,817**	**282,651**	334,275	380,047	344,090
IFDI	263,903	488,280	212,887	367,379	464,228	408,942	438,194	471,475	290,039	262,748	393,910	441,123	407,362

Source: Own compilation based on UNCTAD FDI database (n.d.) and CBR (2019a, 2019b, 2019c, 2019d)

Note: Bold cells indicate years when OFDI stock exceeded IFDI stock

– Not available

[a]UNCTAD moved to use directional principle data (Kálmán Kalotay, email communication, 22 January 2020)

Table 6.3 The top 15 host countries for Russian OFDI stock and the top 15 sources of Russia's IFDI stock, according to the CBR, based on the directional principle, end of period, 2013, 2018 (millions of dollars)

OFDI stock from Russia				*IFDI stock in Russia*			
2013		*2018*		*2013*		*2018*	
Cyprus	**152,702**	**Cyprus**	**172,461**	**Cyprus**	**183,276**	**Cyprus**	**126,366**
BVI	74,412	**Netherlands**	**40,415**	**Netherlands**	**48,948**	**Netherlands**	**40,309**
Netherlands	**45,012**	**Austria**	**26,710**	Bahamas	31,964	Bahamas	39,031
Austria	**25,500**	Switzerland	17,760	Bermuda	29,565	Bermuda	29,830
United States	20,943	BVI	11,277	**United Kingdom**	**21,759**	**Luxembourg**	**19,561**
Switzerland	12,096	Bahamas	8806	BVI	18,925	**France**	**17,291**
Germany	**9607**	Turkey	8229	**Germany**	**18,898**	**Germany**	**16,410**
United Kingdom	**7901**	**Germany**	**8125**	United States	17,979	**United Kingdom**	**14,933**
Bahamas	6416	United States	7332	**Sweden**	**16,176**	Switzerland	11,029
Ukraine	5968	**Spain**	**6441**	**France**	**14,075**	BVI	10,356
Turkey	5277	**United Kingdom**	**6378**	**Luxembourg**	**12,780**	Jersey	9945
Spain	**4772**	Belarus	3960	**Austria**	**11,816**	**Ireland**	**5824**
Jersey	4128	Singapore	3471	Switzerland	6040	**Austria**	**5604**
Belarus	4089	Kazakhstan	3302	**Ireland**	**5210**	**Italy**	**4626**
France	**3629**	Ukraine	3104	Jersey	5013	**Sweden**	**4531**

Source: Own compilation based on CBR (2019a, 2019c)

Note: Bold cells indicate the EU states

BVI British Virgin Islands

concentrated in Kazakhstan and Ukraine. But based on extensive company-level data, Kuznetsov (2017: 79) argues that besides the West (including primarily the United States and a number of EU members), neighbouring Ukraine, Kazakhstan and Belarus are also among the leading recipients of Russian multinational capital, and thus their role is underestimated.

Likewise, Russian FDI stock in Asia is underreported (Kuznetsov 2017: 81). Kuznetsov (2017: 80) notes the rise in the significance of Turkey, Thailand, some other Asian countries and the members of the Eurasian Economic Union. Russia has also dipped a toe in African waters (Panibratov 2017: 284), but the value of Russian FDI has remained insignificant on that continent, though much higher than official statistics suggest (Kuznetsov 2017: 80–81).

6.1.2.1 The Role of the EU

According to Kuznetsov (2011: 11), on the eve of the global financial crisis of 2008–2009 and with the development of Russian multinationals, Russian companies have shifted their focus from Europe to other regions. The geographic distribution of foreign assets of the largest Russian multinationals also suggests a constantly decreasing share in Europe (Skolkovo 2007: 12; 2008: 10; IMEMO 2009: 16; 2011: 24; Kuznetsov 2013: 15). Principally, this has long meant the increasing role of North America. Asia and Africa have also received growing attention. The latter fits into the overall logic of Russian internationalisation and is weakly influenced by the foreign political events of the mid-2010s. However, a radical turn toward the East is impossible. The recent increase in the share of some Asian countries has been due to the exit of a number of Russian investors from the United States and Ukraine, as well as a reduction in the weight of the Caribbean offshore world, rather than the devaluation of the role of the EU (Kuznetsov 2017: 79–80). According to Bulatov et al. (2016: 409), due to the Eurasian Economic Union, growth opportunities are greater in Belarus and Kazakhstan than in the United States.

The gradual reduction of non-CIS Europe's role in favour of North America (the increasing role of the United States, however, has been stopped and reversed) and the developing countries has indicated the evolution of Russian multinationals from regional and bi-regional to real global ones (Kuznetsov 2011: 13). Russian multinationals typically begin their international expansion in other CIS countries (Panibratov 2017: 284). However, UNCTAD (2017: 68) warns that projects in emerging economies do not allow Russian multinationals the same access to cutting-edge technologies as in traditional advanced countries.

Eurostat and the CBR display very different data on the size of Russian FDI in the EU. Both CBR and Eurostat statistics are consistent with the methodology set out in the 6th edition of the IMF's Balance of Payments and International Investment Position Manual (BPM6). Differences in data are in large part a result of the activities of special-purpose entities (SPEs). For end-2017, Eurostat reported Russian FDI stock in the EU28 of EUR 83.4 billion. By comparison,[4] a simple accumulation of country data from the CBR suggests the size of Russian FDI in the EU28 amounted to USD 260.7 billion at the end of 2017 (and USD 256.6 billion at the end of 2018) (Table 6.4). At the end of 2017, Russia's share in the EU28's total IFDI stock by extra-EU28 investing countries was only 1.3 per cent (Eurostat 2019). In contrast, according to the CBR, the EU28's share in Russia's OFDI stock accounted for 68.6 per cent at the end of 2017 (and 74.5 per cent at the end of 2018) (CBR 2019c). The EU's significance for Russia is incontestable, even if we exclude some of the trans-shipment transactions and all the cases of round-tripping.

Stock data from Eurostat (2019) show that at the end of 2017, the largest recipients of Russian FDI in the EU were Cyprus, the Netherlands, Spain and Germany. However, statistics also indicate that Russian FDI stock in the Netherlands is related to the activities of SPEs and the situation should be similar for Cyprus for which SPE data are not available. According to data from the CBR (2019c), Russian FDI stock in the EU at the end of 2018 was by far the largest in Cyprus, followed by the Netherlands, Austria, Germany, Spain and the United Kingdom.

Using a different methodology, IMEMO's FDI project database, incorporating projects for which FDI stock exceeds USD 3 million, perhaps gives a much more accurate picture than official data. Accordingly, at the end of 2016, the main destinations in non-CIS Eurasia were Italy, Germany, Great Britain, Turkey, Switzerland, Iraq and Bulgaria. This database shows minor Russian FDI stock in Cyprus. Likewise, real Russian FDI presence is much smaller in Luxembourg, Spain, Ireland, Latvia and the Netherlands than officially registered (EABR 2017: 24).

[4] End-2018 data are not available from Eurostat.

Table 6.4 Comparing Russian FDI stock in the EU countries using different methodologies, end of period (millions of dollars and millions of euros)

	Eurostat (millions of euros)		*CBR (directional principle) (millions of dollars)*			*IMEMO (millions of dollars)*
	2016	*2017*	*2016*	*2017*	*2018*	*2016*
Total			334,275	380,047	344,318	
EU28	72,809	83,381	220,892	260,668	256,638	–
EU15 plus Cyprus and Malta						
Austria	–[c]	–[c]	21,690	30,944	26,710	1590[a]
Belgium	112	-141	437	527	679	1470[a]
Cyprus	33,656	33,620	141,508	175,217	172,461	50[a]
Denmark	102	49	1028	1205	1214	–
Finland	986	1111	2923	3035	2829	1580[a]
France	1635	1980	2806	3006	2979	1680[a]
Germany	3832	2318	7560	8411	8125	11,690[a]
Greece	26	31	683	733	668	–
Ireland	2298	2003	-17,955	-19,849	-12,510	560[a]
Italy	145	560	2476	2816	2775	16,160[a]
Luxembourg	-38,774	-27,568	-20,048	-19,104	-12,113	10[a]
Malta	44	50	96	126	122	–
Netherlands	36,619	29,188	53,808	48,493	40,415	1060[a]
Portugal	146	171	223	228	231	–
Spain	6968	7499	6321	6382	6441	220[a]
Sweden	179	58	167	183	173	–
United Kingdom	1172	1014	8687	9091	6378	7900[a]
EU-member CEE countries (EU11)						
Bulgaria	2042	2035	3244	3330	3103	4020[a]
Croatia	302	331	388	531	529	–
Estonia	751	747	348	328	369	–
Latvia	1334	1538	1361	1546	1599	880[a]
Lithuania	274	261	303	315	323	–
Romania	139	68	30	29	31	1570[a]
of which ECE countries						
Czechia	613	715	1790	1791	1824	932
Hungary	-62	42	253	259	279	165
Poland	306	370	452	666	538	1144
Slovakia	-214	-173	129	161	160	89
Slovenia	70	176	184	270	309	140
Non-EU-member CEE countries						
Albania	–[c]	–[c]	5	5	6	–

(*continued*)

Table 6.4 (continued)

	Eurostat (millions of euros)		*CBR (directional principle) (millions of dollars)*			*IMEMO (millions of dollars)*
	2016	*2017*	*2016*	*2017*	*2018*	*2016*
Bosnia and Herz.	–	–	615	665	670	–
Kosovo	0[a]	0[a]	–	–	–	–
Montenegro	–(c)	–(c)	1335	1366	1396	–
North Macedonia	39	27	5	9	12	–
Serbia	1355	–	1369	1567	1547	2550[a]

Source: Own compilations based on Eurostat (2019), CBR (2019c), EABR (2017: 24) and IMEMO's database

– Not available

–(c) Confidential

[a]It is rounded by the author

6.1.3 *Industrial Distribution of Russian OFDI*

The CBR does not provide data on the sectoral distribution of Russian OFDI, while Rosstat reports only flow data containing information up until 2013. In the period between 2005 and 2013, these data suggest that manufacturing as well as wholesale, retail and repair sectors tended to attract the most Russian OFDI, leaving only minor shares for the financial sectors (Rosstat 2009, 2014). Following a different classification, one can see that among the top 20 or 25 Russian multinationals, oil and gas as well as metallurgy are predominant. In the service sector, infrastructural companies occupy a dominant position (Bulatov et al. 2016: 405). Between 2004 and 2008, the role of oil and gas declined, but increased again in 2009 and 2011 (Skolkovo 2007: 10; 2008: 8; IMEMO 2009: 15; 2011: 22; Kuznetsov 2013: 19). Out of the 15 leading non-financial Russian multinationals ranked by foreign assets in 2017, four were in metallurgy, four in oil and gas, two in transportation and one in chemicals and one in nuclear energy. Three leading Russian multinationals are conglomerates (UNCTAD 2019: 59). In contrast, the industrial distribution is much more diverse in the second echelon of Russian multinationals (Bulatov et al. 2016: 405). In Europe, Asia and Africa, the sectoral distribution of Russian OFDI is quite diversified, while in North America, Russian FDI has mainly been delivered by metallurgical multinationals (Kuznetsov 2010b: 28; 2017: 82). According to IMEMO's FDI project database, in non-CIS Eurasia, at the end of 2016, most Russian OFDI stock was directed at oil and gas (34.3 per cent), communication and IT (19.7 per cent) and finance (12.9 per cent). Ferrous metals have witnessed the most noticeable decline in their share of the Russian OFDI stock (EABR 2017: 22).

According to Eurostat (2019), the service sector accounted for 80.7 per cent of Russian FDI stock in the EU at the end of 2016. The electricity, gas, steam and air conditioning supply sector (4.0 per cent) and private real-estate activities (3.3 per cent) are still also worth mentioning. Foremost among service sectors are financial and insurance activities (47.9 per cent), though professional, scientific and technical activities (22.4 per cent) play a notable role as well. However, in our view, this gives a distorted picture due to SPEs and transactions via third countries.

6.2 Push and Pull Factors Driving Russian OFDI

Domestic push and international pull factors are equally important when examining the motives behind Russian OFDI. As already discussed, an exodus is caused by negative domestic push factors, while expansion might be related to either international pull or positive domestic push factors. Thus, while exodus refers to a negative phenomenon, the effect of the home country is not necessarily negative.

6.2.1 Push Factors

Russian multinationals challenge some of the premises of traditional FDI theorems (Kalotay et al. 2014), but Dunning's eclectic paradigm or Ownership–Location–Internalisation (OLI) of international production can fit them. The question is whether the role of the Russian state and the Russian economic-policy environment in prompting OFDI can be assimilated under transaction-based ownership-specific advantages (Ot), or a home-country factor (H) has to be added to the OLI legs to OLIH. Kalotay and Sulstarova (2010: 137–138), following Kalotay (2008: 102–103), recommend the latter. Similarly, Anwar and Mughal (2014: 15) argue that Russian OFDI follows the eclectic paradigm to a certain extent, but home-country factors also play a significant role. Kalotay (2010b: 40) divides home-country advantages into the following four groups: home-country-based competitive advantages (Hc), business-environment advantages (Hb), development-strategy advantages (Hd) and state-involvement advantages (Hs).

Home-country-based competitive advantages refers to monopolistic or oligopolistic advantages (a positive domestic push factor accompanied by expansion), arising from dominant positions in the home market. These advantages have often been supported by home-country policies, promoting the formation of national champions (Kalotay 2010b: 40, 42, 45). Notwithstanding, high monopolisation or oligopolisation of the Russian economy frequently drives medium-sized local companies not affiliated with regional or federal authorities to go abroad (a negative domestic push factor accompanied by exodus) (Bulatov 2017: 84–85).

The home-country business environment can be either an advantage or a disadvantage for the company. As a positive effect (an advantage, i.e., a positive domestic push factor), one can refer to an expansion, while in a bad business environment (a disadvantage, i.e., a negative domestic push factor) an exodus is experienced. However, due to a bad Russian business environment, Russian firms possess such firm-specific ownership advantages which can be used abroad (Kalotay 2015: 245).

Home-country development-strategy advantages are linked to the methods and strategies that were applied during the transformation. In Russia, these were based on the building up of national champions, a sustained resistance to IFDI, especially in strategic industries, and an increasing emphasis on promoting OFDI (Kalotay 2010b: 46). The development strategy can also be either a positive or a negative domestic push factor. It is negative if the development strategy is misleading or unsuccessful (Kálmán Kalotay, email communication, 9 July 2015).

State-involvement advantages are related to government policies towards OFDI and state ownership in outward investing firms. Regarding the former, the shift from reservation through acceptance towards some kind of promotion came later in Russia. As to the latter, a tendency towards more state ownership and intervention can clearly be observed (Kalotay 2010b: 47–48). Concerning the state involvement, it is difficult to imagine a negative domestic push factor. Disadvantages that may be experienced while expanding abroad should not be confused with this.

6.2.1.1 The Russian State's Role in Promoting Foreign Expansion

Since the beginning of the 2000s, Russian state leaders have increasingly started to look at OFDI more favourably (Skolkovo 2009: 6). The first real sign of this change was President Vladimir Putin's speech at the 11th St. Petersburg International Economic Forum in June 2007, where he said they were interested in increasing Russian investment abroad and swapping assets with international partners on mutually beneficial terms (Deloitte 2008: 36). The first time Dmitry Medvedev (then first deputy prime minister) spoke about this issue was the speech in Krasnodar in January 2008. He urged Russian companies to copy the Chinese way, claiming that this would reduce dependence on foreign technology, boost production culture, grant the opportunity to diversify investments and win new markets (Belton 2008). However, in October 2009, Medvedev adopted a somewhat different tone, expressing concern over outward foreign investment at a time when the domestic economy was in trouble. Medvedev's concerns were probably fuelled by fear of the political and social consequences of domestic closures and redundancies. In contrast, when Medvedev (as prime minister) offered financial help to Russian steel producers in December 2013, there was no sign of negative governmental attitudes towards foreign assets. The negative attitude regarding OFDI has reportedly been maintained by Putin, including blocking some foreign projects. Nevertheless, launched in 2012, Putin's deoffshorisation campaign is not directed to OFDI but is targeting the ownership of Russian assets or assets with a Russian beneficial owner in foreign jurisdictions (Fortescue and Hanson 2015: 296–296).

Nevertheless, unlike China, there is no specific going-global strategy in Russia (Nestmann and Orlova 2008: 2). Contrary to the Chinese case, Russian outward expansion is mainly driven by private companies (Skolkovo 2009: 6). State support for Russian multinationals is quite weak due to the lack of developed policy instruments. An example for such state support is, nonetheless, the Russian Agency for Export Credit and Investment Insurance (EXIAR), Russia's first-ever such agency, assisting multinationals with export credits and OFDI, which was founded only in late 2011 (Panibratov 2017: 44). In 2013, EXIAR launched a program to insure Russian outward investment against non-commercial risks (Kuznetsov 2014: 130). Here, one can also mention that Russian embassies regularly provide crucial information for Russian companies to establish initial contacts with foreign companies (Panibratov 2017: 43). Additionally, in a broader sense, the Russia-initiated Eurasian Economic

Union is a rare example of government measures that promotes comprehensive support for Russian OFDI. Outside the CIS, the Russian government supports and protects only a few dozen Russian multinationals. Real incentives are still lacking for Russian medium-sized multinationals to engage in OFDI (Kuznetsov 2013: 9–10).

Government involvement can be either an advantage or a disadvantage, but it is an important determinant of the success of internationalisation (Panibratov 2013: 5). State-owned companies enjoy many advantages that can help their internationalisation. Such benefits include financial capabilities, access to loans and administrative support (Panibratov and Kalotay 2009: 3). Good diplomatic relations can be used when expanding abroad. A strong but 'grey' tool is international lobbyism for a company (Panibratov and Michailova 2019). Finally, state ownership can offer a kind of guarantee when participating in a risky project and during a crisis. On the other hand, government involvement in itself can be a disadvantage when expanding into other states, and, in particular, it may have a negative impact during international political conflicts (Kalotay 2010a: 125).

The influence of the Russian state on fully or partially private companies is also often significant (Panibratov 2013: 9; Kalotay 2015: 254). This was evident in the case of bailouts during the 2008–2009 crisis and is also apparent in the acquisition of assets that gives the Russian government an important strategic advantage (Kalotay 2015: 255).

Nonetheless, the role of the state in the expansion of Russian companies is, on the one hand, overestimated (in the case of natural-resource-based sectors) and, at the same time, underrated (in the case of the relatively small companies in less resource-oriented sectors) (Panibratov 2013). According to Panibratov (2013: 14), the state's interest focuses on the expansion of two types of Russian multinationals: those where the business itself requires strict control (such as in the case of nuclear energy) and where foreign policy necessitates it (such as in defence). These are state-owned companies. A special case is apparent when a private Russian multinational is oriented by the Russian government that favours certain countries, especially the CIS, partly because of enduring political ties and informal networks (Liuhto 2015; Panibratov 2017: 43; Panibratov and Michailova 2019). Meanwhile, Kuznetsov (2013: 5) argues that although some natural-resource-based private companies are politically linked to the Kremlin by personal contacts, their foreign activity is rarely affected by Russian economic diplomacy. Similarly, regarding the largest Russian steel producers, Fortescue and Hanson (2015: 296) do not see any indication of intentions to serve Russia's foreign policy. Likewise, Tepavcevic (2013: 206–207) finds that business interests prevail over Russian national interests in most instances of Russian OFDI. Russian companies do not follow the official Russian foreign policy reflecting broader national interests.

6.2.2 *Pull Factors*

In general, the (pull) motives behind Russian OFDI are typically resource-seeking and market-seeking. One can also observe strategic-asset-seeking FDI, and this motive is especially present among Russian machinery companies outside the top 20 Russian multinationals (Kuznetsov 2013: 3). According to Kuznetsov (2013: 4), efficiency-seeking FDI is more typical for medium-sized Russian multinationals. Finally, image-building and aspirations to achieve better global recognition are also decisive in Russian expansion (Panibratov and Kalotay 2009: 3).

In the EU, the most important motives of Russian multinationals consist of sales promotion, access to, and retention of, markets. Most Russian multinationals are major exporters, while the EU is Russia's main trading partner. Compared to the domestic market and developing countries, Russian OFDI investors note the poor prospects in Western Europe and Central and Eastern Europe (CEE)[5] for access to raw materials and increasing efficiency by lower labour costs (Kuznetsov 2011: 10). According to Kuznetsov (2011: 10), the role of strategic-asset-seeking FDI (access to new technologies or the development of cross-border production chains) is small, though it would be important for the modernisation of the domestic economy. Russian energy multinationals have headed towards the vertical integration of supply chains (oil companies by purchasing foreign refineries and filling stations, while the state-controlled gas giant Gazprom by investing in infrastructure). However, this direction has recently been challenged. In the oil sector, Lukoil, Russia's biggest non-state oil producer, has sold a part of its European downstream assets and Rosneft, Russia's state oil champion, has also downsized its European investment programmes. In the gas sector, the creation of the single gas and electricity markets in the EU (including the EU's Third Energy Package) and ambitious climate governance constitute an abrupt

[5] We argue that CEE consists of 17 countries listed in Table 6.4. As in the other chapters of this volume, East Central Europe (ECE) refers to five CEE countries, including Czechia, Hungary, Poland, Slovakia and Slovenia.

transformation of a long-standing model of cooperation between Russia and the West (Deák 2017).

Many Russian metallurgical multinationals tend to have research and development centres in Europe, but their research and development spending has been very small, and technology transfer has been more frequent in North American plants (Kuznetsov 2011: 10–11). Russian steel exporters are subject to import regulation and market protection on the EU market. With Russia's accession to the WTO in 2011, EU quotas for Russian steel products ceased to exist, though Russia had not fully utilised the quotas even before that. Nevertheless, anti-dumping procedures continue to be a problem for Russia in the EU.

Kuznetsov (2011: 11) claims that it was common for Russian multinationals to strengthen their position in the EU before listing their shares or depositary receipts on European stock exchanges. More concretely, Russian companies bought subsidiaries in the EU in 2006–2007 to make their initial public offering (IPO) abroad comfortably (Alexey Kuznetsov, email communication, 4 December 2015). The motive of attracting much cheaper sources of financing as compared to domestic funds was typical for the period prior to the 2008–2009 crisis, owing to the underdeveloped domestic stock market. In contrast, today, the EU's sanctions against Russia over its actions in Ukraine limit access to EU primary and secondary capital markets for certain Russian banks and companies. Finally, for many Russian multinationals, the EU is still attractive because of its political stability, treated as a means to secure themselves against the possible nationalisation of assets in Russia (Kuznetsov 2011: 11).

6.3 Patterns and Trends of Russian FDI and Multinationals in ECE Countries

CBR statistics show that at the end of 2018 Bulgaria was the largest host country of Russian FDI stock within CEE at USD 3.1 billion, followed by Czechia (USD 1.8 billion), Latvia (USD 1.6 billion), Serbia (USD 1.5 billion) and Montenegro (USD 1.4 billion). The CEE region accounted for 3.7 per cent of the Russian OFDI stock, while ECE countries accumulated only 0.9 per cent (CBR 2019c). Thus, Russian official statistics indicate they played a minor role. Only Czechia held a relatively larger Russian FDI stock as of end-2018. Poland, Slovakia, Hungary and Slovenia combined have attracted less Russian FDI than Czechia alone. However, as compared to CBR data, IMEMO calculates much lower Russian FDI in Czechia but much higher in Poland (Table 6.4) (EABR 2017: 24). At the end of both 2009 and 2010, Hungary took a leading position in CEE in terms of attracting Russian FDI. This proved to be temporary and was only due to one item, that is, the acquisition of shares in the Hungarian oil and gas company Mol by Russia's Surgutneftegaz, Russia's third-largest oil producer. Due to local resistance to the 2009 takeover, Surgutneftegaz sold the stake to the Hungarian government in 2011.

6.3.1 Poland

Russia is a surprisingly small investor in Poland, despite the common economic heritage and geographic proximity of the two countries and also despite the fact that Poland was the second main destination of Russian OFDI behind the United States in 1995–1999 (Kalotay 2003: 11–13).

Russian oil and gas as well as metal multinationals have been represented in Poland through the FDI activities of Gazprom, Lukoil and Severstal. However, Lukoil divested its downstream assets in 2016.

Gazprom's main interest in Poland is its ownership in EuRoPol GAZ joint venture, the owner of the Polish section of the Yamal-Europe gas pipeline, running from Russia to Germany across Belarus and Poland. EuRoPol GAZ was formed in 1993 to design, construct and operate the Polish pipeline section. Yamal-Europe was commissioned in 1999, following which Poland became an important gas transit country.

In addition to the midstream business, Gazprom has a new market in Poland, since it is attempting to promote the use of natural gas—both compressed and liquefied natural gas (CNG and LNG)—as a fuel for vehicles in Europe. Gazprom's expansion has been achieved in different ways, such as through the development of its own filling stations, through supplying other filling stations and through specific joint projects; the latter are related to LNG-powered buses in Olsztyn and Warsaw.

Lukoil opened its first petrol station in Poland in 1996 and owned 116 Polish units when it sold its fuel retail businesses in Lithuania, Latvia and Poland in 2016 (petrolnet.pl 2016). By that time, Lukoil had already withdrawn from the Czech, Hungarian and Slovakian markets.

Severstallat, the Latvian subsidiary of Russia's largest steel company Severstal, controlled by billionaire Alexey Mordashov, established the pipe producer and steel distributor Severstallat Silesia in Poland in 2008 (called Severstal Distribution since 2014), when Severstallat acquired the assets of the Polish Technologie Buczek, including four pipe mills, two longitudinal cutting lines, a 50.72 per cent stake in Buczek Automotive (a producer of stock for car exhaust silencers) and a 100 per cent stake in Przedsiębiorstwo Usług Transportowych Samkol (a transportation company). These companies employed a total of 260 people at that time (Severstal 2008). Severstallat argued that Poland was an important market with high growth rates, and also that it was a net importer in the flat products segment because domestic production did not meet demand. Severstallat planned for the service centre in the Polish city of Sosnowiec to serve customers within a radius of around 300 kilometres, including in Czechia and Slovakia (Puls Biznesu 2008).

Besides resource-based companies, software and information technology constitute another important part of Russian FDI in Poland, including the activities of Luxoft and Kaspersky Lab. Luxoft is a leading global provider of software development services and IT solutions, controlled by Anatoly Karachinsky's IBS Group. Luxoft has experienced dynamic expansion in Poland. It has offices in Krakow (2010), Wrocław (2013, 2015), Gdańsk (2015) and Warsaw (2016). Krakow holds the highest position in terms of employment in the business services industry in Poland (wnp.pl 2014). Wrocław was chosen because of its great location, reasonable costs, the quality of living, easy access to highly qualified IT staff and (local) government support (Gazeta Wrocławska 2015; Luxoft n.d.). Very similar factors attracted Luxoft to Krakow and Gdańsk. Warsaw was selected so as to keep track of legislative decision-making and vital business processes. Luxoft emphasised that Warsaw also had a vast talent pool of seasoned programmers and numerous cultural and geographic benefits (Luxoft 2016). Thus, in addition to market-seeking, efficiency-seeking motives are also vital in Poland (Kalotay et al. 2014: 17). Furthermore, political stability and strong rule of law, strengthened by EU membership, were also important factors (Gera 2013). In 2016, Luxoft had over 2000 employees in Poland (Gazeta Wyborcza 2016).

Kaspersky Lab is a well-known cybersecurity and anti-virus software provider, owned by ex-Soviet intelligence officer Eugene Kaspersky. Through Kaspersky Lab Polska, Kaspersky Lab has been active in Poland since 2001. It has two offices—in Warsaw and Częstochowa, employing a total of more than 50 specialists (Kaspersky n.d.).

Russia's Ekoton represents the engineering sector. It has been operating in Poland since 1998 and serving clients throughout the country and abroad. Ekoton focuses on assisting in applications for integrated pollution prevention and control (IPPC) permits, as well as preparing environmental impact assessments (EIA), ecological/environmental audits, Natura 2000 reports, environmental programs, asbestos removal plans and regional development strategies, including tourism development strategies (Prusińska 2010; Ekoton n.d.-b). Ekoton currently has plants in Russia, Ukraine and Poland, producing equipment for wastewater treatment (Ekoton n.d.-a).

Finally, it is important to mention the 2013 acquisition of the vodka producer and spirits distributor Central European Distribution Corporation (CEDC) of Poland by the Russian Standard Corporation. Russian Standard claimed that they had greater potential as one large company, with complementary brands, segments, import portfolios and export markets (Roust 2013).

In addition to these, Poland has also been the target of a couple of unsuccessful takeover attempts made by Russian firms.

6.3.2 *Czechia*

It is estimated that there are some 20,000 firms operating in Czechia that have a Russian owner, but the overwhelming majority of them are rather insignificant.[6] Although Russia's share in the IFDI stock of Czechia is small, there are several important companies that are in Russian hands.

Regarding the oil and gas sector, Gazprom is involved in different segments of the Czech gas sector. Through its Czech subsidiary Vemex, it supplies final gas and electricity customers, owns public CNG stations, supplies CNG stations controlled by independents and co-owns an underground gas storage facility in Damborice. The latter was put into operation in 2016 and was to be used both to meet demand fluctuations and to support the functions of the trans-Baltic Sea Nord Stream, as well as Germany's Jagal and Opal gas pipelines (Gazprom Germania 2015). Vemex minority shareholder MND, owned by Czech tycoon Karel Komarek's KKCG investment group, is Gazprom's partner in the joint venture Moravia Gas Storage. Gazprom was also engaged in the Czech gas wholesaler Gas-Invest, which was liquidated and then terminated in 2011.

[6] Such information is available in an unpublished Czech country study by the Prague Security Studies Institute, prepared for the project "Raising awareness of Russian soft power in Central Europe" (2016–2017), supported by the US National Endowment for Democracy (http://www.pssi.cz/russia-s-influence-activities-in-cee/kremlinleverage).

In contrast, Lukoil has not been successful in Czechia. Lukoil has already left the Czech retail fuel market twice. In 2003, it sold its three petrol stations. Between 2006 and 2014, Lukoil again owned petrol stations in Czechia, after it had acquired a network of 44 petrol stations at the end of 2006 (E15.cz 2014). Lukoil was also a jet fuel supplier through the company Lukoil Aviation Czech, founded in 2007 and ultimately terminated in 2016.

Russia holds a strong position in the Czech steel sector. Controlled by Roman Abramovich, Alexander Abramov and Alexander Frolov, Evraz, a major metallurgical and mining company, bought the Czech Vítkovice Steel, a manufacturer of rolled steel products, during the privatisation process conducted in 2005 through its Cyprus-registered subsidiary Mastercraft. Vítkovice Steel took on the new name Evraz Vítkovice Steel (EVS). The aim of entering the 'closed' European market was said to be the motivation behind this acquisition. Evraz sought to increase its market share, secure its client base and acquire additional margins from the sale of higher value-added steel products (Evraz 2005; Krainová 2005). Subsequently, the company grew for a few years, but was severely affected by the 2008–2009 crisis. In 2014, a private investor group, including five Cyprus front companies, bought EVS (Helmer 2014). In 2007, EVS acquired the Czech company Nikom, which converts vanadium oxide produced by Russia's Evraz Vanady Tula into ferrovanadium, used by the steel industry worldwide. Renamed to Evraz Nikom in mid 2012, the company has been in the hands of the Luxembourg Evraz Group since the end of 2012.

In 2004, the year of Czechia's accession to the EU, OMZ, whose principal shareholder is Gazprombank,[7] acquired three Skoda Holding subsidiaries: Skoda Jaderne Strojirenstvi (Skoda JS), a supplier of technologies for the nuclear power industry; Skoda Hute, a company with a focus on the production of steel and pig-iron forgings; and Skoda Kovarny, a dominant world leader in the manufacture of four-stroke diesel motor cranks and wind power station shafts (New Europe 2004). The related technology and easier access to East European markets were reportedly the reasons behind the Russian industrial group entering the Czech market (Power Machines 2004). In comparison to the highly profitable Skoda JS, Skoda Hute and Skoda Kovarny were subsidiaries that did not bring in much profit and instead incurred debt. In 2007, the latter two were

[7] Gazprom has not had control over Gazprombank for many years.

merged and renamed Pilsen Steel, which was finally bought in 2010 by the Luxembourg-registered United Group, established in 2008, with an operating office in Moscow and belonging to Russian investor Igor Shamis. At the time, the share of Russian orders of Pilsen Steel was less than 15–20 per cent, which the new owner wanted to increase (Pilsen Steel 2010). Skoda JS has a branch in Slovakia (see Sect. 6.3.4), and holds ownership stakes in the Czech ÚJV Řež (concentrating primarily on design and engineering, supporting the safe and efficient operation of nuclear and classical power plants, fuel-cycle chemistry, as well as on providing complex services for radioactive waste management) and the Russian MKHO Interatomenergo (providing services for the design, installation and maintenance of integrated security systems). In 2007, OMZ acquired the Brno-based Cheteng Engineering (formerly Chepos), active in engineering services in crude oil and gas refining. However, Cheteng ended in liquidation.

In addition, Russian FDI investors have been engaged in a couple of other important FDI projects in the Czech machinery sector. The first foreign assets of ChTPZ Group (Chelyabinsk Tube-Rolling Plant) or ChelPipe, controlled by Andrei Komarov, was MSA, a manufacturer of pipeline valves in Czechia, which ChelPipe's asset manager, the Luxembourg-based Arkley Capital, acquired in 2006 (New Europe 2006). MSA was important for ChelPipe as MSA's products meet the needs of Russian companies operating trunk pipelines (MetalTorg.ru 2006).

Urals Mining and Metals Company (UMMC, also known as UGMK according to its Russian acronym) acquired a 51 per cent stake in the Czech aircraft manufacturer Aircraft Industries, formerly LET Kunovice, in 2008, which it increased to 100 per cent in 2013. Established in 1999, UGMK is a top Russian producer of copper, zinc, coal, gold and silver. Its principal owner is Iskander Makhmudov. Aircraft of the L 410 series are Aircraft Industries' main products. It also deals with the service and maintenance of L 410 aircraft, selling spare parts, aircraft modification and modernisation. Aircraft Industries possesses unique know-how, a well-developed technological background and a highly qualified staff (OS KOVO 2016). With the acquisition, UGMK sought to diversify and branch out into new businesses, including regional air services and short-range aircraft (Finance.cz 2008). The company employs around a thousand people. Aircraft Industries also operates Kunovice's private international airport and an aviation high school (Aircraft Industries n.d.).

There is one other Russian-involved company in Czechia related to the nuclear sector. In 2011, TVEL, belonging to the Russian Rosatom Group, and the Czech engineering company Alta Invest formed a joint venture, Alvel, majority owned by Alta, with the aim of localising fuel services for Czech and European nuclear power plants and promoting TVEL fuel types designed for Western reactors (Nuclear Engineering International 2011). Rosatom's representative office responsible for the Central European region is based in Czechia (called Rosatom Central Europe), with a branch located in Hungary.

The next important Russian-owned company deals with software solutions and electronic production. Sistema's company in Czechia, NVision Czech Republic, formerly called Strom telecom, is the main research and development centre of Russia's NVision Group OSS/BSS (operations support systems, OSS; business support systems, BSS) division. Controlled by Vladimir Yevtushenkov, the Russian Sistema conglomerate is mainly interested in information technology, telecommunications and microelectronics in the EU. NVision Czech Republic is both a supplier of end-to-end systems and services to telecom operators and a manufacturer of computing and telecommunication equipment. The Czech company has for years been a prime asset of the NVision Group, while previously—of the Sitronics Group. Sitronics was established in 2002 as Kontsern Nauchnyy Tsentr (in English—Concern Scientific Centre), consisting of the Russian microelectronics producer NIIME & Micron and Strom telecom (TASS 2011).

In the light industry, the Russian workwear manufacturer Vostok-Service has pursued successful international expansion through the Czech company Cerva Export Import, bought by Vostok-Service in 2006. Cerva was the first foreign asset of Vostok-Service, owned by former Russian parliamentarian Vladimir Golovnev. Vostok-Service chose Cerva because it was growing quite fast and Vostok-Service considered it to have potential for further development, as Cerva had been oriented toward a market interested in cheap products, with its main product being gloves. Vostok-Service believed that Cerva could tap into the market of better-quality products and expand its range of products (Pražský Telegraf 2013). Indeed, Cerva turned into an international holding company (Dmitriyeva 2017). It has bought several production assets abroad and either established 100 per cent subsidiaries and joint ventures or made acquisitions in sales, marketing and distribution abroad.

Two Russian banks—the First Czech–Russian Bank (FCRB) and Sberbank—have owned subsidiaries in Czechia. The Czech central bank granted an operating license to the FCRB subsidiary, ERB, in 2008. FCRB was founded in 1996 with majority shares by the now-defunct Czech Investment and Post Bank (IPB Bank) and was later controlled by Russian businessman Roman Popov. In 2009, ERB opened its headquarters in Prague. ERB aimed to break into the European trade-finance market. They considered themselves to have a good understanding of Russian risks, the Russian way of doing business and the mentality of Russian clients. Also, they did not see much Russian competition in Czechia (Global Trade Review 2009). However, Western sanctions and Russian counter-sanctions have seriously hit ERB Bank. The CBR revoked FCRB's licence in July 2016, and ERB Bank also lost its license in October 2016 (bne IntelliNews 2016). At that time, 22 per cent of the total 5400 clients were foreigners from 48 different countries, but mostly from Russia (EFDI 2017). ERB Bank was one of the smallest players on the Czech market. It only had branches in Prague and Karlovy Vary in Czechia (Blesk.cz 2016).

In 2012, Sberbank, Russia's largest lender controlled by the CBR, became the owner of Volksbank International AG (excluding the Romanian subsidiary). It bought operations in Slovakia, Czechia, Hungary, Slovenia, Croatia, Serbia, Bosnia and Herzegovina and also Ukraine. In Czechia, Sberbank has 28 branches with around 840 employees (Sberbank Europe n.d.). Although Russian clients were said to be important for Sberbank, it has made it clear since the beginning that they are not its sole focus in Czechia (Hovorka 2013).

Finally, Russians have established a palpable presence in the Czech real-estate industry. First of all, they have very significant capital investment in hotels and other real estate in the famous Karlovy Vary spa resort.

6.3.3 Hungary

Statistics on Russian FDI in Hungary show only a few major transactions, including the unsuccessful takeover attempt of Mol by Surgutneftegaz, and a few changes connected to the Rakhimkulov family, namely Megdet Rakhimkulov and his two sons.

For almost 20 years after 1989, Russian corporate presence in Hungary was facilitated through the activities of Megdet Rakhimkulov. He established his fortune in the first half of the 1990s as a senior manager at Gazprom and as its Hungarian representative. In those years, Budapest was by far Gazprom's biggest export destination in the CEE region and the company's management attempted to maintain some of its revenues in Hungary. Not surprisingly, Gazprombank (at the time Gazprom's subsidiary) purchased a Hungarian bank, General Banking and Trust (ÁÉB), as early as in 1996, which was later gradually taken over by the Rakhimkulov family's companies. Rakhimkulov was involved in facilitating the purchase of stakes in two Hungarian (petro)chemical plants: TVK (now Mol Petrochemicals) and BorsodChem.[8] Rakhimkulov was also associated with Surgutneftegaz's 2009 attempt at a hostile takeover of Mol. His influence reached its zenith in the mid-2000s. Over the next years, he gradually retired and formally moved back to Moscow. His two sons took over much of the family's business activities in Hungary and Cyprus. In the 2000s, the Rakhimkulov family rationalised its portfolio. All the chemical and machine-industry plants and even ÁÉB were sold in the mid-2000s. Today, the Rakhimkulov family primarily seems to play the role of financial investors. For a long time, Megdet Rakhimkulov and his two sons had held a combined stake of around 8.5 per cent in Hungary's leading retail bank, OTP Bank, considered a portfolio investment, constituting by far the biggest item on the list of Russian investments in Hungary (Deák and Weiner 2016). End-2019 data show that Kafijat, the well-known Hungarian company of the two Rakhimkulov brothers, has a 6.9 per cent stake in OTP (OTP Bank n.d.).

Gazprom's main ownership interest in Hungary is Panrusgáz, an intermediary joint venture for Russian gas imports via Hungary's major long-term gas supply contract. The original motivation behind Panrusgáz's complicated scheme was likely Gazprom's desire to keep the gas sale revenues abroad, outside Russia, as generally suggested above. Nonetheless, today, it does not pursue any practical activities except for transferring wholesale gas with relatively low margins.

Among the Hungarian gas traders, one has a Russian owner. WIEE Hungary is a subsidiary of the Swiss Gazprom Schweiz. Until recently, Centrex Hungary was also certainly in Russian hands, since its parent company, the Vienna-based Centrex Europe Energy & Gas, was owned by Gazprombank.[9] Further, there was a trader, an obscure one, called MET Hungary, which had some Russian interest.

[8] Since 2003, Gazprom has not held any stakes in either company.

[9] We do not have information on the final beneficiary of the 2019 transaction.

Gazprom's other plans and projects in Hungary include failures. Investment in Hungary's oil industry has also involved many failed efforts, such as those of Yukos, Surgutneftegaz, Lukoil and Gazprom Neft. Yet, Gazprom Neft, Gazprom's oil arm and Russia's fourth-largest crude producer, is still active in Hungary via Serbia's NIS oil company, the majority of which is owned by Gazprom Neft.

Apart from Russia's presence in the energy sector, there are only a limited number of important assets under Russian ownership. In Hungary, there have only been two Russian-owned banks, including, in the past, ÁÉB, and, now, a subsidiary of Sberbank. Besides these, Russian banks set up representative offices in Hungary, and in 2019 the International Investment Bank, a multilateral development bank, also moved its headquarters to Budapest from Moscow.

According to Megdet Rakhimkulov, at the time when Gazprombank acquired ÁÉB, Gazprom identified Hungary as a strategic country and Mol as a strategic partner. Several large-scale international projects between Russia and Hungary were agreed upon at the governmental level. Gazprom thus purchased ÁÉB. However, in the end, according to Rakhimkulov, Gazprom's new management changed its investment strategy for Hungary and the region, and ultimately lost interest in ÁÉB (Figyelő 2004). Gazprombank pulled out of ÁÉB in 2005. Following this decision, commercial banking business was not pursued for a number of years. ÁÉB was the eighth largest bank in Hungary (New Europe 2003). At the end of 2005, ÁÉB had a total of only 17 branches. Previously, about 70 per cent of ÁÉB's operations had been devoted to Gazprom and Gazprombank. In 2004, this proportion accounted for only about 8–10 per cent, but a large part of the operations were still linked to Russian clients (Simon and Szép 2005). ÁÉB branches were taken over by Hungarian Volksbank, which was a subsidiary of the Austrian Volksbank.

Traces of historical continuity can be observed in the fact that some of the Hungarian branches of Sberbank Hungary were previously owned by ÁÉB. Initially, the primary objective of Sberbank Hungary was to provide comprehensive services to Russian private and corporate clients, and to enhance trade between CEE countries and the CIS (Kalotay et al. 2014: 28–29). Sberbank currently operates only 27 branches in Hungary (Sberbank Hungary n.d.).

Additionally, there is a strong Russian presence in Hungarian metallurgy, and there have also been a few Russian capital-related projects in Hungary's machinery worth mentioning. One large industrial investment is the ISD Dunaferr steel plant in Dunaújváros situated some 70 kilometres south of Budapest. By the end of the 1990s, Hungarian metallurgy was struggling, due to their low scale of economy, lack of capital and inefficient management. For external producers, these capacities offered a means of bypassing EU protectionism of the steel market (Deák and Weiner 2016). In 2003, Dunaferr was tendered and privatised by a consortium, consisting of Ukraine's Industrial Union of Donbass (ISD) and the Swiss Duferco International Trading Holding. Severstal also submitted a bid. However, a change of ownership occurred in 2009, when Russian investors obtained a 50 per cent plus two stake in the metallurgical assets of ISD. Later, as a creditor, Russia's state-owned Vnesheconombank (VEB) practically controlled ISD, but in 2017, Hungarian media sources suggested that Dunaferr had a new Russian owner, Suleyman Kerimov, a Russian billionaire and representative of the Republic of Dagestan in the Federation Council of the Federal Assembly of Russia, though this has never been confirmed.

A further Russian-related company is VBH Budapest, established in 1992, a wholesaler and retailer of metal fittings. It is the Hungarian subsidiary of the German VBH Holding, a market leader in the fittings industry in Europe, majority-owned by the Russian businessman Viktor Trenev.

In the Hungarian machine-building industry, in light of the construction of new units at Hungary's Paks Nuclear Power Plant (Paks II) by the Russians, the most relevant company with Russian involvement is Ganz Engineering and Energetics Machinery, owned by TsKBM, a part of Rosatom's machine-building division Atomenergomash. Ganz Engineering and Energetics Machinery is involved in the manufacture and installation of hydromachines, nuclear power station machinery and oil drilling equipment.

Another Russian–Hungarian big business could be reached in the sector if, through the Russian–Hungarian TMH Hungary Invest, Transmashholding—Russia's largest railway machine-building company, majority owned by Iskander Makhmudov, Andrei Bokarev, Dmitry Komissarov and Kirill Lipa—acquires 50 per cent of the state-controlled Hungarian Dunakeszi Jarműjavító where half of a 1300 passenger car order is to be manufactured for the Egyptian National Railways according to a 2018 contract between the Russian–Hungarian Transmashholding Hungary and the Egyptian National Railways.

The activities of Uraltrak are also related to the machine industry. Established in 1990, it is the only official Hungarian dealer of Russia's

Chelyabinsk Tractor Plant–Uraltrak, owned by the Russian state-owned tank and railway car manufacturer Uralvagonzavod. Chelyabinsk Tractor Plant is involved in the engineering and production of industrial tractors and engines.

Renova Group, whose beneficial owner is Viktor Vekselberg, a Russian tycoon, has been present in Hungary over the years with three Swiss high-tech and engineering groups (Oerlikon, Schmolz + Bickenbach and Sulzer), in which it now owns at most only minority stakes. Of the production sites of the Oerlikon Group, one is located in Hungary. Oerlikon Eldim (HU) produces honeycomb products used in aero engines. The second subsidiary, Schmolz + Bickenbach Magyarország, is a wholesaler of specialty steels deriving from the group's mills. In contrast, Sulzer's Hungarian subsidiary, Sulzer Pumps Wastewater Hungary, was sold in 2013. Under its new name, Zultzer Pumpen, the company continues its activities in the sales, service and operation of pumps, mixers, flow boosters, fans and blowers.

One more relatively widely known Russia-owned company is LIT Budapest, incorporated in 2006, dealing with disinfection technologies, including the use of UV in the treatment of drinking water, wastewater, technological water and water for swimming pools and spas. The company's main activities encompass the sale and installation of equipment, maintenance and servicing. Russia's LIT is reportedly among the world's top three developers and manufacturers of UV systems for water, air and surface disinfection.

The activities of Russian investors in the Hungarian logistics and transportation industry have been paved with failures. An exception is GEFCO Hungary, a subsidiary of the French GEFCO, 75 per cent owned by Russian Railways RZD. GEFCO Hungary was established in 2006. With its headquarters in Budapest, its logistics base is located in Biatorbágy, a village near the capital. In 2019, the number of employees rose to reach over 90 (GEFCO n.d.). GEFCO offers a wide range of logistics services and transport solutions by road, sea, air and rail.

The presence of Russian residents in Hungary's real-estate market is a visible phenomenon. Budapest and Zala County in the country's westernmost region (with special focus on the spa city of Hévíz) are the most attractive destinations for Russian residential real-estate owners. In contrast, the 232-room Lotus Therme Hotel & Spa, the only five-star hotel in Hévíz, can serve as an example of the presence of Russians in the Hungarian hotel and spa industry. Hungary is interesting for Russian tourists primarily because of medical tourism.

Russian FDI in Hungary could have been much larger than it is at present, but—similarly as in the case of Poland—Russian investors have been involved in a couple of unsuccessful takeover attempts in Hungary, which failed due to local resistance to Russian capital.

6.3.4 *Slovakia*

In Slovakia, Russia has quite moderate FDI activities and involves more stories of failure than success. However, the share of FDI from countries with lax transparency standards for ownership structures (Cyprus, Lichtenstein and Luxemburg) and, therefore, the possible involvement of Russian capital remain relatively high in Slovakia (Takáč 2019: 222).

In the gas sector, Gazprom is active only through Vemex Energo, founded in Czechia in 2003 to trade in gas and electricity. The Gazprom joint venture Slovrusgas, a middleman gas trader, went into liquidation in 2005 and was dissolved in 2010. Slovrusgas was established during the last months of Vladimir Meciar's premiership in 1998 (Nosko 2013: 147–148). It received the right to import gas above the volume agreed upon in the Russian long-term gas supply contract. It was also agreed that Gazprom would spend up to 40 per cent of its gas sales revenues on buying Slovakian goods and services and selling them on the Russian market. However, this deal proved to be problematic (Orbán 2008: 51, 57). Nonetheless, Gazprom could have played a role in Slovakian gas transit, but in 2005 it decided not to exercise the option to buy a 16.3 per cent stake in the Slovak Slovensky Plynarensky Priemysel (SPP), due to the unclear benefits of the deal and plans to develop the North European gas pipeline (later called Nord Stream). In the mid-2000s, SPP, an integrated gas company (excluding exploration and production), covering gas storage, transmission, distribution and trade, launched an extensive restructuring (unbundling) operation in accordance with EU requirements (Weiner 2006: 20).

In the oil sector, although Yukos took over a 49 per cent stake in Slovakia's oil transporter Transpetrol during the privatisation process conducted in 2002, the Slovakian state bought it back in 2009. In 2001, Yukos emphasised that increasing oil production and securing sales for Russian and Kazakh oil were Yukos' main motives for interest in Transpetrol. Yukos stated that extensive technical measures had to be taken to utilise Transpetrol's unused capacities and a strong oil producer was the guarantee for such an investment. Furthermore, Yukos believed that Transpetrol, which was at the heart of the regional oil pipeline system, would make it possible to work with neighbouring oil pipelines and open new oil transport opportunities, above all, reversing the flow of the Adria oil pipeline between Hungary and Croatia to gain access to the Croatian oil terminal Omišail and from there to the Balkans and, for example, to the United States. In addition, Yukos thought that by accessing Transpetrol it could improve its position in negotiations with Czechia and Germany on oil deliveries to Germany (Špáni 2001). Another failure relates to Lukoil, which, as mentioned, sold its Slovakian filling stations.

Sberbank's activities were also discontinued in Slovakia. In August 2017, its subsidiary Sberbank Slovensko was merged into Prima banka Slovensko. Sberbank had 39 offices in Slovakia.

In contrast, Slovakia has performed an important role in the activities of UTair, Russia's No. 1 helicopter operator and world leader in the helicopter market in terms of fleet size and carrying capacity. UTair has been represented in Slovakia by its subsidiary UTair Europe since 2006. UTair's main base in Europe is the international airport at the spa town of Piešťany in Slovakia. UTair Europe's helicopters are used for aerial work mostly in inaccessible terrain.

Finally, as indicated, Skoda JS of Czechia runs a branch in Slovakia. Until recently, it also owned a separate subsidiary Skoda Slovakia, but this merged into Skoda JS in 2019. Skoda Slovakia was founded in 1995. Skoda Slovakia and thus the new Slovakia Division deal with the construction, maintenance, repair, modernisation and decommissioning of facilities in nuclear energetics and of hydropower plants and in classical energetics, chemical, petrochemical and heavy industry, as well as trading and transport.

6.3.5 *Slovenia*

Finally, Slovenia has also attracted some Russian FDI. The first serious Russian FDI investor in Slovenia was the Kemerovo coking coal plant, known as Koks, one of Russia's leading producers and exporters of merchant metallurgical coke. Koks is part of the Industrial Metallurgical Holding, owned by the family of the late Boris Zubitsky, a former State Duma deputy. In 2007, through privatisation, Koks bought the majority of the SIJ Group, the largest Slovenian vertically integrated metallurgical group. SIJ was one of the few non-global steel companies in the EU. As a raw material supplier, it was Koks' goal to enter the market of finished products, used by the Slovenian industry (Lesjak Tušek 2007). On the other hand, vertical integration was crucial for the development of SIJ, as it is very sensitive to fluctuations in raw material and energy prices (SPIRIT Slovenia 2007). It was contended that Koks and the SIJ Group were complementary and not in competition (Warga 2007). Among the synergy effects, the possibility of increasing sales in Russia was mentioned, as SIJ's focus was on Western markets (Lesjak Tušek 2007). In 2012, Koks explained that making steel in Russia would be too expensive, and producers in Russia also lacked the know-how necessary for the production of special kinds of steel (SPIRIT Slovenia 2012).

In Slovenia, Sberbank operates a network of only 12 branch offices. The Slovenian Sberbank unit achieved portfolio growth when in 2014 it took over the retail loan portfolio of Slovenia's Probanka during the latter's controlled liquidation (Ljubljanska borza 2014).

In addition, Russia has some interest in Slovenian tourism. In 2012, Platanus, a Slovenian firm then reportedly owned by a Russian citizen and incorporated in 2010, bought a majority stake in the Maribor-based tourism company Terme Maribor, at that time owner of hotels, travel shops and a medical centre (The Slovenia Times 2012). Since 2014, Platanus has been controlled by the Gazprom Group.

Slovenia is one of Gazprom's smallest gas markets, but it could have received significant amounts of Russian FDI and gained an important transit role if the South Stream gas pipeline, aimed at running under the Black Sea to Bulgaria and then onwards, had been built. Thus, in 2012, the Slovenian–Russian joint project company Južni tok Slovenija was established to supervise the Slovenian South Stream section. Other plans were also considered relating to the South Stream project. However, in 2012, Gazprom Telecom, offering telecommunication and internet connectivity services and operating as a subsidiary of Gazprom, and Slovenia's Comita, developing technologies in the energy and telecommunications sectors, created the South Stream Telecom joint venture in Switzerland for the operation and provision of integrated telecommunications services at main communication lines along the entire South Stream gas pipeline (Gazprom 2012). In 2014, plans between Comita and Gazprom were further developed with the possibility of setting up a joint venture aimed at comprehensively developing the natural gas vehicle (NGV) sector in the

South Stream project countries (Gazprom 2014). After abandoning South Stream, Comita said in 2015 that they were examining the option of implementing the joint South Stream Telecom project with Gazprom within the TurkStream framework, a project substituting South Stream, and runs from Russia to Turkey across the Black Sea (TASS 2015).

In 2009, media suggested that Gazprom might be interested in acquiring Slovenia's largest fuel retailer Petrol, but this was never carried out. In the early 2010s, plans to cooperate in terms of the supply and distribution of oil products in Southern Europe and the Balkan states were also disseminated. For this purpose, Gazprom Neft and Petrol signed a memorandum of understanding in 2011 (Gazprom Neft 2011).

6.4 Summary and Conclusions

Investigating the Russian economic footprint through OFDI and the activities of Russian multinationals has not become either outdated or less interesting, even though most of the current attention on Russian influence in Europe has been focused on direct interference in political affairs.

Russia has a long history of OFDI, with the golden era ending with the global financial meltdown. By that time, Russian multinationals had become significant factors in international capital flows, though they have never been ranked among the largest multinationals. Having faced two financial crises over the past 12 years that interrupted the upward trend, the current period is about their withdrawal or survival.

Among the important features of Russian OFDI, the most well-known ones are round-tripping and trans-shipping that allow Cyprus to lead the list of Russian FDI recipients. Round-tripping leads to Russian FDI being overestimated in both directions. Round-tripping and the offshore orientation of Russian OFDI are strongly related to the tax minimisation strategies of Russian multinationals and to negative domestic push factors. Domestic push factors are very important in driving corporate decisions to invest abroad. Concerning a typical positive push factor, the Russian state's role in directly promoting foreign expansion, one can argue that the state supports only the largest Russian multinationals but Russian OFDI is not dominated by state-controlled companies. State-owned companies possess many advantages that can help them internationalise. However, the Russian state's influence on private companies is also frequently quite significant.

Due to the specific features of Russian OFDI and the lack of statistics referring to the ultimate host/investing country, the role of certain host countries is underestimated, while that of others is overstated. Nevertheless, Europe's leading role in Russian OFDI remains unchallenged, though Europe's share has been falling. This began many years ago and was not directly linked to EU–Russia relations, which—in turn—have definitely reached a very low point at present. Russia's pivot towards Asia as a means of diversifying away from Europe had been formulated before the events in Ukraine. Nonetheless, despite some steps in this direction, a dramatic increase in Russian expansion has not been witnessed and is not projected.

In Europe, possibly Italy, Germany and the United Kingdom are the largest recipients of Russian FDI. In CEE, Bulgaria, Serbia and Romania can be mentioned. ECE countries are not among the main destinations, though Russian FDI in Czechia or Poland is also not negligible. Even Slovenia has received notable Russian-involved companies. Nevertheless, company data demonstrate that the activities of Russian investors in ECE countries have been paved with failures. These have been evident in both divestments and unrealised plans. The low share of Russian investment in ECE countries may be referred to as business opportunities that the Russian parties have failed to exploit.

Generally speaking, Russian investment in ECE countries is dominated by market-seeking and, to a lesser extent, efficiency-seeking projects carried out by state owned or state-related private firms. Most Russian FDI has been done in hydrocarbons, iron, steel and machinery, but banking, software solutions, electronic production, real estate and even the light industry have also been targeted.

As extant theories of international investment—with the exception of Dunning's eclectic paradigm—have limited explanatory power concerning the activities of Russian multinationals in ECE countries, and can hardly even explain the existence of such firms, we—following Kalotay et al. (2014)—analysed the ownership advantages of Russian investors primarily by using the eclectic paradigm, duly adapted to the specifics of the discussed group of companies.

Contrary to findings in the literature on other emerging multinationals (Mathews 2002; Narula 2006), we found only traces of acquiring competitive advantages or ownership advantages. Rather, we identified investment aiming at exploiting existing advantages. This may be due to the fact that there is a very small number of this type of acquisition targets in ECE countries. As for Russian firms' asset-based advantages, it is obvious that their access to domestic raw materials and related technical knowledge is very important for their investments in ECE countries, as investments in oil, gas and metals are predominant. Another industry performing similarly is nuclear energy production. The asset-based advantages of Russian firms in ECE countries are closely related to their transaction-based advantages. The most evident case is that of the financial services sector. Both the asset and transactional ownership advantages of Russian firms are reinforced by the location advantages of ECE countries as these countries heavily rely on certain Russian natural resources, though to different extents. Similarly to hydrocarbons, iron and steel, as well as nuclear energy industries, the machinery industry also shows an interconnection of ownership and location advantages. For technology-based companies, the location advantages are not specific to ECE countries in the case of market-seeking motivations; but such factors are involved when it comes to efficiency-seeking motivations. Investigating the motives for and patterns of Russian investment in ECE countries, we can state that the technology-based firms show characteristics similar to developed-country multinationals. Other large state-owned and natural-resource-based firms are not similar to traditional multinationals. Yet others, for example real-estate investors, fall under no straightforward categorisation. A location disadvantage is also at play. Several examples of negative approaches towards Russian capital in ECE countries could be found, though the reactions of the host governments to Russian multinationals have been mixed (see Kalotay et al. 2014).

We suggest that the main elements of the OLI paradigm could be applied when explaining Russian FDI in these countries, but its extension with home-country factors seems to be necessary. This refers first of all to natural-resource-based multinationals, mainly oil, gas and steel, but home-country interest is also prevalent in other industries. In the case of Russian multinationals active in innovative industries, home-country factors play a minor role (see also Kalotay et al. 2014).

Opposition to Russian investment could continue to grow in the EU. While examples of Russian pressure on companies to sell to them have been known to occur in CEE countries within the EU, there are also already precedents in Western EU states for transactions that have failed because of resistance to Russian investment. In general, there is no need to worry about Russian OFDI, but some of the expressed concerns have certainly been attested. We believe that it is the Russian party who would benefit most from alleviating these fears.

References

Aircraft Industries. (n.d.). Company Profile. Retrieved from http://www.let.cz/documents/companyprofile.pdf.

Anwar, A., & Mughal, M. Y. (2014). *Why do Russian Firms Invest Abroad? A Firm Level Analysis.* MPRA Paper, No. 58178. Munich Personal RePEc Archive. Retrieved from https://mpra.ub.uni-muenchen.de/58178/1/MPRA_paper_58178.pdf.

Belton, C. (2008). Copy China and Invest Abroad, Says Medvedev. *Financial Times*, 31 January. Retrieved from https://www.ft.com/content/850ccda0-d02e-11dc-9309-0000779fd2ac.

Blesk.cz. (2016). Vklady klientů ERB bank budou vyplácet od čtvrtka pobočky ČS. 17 October. Retrieved from http://www.blesk.cz/clanek/zpravy-live-ekonomika/424993/vklady-klientu-erb-bank-budou-vyplacet-od-ctvrtka-pobocky-cs.html.

bne IntelliNews. (2016). Czech National Bank Shutters Russian Exports Lender ERB. 24 October. Retrieved from http://www.intellinews.com/czech-national-bank-shutters-russian-exports-lender-erb-108735/.

Bulatov, A. (2017). Offshore Orientation of Russian Federation FDI. *Transnational Corporations, 24*(2), 71–89.

Bulatov, A., Kuznetsov, A., Kvashnin, Y., Maltseva, A., & Seniuk, N. (2016). Russian MNCs: Empirical and Theoretical Aspects. In R. van Tulder, A. Verbeke, J. Carneiro, & M. A. Gonzalez-Perez (Eds.), *The Challenge of BRIC Multinationals (Progress in International Business Research, 11)* (pp. 395–421). Emerald Group Publishing Limited.

CBR. (2019a). Direct Investment in the Russian Federation: Inward Positions by Instrument and Partner Country (Directional Principle). Retrieved from http://www.cbr.ru/vfs/eng/statistics/credit_statistics/direct_investment/10e-dir_inv.xlsx.

CBR. (2019b). Direct Investment in the Russian Federation: Positions by Instrument and Partner Country (Asset/Liability Principle). Retrieved from http://www.cbr.ru/vfs/eng/statistics/credit_statistics/direct_investment/dir-inv_in_country_1_e.xlsx.

CBR. (2019c). Direct Investment of the Russian Federation Abroad: Outward Positions by Instrument and Partner Country (Directional Principle). Retrieved from http://www.cbr.ru/vfs/eng/statistics/credit_statistics/direct_investment/16e-dir_inv.xlsx.

CBR. (2019d). Direct Investment of the Russian Federation Abroad: Positions by Instrument and Partner Country (Asset/Liability Principle). Retrieved from http://www.cbr.ru/vfs/eng/statistics/credit_statistics/direct_investment/15e-dir_inv.xlsx.

CBR. (2020a). Direct Investment of the Russian Federation by Institutional Sector. Retrieved from http://www.cbr.ru/vfs/eng/statistics/credit_statistics/direct_investment/21e-dir_inv.xlsx.

CBR. (2020b). Direct Investment of the Russian Federation by Instrument (Directional Principle). Retrieved from http://www.cbr.ru/vfs/eng/statistics/credit_statistics/direct_investment/22e-dir_inv.xlsx.

Deák, A. (2017). *Emerging Diversity in Russia's Energy Relations: What Role for Europe?* The First Ghent Russia Colloquium, "EU–Russia Relations: How to Get Out of the 'Midlife' Crisis?" Ghent: Ghent University, 22 September.

Deák, A., & Weiner, C. (2016). *Country Report: Hungary.* Unpublished manuscript prepared for the project "Russian Economic Influence in New Europe", Center for the Study of Democracy (Sofia) and Center for Strategic and International Studies (Washington, DC).

Deloitte. (2008). *Russian Multinationals: New Players in the Global Economy.* Moscow: Deloitte CIS.

Dmitriyeva, A. (2017). Petr Khorak: Serva Group—25 let na rynke. Bolshaya yevropeyskaya mechta. *Getsiz.ru*, 22 May. Retrieved from http://getsiz.ru/bolshaya-evropeyskaya-mechta-serva-group-25-let-na.html.

E15.cz. (2014). Lukoil odchází z Česka, benzinky prodá maďarské Mol. 4 August. Retrieved from https://www.e15.cz/byznys/prumysl-a-energetika/lukoil-odchazi-z-ceska-benzinky-proda-madarske-mol-1107239.

EABR. (2017). *YeAES i strany Yevraziyskogo kontinenta: monitoring i analiz pryamykh investitsiy.* Doklad, No. 47. Saint-Petersburg: Tsentr integratsionnykh issledovaniy Yevraziyskogo banka razvitiya.

EFDI. (2017). *EFDI PR Committee Meeting: Changes ante portas… (27 Feb, Prague, Czech Republic).* Newsletter, No. 7: 7. Retrieved from http://www.efdi.eu/sites/default/files/publications/2017_efdi_newsletter_no_7.pdf.

Ekoton. (n.d.-a). About Company. Retrieved from https://ekoton.com/about.

Ekoton. (n.d.-b). O nas. Retrieved from http://www.ekoton.pl/FIRMA/o-nas.

Eurostat. (2019). EU Direct Investment Positions, Breakdown by Country and Economic Activity (BPM6) [bop_fdi6_pos]. Last update June 17, 2019. Retrieved from http://appsso.eurostat.ec.europa.eu/nui/show.do?dataset=bop_fdi6_pos&lang=en.

Evraz. (2005). Evraz Group S.A. Completes Acquisition of Vitkovice Steel. News, 15 November. Retrieved from https://old.evraz.com/media/news/1711/.

Figyelő. (2004). Rahimkulov a Gazprom-szálról. 4 November. Retrieved from https://24.hu/belfold/2004/11/04/rahimkulov_gazprom_szalrol/.

Filippov, S. (2008). *Russia's Emerging Multinationals: Trends and Issues.* UNU-MERIT Working Paper Series, No. 62. Maastricht: United Nations University, Maastricht Economic and Social Research and Training Centre on Innovation and Technology. Retrieved from http://www.merit.unu.edu/publications/wppdf/2008/wp2008-062.pdf.

Finance.cz. (2008). Russian Miner UMMC Buys 51 pct of Czech Plane Maker. 2 June. Retrieved from https://www.finance.cz/zpravy/reuters/MTFH41497nL02531220-russian-miner-ummc-buys-51-pct-of-czech-plane-maker/.

Fortescue, S., & Hanson, P. (2015). What Drives Russian Outward Foreign Direct Investment? Some Observations on the Steel Industry. *Post-Communist Economies, 27*(3), 283–305.

Gazeta Wrocławska. (2015). Luxoft Poland otworzył swoje drugie centrum IT we Wrocławiu. 16 March. Retrieved from http://www.gazetawroclawska.pl/strefa-biznesu/firma/a/luxoft-poland-otworzyl-swoje-drugie-centrum-it-we-wroclawiu,10153778/.

Gazeta Wyborcza. (2016). Luxoft—juě 2000 pracowników w Polsce, zatrudni jeszcze kilkaset. 15 April. Retrieved from http://krakow.wyborcza.pl/krakow/1,44425,19926779,luxoft-juz-2000-pracownikow-w-polsce-zatrudni-jeszcze-kilkaset.html?disableRedirects=true.

Gazprom. (2012). Gazprom and Comita Discuss Work Plans for South Stream Telecom AG JV. Release, 26 December. Retrieved from http://www.gazprom.com/press/news/2012/december/article152915/.

Gazprom. (2014). Gazprom and Comita May Set up NGV Joint Venture in South Stream Project Countries. Release, 23 May. Retrieved from http://www.gazprom.com/press/news/2014/may/article191729/.

Gazprom Germania. (2015). 2014 Group Annual Report. Retrieved from https://www.gazprom-germania.de/fileadmin/templates/pdf/Geschaeftsberichte_2014/GPG_IFRS_2014_E_web.pdf.

Gazprom Neft. (2011). Gazprom Neft and Slovenian Petrol Sign Memorandum of Understanding. Press Release, 22 March. Retrieved from https://www.gazprom-neft.com/press-center/news/3912/.

GEFCO. (n.d.). GEFCO Magyarország. Retrieved from https://hu.gefco.net/hu/orszag/gefco-magyarorszag.

Gera, V. (2013). Poland Emerging as Major European Outsourcing Hub. *U.S. News*, 27 February. Retrieved from https://www.usnews.com/news/world/articles/2013/02/27/poland-emerging-as-major-european outsourcing-hub.

Global Trade Review. (2009). New Russian Bank Secures First for Europe. 7 May. Retrieved from https://www.gtreview.com/news/europe/new-russian-bank-secures-first-for-europe/.

Helmer, J. (2014). Evraz Plays the Hidden Hand: Vitkovice Steel Sale is a Related-Party Transaction. *johnhelmer.net*, 17 April. Retrieved from http://johnhelmer.net/evraz-plays-the-hidden-hand-vitkovice-steel-sale-is-a-related-party-

transaction-in-which-sergei-taruta-acting-donetsk-governor-gets-a-reward-he-cant-afford/.
Hovorka, J. (2013). Russian bank giant Sberbank aims high in Czech Republic. *Aktuálně.cz*, 1 March. Retrieved from https://zpravy.aktualne.cz/russian-bank-giant-sberbank-aims-high-in-czech-republic/r~i:article:772811/?redirected=1503136678.
IMEMO. (2009). *Russian Multinationals Continue Their Outward Expansion in Spite of the Global Crisis.* EMGP Report, 2 December. Moscow/New York: IMEMO and Vale Columbia Center on Sustainable International Investment. Retrieved from http://ccsi.columbia.edu/files/2013/10/Russia_2009.pdf.
IMEMO. (2011). *Investment from Russia Stabilizes After the Global Crisis.* EMGP Report, 23 June. Moscow/New York: IMEMO and Vale Columbia Center on Sustainable International Investment. Retrieved from http://ccsi.columbia.edu/files/2013/10/Russia_2011.pdf.
Kalotay, K. (2003). Outward Foreign Direct Investment from Economies in Transition in a Global Context. *Journal for European Management Studies, 8*(1), 6–24.
Kalotay, K. (2008). Russian Transnationals and International Investment Paradigms. *Research in International Business and Finance, 22*(2), 85–107.
Kalotay, K. (2010a). Takeoff and Turbulence in the Foreign Expansion of Russian Multinationals. In K. P. Sauvant, W. A. Maschek, & G. A. McAllister (Eds.), *Foreign Direct Investments from Emerging Markets: The Challenges Ahead* (pp. 113–145). New York: Palgrave Macmillan.
Kalotay, K. (2010b). The Future of Russian Outward Foreign Direct Investment and the Eclectic Paradigm: What Changes After the Crisis of 2008–2009? *Competitio, 9*(1), 31–54.
Kalotay, K. (2015). Acquisitions as Engines of Foreign Expansion of Russian Multinationals. In M. Demirbag & A. Yaprak (Eds.), *Handbook of Emerging Market Multinational Corporations* (pp. 239–259). Cheltenham/Northampton: Edward Elgar.
Kalotay, K., & Sulstarova, A. (2010). Modelling Russian Outward FDI. *Journal of International Management, 16*(2), 131–142.
Kalotay, K., Éltető, A., Sass, M., & Weiner, C. (2014). *Russian Capital in the Visegrád Countries.* Working Papers, No. 210. Budapest: Institute of World Economics, Centre for Economic and Regional Studies, Hungarian Academy of Sciences. Retrieved from http://real.mtak.hu/19519/.
Kaspersky. (n.d.). O nas. Retrieved from https://www.kaspersky.pl/o-nas.
Krainová, P. (2005). Akcie Vítkovice Steel byly převedeny. *Ministerstvo financí České republiky*, 14 November. Retrieved from https://www.mfcr.cz/cs/archiv/transformacni-instituce/agenda-byvaleho-fnm/archiv-komunikace-fnm/2005/akcie-vitkovice-steel-byly-prevedeny-15445.

Kuznetsov, A. (2010a). *Industrial and Geographical Diversification of Russian Foreign Direct Investments*. Electronic Publications of Pan-European Institute, No. 7/2010.

Kuznetsov, A. (2010b). Masshtaby rossiyskoy investitsionnoy ekspansii v Yevrope. In A. Kuznetsov (Ed.), *Vliyaniye rossiyskoy investitsionnoy ekspansii na obraz Rossii v Yevrope* (pp. 19–28). Moscow: IMEMO RAN.

Kuznetsov, A. (2011). Evolyutsiya rossiyskikh TNK: ot regionalnykh kompaniy k globalnym. *Vestnik federalnogo gosudarstvennogo uchrezhdeniya "Gosudarstvennaya registratsionnaya palata pri Ministerstve yustitsii Rossiyskoy Federatsii"*, No. 4: 4–14.

Kuznetsov, A. (2013). Global Expansion of Russian Multinationals after the Crisis: Results of 2011. EMGP Report, 16 April. Moscow/New York: IMEMO and Vale Columbia Center on Sustainable International Investment. Retrieved from http://ccsi.columbia.edu/files/2015/04/Russia_2013.pdf.

Kuznetsov, A. (2014). Russian Multinationals FDI Outflows Geography: The Emerging Dominance of Greater Europe. *European Research, 67*(1–2), 130–135.

Kuznetsov, A. (2017). Prospects of Diversifying Russian Direct Investment Abroad. *Studies on Russian Economic Development, 28*(1), 79–86.

Lesjak Tušek, P. (2007). Ruski Koks in SIJ združila interese. *Vseslovensko Združenje Malih Delničarjev*, 3 March. Retrieved from http://www.vzmd.si/novice/mediji-o-vzmd/ruski-koks-in-sij-zdruzila-interese.

Liuhto, K. (2015). Motivations of Russian Firms to Invest Abroad: How do Sanctions Affect Russia's Outward Foreign Direct Investment? *Baltic Region, 7*(4), 7–26.

Liuhto, K. (2016). Does Ownership Matter in an OFDI Decision of a Russian Firm? The Case of Russia's Ten Largest Investors Abroad. In K. Liuhto, S. Sutyrin, & J.-M. F. Blanchard (Eds.), *The Russian Economy and Foreign Direct Investment* (pp. 248–265). Abingdon/New York: Routledge.

Liuhto, K., & Majuri, S. (2014). Outward Foreign Direct Investment from Russia: A Literature Review. *Journal of East–West Business, 20*(4), 198–224.

Ljubljanska borza. (2014). Probanka, d. d., Maribor. Information on successful sale of assets. Public Announcements, 24 July. Retrieved from http://seonet.ljse.si/default_en.aspx?doc_id=55244&language=en.

Luxoft. (2016). Luxoft invests in Warsaw adding new IT jobs in Poland. Press, 30 May. Retrieved from https://www.luxoft.com/pr/luxoft-invests-in-warsaw-adding-new-it-jobs-in-poland/.

Luxoft. (n.d.). Luxoft Corporate Profile. Retrieved from https://emn.gov.pl/download/75/18651/Luxoft.pdf.

Mathews, J. A. (2002). *Dragon Multinational: A New Model of Global Growth*. Oxford: Oxford University Press.

MetalTorg.ru. (2006). Gruppa ChTPZ priobrela kontrol nad 100% aktsiy cheshskogo zavoda MSA a.s. 6 June. Retrieved from https://www.metaltorg.ru/analytics/publication.php?id=2373.

Narula, R. (2006). Globalization, New Ecologies, New Zoologies, and the Purported Death of the Eclectic Paradigm. *Asia Pacific Journal of Management, 23*(2), 143–151.

Nestmann, T., & Orlova, D. (2008). Russia's Outward Investment. *Deutsche Bank Research*, 30 April.

New Europe. (2003). AEB Bank Expanding Horizons. 13 July. Retrieved from http://www.neurope.eu/article/aeb-bank-expanding-horizons.

New Europe. (2004). Skoda Holding Dumps 3 Units. 2 May. Retrieved from https://www.neweurope.eu/article/skoda-holding-dumps-3-units/.

New Europe. (2006). Arkley Capital acquires Czech's MSA. 11 June. Retrieved from https://www.neweurope.eu/article/arkley-capital-acquires-czech%E2%80%99s-msa/.

Nosko, A. (2013). *Energy Security in Transition: Coping with Energy Import Dependence in the Czech Republic, Slovakia and Hungary*. Ph.D. Dissertation. Budapest: Central European University. Retrieved from http://www.etd.ceu.hu/2013/nosko_andrej.pdf.

Nuclear Engineering International. (2011). Through New Czech JV, TVEL Creeps up to Europe. 26 December. Retrieved from http://www.neimagazine.com/news/newsthrough-new-czech-jv-tvel-creeps-up-to-europe.

Orbán, A. (2008). *Power, Energy, and the New Russian Imperialism*. Westport, CT/London: Praeger Security International.

OS KOVO. (2016). Kunovice: Ministr Mládek chce jednat s majiteli Aircraft Industries. Retrieved from http://www.oskovo.cz/aktuality/kunovice-ministr-mladek-chce-jednat-s-majiteli-aircraft-industries.

OTP Bank. (n.d.). Tulajdonosi struktúra. Retrieved from https://www.otpbank.hu/portal/hu/IR_Tulajdonosi_struktura.

Panibratov, A. (2013). *The Influence of the State on Expanding Russian MNEs: Advantage or Handicap?* Russie.NEI.Visions, No. 73. Paris: Ifri. Retrieved from http://www.ifri.org/sites/default/files/atoms/files/ifriandreypanibratovrussiancompagniesengdecember2013.pdf.

Panibratov, A. (2017). *International Strategy of Emerging Market Firms: Absorbing Global Knowledge and Building Competitive Advantage*. Abingdon/New York: Routledge.

Panibratov, A., & Kalotay, K. (2009). Russian Outward FDI and Its Policy Context. Columbia FDI Profiles, 13 October. New York: Vale Columbia Center on Sustainable International Investment. Retrieved from http://ccsi.columbia.edu/files/2014/03/FDI_Profile-_Russia.pdf.

Panibratov, A., & Michailova, S. (2019). The Role of State Ownership and Home Government Political Support in Russian Multinationals' Internationalization. *International Journal of Emerging Markets, 14*(3), 436–450.
petrolnet.pl. (2016). Lukoil niespiesznie opuszcza Polskę. 20 September. Retrieved from http://www.petrolnet.pl/Lukoil-niespiesznie-opuszcza-Polske/.
Pilsen Steel. (2010). The Holding Group "United Group" Expects Threefold Increase in Sales Volume. Press Releases, 2 November. Retrieved from http://www.pilsensteel.cz/?mt=&m=700&id=253&lang=1.
Power Machines. (2004). OMZ—Power Machines Group purchased Skoda Holding Subsidiaries. News, 23 April. Retrieved from http://www.power-m.ru/en/press-center/news/omz-power-machines-group-purchased-skoda-holding-subsidiaries/.
Pražský Telegraf. (2013). Červa Export Import: brend Chekhii v Yevrope. 7 November. Retrieved from http://ptel.cz/2013/11/cerva-export-import-brend-chexii-v-evrope/.
Prusińska, O. (2010). Białystok. Ekoton pracuje z Aton-Ht nad polską propozycją do Ekonobla. *Poranny.pl*, 21 July. Retrieved from http://www.poranny.pl/strefa-biznesu/wiadomosci/z-regionu/a/bialystok-ekoton-pracuje-z-atonht-nad-polska-propozycja-do-ekonobla,10277994/.
Puls Biznesu. (2008). Severstallat zainwestuje w Sosnowcu blisko 20 mln euro. 21 May. Retrieved from https://www.pb.pl/severstallat-zainwestuje-w-sosnowcu-blisko-20-mln-euro-429260.
Rosstat. (2009). *Investitsii v Rossii 2009*. Moscow: Rosstat.
Rosstat. (2014). *Finansy Rossii 2014*. Moscow: Rosstat.
Roust. (2013). Russian Standard Acquires CEDC. News, 5 June. Retrieved from http://roust.com/news/russian-standard-becomes-2nd-largest-vodka-producer-in-the-world-with-acquisition-of-central-european-distribution-corporation-.
Sberbank Europe. (n.d.). Czech Republic. Retrieved from https://www.sberbank.at/sberbank-europe-ag/sberbank-cee/czech-republic.
Sberbank Hungary. (n.d.). About Us. Retrieved from https://www.sberbank.hu/en/headline/about.html.
Severstal. (2008). AO «Severstallat» v rezultate pismennykh ofertnykh torgov priobrelo imushchestvo predpriyatiya «Technologie Buczek S.A.», nakhodivshegosya v sostoyanii bankrotstva,—soobshchil Predsedatel Soveta AO «Severstallat», chlen soveta direktorov OAO «Severstal» Anatoliy Kruchinin. Novosti, 26 March. Retrieved from https://www.severstal.com/rus/media/news/document3204.phtml.
Simon, E., & Szép, I. (2005). Meg kell őszülni a sikerhez. Beszélgetés Medget Rahimkulovval, az Általános Értékforgalmi bank többségi tulajdonosával. *Figyelő, 48*(45), 68–71.

Skolkovo. (2007). *Russian Multinationals Bullish on Foreign Markets*. Moscow/New York: Skolkovo—Columbia Program on International Investment, 10 December. Retrieved from http://www.skolkovo.ru/images/stories/book/SKOLKOVO_PRESS-RELEASE_071210_TOP_25_RANKINGS_Eng.pdf.

Skolkovo. (2008). *Emerging Russian Multinationals: Achievements and Challenges*. Moscow/New York: Skolkovo and Columbia Program on International Investment, November. http://www.skolkovo.ru/images/stories/book/SKOLKOVO_Research_Emerging_Russian_Multinationals_Eng.pdf.

Skolkovo. (2009). *Global Expansion of Emerging Multinationals: Post-Crisis Adjustment*. SIEMS Monthly Briefing, May. Skolkovo Institute for Emerging Market Studies. Retrieved from http://www.skolkovo.ru/images/stories/book/SIEMS_Monthly_Briefing_2009-05_eng.pdf.

Špáni, I. (2001). Yukos chce Transpetrol lepšie využiť. *Hospodárske noviny*, 13 December. Retrieved from https://dennik.hnonline.sk/podniky-a-trhy/44400-yukos-chce-transpetrol-lepsie-vyuzit.

SPIRIT Slovenia. (2007). Majority Stake in Steel Group Sold to Russian Company Koks. 5 March. Retrieved from https://www.sloveniapartner.eu/hot-topics/slovenia-business-week-no-09-majority-stake-in-steel-group-sold-to-russian-company-koks-7377.

SPIRIT Slovenia. (2012). Steel Group Owners Happy with Business in Slovenia. 28 December. Retrieved from https://www.investslovenia.org/news-and-media/business-news/steel-group-owners-happy-with-business-in-slovenia-3929.

Takáč, K. (2019). Slovakia: Energy Dependence Vulnerabilities. In O. Shentov, R. Stefanov, & M. Vladimirov (Eds.), *The Russian Economic Grip on Central and Eastern Europe (Routledge Contemporary Russia and Eastern Europe Series)* (pp. 221–231). Abingdon/New York: Routledge.

TASS. (2011). Russia's Sitronics Enters 100 Top World High-Tech Companies. 1 November. Retrieved from http://tass.com/archive/663559.

TASS. (2015). Slovenian Comita May Implement JV South Stream Telecom within Turkish Stream Project. 1 April. Retrieved from http://tass.com/economy/786472.

Tepavcevic, S. (2013). *Russian Foreign Policy and Outward Foreign Direct Investments: Cooperation, Subordination, or Disengagement?* Ph.D. Dissertation. Budapest: Central European University. Retrieved from http://www.etd.ceu.hu/2014/tepavcevic_sanja.pdf.

The Slovenia Times. (2012). Terme Maribor Sold to Russians. 2 April. Retrieved from http://www.sloveniatimes.com/terme-maribor-sold-to-russians.

UNCTAD. (2015). *World Investment Report 2015: Reforming International Investment Governance*. New York/Geneva: United Nations.

UNCTAD. (2016). *World Investment Report 2016: Investor Nationality: Policy Challenges*. New York/Geneva: United Nations.

UNCTAD. (2017). *World Investment Report 2017: Investment and the Digital Economy*. New York/Geneva: United Nations.

UNCTAD. (2019). *World Investment Report 2019: Special Economic Zones*. New York/Geneva: United Nations.

UNCTAD FDI Database. (n.d.). Retrieved from http://unctadstat.unctad.org/wds/ReportFolders/reportFolders.aspx.

Vahtra, P., & Liuhto, K. (2004). *Expansion or Exodus? Foreign Operations of Russia's Largest Corporations*. Electronic Publications of Pan-European Institute, No. 8/2004.

Vasileva, A. (2014). Continuity and Change in Russian Capitalism. In U. Becker (Ed.), *The BRICs and Emerging Economies in Comparative Perspective: Political Economy, Liberalisation and Institutional Change* (pp. 100–122). Abingdon: Routledge.

Warga, Ž. (2007). The Slovenian Steel Industry: One of the Pillars of the High-Tech Society. *sinfo, 6*, 21–24.

Weiner, C. (2006). *Russian FDI in Central and Eastern European Countries: Opportunities and Threats*. Working Papers, No. 168. Budapest: Institute for World Economics, Hungarian Academy of Sciences. Retrieved from http://real.mtak.hu/80460/.

wnp.pl. (2014). Luxoft zatrudni ok. 600 informatyków w Krakowie i Wrocławiu. 4 December. Retrieved from https://www.wnp.pl/tech/luxoft-zatrudni-ok-600-informatykow-w-krakowie-i-wroclawiu,239874_1_0_0.html.

CHAPTER 7

Turkish Investments in Central and Eastern Europe: Motivations and Experiences

Tamás Szigetvári

7.1 Introduction

With the growing global integration of the Turkish economy, the country has emerged as a capital investor abroad. In this chapter, we would like to analyse the forms of Turkish outward foreign direct investment (OFDI) and the motivations of Turkish multinational enterprises (TMNEs) in this process. We have a special interest in Turkish OFDI towards the Central and Eastern European (CEE) region—what kind of Turkish investment comes to the region, why Turkish firms choose these countries for their investments, do they have specific motivations and what kind of location-specific advantages they may have.

We begin the chapter with an overview of recent changes in Turkish economy and economic policy: how did the structure and the global position of the Turkish economy change and what kind of push factors motivated Turkish firms to invest abroad. Next, we analyse the patterns of

T. Szigetvári (✉)
Institute of World Economics, Centre for Economic and Regional Studies, Budapest, Hungary
e-mail: szigetvari.tamas@krtk.mta.hu

Á. Szunomár (ed.), *Emerging-market Multinational Enterprises in East Central Europe*, Studies in Economic Transition,
https://doi.org/10.1007/978-3-030-55165-0_7

Turkish OFDI and the major motivations of TMNEs. Then, we deal with the CEE region: what is the importance of the region in Turkish OFDI and what kind of Turkish firms have invested in these countries. We next focus on the motivation of these firms and on the advantages and experiences they have earned in the CEE region. In our analyses, we have used international and Turkish statistical databases (United Nations Conference on Trade and Development (UNCTAD), Turkish Central Bank, Amadeus database), and to overview the motivations and experiences of TMNEs, we have widely used the results of previous researches in the literature and also our own investigations and interviews in this field.[1]

7.2 Turkish Economic Policy and Outward Investments

Until the 1980s, Turkey's economy was relatively closed. The import substitution industrialisation followed by Turkey was concentrating on the domestic markets; the mostly state-owned or state-subsidised private companies had little incentive and possibility to enter new markets. The oil price boom and the economic challenges of the 1970s, however, have forced it to open up its economy. With a radical shift in its economic policy, Turkey started to promote export orientation as a basic strategy in its industrial development. Accordingly, the government strongly supported production for export by taking over 30% of the export costs of the enterprises, as well as giving them discounts in respect of energy and transport costs.

The progress that started from 1980 was more convincing than the results achieved in the previous two decades. As a result of the economic opening, private enterprises started to flourish; there was a boom in tourism and also a modest inflow of foreign investments. In the second half of the 1980s, however, signs of imbalances intensified as a result of the quick growth in domestic demand and the failures of economic management. Because of the incompletely implemented structural reforms, huge amounts of money were spent on the financing of unprofitable state enterprises.

To ease the situation, large-scale liberalisation was started again in 1989, within the framework of which larger inflow of foreign capital was

[1] The interviews were done mostly in Hungary, with interviewees working for or dealing with Turkish firms in the region.

made possible. This helped to finance the deficit, but the resulting short-term capital (so-called hot money) made the country vulnerable in times of external crises (Öniş and Şenses 2009). After a couple of years of dynamic progress, however, capital liberalisation resulted in periodic economic setbacks (1994, 1999, 2001), with a decrease of GDP by 5–10% in these years. The development of crises was also fuelled by the deficiencies of the financial institutions and the problems arising from the bank system operating poorly (Cizre and Yeldan 2005).

As a consequence of the 2001 economic crisis, deep and comprehensive reforms started. The implementation of the reforms was supported by the extended stand-by facility of the International Monetary Fund, but similar, if not even more important, factors behind the success were the increasing European political support after 2002 and the forming of a new government by the reform-oriented, moderate Islamic AK party (AKP). The results of crisis management were convincing. The average economic growth remained over 6% from 2002 to 2007 and was able to return to this level after the 2008–2009 crisis again. The chronically high inflation rate, a major sign of the economic imbalance for decades, was reduced to one-digit levels. The stable macroeconomic environment and the prospects of closer integration into the EU encouraged foreign investments; the level of FDI grew from yearly 1–2 billion USD to 10–20 billion USD, flowing mostly into export-oriented manufacturing (Taymaz and Voyvoda 2009). The competitiveness of exports was improved by the depreciation of the currency in the first years. Exports became more diversified, not only in their product structure but concerning target countries as well. After the growing importance of European exports in the period 2002 to 2007, the post-crisis period led to an increasing share of neighbouring regions (the Middle East, the Commonwealth of Independent States (CIS), the Balkans), not only in trade but in investment relations as well.

Turkey has started to shift from an economy largely based on agriculture and on an abundant low-skilled labour force used mainly in textile sector towards an industrial economy. It is today a major European automotive producer, a world leader in shipbuilding and a significant manufacturer of electronics and home appliances, for example, TV and white goods (OECD 2012). In electronics especially the home appliance sector developed dynamically, where domestic brands (Vestel, Beko) are prominent representatives of the exports. Turkish products are not top quality brands, rather low and medium price products, but there is a growing demand for these products both on the domestic markets and in developing and transition countries. In vehicle production, several multinationals (Ford, Renault, Fiat, Hyundai, Toyota, Honda, Opel, Mercedes, MAN) brought part of their production capacity to Turkey, largely due to the customs union agreement with the EU allowing a free export of products to the European single market. In bus production, domestic brands (Otokar, BMC, Temsa) are dominating.

Turkish foreign economic policy has changed both in its philosophy and in the practice based upon it. The key figure of the new foreign policy, Ahmet Davutoğlu, emphasised the importance of strategic depth: instead of being just a periphery of Europe, Turkey, as a country with a strategic location, should use its position to create its own regional importance. As a consequence of this approach, Turkey started a "zero-problem" foreign policy with its neighbours and tried to create a trading state image of a country preferring good economic relations to unfruitful foreign political clashes. Together with the successful economic recovery in the early 2000s, this policy resulted in a growing importance of regional and global ties. After the 2008 crisis, the economic importance of the neighbouring regions (the Balkans, the Caucasus, the Middle East and North Africa, Central Asia) increased further. This meant not only the increase of trade volumes with these regions and countries but also a rising activity of investors.

7.2.1 Turkish OFDI

7.2.1.1 History and State Policy

Before the 1990s Turkish OFDI was not significant. The few such transactions were connected to state economic enterprises that entered into partnership with foreign companies or to larger private firms trying to facilitate international trade. After the 1960s, when Turkish workers began arriving in Europe, countries like Germany and the Netherlands became the destination of Turkish financial and commercial firms, while from the 1970s, the increasing activity of Turkish construction firms especially in the Middle East led to some outward capital flows as well.

In the late 1980s and early 1990s capital liberalisation created a better environment for capital flows. The opening up of the Turkish economy increased domestic competition and turned the attention of Turkish firms towards markets abroad. The rather negative business climate in Turkey (high inflation, economic volatility) was another push factor for OFDI, while the political and economic transformation in Eastern Europe and the dissolution of the Soviet Union during this period created new business opportunities for Turkish firms (Yildirim 2017: 280).

Turkey, as a relatively closed developing country, had few experiences with outward investment. Erosion of home country competitive advantages with greater openness and increased foreign competition forced Turkish firms to evolve into multinational enterprises (TMNEs). Challenged in their domestic market, they began to search for markets and technology to compete successfully in the global economy (Aybar 2016: 80).

The promotion of OFDI by the governments of developing countries became common. The potential advantages based on the internalisation of local companies could help economies to integrate more effectively with the international economy (Egresi and Kara 2015: 182). After the macroeconomic stabilisation in the early 2000s, the Turkish government started to promote outward investments in accordance with its foreign policy. The increasing domestic demand, a strengthening currency and the cheaper funding, however, underpinned TMNEs' outward orientation at the beginning of this period. More recently, the European debt crisis offered new possibilities for Turkish firms to acquire struggling businesses in Europe, particularly in the Balkans and in transition countries. Turkey became one of the four major emerging country investors in transition countries along with China, India and South Korea (UNCTAD 2011: 66).

The Turkish government has taken various steps to help companies' outward investment activities. Besides providing information about local conditions in host countries, the government established an insurance coverage for companies investing abroad; it gives tax relief to holding companies, and a programme "Turquality" was established to encourage the development of Turkish brand names abroad (KHU 2014).

7.2.1.2 OFDI in Statistics

The positive trends in the outward investments are shown by the statistics as well. By 2018, the overall stock OFDI was around 50 billion USD (Table 7.1). Compared to the overall OFDI of developing countries, it was around 0.7%, far behind the largest investors among emerging markets: not only China (1939 billion USD), but South Korea (388 billion USD), Russia (344 billion USD), South Africa (238 billion USD), Brazil

Table 7.1 Turkish inward and outward FDI (million USD)

	1980	*1990*	*2000*	*2010*	*2013*	*2014*	*2015*	*2016*	*2017*	*2018*
IFDI	8801	11,150	18,812	187,016	149,168	168,645	158,994	150,023	196,470	134,524
OFDI	0	1150	3668	22,509	33,373	40,088	35,673	38,662	46,288	49,935
%	0	10.3	19.5	12.0	22.4	23.8	22.4	25.8	23.6	37.1

Source: UNCTAD

(229 billion USD) and India (166 billion USD) are all well ahead of Turkey.[2]

While the inflow of foreign capital (around 11–13 billion USD yearly between 2016 and 2018) still exceeds the outflow of FDI (2.6–3.6 billion yearly in the same period), due to a drastic fall of the exchange rate of the Turkish lira, the ratio of outward to inward FDI stocks has reached 37.1% in 2018.

By looking at the regional composition of OFDI stocks, we can see that more than 80% of the Turkish OFDI went to the EU; the largest target countries were the Netherlands (45.0%), the UK (10.3%), Austria (4.8%), Malta (4.4%) and Germany (4.3%). The special position of the Netherlands is to be explained: many MNEs prefer using a Dutch limited (BV) or joint stock company (NV) as a doorstep for their investments in third countries due to the liberal tax structure in the Netherlands; hence, for Turkish holdings it became common to use Dutch-origin companies to invest abroad. In the case of the UK, the British Virgin Islands was an important destination. Outside the EU, neighbouring countries and regions were the most popular destinations for Turkish capital investments: the Middle East and North Africa (7.6%), the Western Balkans (3.7%), the Caucasian region (1.7%) and Central Asia (1%). Among non-EU countries, the US (4.7%), the United Arab Emirates (2.5%), Algeria (2.3%) and Russia (1.5%) were the most important destinations.[3]

By the sectoral composition of outward capital flows, financial services had the largest share (55%), followed by the oil sector (21%), and only a quarter of it went to manufacturing. An increasing number of OFDI projects are in the areas of mining, energy and infrastructure. This is due to the demand from Turkish manufacturing industries aiming to gain direct access to raw materials (KHU 2014).

Statistical databases sometimes over- or underestimate the amount of OFDI because, for example, of the round-tripping of capital, also common in emerging market MNEs (EMNEs). We can find other relevant sources, however, examining the main characteristics of Turkish investments abroad.

[2] Interestingly, in 1990, the 1150 million USD Turkish OFDI had a similar 0.8% share in the total OFDI of developing countries (based on UNCTAD data).

[3] Based on the 2018 dataset of the Turkish Central Bank (https://evds2.tcmb.gov.tr/index.php?/evds/serieMarket).

In their study, Bakir and Acur collected data on greenfield investments of non-financial TMNEs in the period between 2003 and 2013. Based on their sources, 438 TMNEs invested 46 billion USD in 792 investments during this period, and they created 196,000 work places abroad (Bakir and Acur 2016: 135). The average value of capital investment of these investments was 81 million USD, while the average number of workplaces was 354. Concerning the regional distribution of these investments, 46% (or 21.4 billion USD) happened in transition economies, 29% (or 13.7 billion USD) in developing economies and only 22% (or 10.6 billion USD) in developed economies (Bakir and Acur 2016: 135). It means that 90% of Turkish OFDI (or about 35 billion USD) are greenfield investments, and more than 75% of it is directed towards transition and developing economies.

Yildirim (2017) examined Turkish mergers and acquisitions (M&As) (with Turkish stakes of at least 10%) between 2002 and 2014. Overall, he found 115 such cross-border acquisitions by Turkish firms. Among these 56 were in Western Europe and 32 in Eastern Europe, further 20 on the Balkans and 16 in Central Asia and the Far East. In a country structure, Germany (14), Italy (11) and Russia (8) were at the top, followed by the Netherlands (7) and Romania (6). In the CEE region Bulgaria (3), Hungary (3), Macedonia (3) and Albania (2) had more than one Turkish acquisition. Out of the 115 acquisitions, 64 were in manufacturing and 43 in the service sector, while 5 were in the primary sector. Yildirim also examined the technology level connected to these acquisitions. He found that in manufacturing, 23 out of the 64 acquisitions were high- or medium-high technology, while the remaining 41 were medium-low or low technology. In the case of services, 16 out of 43 were knowledge-intensive.

Over 95% of TMNEs investing abroad are private (mainly family-owned) firms (Bakir and Acur 2016: 135). The number of state enterprises has been reduced to half since the 1990s; their share within the GDP and the number of their employees have been reduced to a fraction. For the time being, enterprises still owned by the state produce less than 1% of the GDP and employ a little more than 100,000 employees, which can be considered negligible in a country with a population of 80 million.

In a research made in the framework of the Emerging Market Global Players project, the Columbia Center on Sustainable Investment analysed the largest Turkish OFDIs (KHU 2014). Until 2012, they found 29 Turkish non-financial MNEs investing more than 100 million USD abroad. The 29 MNEs had 426 subsidiaries, with a clear dominance of neighbouring countries and regions: 326 of them were in Europe and Central Asia, 53 in the Middle East and Africa, 31 in East and South Asia, and 16 in the Americas. By the TMNEs involved, the share of foreign assets was around 12.5% of the total assets and foreign sales were 17.8% of the total sales, while by employment, 23% of the employees worked in the affiliates abroad (overall 115,539 in 2014) (KHU 2014: 10).

There is a huge variance in the transnationality ratio (TNI) of these firms; Tekfen Holding has a 64% average TNI ratio, while that of Türk Telekom and Sabanci Holding was only around 3%. Four companies had an over 50% TNI and further seven an over 40% TNI (the average TNI of the 29 companies is 31%).

7.3 Motivations of TMNEs for Investing Abroad

In this section, we look for the main motivations of TMNEs to invest abroad, with an overview of the recent literature on this topic.

Kayam and Hisamciklilar analysed pre-2007 investments and found that Turkish OFDI is rather market seeking (Kayam and Hisarciklilar 2009). Foreign markets are used as substitutes for the domestic market by TMNEs. Especially firms that produce low quality alternatives to high quality products in host countries have a decreasing OFDI if incomes in host countries increase. Turkish OFDI has become more vulnerable to external developments (KHU 2014).

On the other hand, economic instability also has an impact on Turkish OFDI; that is push factors are effective in determining FDI. The large current account deficit of Turkey (with the depreciation of the currency) deteriorates the OFDI potential; recent domestic political disturbances, however, may give incentive to TMNEs to search for investment opportunities abroad.

Başar and Özkılbaç have found that OFDI has a positive effect on domestic investment, creating a positive impact on unemployment through transfer of profits and employment of the unemployed youths abroad in areas where investments are realised. As a result, growth can be said to be affected positively (Başar and Özkılbaç 2016: 245).

Demirbag and Tatoglu made a research with the use of a different sample, 79 large-size Turkish manufacturing firms operating in EU markets. They found that the TMNEs were principally concerned with growth strategies aiming to extend current product lines with related products through enabling standardisation and technology sharing. Turkish manufacturing firms were also focused on enabling integration. The integration of information within manufacturing and across different business functions indicated a horizontal integration with the rest of the firm (Demirbag and Tatoglu 2008: 741).

Demirbag et al. found that TMNEs entering developed countries, with the asset-seeking motive as a main driver, have a much higher investment size and commitment (springboard), whereas they have a much lower significance in emerging markets (Demirbag et al. 2008: 459). TMNEs may use this strategy to secure preferential treatment offered by emerging country governments and also to bypass trade barriers into developed country markets; for example TMNEs in the textile sector invested in Jordan to get a free access to the US market.

Bakir and Acur investigated the motivations of greenfield investments. Their study found that TMNEs are mainly motivated by market seeking, but efficiency seeking (cost and tax advantages) and resource seeking are also relevant factors. By contrast, in acquisitions strategic asset seeking (global brands, competitive technology, international experiences, distribution networks) seems to be the dominant factor (Bakir and Acur 2016: 129). They have also found that TMNEs mainly exploit firm-specific advantages obtained at home (managerial and market knowledge, expertise, technology, local/regional brands and distribution channels, expertise in operating in relatively weak institutional environment), but country-specific advantages, such as geographic, cultural and institutional proximity or leadership in the home market, are also exploited (Bakir and Acur 2016: 130).

In the case of Turkish acquisitions studied by Yildirim, the dominance of lower technology level suggests that Turkish firms are primarily motivated to access new markets, and they do not have the capacity to buy high technology and knowledge-based firms in advanced countries (Yildirim 2017: 289).

The results of Vardar slightly contradict the findings of Yildirim. Vardar had questioned 38 companies interested in OFDI activities towards EU countries, and in his factor analysis he found eight main factors explaining 70% of total variance (Vardar 2016: 98). The following were the major motivations of Turkish investors (in order of importance): (1) looking for international brand, (2) satisfying niche markets (e.g. the more than five million consumers of Turkish origin in Europe, and even more with a Muslim origin), (3) value chain, for example, having own distribution market, (4) looking for a less risky market, (5) increasing global market shares, (6) having financial and cost advantages, (7) making use of feasible investment opportunities and (8) making use of geographic and psychic proximity. On analysing managers' perceptions, the three major motivations were found to be technology and branding, competitiveness, and better production and financing possibilities, the first being the most important motivation. Instead of fixed assets, intangibles (know-how, patents, trademarks, global brand building activities) were the key priority. Uray et al. (2012) also found that TMNEs' OFDI activities are generally centralised around branding efforts. Many of them are interested in acquiring an international brand for their global presence and then they focus on acquiring technology, innovation and design (Uray et al. 2012: 330).

In the empirical analysis of Turkish OFDI over the 2002–2011 period, Aybar found that absolute size of the market, natural resource endowment and cultural proximity play the most important roles in the decisions of TMNEs' investments, though Turkish OFDI has different motivations for EU and non-EU countries (Aybar 2016: 90).

Another research found that source and host country incomes, distance/transport costs, market size and openness appear to be the main determinants of Turkish FDI abroad (Kayam and Hisarciklilar 2009: 14).

It also indicates that Turkish FDI seems to be mostly market seeking. Foreign markets are used as substitutes for the domestic market by Turkish FDI firms.

A further finding of previous research shows that firms that perceive location selection factors such as "geographical proximity", "the growth rate of economy" and "level of unionisation" to be highly significant prefer the greenfield investment type (Anil Keskin et al. 2012: 277).

Demir and Moiz had a different approach: they were looking for pull factors in the top ten investment destinations for Turkish OFDI. The most important "host country factors" correlating with Turkish OFDI were innovation (Netherlands, Russia), technological readiness (Russia, UK), labour market efficiency (Netherlands), infrastructure (Netherlands) and exports (UK) (Demir and Moiz 2017). Aybar found that market-seeking motive is an important driving factor for Turkish OFDI, but economic and non economic factors such as profit seeking, cultural proximity, bilateral trade agreements and natural resource endowments may also play important roles in the geographical preferences of the TMNEs (Aybar 2016).

Anil et al. found five determinants with high importance relative to location selection for outward Turkish FDI. These are the advantage of being the first mover, level of industry competition, growth rate of economy, market size and low cost inputs, successively (Anıl et al. 2011: 145).

On the other hand OFDI has different motivations for EU and non-EU countries, which is because of the different conditions in the two country groups. Kaya's results suggest that TMNEs seeking favourable business environment and strategic assets prefer to invest in developed countries, while TMNEs that want to exploit the cultural assets of the home country and production efficiency in the host country invest in developing countries. Therefore, motives of the firms to a great extent affect the firms' location choice depending on the host country's development level (Kaya 2014: 383). As Anil et al. (2014) emphasise, a poor domestic institutional environment may be an advantage for TMNEs (and EMNEs in general) when investing in emerging countries with a similar institutional infrastructure. Unlike MNEs from developed countries, EMNEs benefit from inward FDI at home by using different linkages such as joint venturing or original equipment manufacturing with global players that transmit technological and managerial skills (Anil et al. 2014).

Anil et al. emphasise the importance of joint ventures as common initial strategies to mitigate risk and gain access to superior technological and managerial know-how of their foreign partners. Following experiential learning and developing their own R&D in joint ventures, TMNEs prefer full ownership by buying out foreign partners (Demirbag et al. 2008: 459). Also, they prefer to set up greenfield investment or acquire full ownership of indigenous firms in emerging host countries. TMNEs may also use global expansion through higher equity modes as a springboard to secure preferential treatment offered by host country governments and also to bypass trade barriers into developed country markets such as other EU countries (Anil et al. 2014).

As Uray et al. (2012: 330) also underlined, TMNEs first decided to compete internationally through exports, then through license agreements and only finally through OFDI, starting with nearby countries.

In another research based on the largest TMNEs having foreign assets over 100 million USD, the main drivers in the investment decision of these largest investors were new markets and market diversification (75%), followed by sustainability of growth (60%), risk management (50%), accessing natural resources (40%) and reducing costs (40%) (KHU 2014). There are several examples on the different motivations of these large TMNEs. Some firms invested abroad in order to gain access to natural resources, including Şişecam, one of the largest flat-glass producers in Europe, with large production facilities in Bulgaria and Russia; the fertiliser producer Gübretas, with investments in Iran; and Kürüm Holding, which specialises in iron and steel production and invests in Albania. The Turkish conglomerate Yildirim Group bought Mechel Chrome, the chrome division of Russian Mechel, and the TMNE is now the owner of the vertically integrated Voskhod Mining Plant in Kazakhstan and Tikhvin Ferroalloys Plant (TFP) in Russia. With the ownership of Vargön Alloys in Sweden, Yildirim is already the world's largest hard lumpy chrome ore producer. Market seeking is the motivator for some firms. Tosyalı Holding and Kürüm Holding, for instance, with steel operations in the Balkans and North Africa aim to become important steel suppliers in those regions. Turkish manufacturing companies move their production facilities abroad seeking cost minimisation as well as market access. Teklas, an auto parts manufacturer, expanded its production to Bulgaria, Serbia, Russia and China; soap and cosmetic industry giant Evyap has production facilities in Malaysia and Egypt; and Eroglu Holding, one of the biggest denim producers of Turkey, has a factory in Egypt and owns shop networks for brand marketing in Russia, Ukraine, Belarus, Romania and Germany. In the last decade, some of the most aggressive/innovative TMNEs focusing on OFDI were Yıldız Holding, Yildirim Group, Eczacibaşi, Arçelik and Anadolu Group.

7.3.1 TMNE Case studies

Yıldız Holding has over 300 brands available in more than 130 countries. With a focus on biscuits, cakes and confectionery, the company has become number two in the world in the sweet biscuits category and number seven in the chocolate category by revenue. The company employs 56,000 people and has 83 factories (24 of which are outside Turkey). It acquired the Belgian Godiva Chocolatier for 850 million USD, after which Godiva entered new markets in China, the Middle East and North Africa region and Central Asia. As Bakir and Acur (2016: 142) point out, a mature MNE may learn from an EMNE, for example, how to operate in a weak institutional environment. As a result of the acquisition, the firm-specific advantages of the parent company (Yıldız) helped the subsidiary (Godiva) to operate in new markets. At the same time, Yıldız acquired unique resources and dynamic capabilities from Godiva (global brand, managerial and marketing skills, knowledge and experience).

Yıldız is one of the most active TMNEs in the strategy to create global brands and to become a global player. The company entered the cereal market with Kellogg's, creating Ulker Kellogg's in 2005. In 2009, it combined operations with Danish gum technologist Gumlink. In 2014, Yıldız Holding purchased DeMet's Candy Company in the US. In the same year, its acquisition of British United Biscuits for 2 billion GBP (3.2 billion USD) was the largest foreign acquisition of a TMNE, and Yıldız become the world's third-biggest biscuit maker (Bakir and Acur 2016: 142).

Yildirim, a Turkish family-owned company, started its international acquisitions only in 2008 (with the earlier-mentioned Swedish company, Vardör). Since then, however, it has showed an astonishing appetite. Besides becoming one of the world's leading chrome producers by Russian and Kazakh acquisitions, in 2010, it bought a 24% share in French CMA CGM, one of the world's leading shipping groups, for 500 million USD. It established Yilport, a subsidiary company that continues the TMNE's global expansion by buying ports. After acquiring the Malta Freeport (2011), the Port of Oslo (2014) and the Gavle Container Terminal in Sweden (2014), with its latest acquisition it bought a Portuguese port management company, TERTIR, for a total of 335 million EUR. Yilport currently operates 26 maritime terminals worldwide. Yildirim now plans to sell its share in CMA CGM to finance the acquisition of Ports America and thus become one of the ten biggest container terminal operators by 2025.

Eczacıbaşı's core sectors are building products, pharmaceuticals and consumer products. Additionally, the group is active in finance, information technology, welding technology and real estate. Globally, Eczacıbaşı has established itself among the world's top providers of bathroom and tiling solutions for homes and commercial venues with its VitrA and with its global brands based on three prestigious German companies, Burgbad, Villeroy & Boch, and Engers, acquired between 2005 and 2007. International partnership is a central component of the Eczacıbaşı Group's growth strategy. Eczacıbaşı has four international joint ventures and numerous cooperation agreements with international companies.

Arçelik A.Ş. is Europe's fourth largest home appliances maker. It is active in more than 100 countries including China and the US through its 13 international subsidiaries and over 4500 branches in Turkey. The company operates 15 production plants in Turkey, Romania, Russia, China, South Africa and Thailand including refrigerator, washing machine, dishwasher, cooking appliances and components plants. It offers products under its own 12 brand names, namely Arçelik, Beko, Grundig, Dawlance, Altus, Blomberg, Arctic, Defy, Leisure, Arstil, Elektra Bregenz and Flavel. Arçelik merged with the German consumer electronics manufacturer Grundig in 2009, while South African Defy Appliances was acquired for 327 million USD in 2011.

Anadolu Group (AG) has focused its activities in the areas of beverages, automotive and retail. Together with brands which are respected on a global scale, it is also extending its fields of business with the investments it has undertaken in the sectors of agriculture, real estate, energy and health in recent years. The group continues its activities in 19 countries—including Turkey—with approximately 80 companies, 61 production facilities and more than 50,000 employees. As a part of AG, Anadolu Beverage Group, consisting of Anadolu Efes and Coca-Cola İçecek, is operating beer and soft drinks in a wide geography of 14 countries across Eurasia with its 20.000 employees. The Group's activities include production, bottling, distribution and sales of both alcoholic and non-alcoholic beverages. In the alcoholic beverages market, Anadolu Efes currently continues its operations as a global company, which exports three quarters of its production. In terms of sales volume, it is the 6th largest brewer in Europe and the 11th largest in the world. Exporting products to over 70 countries, Anadolu Efes is one of the key players in the region with a total of 15 breweries, 6 malt production facilities and 1 hops processing facility across Turkey, Kazakhstan, Russia, Moldova, Georgia and Ukraine, and offers more than 40 local and foreign beer brands to its consumers. In the non-alcoholic beverages market, Coca-Cola İçecek (CCI), the fifth largest bottler of the Coca-Cola Company in terms of sales volume, operates with 25 plants in a geography of 10 countries (Turkey, Pakistan, Kazakhstan, Azerbaijan, Kyrgyzstan, Turkmenistan, Tajikistan, Iraq, Jordan and Syria). CCI offers more than 25 local and foreign brands of the Coca-Cola Company to its consumers.

7.3.2 *Political Incentives: New Foreign Policy Doctrine and EU Relations*

In its modern history Turkey had quite limited relations with its direct neighbourhood. With its strong Western orientation, being a member of NATO, it had limited will and also possibility to create deeper cooperation with neighbouring countries. Eastern Europe had belonged to the Soviet Bloc. For long decades the attitude of Turkey towards the Balkans was quite passive and the relations were aggravated by both historical and ideological controversies (Tolay and Linden 2012). With the end of the Cold War, Turkey had to rethink its foreign policy doctrine.

Davutoğlu, who had become the main foreign policy ideologist of the AKP, set forth his ideas about Turkey's future in his work *Strategic Depth*. The most distinct characteristic of the new foreign policy was not a break with former Western allies but the attempts to normalise and intensify relations with the neighbouring countries (Davutoğlu 2010). The concept of "zero problems" was introduced as a basic principle: Ankara sought to normalise its relations with even those countries it had tended to confront previously (e.g. Armenia, Greece).

Kirişci (2009) claims that the AKP's zero-problem policy is attributable to the growing emphasis on economic interests. When discussing the foreign policy options of other countries, even Davutoğlu remarks that a prerequisite of a successful export-oriented model of external economy is that the representation of economic interests be a part of foreign policy. Under the "zero problem to neighbours policy" Turkey has tried to improve its relations with all neighbours and also to promote Turkish business activity abroad.

The new foreign policy doctrine defined Turkey as a regional power, a natural heir of the Ottoman Empire that has neglected its historic backyard, the neighbouring regions, for too long. The new type of Turkish foreign policy activism is sometimes accused of being a kind of "neo-ottomanism". Although the official Turkish standpoint refuses it because of its negative connotations, it is obvious that the core areas of Turkish activism are in the neighbouring regions once part of the Ottoman Empire: the Balkans, the Middle East and the Caucasian region.

After the 2008 crisis, the EU's economic difficulties and declining demand urged Turkey to diversify its trade relations and to search for new markets, be it in Africa, the Middle East, the post-Soviet region or Asia. Although opening up to the East and to the South brings opportunities involving long-forgotten neighbouring regions or remote markets of Asia and Africa, for the time being they only constitute ancillary benefits rather than a real alternative for EU relations. Regarding the opportunities outside Europe, some of the rhetoric is exaggerated and does not reflect economic rationale. Retaining close European economic ties remains a top priority for Turkey, partly because Turkey has already been embedded in the production value chains of the European multinational companies, which contribute three quarters of FDI, but also because the advantages of the customs union and cooperation in research, development and innovation are crucial for the state.

On the other hand, Turkey's geopolitical weight and role is also growing. It is a hub in the energy sector, especially with regard to the gas supply of Europe, and "the epitome of the Muslim state", whose economic success and democratic structures may serve as a positive example for other countries in the region. This makes Turkey strategically important for the EU.

7.4 Eastern Europe and the Turkish OFDI

As was already mentioned, Europe and the EU have a special position in the Turkish OFDI. One-third of the Turkish OFDI is directed towards the Netherlands to take advantage of the specific Dutch regulations and tax regime, but Ireland and Malta are also popular for similar reasons, while the UK (Jersey) and Luxembourg have a prominent role in the case of Turkish financial investments. If we consider non-financial OFDI, however, then Germany and Austria are the main target countries, along with Switzerland and the Netherlands, which also shows some correlation with the share of Turkish population in Western European countries.

If we consider Eastern European countries, the main target countries of Turkish investors among these transition countries are Russia, Azerbaijan, Romania, Bulgaria and recently the countries of the Western Balkans. Though the Visegrad countries are not among the top investment countries for Turkish investment, the region has also had some experience with Turkish investments worth analysing.

The economic transformation of Eastern Europe in the transition period has created new business opportunities for Turkish firms, while the close geographic and cultural proximity to Turkey further spurred this process (Yildirim 2017: 280). The share of Eastern Europe in total Turkish OFDI went up from 20% in 2001 to 35% in 2007, but it has been decreased

Table 7.2 Turkish FDI in Eastern Europe (million USD, stock)

Country	*2001*	*2007*	*2017*
Post-Soviet Eastern Europe	**776**	**2636**	**1133**
Russia	166	180	233
Ukraine	7	39	94
Azerbaijan	569	2364	400
Georgia	34	53	314
Central and Eastern Europe	**46**	**164**	**58**
Czech Republic	0	84	0
Hungary	43	70	25
Poland	3	8	31
Slovakia	0	2	2
Slovenia	–	–	–
South-Eastern Europe	**112**	**313**	**2419**
Albania	0	53	610
Bosnia	0	44	226
Bulgaria	30	54	697
Croatia	0	0	166
Kosovo	0	0	201
North Macedonia	0	0	147
Montenegro	0	0	24
Romania	82	162	203
Serbia	0	0	145
Total Eastern Europe	**934**	**3113**	**3610**
Total World	**4581**	**8806**	**37,989**

Source: Turkish Central Bank

to under 10% by 2017 (Table 7.2). While in the first period Azerbaijan was the top target of Turkish FDI in the region, by 2017 the Balkan countries took over its place. Indirect investments make it harder to detect the final destination of investments: many Turkish investments in Eastern Europe (especially in EU member countries) happen through companies registered in other countries.[4]

[4] The Dutch investment protection and tax policies make the Netherlands an attractive trans-shipping point of foreign investments. On the "Dutch Sandwich" and the reliability of FDI data see more in: Antalóczy & Sass (2015: 41–43). The Hungarian National Bank has data revealing the ultimate controlling parent of FDI. It shows that Turkish investments in Hungary are more than double the UNCTAD figure, 55 million USD instead of 25 million USD, a large part of them coming through Dutch companies. And based on single investment reports of companies, even these data seem to be underestimated.

Though the overall amount of investment is lower, more firms have invested in Eastern Europe than in Western Europe. It means that in general smaller size, risk-taking TMNEs invested in Eastern Europe, while capital-intensive TMNEs with market knowledge and experience invested more in Western Europe (Culpan and Akcaoglu 2018). The TMNEs investing in Eastern Europe were more adaptable to local conditions; they were not deterred by legal uncertainties and bureaucratic difficulties around obtaining licences and permits, because they have experiences with similar problems at home (Culpan and Akcaoglu 2018). It can be observed that these firms use their firm-strategic advantages, coming from the know-how gained in their operation in Turkey and its neighbouring regions, but country-specific factors such as geographical and cultural proximity and an access to cheap and skilled labour are also among their core advantages.

Before focusing on the example of the five CEE countries, let us take a look at the Turkish investment in the East and South-East European region. Russia, as one of the fastest growing markets in the world, became popular for foreign investors, but the specificities of the Russian market (e.g. weak institutional environment) required specific approach from investors. Turkish investors seemed to be successful to cope with these obstacles. During 2003 and 2013, TMNEs made 105 investments (13% of their total worldwide greenfield investments) in Russia and invested about 10 billion USD and created jobs for over 55,000 people (Bakir and Acur 2017: 215). In recent years, Ukraine and Belarus, two very similar, relatively big and underinvested, regions in the Post-Soviet Eastern Europe (PSEE) region have also become popular for Turkish investors. In these countries real estate development is the top sector of Turkish activity, but investments in the financial sector and in manufacturing are also among the top targets.

In the Caucasus region, Azerbaijan has been the top investment target for Turkish companies since the 1990s. In 2000, more than 1300 Turkish firms were operating in Azerbaijan. Until the end of 1990s, Turkish businesspeople had no rivals in the chaotic, but unexploited, Azerbaijani market: Turkish experiences with market economy, ability to do business in corrupt environment and cultural proximity were strong assets (Bedirhanoglu 2016). They acted as intermediaries between Azeri and Western companies. Azerbaijan offered high profits, secure payment and, due to CIS, free access to other post-Soviet countries. The peak period of high profits was between 2005 and 2007, but even today the prospects of

Azeri markets are good in a regional comparison. But there are risks as well, partly due to political pressure: Koc Holding sold its supermarket chain Ramstore to local Azersun and left the market; a factory of DHT Metal was appropriated, and some leading businessmen were arrested (Bedirhanoglu 2016).

South-Eastern Europe (the Balkans) has an even larger importance for Turkish investors nowadays: many companies invest in the region as a first step towards becoming regional players (Djurica 2015: 46). They mainly invest in infrastructure (communication, finance, retail trade, tourism, road construction), but manufacturing has a growing importance as well. All things considered, however, Turkey is a latecomer to the region. The EU firms seized control in crucial sectors (like German Deutsche Telekom in the telecom sector or Greek OTE in the banking sector). Greece keeps on playing a key economic role in the region, even though it has been particularly hit by the financial crisis. Turkey has lagged at targeting strategic sectors, being undercut also by Russian plans, for example, in the energy industry.

There are several characteristics of the Turkish investment strategy in the South Eastern Europe (SEE) region, some of which are applicable for other neighbouring regions. Financial investments have a crucial importance; the entry of Turkish banks into a country used to pave the way for further economic ties by offering valuable country-related knowledge to Turkish investors.

Brownfield investments are a popular form for Turkish investors to enter these economies. Compared to greenfield investments, in this form there are less administrative barriers (permits needed for construction, registering property). Furthermore, acquiring active facilities allows investors to take over the existing workforce, significantly reducing the time until operations can start (Djurica 2015: 47). However, as investment climate reforms speed up, and the EU accession talks of Western Balkan countries progress, greenfield investments may increase.

In the small market economies of the Balkans, the culture of doing business is similar to that in Turkey. Investing in these countries appears to be a low cost, low risk and high reward enterprise, so in many respects it is ideal for Turkish companies as a first location for going abroad, to streamline their internationalisation process in management and production practices and to step further in more competitive EU-28 markets (Djurica 2015: 50). A further advantage of SEE countries for investors is that multiple daily flights operated by Turkish Airlines to all capitals in the region facilitate integration. In many Balkan countries, Turkish universities offer important opportunities to find Turkish-speaking high quality human capital (Djurica 2015: 45).

Two SEE countries, Romania and Bulgaria, joined the EU in 2007, thus offering special opportunities for investment. Though Romania ranks only 11th in terms of total stock of Turkish OFDI, it is the 3rd regarding the number of investors, which means that the majority of Turkish investors are rather small and medium size. Turkish investors entered Romania with the purpose of either exploiting their firm-specific resources and capabilities or acquiring and exploring new resources and capabilities which provide them with required competitive advantages (Anil et al. 2014: 441). Their role in the Bulgarian economy—both in production and in employment—has grown significantly. In addition to two Turkish capital-based banks, there are close to 1500 small-medium and large Turkish firms operating in Bulgaria: 36 large projects were completed or are underway by Turkish construction companies amounting up to 1.5 billion USD (Daily News 2018).

Egresi and Kara (2015) found in their study on Turkish OFDI towards the Balkans a higher intensity with those countries that have stronger cultural ties with Turkey: countries with a Muslim majority such as Kosovo, Albania, Bosnia and Herzegovina or a significant minority such as Macedonia and Bulgaria. Beside cultural and historical elements, however, political factors played an equally important role in the new priorities of Turkish foreign policy.

There is a shift of Turkish interest in the Balkans towards economically more prosperous businesses. As a Bosnian politician said: "Turkey gives Bosnia love, and Serbia investments" (Colborne and Edwards 2018). Turkish companies are aiming to get closer to the European market through Serbia's capital, Belgrade. İrfan Özhamaratlı, vice chairman of the Istanbul Chamber of Industry (ICI), said Turkish companies have invested in Serbia to be close to the European market, noting that he sees the presence of Turkish companies in Serbia as a breakthrough with the intent of strengthening (Daily Sabah 2018). "Turkish companies do not intend to stay there. Investments are being made to increase additional capacity," he said. "Being in Serbia means moving fast and conducting flexible and low-capacity production. The terms are also suitable for investing there." For companies that want to reduce their logistics costs and time, and increase their capacity, Serbia's favourable incentive system, high training power and lower minimum wage increase the attractiveness

(Daily Sabah 2018). Currently there are Turkish direct investments totalling around 145 million USD in Serbia, mainly in the textile and food sectors, in retail trade and in entertainment. Serbia welcomes Turkish investors, because unlike Western investors, they go to underdeveloped areas (Sekularac 2018).

7.4.1 TMNEs in the CEE Region

According to official statistics of the Turkish Central Bank, the Turkish OFDI in the CEE countries is not too relevant: in 2017, Poland had 31 million USD of Turkish investment, Hungary had 25 million USD, Slovakia 2 million USD and the Czech Republic and Slovenia have less than 1 million USD of Turkish investment. On making a deeper investigation based on other relevant sources, we can see, however, that a higher amount of Turkish capital and more TMNEs are present in the region.

Based on the Amadeus database, 316 Turkish firms have invested in the 5 CEE countries. Out of these firms, 141 were in the Czech Republic, 119 in Slovakia, 35 in Poland, 13 in Slovenia and only 8 in Hungary. By taking a look at the size of the companies listed in the Amadeus database, we can see that while in Poland, Hungary and Slovenia only larger size firms are on the list, in the Czech Republic and Slovakia there are mostly micro-firms listed, lot of them without any reported activity. In the following part we take an in-depth look at the largest Turkish-owned companies in each of the CEE countries.

7.4.1.1 Poland

According to PAIH, the Polish Investment Promotion Authority, the total worth of Turkish investments in Poland amounts to 112.3 million USD (Table 7.3). Nearly 1300 workplaces were created, mostly in textile, automobile and R&D sectors, as a result of these investments (Polandin 2019).

Data from 2017, if otherwise not indicated.

In Poland the largest Turkish investor is Arçelik, a firm belonging to Koc Holding. Arçelik is the fourth largest home appliance company in Europe. Its affiliate in Poland, Beko Poland, aims at helping the brand marketing and sales of products in the region. With an over 200 million USD turnover, and almost 100 million USD of assets, Beko Poland is the largest Turkish-owned firm in the whole CEE region. The production facilities of Arçelik are in lower wage countries of the region, however:

Table 7.3 Largest Turkish-owned firms in Poland, 2017

Company	*Sectors*	*HQ*	*Owner*	*Turnover (m)*	*Assets (m)*	*Net income*	*Employees*
Beko Poland	Wholesale of electrical household appliances	Warsaw	Koc	214	97	6.7	115
Coral Travel Poland	Other reservation services	Warsaw	OTI Holding	98	27.4	1.1	n.a.
Tema retail	Retail sale of clothing in specialised stores	Warsaw	LC Waikiki	54 (2016)	5.6 (2016)	0.4 (2016)	5 (2012)
Vestel Poland	Wholesale of electrical household appliances	Warsaw	Zorlu Holding	50 (2016)	26.6 (2016)	0.3 (2016)	n.a.
Konveyör Polska	Manufacture of electric domestic appliances	Kalisz	Konveyör AS	14	9.5	1.1	216

Source: Amadeus database

they have a refrigerator and washing machine plant in Kirzhach, Russia, and a refrigerating appliances plant in Gaesti, Romania.

Coral travel is among the leading tour operators in Eastern Europe; it orginises flights form Russia, Poland, Ukraine, Belarus, Turkey and Georgia to over 65 destinations in 38 countries. Coral Travel started its regional activities in Moscow and took its place among the most reliable brands in the Russian, Ukrainian and Belorussian markets via its sector experience and service concept of good quality. It performs its activities in eight cities of Poland and its central office is in Warsaw. The owner of Coral Travel, Turkish OTI Holding, is serving in various sectors of tourism business and includes numerous internationally acknowledged brands of the tourism sector.

The Istanbul-based Tema Group was founded at the end of the 1980s. In 1997, it took French LC Waikiki brand under its umbrella. Today Tema is a market leader in Turkey, while LC Waikiki Retail Company is a leading fashion retail company with a turnover of 3 billion USD in around 910 stores in 44 countries

In addition to its retail operations, the Tema Group also manufactures textiles, predominantly in the Middle East/Egypt and India/Bangladesh. The group operates more than 400 own stores, mainly in Turkey, but also in other countries such as Bulgaria (5 stores), Romania (6), Kazakhstan (2), Albania (2), Bosnia (1), Syria (1), Russia (5) and Iraq (2). Its expansion into Western Europe was initially focused on Germany, but it has also started to open stores in Poland and Hungary.

Founded in 1984, Vestel is a Turkish domestic and business appliance manufacturing company that consists of 18 companies specialising in electronics, major appliances and information technology. It controls around 20% of the European market for flat screen TVs and is one of the leading enterprises in Turkey. Vestel has also managed to become one of the ten biggest household appliance manufacturers in Europe. It exports television sets, washing machines, refrigerators and LED lights to all over the world under various European and Japanese brands (Goodmans, Digihome, Hitachi and Grundig). The company is constantly expanding in terms of capacity, export activities and market share. In addition to its sites in Turkey, it also has many locations worldwide. In Poland, its factory is situated near Wroclaw, where 330 workers produce LCD televisions. The assembly plant was bought in 2016 from Taiwanese Compal Electronics. The production here is based on a brand licensing agreement with Toshiba. Vestel is responsible for the production, sales, marketing and supply chain functions in the European market for Toshiba-branded TVs while working closely with Toshiba research, development and quality assurance resources. Vestel Poland was established in 2014 for the purpose of marketing Vestel products throughout Poland, while another affiliate, Vestel Polska Technology, is responsible for the manufacturing.

Another Turkish home appliance manufacturer in Poland is Konveyör. The Turkish firm was founded in 1979 to produce conveyor systems. Though the conveyor business was finally ended in 1992 and the firm became an entirely white goods supplier, the name "Konveyör" remained. After reaching a certain maturity, it started to look for investment opportunities abroad and first started checking out Bulgaria and Romania (Beysad 2018). In 2018, it acquired an active factory in Kalisz, Poland, from Bundy Refrigeration. The operation, named Konveyör Polska after the acquisition, has 10,000 square metres of covered area and over 200 employees.

A further Turkish manufacturing FDI in Poland was Polimer Kaucuk's rubber and plastic article plant in Krakow. The originally Turkish-owned firm started its activity in Poland in 2010, but in 2012 the US-based power management company Eaton Corporation had acquired the Turkish parent company; its Polish plant Niff Rubber has continued its activity as part of Polimer Kaucuk.

Turkish construction companies are also well presented in the flourishing Polish real estate market. Turkish Mesa Mesken (Euro Power Centrum) and Yenigün Construction (Yenigün Polska) are active in the Warsaw construction and real estate market, while Gülermak, another Turkish construction firm, took part in the metro building project in Warsaw.

7.4.1.2 Hungary

The Turkish prime minister Binali Yıldırım, in his speech at the Turkey-Hungary Business Forum in Ankara, put the number of Turkish investors in Hungary at over 500, having more than 100 million USD in investments in Hungary (Daily Sabah 2017) (Table 7.4).

Şişecam, one of Europe's leading flat-glass companies (with 44 plants, 18 in Turkey and 26 abroad, e.g. in Bulgaria and Russia) acquired 100% of the German Richard Fritz Gmbh in 2013, in order to further expand its position as a key supplier to the auto glass industry. Richard Fritz is a supplier to all major automobile producers; it has over 1200 employees and has subsidiaries both in Hungary and in Slovakia. The Hungarian firm has around 300 employees, with annual revenues of over 50 million USD.

Türk Telekom, a major Turkish telecommunication company,[5] bought 100% of data service provider Invitel International for 243 million USD in 2010, to increase the firm's competitiveness by entering new markets. The TMNE gained control of a 27,000-kilometre fibre-optic network, a network of operations in 16 countries, and Invitel International subsidiaries AT-Invitel (Germany), Invitel International Hungary and EuroWeb Romania.

[5] OTAS, a unit of the Dubai-based Oger Telecom, had taken out a 4.75 billion USD loan in 2013 to acquire a 55% stake in Türk Telekom. But it failed to keep up payments on what at the time was Turkey's largest corporate loan. In 2018, as part of debt restructuring, Levent, a special purpose vehicle (SPV), now holds a 55% stake in Türk Telekom (25% belongs to the Turkish State Treasury). Levent is controlled by Akbank (35.56%), Garanti Bank (22.13%), and Iş Bank (11.60%). Currently the main goal is to transfer the Türk Telekom shares to a "competent" investor.

Table 7.4 Largest Turkish-owned firms in Hungary, 2017

Company	*Sectors*	*HQ*	*Owner*	*Turnover (m)*	*Assets (m)*	*Net income*	*Employees*
Richard Fritz Kft	Manufacturer of vehicle parts	Aszód	Iş Bank	53.7	21.4	-0.6	298
Türk Telekom	Wired telecommunication	Budaörs	Levent	37	75	0.2	78
Çelebi	Service for air transport	Budapest	Çelebi	31	22.6	4.7	629
New MGM	Manufacturing of bearings, gears	Diósd	Bera Holding	3.9	6.5	0	34
Diet Tobacco	Manufacture of tobacco products	Sátoraljaújhely	Birgul Sandal	0.1	0.1	0	n.a.

Source: Amadeus database

Among the largest Turkish investors we can find Çelebi Ground Handling. The firm was established in Hungary in 2005; it has an own capital of over 3 million USD, annual revenues of over 30 million USD and over 600 employees. Besides the Budapest International Airport, Çelebi offers ground-handling services in Mumbai and Delhi (India) and in Vienna (Austria), and it provides cargo management in Frankfurt (Germany) as well.

Another Turkish company coming under Turkish ownership, partly indirectly, is MGM (Magyar Gördülőcspágy Művek). In 2007, the Romanian firm Rulmenti Barlad (49%) and Turkish legal personalities bought MGM from South Korean Hanwha for 3.5 million USD. Rulmenti Barlad was one of the most successful Romanian companies, acquired by the Turkish Kombassan (or today Bera Holding) in 2000, so this is a partly Romanian FDI in Hungary with Turkish owners in the background.

Diet Tobacco Europe Kft (DTE) was established by Sangroup in partnership with Continental Tobacco Corporation in 2017. Diet Tobacco has installed new DIET (dry iced expanded tobacco) production lines in Sátoraljaújhely, situated in one of the most underdeveloped regions of Hungary. Tobacco retail trade was strongly regulated in Hungary recently, and the Fidesz-friendly Hungarian Continental Group was awarded a lot of concessions, which makes the collaboration with Continental in production useful for Diet Tobacco.

There are several other larger Turkish investments in Hungary worth mentioning. Ekol is an integrated logistics company founded in 1990, providing international freight, warehousing, domestic distribution, foreign trade, customs and supply chain management services in 15 countries. It is one of Europe's major logistics providers, active in Poland, Hungary, the Czech Republic, Slovakia and Slovenia. In Hungary, Ekol Logistics launched its operation in 2013, and currently it employs 360 people. The headquarters is in Budapest, but it has a presence in three other locations nationwide, along the main corridors connecting the west, south-west and south-east of Europe. Most of Ekol's customers come from the automotive, hi-tech, fashion, retail, industry, FMCG and healthcare sectors. The company has the know-how of the fashion sector as 16% of the global turnover comes from this industry (EFT 2018). Fashion is more and more demanding for logistic solutions as changes of collections are more frequent nowadays.

Another Turkish firm present in the logistics sector in Hungary is Barsan. Founded in 1982, Barsan is today a global brand that gives integrated logistics service with 81 logistics centres in 39 countries. In 2009, Barsan Global Logistics bought a 50% stake in Transemex, which became a part of the global transportation and logistical network of the TMNE. Transemex was founded in Hungary by a Turkish-born Hungarian businessman Sismanoglu Melih. Transemex Hungary has 140 employees and annual revenues of over 15 million USD.

Polat Group became an active participant of the Hungarian economy not only because of EGE Seramik, one of the largest producers of high-quality ceramic tiles but also due to its good ties to the Hungarian political elite and its real estate businesses. But here as well, the real estate business of Polat Group and its leader Adnan Polat are represented in Hungary indirectly, by a Dutch firm, ALX, owned by Polat. Polat also started to build a network (Polat-HWSE) in the solar energy industry.

Metyx Composites is a rapidly growing division of Telateks,[6] a manufacturer of high-performance technical textiles Metyx. In 2013, it acquired NABI's (North American Bus Industries) former production facilities in Kaposvár and launched a 17,000-square metre manufacturing centre, employing almost 200 people.

Ravaber Building Material Industry was created when Belgian Ravago and the Turkish Besler Tekstil joined forces in 2013, leaving Ravago Group and Besler Tekstil with 50% share each. Worth 20 million EUR, this investment will create 90 direct jobs in Alsózsolca, but this number will be higher considering the indirect implications of the extraction of the basic material in Hungary. The investment will produce rock-wool with an annual capacity of 36,000 tons in Hungary. For the production of the insulation material, Ravaber is going to use a high volume of basalt, diabase and coke partly to be purchased from a Hungarian source, the Egerbakta mine.

7.4.1.3 Slovakia

In Slovakia, Enpay Transformer is the largest Turkish-owned company (Table 7.5). Enpay started to produce transformer components in 1989 and in the new millennium it started to make its presence felt in international markets, exporting to Germany and later other European countries.

[6] Telateks A.S. was founded in 1940 by Emin Ustunel, a pioneer in the manufacture of haircloth interlining. Telateks has evolved into an internationally recognised textile company. Metyx Composite products are currently provided from its four factories in Turkey, Hungary and the US.

Table 7.5 Largest Turkish-owned firms in Slovakia, 2017

Company	*Sectors*	*HQ*	*Owner*	*Turnover (m)*	*Assets (m)*	*Net income*	*Employees*
Enpay Transformer	Manufacture of electric motors	Krskany	Murat Yurekten	31.5	25.8	0	275
ATO Trans	Freight transport by road	Nove Zamky	Serafettin Aras	20	11	0.3	125
Beko Slovakia	Wholesale of electrical household appliances	Bratislava	Koc	15	7	0.1	1
UTS	Business and management consultancy	Samorin	Zorlu Holding	4	1	1	38
Türk Telekom	Wired telecom-munication	Bratislava	Levent	2	5	0	3

Source: Amadeus database

Enpay has achieved a respectable place in the electricity industry. Responding to customer demands on a wide scale with its facilities it commenced production in Slovakia (2005), in India (2007) and in Bulgaria (2010). Today, it has become a global manufacturer with its products marketed to over 50 countries.

The road freight transport company ATO Trans was established in 2007. Currently it has over 200 vehicles, and it focuses its activity in Eastern Europe and the Middle East (Iraq, Iran). The two Turkish giants, Beko (Arçelik) and Türk Telekom, are also present in Slovakia, but their size and presence in Slovakia is much lower compared to both Poland and Hungary.

The last firm among the top five Turkish investors, UTS, is owned by Zorlu, the owner of Vestel. The company itself is an Abu Dhabi-based firm, providing business and management consulting activities. Its Slovakian headquarters in Samorin was established in 2016. With around three dozen employees it deals mostly with the management of returned electronics.

7.4.1.4 *Czech Republic*

In the Czech Republic, Cross Jeans is the largest Turkish-owned subsidiary (Table 7.6). The parent, Cross Textile, has more than 3200 points of sales, 30 monobrand stores and strong wholesale/online partners such as Zalando, Otto and Amazon. Its European headquarters are in Berlin and Warsaw; its Prague branch with the headquarters in Brno (and not in Prague) has an important role in the value chain as a distribution centre. Cross Jeans owns a producer backing as well: its own factories and production facilities in Turkey and Egypt ensure Cross Jeans a solid position on the market.

Palmerino Colamarino, the owner of Viva Casino, is the Italian husband of Sudi Özkan's daughter, Venus. Sudi Özkan, the owner of Princess Hotels and Casinos, is known as the "Casino King" in Turkey. In the early 2000s, due to debates with the authorities, 18 casinos were transferred to Switzerland by Özkan's daughter. Similar to Türk Telekom, Ekol Logistics is present in most countries of the region. Ekol opened its Prague branch in 2016, followed by one in Ostrava the next year. It offers intermodal transport services, operating trains connecting Trieste with Ostrava. In the Czech Republic it had 15 employees and a three million USD turnover in 2017.

7.4.1.5 *Slovenia*

In Slovenia, Ayen Energy is the most important Turkish investor (Table 7.7). It carries out trade activities in Central and South-Eastern Europe (in ten countries: Slovenia, Austria, Hungary, Croatia, Serbia, Montenegro, Albania, Greece, Kosovo and Turkey). In accordance with the different regulations of the European countries, these companies operating in Central and South-Eastern Europe perform short- to medium-term electricity trading in regulated markets on one hand and build partnerships through bilateral agreements for the purpose of electricity trading on the other.

Wood-processing company Lesna TIP had been struggling with liquidity for years, ending 2010 with a loss of 3.9 million EUR. Its first Turkish owner Dortek (subsidiary of Miador) acquired a majority stake back in 2011. Despite the efforts to get out of the red, Lesna TIP, at the time the only producer of particle boards in Slovenia, entered a debt-restructuring process in 2013 and went into receivership in March 2016 (Slovenia Times 2018). In 2018, another Turkish firm, Yildiz Entegre Adria, had become

Table 7.6 Largest Turkish-owned firms in the Czech Republic, 2017

Company	*Sectors*	*HQ*	*Owner*	*Turnover (m)*	*Assets (m)*	*Net income*	*Employees*
Cross Jeans	Wholesale of clothing and footwear	Brno	Furkan Kolunsag	9	18	0	5
Türk Telekom	Wired telecommunication	Prague	Levent	4.2	12	0	7
Viva Casino	Gambling and betting activities	Prague	Palmerino Colamarino	3.6	11.7	1	59
Ekol Logistics	Collection of non-hazardous waste	Prague	Ekol Lojistic	3.1	n.a.	n.a.	15
Verdadero	Other retail sale	Prague	Ali Erdem	2.7	2.5	n.a.	n.a.

Source: Amadeus database

Table 7.7 Largest Turkish-owned firms in Slovenia, 2017

Company	*Sectors*	*HQ*	*Owner*	*Turnover (m)*	*Assets (m)*	*Net income*	*Employees*
Ayen Energija	Trade of electricity	Ljubljana	Aydiner Insaat	58	3.5	0.5	1
Lesna Tip	Manufacture of veneer sheets	Sentjanz	Miador Orman/ Yildiz Entegre	14 (2015)	10	1	88
Tumay Europa	Wholesale of food	Koper	Tumay Balikcilik	6.5	1.1	0	n.a.
Cetin Gostinsvo	Maintenance of motor vehicles	Ajdovcina	Hasan Cetin	5	1.7	0	8
EFE Logistika	Sale of other motor vehicles	Ljubljana	Kamil Uluer	1.7	1.4	0	3

Source: Amadeus database

the owner of Lesna TIP after paying 7.5 million EUR for its bankruptcy estate. If production is successfully launched, around 500 new jobs will be created in the following years.

7.5 Pull Factors of CEE for TMNEs

In this part we analyse the major factors that attract Turkish firms to the CEE region. For many companies, the gain from international corporation status itself was an important factor in investing abroad. Many export-oriented SMEs or large firms wanted to strengthen their value chains and facilitate regional integration with their investments abroad. Though for most Turkish firms the Balkans used to be the first step abroad, for those trying to open up for European markets the CEE countries may also offer a good option (see, e.g., the motivations of Konveyör; see Beysad 2018). When firms achieve well-established positions at home (Arçelik) they become more outward oriented, seeking new markets abroad (Ayden et al. 2018: 192).

After 2004, the attractiveness of the new EU-member CEE countries increased. Free trade between the CEE countries and the EU existed since the early 1990s, but the full-fledged membership offered a different quality of trade integration. Though Turkey as part of the EU customs union was exempt from EU customs for a wide range of (industrial) products, the CEE countries as part of the single market became even more attractive. We can see it in cases such as Vestel, which opted for the CEE region as a production location for TV sets partly due to custom reasons (Glowik 2009: 107).

Another EU membership-related advantage of the region was generated by increased EU financial support to infrastructural investments. Especially compared to CIS and SEE regions, the improving infrastructural set-up in the CEE region created a much better business environment. Additionally, Turkish construction companies also took part in the partly EU-financed investments, for example, Gülermak in constructing Warsaw Metro line and motorways in Poland. The increased investment and consumption activity of the private sector was also attractive for Turkish firms; they have initiated or participated in several commercial construction projects (shopping malls, business and residential buildings).

Investment benefits granted by national and local authorities became a similarly decisive factor. Most countries in the region try to attract FDI, especially to the manufacturing and technology-intensive service sectors, and the investment promotion authorities grant different kinds of incentives. As one recent case from 2018, HIPA (Hungarian Investment Promotion Agency) secured a 50% matched government funded incentive package to support a multimillion euro investment project of Metyx to expand its composite material production facility in Kaposvár.

The availability of qualified employees and relatively lower labour costs were also among the attractive factors. The minimum wage and the overall personnel costs are around 10% higher than it is in Turkey, which means that labour-intensive investments were opting rather for low-wage Southern and Eastern European countries. A recent problem mentioned by several investors is the inability to find sufficient labour in CEE countries, however. Young people move to West Europe for work, while the deficit for labour is tried to be met by temporary labourers from the neighbouring countries (Ukraine, Belarus). In the case of, for example, Konveyör in Poland, temporary labourers make up to 25% in its factory (Beysad 2018). As Konveyör owner Hasan Aksu said, "if this was not the case, it would be possible to double up your turnover in only 1–2 years; that is the business potential is quite high" (ibid.).

Many TMNEs investing in CEE countries seemed to prefer taking advantage of growing markets and acting with cost-cutting concerns; in reality, however, their aim was rather to manage brand more effectively and to improve EU costumers' perceptions and attitudes towards their products (Uray et al. 2012: 332). The direct market access and proximity to European customers was an important advantage for companies with design expectations. Turkish brands such as Cross Jeans and TEMA/LC Waikiki opened stores and regional distribution centres in CEE countries (especially in Poland and the Czech Republic). Increased market response flexibility and more effective after-sales service were decisive motivations for home appliance producers Vestel, Arçelik (Beko) and Konveyör. The need for strategic assets such as brand and technology becomes clearer as firms target sophisticated markets. Vestel has acquired several local brands in Europe in order to realise growth. The most notable ability of the firm is in transforming old but rooted brands into new generation brands through its strong production skills and market knowledge (Ayden et al. 2018: 180). While Arçelik targets with the brand Beko the middle segment of the market, it has transformed Grundig from a consumer electronics brand to a global home appliances brand following acquisition. The company offers Grundig-branded products produced with high technology and stylish designs to the upper segment (Ayden et al. 2018: 190).

Poland, as the second biggest white goods producer in Europe after Turkey, has a strategic importance here; the country could offer new business and client opportunities and create an attractive environment for such companies.

While Poland is attractive for investments due to the size of its market, which makes it a favourable target also for retail ventures, construction projects and real estate development, Slovakia may raise attention due to its Eurozone membership and proximity to Vienna. As a representative of TUİD in Istanbul, Mehmet Seyfettin Küçük, said "Slovakia, which is only 70 km away from Vienna and which, in contrast with Hungary, the Czech Republic and Poland exists in euro zone, must be in the agenda of Turkish businessmen" (Berktay 2013).

Due to its proximity to Turkey, and partly due also to historical ties, Hungary was one of the most important targets for Turkish transportation and logistical companies. Osman Şahbaz, president of the Turkish Hungarian Businessmen Association, called Hungary as the country best suited to be a bridge linking Turkey to Europe. "We should perceive Hungary as Turkey's door to the West," he commented, noting that the country is not only a member of the EU but is also well situated in Central Europe to play the role of a transit country in Turkey's trade with Western and Eastern Europe (Turkmacar 2013). In telecommunication, location has the same advantages. The acquisition of Invitel International by Türk

Telekom International was aimed at the size of the infrastructure and network of Invitel in the region to improve Türk Telekom's position in terms of geographical connection and also to increase the company's international competitiveness by allowing it to enter new markets (Bakir and Acur 2016: 145).

It is worth mentioning that Turkish banks and financial companies investing broadly in the Southern and Eastern European countries are almost totally missing from the CEE region. The presence of Turkish banks in Eastern Europe has created two crucial advantages for Turkish investors. These banks made it possible for Turkish investors to get in contact with bank managers and commercial banking representatives who can speak their language. Since one of the most significant constraints for growth in the case of Turkish SMEs is language skills, the existence of Turkish-speaking financial institutions in foreign markets appeared to be a valuable asset (Djurica 2015). Furthermore, these banks can provide market intelligence for investors who are seeking to expand their operations to new destinations. As local players, senior-level managers of these banks know in detail the national investment climate, the sectoral situation, potential barriers to entry and ways to overcome them. Additionally, they have a network of key economic and political actors that they can mobilise for serious investors (ibid.). Maybe due to the higher saturation of CEE financial markets by the early 2000s, Halkbank was the only Turkish bank trying to make financial investments in the region. Halkbank had a minority share in Hungarian Volksbank, which was acquired and renamed in 2013 by Russian Sberbank. Halkbank still owns a 1% share (1.5 million USD) in Sberbank Hungary.

In manufacturing, electronics, textile and vehicle components are the major sectors of Turkish activities in the CEE region. In general, Turkish investors kept working with the local labour force, but initially brought plant managers from Turkey. However, as the know-how transfer intensified, the number of Turkish managers and engineers significantly declined (Djurica 2015). The integration of locals into top management positions created harmony and increased efficiency of the workforce.

7.5.1 *Institutional Factors*

The importance of government support has an increasing importance in attracting FDI. Most CEE countries try to promote investors, and Turkey—due to its proximity, its dynamic economic performance and its growing interest in investing in the Eastern European region—is one of the most important target countries.

If we take a look on the foreign policy priorities of the CEE countries, we can find that these countries mostly have a pragmatic, positive approach towards Turkey. Turkey has been percieved as one of the rising economies and as an important economic partner, so the "business should come first" approach has in most cases overcome political concerns. Turkey represents a large market and a great investment opportunity for Hungarian companies; for this reason, it has become one of the main destinations of the Hungarian government's "Eastward opening policy" (Egeresi and Szigetvári 2017).

Compared to Ukraine, Turkey is of secondary importance for Poland and EU-Turkey relations never figured prominently on the Polish foreign affairs agenda (Cianciara 2017). Although all political forces in Poland agree that important economic benefits could be reaped, there is clear shortage of tangible results. Construction, infrastructure, energy and defence sectors are usually identified as particularly fruitful areas for bilateral cooperation.

Bilateral relations between Turkey and the Slovak Republic are mostly free of political disputes, and one could speak of a friendly partnership between the two countries. Slovakia has launched a process of liberalisation and intensification of relations with Turkey in 2013, a priority of which is of course the intensification of business and trade relations (Satir 2017). In the case of Slovenia and the Czech Republic, we can find a similar approach to Turkey.[7]

On the other hand, political ties and connections to the local political elites have always been important for investors. Sometimes these ties, however, seem to be decisive regarding the opportunities companies may get in a country.

As an eminent and well-documented case in Hungary, we should mention the good political ties of a group of Turkish businessmen to Hungarian government circles. Adnan Polat, a Turkish businessmen and former president of the Istanbul-based football club Galatasaray, is in close relationship with the government-supported new Hungarian elite. Polat's solar business in Hungary is being developed in strong government tail-wind (Bódis 2018). The Polat–HSWE is about to establish a 1000-megawatt solar park

[7] For the approaches of CEE countries towards Turkey, see FEUTURE site on http://feuture.eu.

network in Hungary. During Viktor Orbán's visit to China, Polat was a member of the Hungarian prime minister's delegation and has signed a contract with state-owned PowerChina on using Chinese technology. Several other Istanbul tycoons (such as the Derelis and Demirer families) were also pulled by Polat into the Hungarian solar energy production business (ibid.).

The good relationship of Polat with the government circles was also honoured by an official representation of the Hungarian Export Promotion Agency (HEPA) in Turkey and Greece. In 2015, the Polat Holding established local HEPA offices in both countries. By granting Polat's real estate development project in Budapest the grade of "special importance for the national economy", the cabinet has cleared the administrative barriers (e.g. that of local authorities) to his large-scale construction.[8] Here as well, Nurol Group and Özaltin Holding (two well-known Turkish family business conglomerates) have joined him.

7.6 Conclusions

In recent years, Turkey has become one of the leading investors among emerging economies in its neighbouring regions. The rising presence of Turkish investments abroad is due both to economic and to political reasons. The rapidly growing Turkish economy and the structural changes in Turkey created a bunch of internationally competitive sectors and firms, while the changing Turkish foreign policy also promoted the active presence of Turkish companies in neighbouring countries, as part of its new strategy aimed at increasing the central position of Turkey in the region.

These trends can be witnessed by the Turkish OFDI statistics as well. The majority of Turkish OFDI went to European countries, but it is not concentrated solely in developed Western European countries; a lot of Turkish capital has flown to Eastern Europe and the Balkans.

By looking at the motivations of TMNEs, we found different reasons depending also on the type of firms and the sectors they are active in. There are Turkish firms making resource-based investments, especially in Russia, in Central Asia and in the Middle East and North Africa. Market seeking is also a common motivation of Turkish companies, and they are able to exploit their country-specific advantages: the experiences earned

[8] According to the plans, 1232 flats, 45.000 square metres of office, 200 hotel rooms, underground garages, restaurants and malls will be built (Bódis 2018).

on the relatively competitive but institutionally underdeveloped Turkish domestic market. A continuously increasing motivation of TMNEs for outward investment is brand building, and the upgrading of their technologies, to be able to compete on more developed markets as well.

The chapter examined the special characteristics of Turkish OFDI in the Central European countries. On the one hand, we could find here several of the above-mentioned specificities of TMNEs' motivations. They invest in these countries to enter new markets; in many cases they use other, mainly Dutch, firms as the direct investor company. It was also common that through such investments they aimed to manage their brands more effectively and to improve EU costumers' perceptions and attitudes towards their products.

CEE partners may offer Turkish firms a broad field of cooperation with CEE partners in many aspects. By forming joint ventures with local firms they can both reach a better position on the local market and increase their competitiveness in the global economy. They may consider relocating part of their value chains to CEE to get closer to the Western European markets. Visegrad countries are not only closely connected to the core European markets but they also share several institutional weaknesses common to the Turkish domestic market. One of the institutional similarities is the growing importance of political ties in the business life. Turkish business people having good relationship with the local political elite may enjoy special opportunities in these countries, as especially the Hungarian examples prove it.

References

Anil Keskin, D., Anil, I., Canel, C., & Porterfield, R. (2012). A Study on the Entry Strategies Related with Risk Management of Turkish Companies to the Emerging Economies. *International Journal of Business and Social Science, 3*(7), 272–282.

Anıl, İ., Cakir, O., Canel, C., & Porterfield, R. (2011). A Comparison of Inward and Outward Foreign Direct Investment Determinants in Turkey. *International Journal of Business and Social Science, 2*(20), 141–155.

Anil, I., Tatoglu, E., & Ozkasap, G. (2014). Ownership and Market Entry Mode Choices of Emerging Country Multinationals in a Transition Country: Evidence from Turkish Multinationals in Romania. *Journal of East European Management Studies, 19*(4), 413–452.

Antalóczy, K., & Sass, M. (2015). Through a Glass Darkly. The Content of Statistical Data on Foreign Direct Investment. *Külgazdaság*, Special Issue, 34–61.

Aybar, S. (2016). Determinants of Turkish Outward Foreign Direct Investment. *Transnational Corporations Review, 8*(1), 79–92.

Ayden, Y., Demirbag, M., & Tatoglu, E. (2018). *Turkish Multinationals. Market Entry and Post-Acquisition Strategy*. Cham: Palgrave Macmillan.

Bakir, C., & Acur, N. (2016). Greenfield Investments and Acquisitions of Turkish Multinationals: Trends, Motivations and Strategies. In L. Brennan & C. Bakir (Eds.), *Emerging Market Multinationals in Europe* (pp. 129–156). London; New York: Routledge.

Bakir, C., & Acur, N. (2017). Turkish Multinationals in Russia. In K. Liuhto, S. Sutyrin, & J.-M. F. Blanchard (Eds.), *The Russian Economy and Foreign Direct Investment* (pp. 213–229). London; New York: Routledge.

Başar, S., & Özkilbaç, S. C. (2016). Effects of Outward Foreign Direct Investment of Turkey on Economic Growth and Domestic Investment. *Atatürk Üniversitesi SBF Dergisi, 71*(1), 231–247.

Bedirhanoglu, P. (2016). State-Business Relations in Azerbaijan through the Eyes of Turkish Businesspeople. In M. Ismayilov & N. Graham (Eds.), *Azerbaijan and Turkey: One Nation-Two States?* Routledge.

Berktay (2013). The Turkish – Slovakian Relationship Experiences Its Golden Era. TUID, 5 October, Retrieved from http://tuid.org.ua/en/the-turkish-slovaki-anrelationship-experinces-its-golden-era/ last accessed 27/02/2019.

Beysad. (2018). Beysad News., 25 December. Retrieved from https://www.beysad.org.tr/en/konveyor-and-beysad-co-founder-mr-hasan-basri-aksu-and-a-very-successful-2nd-generation-executive-of-the-company-and-beysad-board-member-mrs-d-yasemin-aksu.

Bódis, A. (2018). *The Friend of Erdoğan Conquers Hungary's solar Energy Sector*. Válasz Online.

Cianciara, K. A. (2017). EU 28 Country Reports—Poland. *FEUTURE*. Retrieved from http://feuture.eu.

Cizre, Ü., & Yeldan, E. (2005). The Turkish Encounter with Neo-Liberalism: Economics and Politics in the 2000/2001 Crises. *Review of International Political Economy, 12*(3), 387–408.

Colborne, M., & Edwards, M. (2018). Erdogan is Making the Ottoman Empire Great Again. *Foreign Policy*, 22 June. Retrieved February 27, 2019, from https://foreignpolicy.com/2018/06/22/erdogan-is-making-the-ottoman-empire-great-again/.

Culpan, R., & Akcaoglu, E. (2018). An Examination of Turkish Investments in Central and Eastern Europe and the Commonwealth of Independent States. In S. T. Marinova & M. A. Marinov (Eds.), *Foreign Direct Investment in Central and Eastern Europe* (pp. 181–200). London; New York: Routledge.

Daily News. (2018). Turkish Trade Minister to Visit Bulgaria in Bid to Boost Bilateral Ties. *Hürriyet Daily News*, 18 November. Retrieved February 25, 2019, from http://www.hurriyetdailynews.com/turkish-trade-minister-to-visit-bulgaria-in-bid-to-boost-bilateral-ties-138972.

Daily Sabah. (2017). Turkey, Hungary Pledge to Reinvigorate Economic Ties. *Daily Sabah*, 1 July. Retrieved February 27, 2019, from https://www.dailysabah.com/economy/2017/07/01/turkey-hungary-pledge-to-reinvigorate-economic-ties.

Daily Sabah. (2018). Turkish Companies Invest in Belgrade for Easier Access to Europe. *Daily Sabah*, 15 March. Retrieved from https://www.dailysabah.com/business/2018/03/16/turkish-companies-invest-in-belgrade-for-easier-access-to-europe.

Davutoğlu, A. (2010). Turkey's Zero Problems Foreign Policy. *Foreign Policy*, May20. Retrieved from http://www.foreignpolicy.com/articles/2010/05/20/turkeys_zero_problems_foreign_policy.

Demir, A. O. & Moiz, M. (2017). Outward Foreign Investment in Emerging Economies: A Case of Turkey. In Dorozynski, T. & Kuna-Marszalek, A. (Eds.) *Outward Foreign Direct Investment (FDI) in Emerging market Economies* (pp. 244–257), Hershey (PA): IGI Global.

Demirbag, M., & Tatoglu, E. (2008). Competitive Strategy Choices of Turkish Manufacturing Firms in European Union. *Journal of Management Development, 27*(3), 727–743.

Demirbag, M., Tatoglu, E., & Glaister, K. W. (2008). Equity-Based Entry Modes of Emerging Country Multinationals: Lessons from Turkey. *Journal of World Business, 44*, 445–462.

Djurica, D. (Ed.). (2015). *Strengthening Economic Cooperation between South East Europe and Turkey*. Sarajevo: Regional Cooperation Council.

EFT. (2018). Ekol Poland Starts Comprehensive Logistics Services with Regatta Ltd. *Eyefortransport*, 9 February. Retrieved from https://www.eft.com/content/ekol-poland-starts-comprehensive-logistics-services-regatta-ltd.

Egeresi, Z., & Szigetvári, T. (2017). EU 28 Country Reports—Hungary. *FEUTURE*. Retrieved from http://feuture.eu.

Egresi, I., & Kara, F. (2015). Foreign Policy Influences on Outward Direct Investment: The Case of Turkey. *Journal of Balkan and Near Eastern Studies, 17*(2), 181–203.

Glowik, M. (2009). *Market Entry Strategies: Internationalization Theories, Network Concepts and Cases of Asian firms*. München: Oldenbourg.

Kaya, H. (2014). *Strategic Motives of Turkish Foreign Direct Investment Firms: An Empirical Study on Manufacturing Sector*. Istanbul University.

Kayam, S. S., & Hisarciklilar, M. (2009). *Determinants of Turkish FDI abroad*. MPRA Paper No. 17813.

KHU—DEIK—VCC. (2014). Turkish OFDI Continues to Grow. *Report*, March 24.

Kirişci, K. (2009). The Transformation of Turkish Foreign Policy: The Rise of the Trading State. *New Perspectives on Turkey, 40*, 29–57.

OECD. (2012). OECD Economic Surveys: Turkey 2012. Paris: OECD Publishing.

Öniş, Z., & Şenses, F. (2009). The New Phase of Neo-Liberal Restructuring in Turkey: An Overview. In Z. Önis & F. Şenses (Eds.), *Turkey and the Global Economy. Neo-Liberal Restructuring and Integration in the Post-Crisis Era* (pp. 1–11). London; New York: Routledge.

Polandin. (2019). Polish-Turkish Economic Forum to start in Warsaw. *Poland In*, 7 March. Retrieved from https://polandin.com/41637324/polishturkish-economic-forum-to-start-in-warsaw.

Satir, B. (2017). EU 28 Country Reports—Slovakia. *FEUTURE*. Retrieved from http://feuture.eu.

Sekularac, I. (2018). Spurned by EU investors, Balkans looks to eager Turkey. *Reuters*, 18 May. Retrieved from https://www.reuters.com/article/us-balkan-sturkey/spurned-by-eu-investors-balkans-looks-to-eager-turkey-idUSKCN1I-J20Y last accessed 07/09/2020.

Slovenia Times. (2018). Lesna TIP Gets New Turkish Owner. *Slovenia Times*, 28 February. Retrieved from http://www.sloveniatimes.com/lesna-tip-gets-new-turkish-owner.

Taymaz, E., & Voyvoda, E. (2009). Industrial Restructuring and Technological Capabilities in Turkey. In Z. Önis & F. Senses (Eds.), *Turkey and the Global Economy: Neo-Liberal Restructuring and Integration in the Post-Crisis Era* (pp. 145–172). London: Routledge.

Tolay, J., & Linden, R. H. (2012). Understanding Turkey's Relations with its Neighbors. In R. H. Linden et al. (Eds.), *Turkey and Its Neighbors. Foreign Relations in Transition* (pp. 1–12). Boulder, CO: Lynne Rienner.

Turkmacar. (2013). Turkey and Hungary Set To Boost Ties. turkmacar.org. Retrieved from http://www.turkmacar.org.tr/index.php/component/content/article/258 last accessed 25/02/2019.

UNCTAD. (2011). World Investment Report: Non-Equity Modes of International Production and Development. United Nations, New York and Geneva.

Uray, N., Vardar, N., & Nacar, R. (2012). International Marketing-Related Outward FDI Motives: Turkish MNCs' Experience in the EU. In R. van Tulder, A. Verbeke, & L. Voinea (Eds.), *New Policy Challenges for European Multinationals* (pp. 305–338). Bingley: Emerald Group Publishing.

Vardar, N. (2016). Turkish EMNCs with Foreign Direct Investment in the EU. Their Motivations, Degree of Internalisation and Company Performances. In L. Brennan & C. Bakir (Eds.), *Emerging Market Multinationals in Europe* (pp. 95–111). London; New York: Routledge.

Yildirim, C. (2017). Turkey's Outward Foreign Direct Investment: Trends and Patterns of Mergers and Acquisitions. *Journal of Balkan and Near Eastern Studies*, *19*(3), 276–293.

CHAPTER 8

Motivations of Brazilian Firms to Invest in East Central Europe: Specific Home-Country Advantages and Some Host-Country Specificities Dominate

Judit Ricz

8.1 Introduction

This chapter widens the geographical focus of this volume to the Latin American continent, by focusing on outward investment activities of the largest Latin American economy, Brazil. By examining the European expansion strategies of Brazilian multinational enterprises (BMNEs), it aims to provide a better understanding of investment motivations and operational practices of emerging market multinationals (EMNEs). As we shall see by the end of this chapter the Brazilian case is a good laboratory for analysing non-European EMNEs, as it reveals some important similarities with other EMNEs (mainly from Asia), but also draws attention to some unique (Latino) specificities.

J. Ricz (✉)
Institute of World Economics, Centre for Economic and Regional Studies, Budapest, Hungary

Institute of International, Political, and Regional Sciences, Corvinus University of Budapest, Budapest, Hungary

Á. Szunomár (ed.), *Emerging-market Multinational Enterprises in East Central Europe*, Studies in Economic Transition, https://doi.org/10.1007/978-3-030-55165-0_8

Brazil is the fifth largest country in the world by area and population and the ninth largest economy in the world by nominal GDP (and the eighth largest by purchasing power parity). It is the leading economy of South America and a prominent member of the elite club of emerging economies, the BRICS (Brazil, Russia, India, China and South Africa), and at least during the first decade of the twenty-first century it has shown strong ambitions and geopolitical aspirations to become a leader of the Global South. Even though during the recent years the global aspirations of Brazil have faded, and the country has turned towards problems arising domestically, it has submitted a formal request to join the OECD in May 2017, signalling its ongoing commitment to get into the club of the more developed countries. An important aspect of the ascendance of the Brazilian economy and development during the 2000s has been the emergence of outward foreign direct investment (OFDI) flows from Brazil to conquer in international markets.

Based on the political economy changes starting after the turn of the new millennium, Brazil—along with other BRICS economies—has been characterized as a state-permeated market economy (Nölke et al. 2019). Looking however deeper into the organizational structure of economic relations (and taking into account historical path dependencies) in Brazil, the Brazilian variety of capitalism is probably better described by the Hierarchical Market Economy model (Schneider 2013).

The main characteristics of hierarchical market economies are the large and mostly family-owned diversified business groups, high presence of foreign multinationals, concentrated ownership structures and the dominance of hierarchical coordination mechanisms. These latter are further strengthened by the fact that governments throughout hierarchical market economies tended to be historically highly interventionist, and as a historical heritage their market used to be largely dominated by state-owned companies, with important imprints upon their market structure and state-business relations even after several waves of privatization. A further striking feature of hierarchical market economies is that these countries tend to have low skills and low levels of investment into education (combined with large informal sectors). In addition, atomistic labour relations with low union density have not only resulted in a highly fragmented labour market but also reinforced the traditionally dualistic economic structures (Schneider 2013).

All in all Brazilian companies embedded into these hierarchical market conditions are until today heavily affected by the above-mentioned factors, both in their internal decision-making processes and when constructing and implementing their internationalization strategies. Thus Brazilian companies often cannot escape their faith and the heritage of the traditional Brazilian economic and political organizational structures. Thus in social and institutional memories the more than half century long import substitution industrialization (ISI) era, combined with bureaucratic authoritarianism, is still often present, leading to the dominance of centralizing, autocratic and hierarchical coordination mechanisms even if operating outside Brazil (Aguzzoli and Hunek 2019).

Many stories can be found in economic and management literature on the specificities of the "Brazilian way" of doing business, and in this chapter we explicitly aim to look at investment activities of Brazilian firms outside their country borders, with a special focus on Europe and more concretely on the Visegrad countries. According to our preliminary expectations even if BMNEs show some similarities with other EMNEs when investing in this region, there are also some unique (Latino) features.

Studies analysing European activities of "multilatinas" (companies originating from Latin America) are rather scarce.[1] This chapter aims to add to this literature, with a special focus on the Brazilian investment activities in the East Central European (ECE) countries.

Our data collection comprises of a diverse range of sources to explore Brazilian companies in the ECE region and reveal their main investment motives. Interviews were conducted with investment promotion agencies, experts of Foreign Affairs Ministries, Embassies and Consulates (both in ECE countries and in Brazil), and some companies in the region; however in this latter area we rather faced difficulties. Secondary sources were also thoroughly analysed, and information mainly based on media sources (articles in magazines, newspapers and websites) was complemented by company documents (annual reports, websites and other).

The remainder of this chapter is in four sections. First the specificities of the internationalization of Brazilian companies are presented in a historical and comparative perspective. The next two sections present the push and pull factors of Brazilian OFDI, respectively, while highlighting the role of the ECE region and presenting some illustrative cases from the region. The final section provides the conclusions.

[1] A few exceptions: Fleury et al. (2011), Santiso (2013), Éltető (2014), Aguzzoli and Hunek (2019).

8.2 BMNEs Going Global—A Historical and Comparative Perspective

By 2020 it is clear that after a relatively good start, Brazilian companies are lagging behind in the global race of emerging economies in terms of OFDI flows. On the global scene Brazil was among the new significant emerging foreign investors that had shown impressive investment growth in the 2000s. In 2000 Brazil had outperformed even China in both absolute terms of OFDI flows (Fig. 8.1) and in its share of global or developing OFDI flows. By 2010 it was third among the BRICS, only after China and Russia, while since then it has been gradually falling behind and became the laggard in the group, with negative figures—divestment amid a severe economic crisis—since 2012. In terms of OFDI stock, however, if the share of total developing country OFDI stock is considered, Brazil was still on the third place in 2015 with 6.5 per cent, compared to 36 per cent

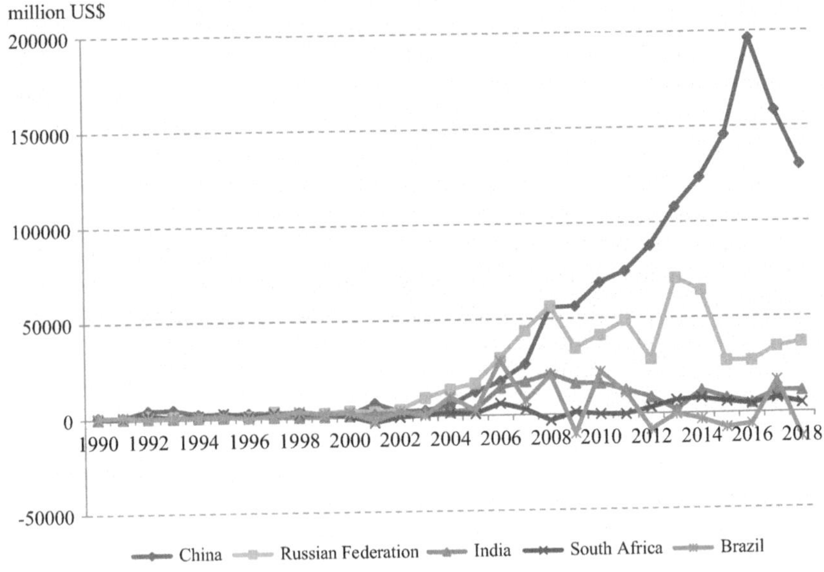

Fig. 8.1 FDI outflows in BRICS economies, 1990–2018 (millions of US dollars) (Source: own construction based on the United Nations Conference on Trade and Development (UNCTAD) data (UNCTAD 2019))

of China and 9 per cent of Russia, and followed by 5.8 per cent in the case of South Africa and 4.9 per cent for India (UNCTAD 2019).

Historically, Brazilian companies (both state- and privately owned ones) were rather focusing on local (and regional) markets. There is a complexity of reasons beyond the relatively closed Brazilian domestic market, not only in commercial terms but also in terms of firms' outward investments; the long period of import substitution industrialization and the large domestic market as well as the abundance of natural resources are the primary reasons beyond this. As a result Brazilian companies in general have had little incentive (and often also important competitiveness constraints) to expand towards foreign markets.

This picture changed significantly in the early 2000s, when the boom in OFDI started and (as many have thought) marked the beginning of a new era. It can be seen from the data in Fig. 8.2 that in the middle of the 1990s, after the economic stabilization and market-oriented reforms, Brazil emerged as an important recipient of FDI flows. It was however only after 2003 when Brazil became a significant investor abroad—in parallel with other emerging countries—OFDI flows from Brazil started to

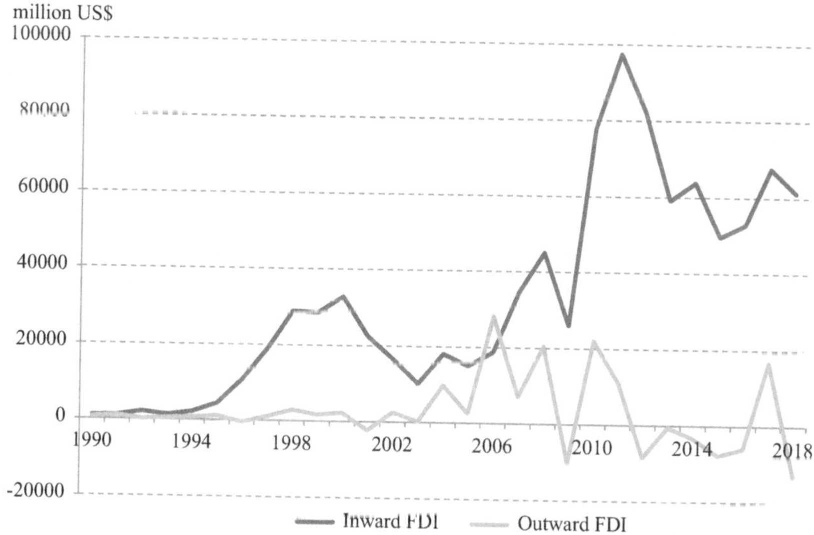

Fig. 8.2 Inward and outward FDI flows in Brazil (1990–2018, millions of US dollars) (Source: own construction based on UNCTAD data (UNCTAD 2019))

gain momentum as a result of several (coinciding) events. *First*, in the economic front the export boom (based mainly on primary commodities export) generated increasing trade surplus, and this hand in hand with large flows of incoming FDI and the appreciation of the Real (the Brazilian currency) has boosted foreign exchange reserves, which has meant a favourable scenario for Brazilian firms to invest abroad. Mostly export-led Brazilian companies in industries where Brazil traditionally enjoyed competitive advantages (iron ore, steel, meat, soybeans, etc.) have benefitted from improved access to domestic financial markets for financing their (mainly) market-seeking investments abroad (Campanario et al. 2011). In more general terms, the global market opportunities have also favoured these firms, as commodity prices were booming, fuelled by increasing demand from China, and led to (overly) optimistic atmosphere in global markets and rising investors' confidence. Not surprisingly, looking at the sectoral division we can see an increase towards the natural resources sector (metals, mining, oil, gas and steel) (Resende et al. 2010).

Second, on the policy front, these favourable economic conditions were accompanied by a fundamental shift in Brazilian policy attitude towards global markets (Casanova and Kassum 2014: 68). This can be best illustrated with the address of the former Brazilian president Lula urging Brazilian companies to go global in 2003 (at a meeting of the Portuguese Industrial Association in Lisbon): "It is time for Brazilian businessmen to abandon their fear of becoming multinational businessmen" (UNCTAD 2004: 1).

It can be revealed from the data that in 2006 the total Brazilian direct investments abroad outweighed the incoming FDI in Brazil. This unprecedented event has underlined the internationalization aspirations of a country that explicitly aimed at consolidating its position as a global player also in terms of outward direct investment flows. However, this was an exceptional year, and this performance can easily be explained by Vale's acquisition of the Canadian Inco for an estimated 17 billion US dollars (Resende et al. 2010: 99).

It is not unique however that yearly amounts of Brazilian OFDI are dominated by one or two transactions of the given year,[2] as indicated also

[2] In 2004, for example, the merger between Ambev (a Brazilian drinks group) and Interbrew (a Belgium-based brewer) with its value of five million US dollars had accounted for more than half of that year's total Brazilian OFDI (with increased intra-company loans also accounting for 22% of total outward flows that year) (UNCTAD 2004).

by the relatively low volume—most of all in the early 2000s—and relatively high year-to-year volatility. Outward investment flows surpassed the 10 billion US dollar threshold in 2006 in Brazil, with the average being below 1 billion US dollars between 2000 and 2003 on a yearly basis and between 2004 and 2008 the average jumped close to 17 billion US dollars (BCB 2017).

Furthermore, and also less surprisingly, OFDI trends of Brazilian companies tend to highly correlate with the general economic trends of Brazil. It can be seen how OFDI became negative as a response to the 2009 financial crisis, as foreign affiliates of Brazilian multinational enterprises started to repatriate capital to their parent firms mainly via intra-firm lending. Similar—divestment—tendencies can be captured during the last years with the evolution of the recent economic and political crises. Accordingly we can differentiate between two main cycles of outward investment activities as recent waves of internationalization of Brazilian companies: after a boom in OFDI activities between 2005 and 2011 a divestment cycle followed from 2012 until 2016 (Fig. 8.3). Data is however less conclusive on the most recent years, according to recent UNCTAD data (in UNCTAD 2019): as long as incoming FDI flows seem

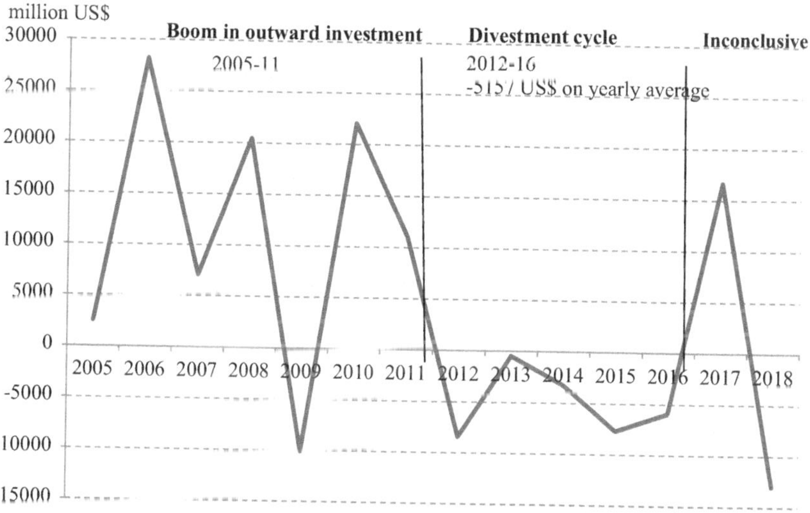

Fig. 8.3 Cycles of OFDI in Brazil (2005–2018, millions of US dollars) (Source: own construction based on UNCTAD data)

to be at a more or less stable level around 60,000 million US dollars on yearly average, outward investment flows turned into positive in 2017 (with 16,677 million dollars) and became negative again in 2018 (resulting in a disinvestment of 13,035 million US dollars). Further negative figures are foreseen by analysts for the upcoming years.

Historically Brazilian firms tended to open up commercial offices to support their export activities as the first step to expand abroad. During the early 2000s greenfield investments were the preferred mode of entry in foreign markets by Brazilian firms, mainly in the mining and energy industry (with Petrobras leading the row through overseas energy investments, but even Ambev entered into other Latin American markets via greenfield investments—mainly for market-seeking reasons) (Sauvant 2006: 344). This trend has changed significantly and with OFDI flows gaining momentum by 2006 cross-border mergers and acquisitions became the main form of BMNEs' investments.

8.2.1 *Size Does Not Matter a Lot if Looking at the Internationalization of Brazilian Companies*

Looking at the largest Brazilian firms, it is easy to see that these have done undoubtedly well during the first decade of the new millennium. In 2003 there were only 4 Brazilian companies in the world's top 500 largest companies (by revenues), while in 2013 this number rose already to 8, where it stood also in 2019.[3] Among the top 100 non-financial MNEs from developing and transition economies (ranked by foreign assets) 5 Brazilian firms were present in the latest available list from 2017.

However not all of these large companies qualify as multinationals, as some of them have rather limited presence in overseas markets. Looking at the list of top 20 Brazilian multinationals,[4] we can see that Vale is on the top of the list, if looking at foreign assets abroad, and JBS is the first if looking at foreign sales or employees. Both are ahead of the largest Brazilian energy giant, the semi-state-owned Petrobras. But looking at rankings of major Brazilian companies by the transnationality index (published by Fundação Dom Cabral),[5] on the first seven places are companies

[3] http://fortune.com/global500/.

[4] http://ccsi.columbia.edu/publications/emgp/.

[5] The transnationality index was originally developed by UNCTAD and is calculated as the arithmetic mean of the ratio of foreign assets to total assets, the ratio of foreign sales to total

that are often less known internationally and that have rarely if at all appeared in the rankings of the largest companies, namely the Fitesa (hygiene business[6]), Iochpe-Maxion (equipment and parts), CZM (equipment and parts), Intercement (cement industry), Stefanini (software company), Artecola (petrochemicals) and Gerdau (steel producer) (FDC 2016: 53). At the same time internationally well-known Brazilian multinationals, such as JBS, Vale and Embraer, only follow at the 8th, 18th and 24th places, respectively. Petrobras is missing from the 2016 list; however, in 2014 it was on the 38th place.

Our look at the largest and the most internationalized Brazilian companies reveals an important insight, which is in line with the results of Kassum (2014: 79): "the biggest Brazilian companies are not necessarily very internationalized, while the most internationalized Brazilian companies are not necessarily very big." This statement might be however a little bit misleading, as the Brazilian companies most active abroad are still large firms, even if not necessarily the biggest ones. Small and medium-sized Brazilian enterprises were still having very low participation in foreign markets as compared to large firms in 2015 (Sheng and Carrera 2017: 12). As we shall see in a later section, most public policies have also been biased towards promoting the internationalization of large firms. There have been no special aims and measures to support SMEs' activities abroad, and the smaller firms are rather disadvantaged not only regarding their outward focused activities but also in the domestic market.

Yet to support our arguments above, we draw attention to the case of Stefanini, the Brazilian IT company, which has been named as one of Brazil's "most global company" on the basis of factors including size, number of employees abroad, number of clients outside Brazil and number of overseas offices (Monteiro and Rozman 2017: 12).

8.2.2 *Extractive Industries Are Leading the Way*

As mentioned already, during the late 2000s mostly export-led Brazilian companies in industries where Brazil traditionally enjoyed competitive advantages (iron ore, steel, meat, soybeans, etc.) have benefitted from

sales and the ratio of foreign employment to total employment.

[6] Fitesa is manufacturing nonwoven fabrics for use in hygiene, medical and industrial specialty applications.

improved access to domestic financial markets for financing their (mainly) *market-seeking investments* abroad (Campanario et al. 2011).

According to an analysis focusing on the top 20 BMNEs (Sheng and Carrera 2018), the following sectors have contributed to 90 per cent of the total foreign assets (by 11 companies) in 2016:[7] oil and gas extraction (Petrobras), food manufacturing (JBS, Marfrig, BRF and Minerva), mining (Vale and Magnesita), primary metal manufacturing (Gerdau and CSN) and paper and allied products (Fibria and Suzano Papel industries). At the lower end of the scale six different industries appear, and add up to the remaining 10 per cent of foreign assets of the ranked firms: transportation equipment manufacturing industry (Embraer, Iochpe-Maxion, Marcopolo and Tupy), chemical manufacturing (Braskem), merchant wholesalers and nondurable goods (Natura), printing and related activities (Valid), leather and allied product manufacturing (Alpargatas) and last but not least machinery manufacturing industry (Metalfrio) (ibid.: 5.)

All in all we can see a very concentrated sectoral composition in extractive and commodities sectors. This is in line with the Brazilian production and export structure, and is less surprising if the home-country endowments are considered, as Brazil is rich in natural resources and has extensive areas suitable for agriculture and livestock. At the same time this concentrated pattern is also present on the firm level: Petrobras, Vale and JBS, the top three companies, have accounted for the major part of total foreign assets (approximately 62 per cent of the total of the top 20 BMNEs) in 2016 (Sheng and Carrera 2018: 1). Nevertheless, not all Brazilian internationalized companies are primarily active in the commodities sector. Resende et al. (2010:99) highlight the service sector's growing share in Brazilian OFDI; examples range from the construction sector (Odebrecht or Guiterrez) to some high-tech companies such as Datasul, Lupatech and Stefanini, which are more and more active outside Brazil. Some other outstanding examples where home-grown technology and innovation has driven the successful internationalization strategies (such as Embraer, Embrapa and the Camargo Correa) are often also mentioned (see, e.g., Casanova 2016: 33; Amann 2009).

[7] In this section of the study we highlight the most recent sectoral composition, which reveals however rather a static pattern, and no significant sectoral changes took place during the last years (for a more detailed discussion see Ricz 2017 or the EMGP successive studies on Brazil, available: http://ccsi.columbia.edu/publications/emgp/).

8.2.3 Europe (but Not the ECE) as an Emerging Destination to Host Brazilian OFDI

Historically Brazilian OFDI is accumulated in its "natural market", composed of its immediate neighbourhood, the Latin American region and some other Portuguese-speaking countries (Portugal and some of its former colonies in West Africa). In a wider sense the Ibero-American world can also be regarded as a natural market for Brazil, as it shares strong similarities in both cultural and institutional terms (Casanova 2016: 31).

Before however looking at rankings and maps of Brazilian OFDI flows, we must clarify (in line with Campanario et al. 2011) whether the outflows are short-term movements in the financial market (such as portfolio investments or other deposits) or long-term capital movements constituting to the real purpose of making FDI transactions (such as mergers and acquisitions). The numbers reveal that the main destination of Brazilian OFDI flows used to be undoubtedly the Latin American region. However, if we focus on real foreign direct transactions, and leave aside the flows into tax havens (such as those in the Caribbean Islands, e.g. the Cayman Islands, the British Virgin Islands and the Bahamas), the European region and the United States gain importance. Still, there is also a strong presence of major BMNEs in the Latin American region (including Argentina, Mexico, Chile, Uruguay, Colombia, Paraguay and Peru). Beyond already mentioned factors, such as geographical, institutional and cultural proximity, and especially for the case of Argentina, the above-addressed issue of following export activities might hold here as well, as Argentina is an important market for Brazilian manufactured goods. In the case of one of the least developed Latin American economy, Paraguay, the low labour costs and favourable taxation policies have also played an important role (Sheng and Carrera 2018).

Looking at accumulated FDI stocks, the EU has overtaken Latin America in 2009 and became the main recipient of Brazilian investments. In Europe, however we have to be cautious because of the strong dominance of countries (Denmark, Netherlands, Luxembourg and more recently Austria) where through setting up special-purpose entities Brazilian firms primarily aim at avoiding the burdensome domestic taxes and bypassing complicated Brazilian regulations.

In 2016 the top foreign investment destinations of the top 20 BMNEs were: (1) United States; (2) Argentina; (3) United Kingdom; (4) China and (5) Mexico. Primary activities in these destinations included production and manufacturing units as well as foreign sales and distribution centres (ibid.). Looking at this list, one might remember that the two main export markets for Brazilian products are traditionally the United States and most recently China. Thus, the large presence of BMNEs in these countries might reflect their market-seeking strategies and the aim to achieve proximity to main customers. According to Sheng and Carrera (2018: 6) even though some changes in foreign asset to total asset (FA/TA) ratio for some companies (notably for Fibria and Marcopolo) in 2016 can be observed, these changes were not due to any major new FDI abroad, but rather due to losses in the domestic market. Amidst a multidimensional economic, social, political and institutional crisis in Brazil, most firms were focusing their resources on defending their domestic activities (or, having been involved in the overarching corruption scandal, paying off the record-breaking fines, such as Odebrecht and Petrobras) and often even withdrawing FDI from overseas.

In general Europe did not represent any special priority in the localization strategies of the Brazilian companies, nor was there any government priority to promote the expansion of Brazilian firms towards the European market. This process was rather driven by the companies themselves and their own priorities or the desire to follow the clients, search for new markets or acquire knowledge. Within the European region the already mentioned United Kingdom has received the most Brazilian FDI in 2016, while traditionally Spain and Portugal have been leading the way (as traditional hubs of multilatinas' investments), but some companies are also present in Germany, France and Italy.

8.2.4 *Brazilian Investments in the ECE Region*

Within Europe, most Brazilian FDI flows to Western European countries, and the ECE region undoubtedly lags behind. A possible explanation might be simply the geographical distance, but also the lack or historically low levels of political, diplomatic or cultural relations might play a role. This relatively low level of Brazilian FDI flows was further negatively impacted by the recent global crisis and the Brazilian economy's crisis since 2014 as well as the following slow recovery.

The ECE region has never been on the geographical radar of Brazilian companies. FDI coming from Brazil to this region is characterized by relatively low volume and high year-to year volatility as these are mostly bound to one or two transactions of BMNEs (Éltető 2014). Furthermore these investments stay mostly below any threshold of international surveys that usually map larger OFDI flows (EPMG, BCG, FDC, etc.) of mainly top 20 Brazilian (non-financial) companies and also those of academic research in this regard.

Another characteristic of Brazilian FDI in the ECE region is that more often than not, these are not real, productive investments, rather just transactions on papers, such as to avoid large tax burden or other regulations at home. This is indicative from the fact that of 29 Brazilian-owned companies in Hungary that are present on paper, only 4 have reported to have more than one employee in 2016.[8] Consequently, there is also a relative scarcity on the data, as most investment coming from Brazil into the ECE region is not included in datasets. The Amadeus database lists only two companies (both settled in Slovakia)—Rudolph Usinados and Micro Juntas—neither of them corresponds to the most important and significant companies in the ECE region or even in Slovakia itself.

In our analysis the following companies have been taken into consideration: KACO (Hungary), Stefanini (Poland and Hungary), BRF (Hungary), Tupy S.A. (Poland),[9] Embraco (Slovakia), CRW Plásticos (Slovakia), Micro Juntas (Slovakia), Rudolph Usinados (Slovakia) and Sellier & Bellot (Czech Republic). These Brazilian companies are according to our best knowledge the most actively present in the ECE countries. There might be some other "real" investments which remained below the radar of our investigations; however, we are convinced that these would not have altered the regional picture.

The economic cooperation between the Brazilian aircraft company Embraer and the Czech aircraft company Aero Vodochody has remained outside the above list, as this does not seem to be a classical acquisition of a foreign company, rather a long-term cooperation. In 2011 the two companies signed a contract to cooperate on the development of KC-390, multi-purpose military transport aircraft of medium size, which is basically developed by the Brazilian company, Embraer. The Czech partner, Aero, mainly supplies rear fuselage sections, crew and parachute doors, emergency doors, hatches and cargo ramps for the plane (Vondra 2011).

[8] Based on data received from the Brazilian Embassy in Budapest. In any other Hungarian sources much lower numbers appear regarding Brazilian companies' presence in Hungary.

[9] Tupy has taken over a plant in Skoczów from FCA and starts to operate in Poland in 2020.

Looking at the above-mentioned investments we can highlight two outstanding features. First of all it is clear that the first firms investing in ECE were mainly active in manufacturing, related to automotive parts and electrical products (like KACO and Embraco). Though this trend is still present (see, e.g., Tupy's most recent investment in Poland), there is a different wave of investment led by Stefanini, the Brazilian IT company.

8.3 Drivers of Internationalization

Before mapping the drivers of internationalization of BMNEs, it is worth remembering the specificities of the Brazilian context (and in more general term the Latin American realities) that have been explained in earlier sections—such as the role of family-owned business, the strong, albeit changing, role of state-ownership with direct and indirect state influence, and a somewhat different but not totally independent characteristic: resource abundance and the role of the primary resources.

In Brazil one of the most important economic policy tendencies that have influenced the hierarchical structure of its market economy (Schneider 2013) has been the aim to promote "national champions". These were either state-owned or (directly or indirectly) state-backed large, specialized domestic firms that were protected from competition and have benefitted from government (export) subsidies and became leaders in their respective industries. These national champions were created and supported to drive the industrialization of the economy and serve as major engines for economic development (including objectives of employment creation, growth promotion, gaining access to and prestige in international markets, etc.) (Casanova 2009). After the years of liberalization and privatization during the 1990s, many of the former national champions maintained and even improved their leading positions in the Brazilian and international markets. The most-known and cited examples are: Embraer, Vale and Petrobras.

As active industrial policies came back to the agenda during the new governments of the Workers Party (PT) in early 2003, not only the different types of state influence were maintained and strengthened (via golden shares, indirect state-ownership via pension funds and the national development bank) but also new credit lines were put in operation, to help the internationalization of these national champions (see the next section).

8.3.1 Historical Driving Forces

The internationalization of Brazilian companies was a sequential process, dating back to the 1960s and 1970s, and we can differentiate five phases of this process. As the following short historical overview demonstrates, for the first major home-country push factor in the internationalization process of Brazilian companies we have to look at *broad macroeconomic factors* that have historically determined the ability and desire of Brazilian companies to start operations abroad.

During the first phase in the 1960s and 1970s some companies started to export and establish operations, mainly in markets with geographical and cultural proximity, the so-called "natural market". After the oil crisis and even more so during the lost decade of the 1980s due to the domestic economic downturn and falling sales and public investments, most of the large (family-owned) Brazilian companies favoured moving abroad as the only viable expansion strategy. In this period the main driving force for internationalization was the bad and worsening outlook in the domestic market. During the second phase, the market-oriented reforms (in line with the Washington Consensus) of the 1990s (in fact until 2002), the main tendency was the heightened competition from foreign multinationals investing in Brazil. During this "*competitive shock*" (Casanova and Kassum 2014: 84) Brazilian companies were forced to reorganize their operations, including turning towards foreign financing and pushing forward their international expansion. Thus the major push factor this time was the *increasing competition within the domestic market* and the inherent need to raise competitiveness, also via expansion of operations abroad.

The third phase of internationalization of Brazilian companies started around 2002–2003 and represents up to today the most aggressive and successful period of Brazilian companies' global expansion. Driven by *high commodity process* and *increasing demand* from Asia (mainly China), mostly resource-based companies (such as Petrobras and Vale) executed large-scale acquisitions in neighbouring and more distant (developed and emerging) markets. The *favourable international conditions and rising demand from Asia* have served rather as important *pull factors*, whereas *domestic economic growth*,[10] rising sales and public investment have also

[10] Major Brazilian companies were also driven by the emergence of a new middle class in Brazil (in line with active social policies under the Lula era) and the subsequent increasing demand for consumer products. The food processing JBS-Friboi and the retailer CBD (Grupo Pão de Açúcar) are good examples, but also Brazilian banks (Banco do Brasil,

acted as push factors as these allowed companies to turn their attention towards international markets (as business has been doing well at home). It was also during this phase when *public policies* started to effectively drive the internationalization project: President Lula explicitly urged Brazilian companies to go global, and *new Brazilian Development Bank (BNDES) credit lines* were opened and supported by other regulatory measures to stimulate the internationalization of (mainly large) Brazilian companies.

The fourth phase started with the global financial crisis in 2008, when amid the financial and economic turmoil in the Global North, emerging markets became major destinations of FDI flows and in more general terms the engines of global growth. As a result major Brazilian firms started to *re-orient their activities from advanced markets, towards emerging markets* or even the domestic market. Finally, the fifth phase[11] started in 2015,[12] when the economic (and political) crisis in Brazil culminated and its effects have been adding up. As long as in 2012 and even in 2014 most authors and analysts had been praising the resilience of Brazilian companies towards economic instability and volatility,[13] while in 2017 reports were already written about *divestment under crises* (Sheng and Carrera 2017). Not only the economic downturn but also huge corruption scandals surrounding major Brazilian firms, as well as changes in the political leadership and the following economic policy turn, have all resulted in a basically new and complex set of framework conditions, inhibiting most large Brazilian companies from going on with their internationalization strategies. Most companies affected by the corruption scandal have announced plans to sell foreign subsidiaries and cancel or decrease future investment plans, in order to be able to pay the leniency fees and fines. The most striking example is obviously Petrobras, which

Bradesco and Itaú-Unibanco) have benefitted from rising levels of consumer credits (Casanova and Kassum 2014: 72).

[11] The literature writes about four phases, mainly based on the work of Casanova (2009, 2014, 2016), these analysis end however by 2014–2015, exactly at the time, when we date the beginning of last phase.

[12] The literature writes about four phases, mainly based on the work of Casanova (2009, 2014, 2016); these analyses end however by 2014–2015, exactly at the time when we date the beginning of the last phase.

[13] With catchy wording Casanova and Kassum (2014: 85) write about the ability of Brazilian firms to tackle the persistent "*voo de galinha*," which means something like chicken flight, and refers to short-term economic downturns.

had announced to cut its investment until 2019 by 25 per cent (the equivalent of 32 billion US dollars).

Besides these main broad macroeconomic trends, other, mainly *firm-specific*, factors have also stimulated (or constrained) the internationalization of BMNEs. These, obviously, differ from case to case, but some commonalities can be revealed (Casanova and Kassum 2014: 84–85). First of all, a main motivation for going abroad was the aim to *secure access to natural resources* in foreign markets, mainly in the case of resource-based companies such as Petrobras and Vale. Second, in the case of companies at the high ends of the value chain, the desire was to *better adapt to local needs* and to *better serve these markets* by becoming more responsive to local specificities. This was typically the case for Embraer (the airplane manufacturer) and Marcopolo (the bus manufacturer), which have opened up commercial offices and subsidiaries in order to be closer to the clients. As the third factor we can mention the aim of Brazilian exporting companies to *avoid tariff and non-tariff barriers* by opening up production units in their end markets (instead of solely exporting). Examples are the steel company Gerdau and the orange juice maker Cutrale. Last but not least, many companies have chosen to internationalize with the aim *to learn and upgrade* by being exposed to higher competition in international markets (in contrast to the rather protected and closed domestic market). The retail sector and food industry can offer good examples for this strategy Casanova and Kassum (2014: 85) mention, for example, the beauty products company Natura and its opening up a retail store in Paris, the international centre for the beauty industry.

Among several specificities of Brazilian companies (mainly related to state ownership or influence, family ownership, the hierarchical market economy structure), an often-highlighted distinctive characteristic is *the so-called resilience to volatility*, meaning the ability to navigate (and do business) under volatile economic conditions. This ability has been achieved by operating in volatile domestic market conditions during the twentieth century, characterized by unstable recurring crises, overregulated markets and infrastructural bottlenecks. Casanova and Kassum (2014: 87) argue that even though these conditions might have negatively affected both the daily operations and long-term development perspectives of the firms, their resulting ability to successfully operate under such perverse conditions might be regarded today as a competitive advantage, if doing business under similar constraints (physical or legal infrastructural deficiencies). A good example is the food processing company BRF, which has developed a world-class distribution network for frozen and refrigerated products and was able to successfully expand towards the Middle East and North Africa region and overcome all the imperfections typical for these Arab markets.

8.3.2 *Current Driving Forces of Internationalization of BMNEs*

According to a recent survey on the top 20 BMNEs ranked in terms of foreign assets, the primary reasons for investing globally were the following (Sheng and Carrera 2017: 10): (1) access to new markets; (2) proximity to clients; (3) cost reduction; (4) access to natural resources and (5) high taxes and institutional voids in Brazil (such as corruption, poor transportation system and unqualified labour force). Some companies have also cited access to new technologies; however, the overall ranking and relevance of this factor was much lower than in the case of the above-mentioned drivers. From this list we highlight the desire to avoid high taxes and institutional voids as an important push factor for Brazilian firms to go abroad, as all the other factors are more in line with traditional push factors present in the cases of more developed countries and thus thoroughly analysed in classic FDI literature.

Looking at the Brazilian internationalization process in a more historical perspective we have argued that in more general terms the macroeconomic context the domestic instability has also pushed the companies to expand in more stable economies, so as to compensate the risks faced at their home markets. Not independently from the broad macroeconomic volatility, high capital costs (high interest rates, expensive credit facilities, high transaction costs and scarcity of long-term credit) at home have also pushed Brazilian companies towards setting up subsidiaries abroad and gaining access to cheaper credit facilities overseas.

Extensive literature addresses the internationalization process of EMNEs as a learning process and claim that these companies do not always begin their expansion abroad with clear competitive advantages, but rather acquire it meanwhile, and the *aim to acquire knowledge* can be considered as an important driving force behind their international activities. This argumentation is also found for Brazil (e.g. Casanova 2016), and a good example is the already mentioned beauty company Natura and its subsidiary in Paris, France.

Another example is Stefanini. The Brazilian IT company, created in 1987 by the current owner and CEO Marco Stefanini, is an outstanding success story among Brazilian firms, yet it reveals many typical features of Latino-type business development: family owned, hierarchical in its structure, taking advantage of complex home-country environment—to just mention a few. The main motives for Stefanini to go global was to be close to its customers and clients and thus to be able to compete with its competitors like IBM, Tata Consultancy Services and Accenture, some of them over 15 times Stefanini's size (Monteiro and Rozman 2017: 1). At the same time Stefanini has also built upon its abilities gained at home, by operating in one of the world's most complex business and political environment, and has proved to be able to deal with extreme crisis situations originated in its home country. This ability to change and adapt might be a valuable source in the current global (and sectoral) environment, when companies are facing perhaps the most dramatic challenges in this industry: the digital revolution. In Stefanini's own words "Nobody knows who will be winners and losers in the digital revolution. The jury is still out for us, and for all companies in our industry. Flexibility and innovation are in our DNA. Now, more than ever, it is time for us to be flexible and innovative. These are the most exciting times in Stefanini's history" (Monteiro and Rozman 2017: 3).

8.3.3 Internationalization as a State-Led Process: Public Policies to Promote OFDI of BMNEs

The rise of EMNEs on the global level is challenging the traditional argumentation of "mainstream" economic theories both in international business and in development economics (Nölke 2014). There is at least one important distinctive feature of the internationalization of EMNEs: the fact that more often than not they have relied on the active support of their respective governments to conquer external markets (Caseiro and Masiero 2014; Goldstein 2007; Johnson 2012). This was certainly the case in Brazil: at the latest from 2003 the Brazilian government has actively tried to encourage OFDI through expensive and often controversial (and debated) public policies, which have also come to the limelight during the currently unfolding corruption scandal.[14]

[14] But we will show that some measures have already been in place since 1998.

Until the 2000s the direct promotion of outward investment had not entered the economic policy agenda. The internationalization of Brazilian companies, as presented above, was largely driven by the companies themselves (Fleury and Fleury 2011); the state had not played a key (direct) role in this (early) process. Since the early 2000s some new forms of BNDES support appeared; however, these remained stand-alone programmes, and there has been no comprehensive strategy to support the global expansion of Brazilian firms. This is in stark contrast with China and some other Asian countries, where the "developmentalist" governments have been the key driving force behind the internationalization of firms.

After 1990 and the liberalization efforts most policy measures were devoted to attract FDI into Brazil—as in the context of foreign exchange scarcity, high indebtedness, low competitiveness of the state-dominated production sector, privatization efforts and so on; foreign capital inflows were to be promoted, while any type of capital outflow was to be prevented (important restrictions were also put in force). OFDI flows from Brazil, and public policies to promote these, came onto the development agenda only after the economic stabilization in the mid-1990s; however, the progressive liberalization of capital accounts have to be regarded as an important prerequisite for these.

The first direct instrument to promote the internationalization of Brazilian companies goes back to 1998, when a separate credit line was introduced by the BNDES to help foreign governments to realize large infrastructure projects (mainly in Latin America and Africa[15]) by hiring Brazilian engineering companies. The BNDES loans may have added up to 85 per cent of the total value of the construction projects, which made these not only available but also lucrative for BMNEs. This was however contingent upon the fact that in each infrastructure project abroad the products manufactured in Brazil had to make up at least 35 per cent of the bank's disbursement (Caseiro and Masiero 2014: 241–242). This requirement was put in place in order to foster exports (of manufactured goods) and to promote positive spillovers in the Brazilian supply chains.

The second instrument aiming at directly financing Brazilian companies to invest abroad was put in place in 2002 and included both loans and subscription of securities. This credit line was first used only in 2005

[15] BNDES loans were essential to make Brazilian companies competitive against the expanding Chinese companies, which were also supported by their government.

(when JBS acquired the Argentine subsidiary of its American competitor, Swift) (Sennes and Mendes 2009). In 2005 as an important complementary measure the Brazilian Central Bank (BCB) removed the prior authorization requirement of all OFDI projects above the five million US dollar threshold, and this has to be regarded as an important milestone in Brazilian OFDI policies.

Until 2007 there was no coherent policy framework in Brazil to support OFDI. There were two instruments and special credit lines (supplemented by the regulatory measure lifting the prior authorization requirement of OFDI projects by the BCB), which tried to promote the internationalization of Brazilian companies. The year 2007 represents however an important turning point as with the adoption of the "Production Development Policy" (PDP), the new industrial policy plan, explicit goals for OFDI support were laid down and a more coherent (however short-lived) policy approach started. The PDP had set the strategic goal of expanding and consolidating the international leadership of Brazilian EMNEs in those strategic industries in which Brazil already possessed international competitiveness, such as aeronautics, oil and gas, petrochemical, ethanol, mining, steel, pulp and paper, and meat (MDIC 2008).[16]

Between 2005 and 2011 the BNDES supported the internationalization of Brazilian companies by 4.9 billion US dollars, and this consisted almost exclusively of securities subscription. In addition, the BNDES continued to finance overseas infrastructural projects with an annual average summing up to 1.1 billion US dollars between 2007 and 2012, when the total number of these projects exploded to 97 (compared to the total of 5 projects and 350 million US dollars between 1998 and 2002) (Caseiro and Masiero 2014: 242). Even though the international expansion of technology-intensive companies also emerged among the goals, in reality these remained restricted, and the overwhelming majority (more than 95%) of the BNDES-financed OFDI projects went to meat processing companies (such as JBS and Mafrig).

After heavy criticisms (and strengthening pressure from Brazilian business elite), and as a consequence of change in the presidency (Dilma Rousseff followed Lula as the president), but also in the light of worsening economic indicators, a new industrial policy document was instated in

[16] "Keep or position the local productive system amongst the top 5 world exporters/global players."

2011, the Bigger Brazil (Brasil Maior) plan. This contained the reorientation of industrial policy priorities, while it was also foreseen not only to support OFDI in already highly competitive industries but to promote obtaining foreign technologies and/or access to new markets. However, no specific goal and no further policy instrument or action was instituted to reach this objective, and thus no implementation followed. Caseiro and Masiero (2014: 244) write about the "interruption of the global champions policy" and cite Luciano Coutinho (the BNDES president at that time) as saying that the number of those sectors in which Brazilian companies are internationally competitive enough to be promoted as potential global champions is limited and he cannot see other sectors with the same potential. Thus, in his opinion, the policy aiming at supporting the internationalization of large BMNEs has run its course and thus it has been concluded.

To sum up we claim that the Brazilian OFDI strategy was rather based on already existing dynamic comparative advantages, and thus it preferred to support industries that were already highly competitive internationally (Caseiro and Masiero 2014). Obviously this investment promotion strategy has lower potential to generate positive spillovers to the domestic economy; hence, it was less successful domestically in developmentalist terms. This is why, even though relatively successful abroad, Brazilian OFDI policies lie (deservedly) at the centre of political and academic debates. In international comparison among the emerging countries the Brazilian OFDI policies seem to be less interventionist (compared to China, e.g.), while it was of course more driven by direct state interventions than the more liberal counterparts, such as Chile or the majority of the more advanced countries. The Brazilian government is exercising direct power over the two state-owned companies (Petrobras and Banco do Brasil), while in other cases it is "only" a minority shareholder. At the same time however it is almost the exclusive provider of long-term (subsidized) credit via the BNDES, which makes the state influence excessively strong, albeit rather via indirect channels. We can state that with the exception of infrastructural projects in Latin America and Africa, the Brazilian government is not directly influencing OFDI allocation decisions.

8.4 Pull Factors: Incentives for Brazilian Companies to Invest in the ECE Region

Turning towards the analysis of host-country determinants of Brazilian OFDI, we first have to admit however that only a few studies look at internationalization strategies of Brazilian companies from the host-country perspective (Amal and Tomio 2012; Calderón 2014; Nunes de Alcântara et al. 2016). In the following discussion we explicitly aim to enrich these results with our own research findings.

8.4.1 Main Drivers of Brazilian OFDI: The Host-Country Perspective

In one of the most comprehensive analysis on host-country determinants of Brazilian OFDI Nunes de Alcântara et al. (2016) identify the following pull factors:

1. reduced or zero tax burdens and simplified corporate and financial rules (the tax haven argument);
2. geographical proximity and Mercosur membership (efficiency seeking argument);
3. cultural proximity (Portuguese as native language);
4. availability of natural resources (natural-resources seeking argument);
5. large pool of available workers (human capital argument);
6. large internal (local) market (market-seeking argument) and
7. government effectiveness.

The pull factors are ranked according to their significance level, meaning that the first five factors are not only positively influencing Brazilian FDI but their effect is considerably large. The last two elements, although having significant and positive relationship, have a rather minimal effect.

This list is not just telling in terms of what it is containing but it is also worth recalling some few missing elements. First and foremost, political stability does not play a role during locational decisions of Brazilian firms. The explanation for this is that Brazilian investors are used to market imperfections and weak institutional environments in their home country, so they have a different interpretation of political risk than their counterparts from more developed countries. To some extent we could argue similarly in relation to government effectiveness.

Analysing the period between 2002 and 2011, Nunes de Alcântara et al. (2016: 177) claim that "Brazilian multinationals do not internationalize their activities in pursuit of cost reduction, efficiency, or to explore new markets or natural resources of the host countries. Results show that Brazilian investments were attracted by the availability of skilled labor, openness of the host market, geographic proximity, improved financial conditions of Brazilian companies, and national companies' strategy of reaffirmation and consolidation as global players."

At the same time Amal and Tomio (2012) highlight a different pattern of internationalization in the case of Brazilian companies than the model of MNEs from Asian countries. They emphasize that Brazilian OFDI is influenced mainly by the *economic performance*, *cultural distance* and *regulatory quality* of the host country.

We have shown earlier that a considerable share of Brazilian OFDI goes into so-called "tax haven" countries (mainly in the Caribbean region, but also some into European countries), with the main motivation being to enjoy preferable, low rates of taxes and other regulations. This regional focus reaffirms convincingly the findings above.

These can be easily paralleled with the above-mentioned pull factors, such as natural resource-seeking, tax haven and market-seeking arguments, while the learning and upgrading motivations were not explicitly included in those studies.

We have also shown that a unique feature of Brazilian companies investing abroad was *the so-called resilience to volatility*, meaning the ability do business under volatile economic and/or political conditions is of special relevance for our current study. Several authors highlight that Brazilian EMNEs are less concerned about political risks and macroeconomic instability in the host markets and even better align to institutional shortcomings. At the same, time several studies have highlighted that Brazilian firms tend to invest in countries that resemble their domestic environment (so-called natural markets, mainly Latin countries), by which we mean that cultural and institutional proximity does play an important role when deciding upon the localization strategy. This preference to invest in so-called *natural markets* (mainly Latin countries), which resemble similar cultural settings close to their domestic environment.

In a somewhat contradictory manner, however in line with arguments of mainstream theories, Martins (2012) has found that *economic freedom*, "good" *institutional setting* and polices to improve *economic openness* are of large importance for Brazilian investors during their localization decisions, while geographic distance in not a major determinant according to his survey.

Somewhat more surprisingly the size of the host economies (GDP of host countries) does not constitute to be a relevant motivation factor for Brazilian companies to invest abroad (the market-seeking argument), as several authors (Martins 2012; Calderón 2014) have found that Brazilian firms still tend rather to prefer to export their goods and services instead of investing in large overseas economies. In a similar vein, the same scholars have found that the technology and human capital levels of the host country do not play a decisive role, suggesting that Brazilian OFDI is not primarily determined by asset seeking or augmenting motivations (even though counterexamples mainly from technology-intensive sectors exist).

Finally, we sum up the main findings of Andreff (2015: 89) related to the Brazilian case from his comparative analysis on OFDI strategies of BRIC (Brazilian, Russian, Indian and Chinese) multinational companies. According to this research BMNEs are predominantly market seeking, to some extent resource seeking and to a much lesser degree, and only more recently, technological asset seeking (which constituted to be less than ten per cent of declared OFDI motives). This study has found no sign of an efficiency-seeking strategy, meaning to relocate production into countries with low unit labour costs. Even though technological upgrading is in general an important driving force for developing and emerging countries' companies, in Brazil technology-seeking OFDI has been relevant only for 7.2 per cent of the surveyed MNEs (ibid.).

Traditionally BMNEs tended to internationalize product development activities with the aim of adapting products to local markets, with the core of R&D activities remaining within Brazil. This was also proven by Maehler et al (2011), who have analysed Brazilian subsidiaries located in Portugal in different industries and have shown the innovations there were typically incremental and occurred mainly in relation with product development (aligning to Portuguese customers' needs via new products' creation).

Even though BMNEs in general might be underrepresented in technology-intensive sectors, some of them have significantly invested in R&D expenditures abroad, even if not yet in the very high-tech ends, like some of their Indian or Chinese counterparts. There are however some examples of foreign expansion of smaller Brazilian IT companies, such as Stefanini, and more recently we find outstanding trans-border mergers (such as the most recent case of Embraer and Boeing suggests), which might signal that BMNEs have started to try to improve their strategic position in the global scene and climb up the value chain through investment in technological assets.

To sum up we might conclude that host-country determinants of Brazilian OFDI are neither totally resembling MNEs from developed countries nor can be totally explained by traditional FDI theories present in the literature, which might lead us to reconsider these in the light of "atypical" behaviour of the BMNEs.

8.4.2 ECE Region in Focus

If we wish to narrow down our regional focus on Europe, more specifically on the ECE region, while analysing main host-country determinants of Brazilian OFDI, we unfortunately encounter a "blind spot" in the literature. To our best knowledge no analysis has been yet focusing on Brazilian companies' investment strategies in Europe from a host-country/region perspective (see, e.g., Brennan's (2011) book on Southern MNEs in Europe and its respective chapters on host-country determinants, which analyse only the Chinese and Indian cases, while the volume of Szent-Iványi (2017) on FDI in Central and Eastern Europe basically only refers to negligible levels of Brazilian FDI in the region).

An obvious reason is undoubtedly that most Brazilian FDI flows to Western European countries; however, these amounts are also relatively low if compared to those of other outward investor emerging economies with similar characteristics (such as China, Russia or India). Referring specifically to the Brazilian case we have already highlighted the possible explanation of prioritizing the "natural market", close in geographical, cultural and institutional terms. Furthermore, and related to the sectoral composition of Brazilian OFDI, we have seen an increase towards the natural resources sector (metals, mining, oil, gas and steel), which also results in different regional priorities than ECE.

All in all we have shown that the ECE region does not represent any special emphasis in the internationalization strategies of Brazilian (or even Latin American) firms. We have found only a few companies which are actively present in this region. To name the most important outstanding examples, we highlight: Kaco, a Brazilian auto parts manufacturer (Hungary); Embraer, the Brazilian aircraft manufacturer (Czech Republic); Embraco, the Brazilian refrigerator producer—which has been followed by three smaller supplier firms—(Slovakia); and Stefanini, the Brazilian IT company (Poland and Hungary) (see also Sect. 8.2.4).

It is clear that even though there are low levels of Brazilian OFDI in the ECE region, these reveal a rather diverse sectoral composition and we find examples at both the lower and higher ends of the value chain. This finding offers some optimistic outlook for further research at the firm level.

The few relevant examples reveal some interesting cases, such as the Brazilian car component manufacturer KACO (formerly known as Sabó), which was founded by a Hungarian immigrant in the 1950s and became a global supplier to Volkswagen. This case might reveal the *role of diaspora, personal ties and informal institutions* acting as an important pull factor (which might show some similarities with the Chinese or Asian cases).

In the case of Embraco, the clear motivation to invest in Slovakia was a rather classical one: to decrease production costs and thus to increase efficiency (Éltető 2014: 18). Embraco, the Brazilian company providing innovative solutions for refrigeration, namely compressors and air conditioning units, was founded in 1971 in Brazil and has set up a factory in Slovakia in 1999 and pursued several reinvestments later. The Slovak factory took over the Most labour-intensive parts of production has been moved from Italy to Slovakia due to the *significantly lower labour costs* in the latter country. The Slovak factory is currently employing around 2600 people and exporting its products mainly to Europe and the United States. The efficiency-seeking motive can easily be revealed from the words of Antonello Lanfranco, the chief operating manager of Embraco Slovakia: "We chose Slovakia because, among other things, it offered us a better opportunity regarding labour costs than either Hungary or the Czech Republic."[17]

To better understand Embraco's locational choice, it is worth highlighting that it operates in Spišská Nová Ves, which is located in the eastern part of Slovakia, with traditionally high levels of unemployment. Embraco represents one of the biggest foreign investments in this region and plays an important role on the regional labour market. From a slightly different (host-country) perspective, Embraco's role is also outstanding in terms of its contribution to decrease inequality between marginalized groups and the others because it employs ten per cent of Roma in East Slovakia (MFEA 2017).

[17] https://spectator.sme.sk/c/20007588/embraco-bullish-on-quality.html

This is however yet only one side of the Embraco success story, as besides the industrial plant, the Brazilian company has also set up a research and development centre in Slovakia with more than 100 employees, working on the development of commercial compressors and of natural refrigerants such as propane and isobutane, environmentally friendly and more efficient than synthetic fluids. This operation was so successful that Embraco has decided to transfer a branch of its R&D operations from Italy to Slovakia.

The case of Embraco reveals a further important dynamic (acting as a pull factor) regarding OFDI flows. Embraco's investment has attracted three other smaller Brazilian companies, the CRW Plásticos (produces plastic components for the automotive industry and appliances, electronics and compressors), Rudolph Usinados (manufactures metal components for the automotive industry) and Micro Juntas (manufactures insulators and seals for compressors), which are also located in the eastern part of the country. There are clear *agglomeration forces* present in this case, as the already operating Brazilian company has acted as a magnet to pull further Brazilian investments into the region.

We can sum up the above-mentioned pull factors through the words of Renato Pellegrini, the general secretary of the Luso Brazilian Business Association: "Located in the heart of central-eastern Europe, Slovakia is an attractive investment destination particularly for Brazilian companies with solid, long-term business relations with customers in this region. … Besides its strategic location, Slovakia offers other important assets to potential Brazilian investors, such as a qualified workforce and access to the common market and the economic cooperation and regional development mechanisms of the EU."[18] Pellegrini has also added that *synergies* with already established Brazilian companies have acted as an important *incentive for new investments* in Slovakia and reveals also some further potential in the future.

The other ECE success story is the case of Stefanini, the Brazilian IT company (as mentioned already earlier in the chapter). Stefanini has successfully expanded globally, by pursuing a differentiated expansion strategy in the more mature markets such as North America and Western Europe. In "Vision 2022", the company's global expansion strategy, Stefanini, the CEO, has explained the recipe for success in the future.

[18] https://spectator.sme.sk/c/20042223/brazil-and-slovakia-seek-ways-to-grow-together.html

According to him there is a "need to transform Stefanini's sales and delivery model and simultaneously expand its global footprint, both in emerging markets as in the more mature markets as North America and Europe. The strength of the firm was to understand how to move from Brazil to other countries, and to understand the local culture and feel comfortable in it" (Monteiro and Rozman 2017: 1).

As Tania Herrezeel, EMEA (European Regional Office) marketing director has rightly put it: "Being global means understanding the world but also your local environment. Europeans buy services very differently from North Americans, and the differences exist even between Germany and Spain in Europe and are significant. We understand both the local and global markets" (ibid.).

More recently the company seems to have understood the specificities of emerging markets, such as the local context of Central and Eastern European countries, as after being present in Poland and Hungary it has opened its second office in Poland in 2018 and one each in Romania and in Ukraine. As Stefanini has highlighted, one of the factors that influenced the decision to invest in Eastern Europe besides its thriving IT market was the very high share of workers with intermediate or high English proficiency,[19] which is a must in the IT sector as well as in multinational environments.

Besides these success stories, it is also worth looking for reasons why BMNFs (and multilatinas in more general terms) have been or are staying away from the ECE region. We have mentioned earlier one obvious reason for this: the prevalence of geographical distance. However, not only being literally far away but also cultural distance plays a role, as well as the lack or historically low levels of diplomatic, political and even economic relations, which also add up to the low and volatile incoming investment flows. To overcome these (and other) shortcomings a recent study by Kugiel (2016) has suggested a new cooperative approach towards emerging markets and a strengthened cooperation between Visegrad countries to be better able to emerge as a potential FDI location on the horizon of the BICS (Brazil, India, China and South Africa) countries. This finding is especially relevant for proactive strategies towards Brazilian companies.

[19] https://www.globenewswire.com/news-release/2019/09/30/1922816/0/en/Stefanini-strengthens-operations-in-Europe-with-expansion-to-Ukraine.html

8.5 Conclusions

In this chapter we have presented the motivations of Brazilian firms to invest abroad, with a special focus on the ECE countries. According to our main results there are some specific home-country advantages resulting from the very complex home-country context of Brazil, and some host-country specificities have also been identified based on the rather few success stories of Brazilian companies actively present in the region.

We have shown that Brazilian OFDI reveals in general a very concentrated pattern in terms of sectoral composition, mainly dominated by the extractive and commodities sectors, and also in terms of company size. We have also drawn attention however to some outstanding examples in other more technologically intensive sectors, such as the case of the former national champion Embraer in the aviation industry and the international success of the privately owned company Stefanini.

In terms of regional distribution, the hegemony of natural markets was to some extent broken down, as leaving aside the Caribbean tax havens, the United States and Europe have emerged as important destinations of Brazilian OFDI. In the most recent years, however, amid a multi-dimensional economic, social, political and institutional crisis in Brazil, most firms were focusing their resources on defending their domestic positions and activities (or paying off leniency fees and fines due to the overarching investigations related to the Petrobras scandal and Operation Lava Jato, such as Odebrecht and Petrobras), and often even withdrawing investments from overseas. However, as the ECE region had already been out of the focus of Brazilian companies during the 2000s, these more recent negative trends were not necessarily felt in the region.

Preceding this recent turmoil, mainly during the 2000s BMNEs undoubtedly became prominent actors on the global level (global players). We have presented some historical antecedents of this success story and highlighted main home-country push factors behind these trends. Among the more classical driving forces of the internationalization process, we have laid special emphasis on the role the Brazilian government has played in this process.

Thus one of our main insights was that government policies have actively (directly and indirectly) influenced Brazilian companies' internationalization decisions, and this was especially spectacular in the mid-2000s. We have argued however that the Brazilian going global policy was a much more defensive and limited one, than, for example, the Chinese strategy, even though compared to some regional counterparts (Chile or Argentina) the proactivity of the BNDES stands out.

In the last part of our study we looked at host-country determinants of Brazilian OFDI. The expansion of Brazilian firms is still very much determined by geographical and cultural proximity and tax issues. Depending on the very specific cases and companies, the availability of natural resources, human capital and large host markets might play very different roles during the locational decisions. At the same time due to their home-country experiences, Brazilian firms tend to be highly resilient to macro-economic and political instabilities and are often less affected by institutional voids. As a rule, Brazilian firms are rarely considering the internationalization strategy as a way of technological upgrading and learning opportunity, though counterexamples also exist.

Looking at the ECE region, we have concluded that it does not represent any special emphasis in the internationalization strategies of Brazilian (or even Latin American) firms; on the contrary, there are only a few companies that are actively present in the region. These investments—more often than not—stay mostly below any threshold of international surveys and databases that usually map larger OFDI transactions (such as Amadeus or EPMG) and also those Brazilian surveys that focus on the top Brazilian companies (such as BCG, FDC). This also explains the lack of focused academic research in this regard.

Among the real driving forces of those few Brazilian companies that have successfully invested in the ECE region, we have highlighted the following: *diaspora, personal ties and/or informal relations* (as in the case of KACO); *relatively low labour costs* (Embraco); *agglomeration forces*, such as the presence of other Brazilian firms (CRW Plásticos, Micro Juntas, Rudolph Usinados); *relatively high skilled labour force* (Stefanini) and a *thriving local market* (Stefanini).

Finally, our results have shown that even though the ECE region was by far not among the main destinations of the Brazilian outward investments, still some outstanding success stories can be found. Thus, the insights of this study might contribute to better capitalizing upon the existing experiences and also enhance the possibilities for intensifying economic relations in terms of investments between Brazil and the ECE region in the future.

References

Aguzzoli, R., & Hunek, I. (2019). How Regional are Regional Headquarters? The "Latinization" of Control in European Structures of a Brazilian MNC. In A. Breinbauer, L. Brennan, J. Jäger, A. G. M. Nachbagauer, & A. Nölke (Eds.), *Emerging Market Multinationals and Europe. Challenges and Strategies.* Cham: Springer.

Amal, M., & Tomio, B. T. (2012). Determinants of Brazilian Outward Foreign Direct Investment (OFDI): A Host Country Perspective. 36. Encontro de EnAnpad, Rio de Janiero. Retrieved from http://www.anpad.org.br/admin/pdf/2012_ESO305.pdf

Amann, E. (2009). Technology, Public Policy, and the Emergence of Brazilian Multinationals. In L. Brainard & L. Martinez-Diaz (Eds.), *Brazil as an Economic Superpower? Understanding Brazil's Changing Role in the Global Economy.* Washington, DC: Brookings Institution Press.

Andreff, W. (2015). Outward Foreign Direct Investment from BRIC Countries: Comparing Strategies of Brazilian, Russian, Indian and Chinese Multinational Companies. *The European Journal of Comparative Economics, 12*(2), 79–131.

BCB. (2017). The Brazilian Central Bank Statistical Data. Retrieved August 3, 2017, from http://www.bcb.gov.br/ingles/economic/SeriehistFluxoInvDir_i.asp

Brennan, L. (Ed.). (2011). *The Emergence of Southern Multinationals. Their Impact on Europe.* Basingstoke: Palgrave Macmillan.

Calderón, A. A. B. (2014). *Outward FDI in Brazil: A Matter of Economic Growth and Institutional Configuration.* Prepared for the FLACSO-ISA Joint International Conference in Buenos Aires, Argentina, July 23–25, 2014.

Campanario, M. A., Stal, E., & Silva, M. M. (2011). *Outward FDI from Brazil and Its Policy Context, from Inward and Outward FDI Country Profiles.* Vale Columbia Center on Sustainable International Investment.

Casanova, L. (2009). *Global Latinas. Latin America's Emerging Multinationals.* Basingstoke: Palgrave Macmillan.

Casanova, L. (2016). Latin American Multinationals Facing the 'New Reality'. In P. F. Perez & A. Lluch (Eds.), *Evolution of Family Business. Continuity and Change in Latin America and Spain* (pp. 23–36). Cheltenham: Edward Elgar.

Casanova, L., & Kassum, J. (2014). The Political Economy of an Emerging Global Power. In *Search of the Brazil Dream.* Basingstoke: Palgrave Macmillan.

Caseiro, L., & Masiero, G. (2014). OFDI Promotion Policies in Emerging Economies: The Brazilian and Chinese strategies. *Critical Perspectives on International Business, 10*(4), 237–255.

Éltető, A. (2014). *Trade and Investment Relations between Central and Eastern Europe and Latin America.* Centre for Economic and Regional Studies HAS Institute of World Economics, Working Paper No. 206.

FDC. (2016). *Ranking FDC das Multinacionais Brasileiras 2016*. Fundação Dom Cabral.

Fleury, A., & Fleury, M. T. L. (2011). *Brazilian Multinationals. Competences for Internationalization*. Cambridge: Cambridge University Press.

Fleury, A., Fleury, M. T. L., & Reis, G. G. (2011). Europe in the Internationalization Strategies of the Multilatinas. In L. Brennan (Ed.), *The Emergence of Southern Multinationals*. London: Palgrave Macmillan.

Goldstein, A. (2007). *Multinational Companies from Emerging Economies: Composition, Conceptualization and Direction in the Global Economy*. London: Palgrave Macmillan.

Johnson, L. (2012). Absent from the Discussion: The Other Half of Investment Promotion. Columbia FDI Perspectives, No. 79, Vale Columbia Center on Sustainable International Investment, New York, NY.

Kugiel, P. (Ed.). (2016). *V4 Goes Global: Exploring Opportunities and Obstacles in the Visegrad Countries' Cooperation with Brazil, India, China and South Africa*. Warsaw: PISM.

Maehler, A. E., et al. (2011). Knowledge Transfer and Innovation in Brazilian Multinational Companies. *Journal of Technology Management and Innovation, 6*(4), 1–14.

Martins, T. (2012). *Emerging MNE from Emerging Economies: OFDI from Brazil*. Paper presented at the Third Copenhagen Conference on "'Emerging Multinationals': Outward Investment from Emerging Economies", Copenhagen, Denmark, 25–26 October 2012.

Masiero, G., Ogasavara, M. H., Caseiro, L., & Ferreira, S. (2014). Financing the Expansion of Brazilian Multinationals into Europe. The Role of the Brazilian Development Bank (BNDES). In A. Nölke (Ed.), *Multinational Corporations from Emerging Markets. State Capitalism 3.0* (pp. 130–152). Basingstoke: Palgrave Macmillan.

MDIC. (2008). Política de desenvolvimento produtivo. Ministério do Desenvolvimento, Indústria e Comércio Exterior. Retrieved July 3, 2017, from www.mdic.gov.br

MFEA. (2017). Ministry of Foreign Affairs and Trade of Hungary. V4-Brazil Meeting in Budapest on 11-21-2017. Retrieved from https://www.kormany.hu/en/ministry-of-foreign-affairs-and-trade/news/v4-brazil-meeting-in-budapest

Monteiro, F., & Rozman, G. (2017). *Stefanini and the Digital Revolution: Transforming and Being Transformed*. INSEAD Case Study 1425.

Nölke, A. (Ed.). (2014). *Multinational Corporations from Emerging Markets. State Capitalism 3.0*. Basingstoke: Palgrave Macmillan.

Nölke, A., ten Brink, T., Claar, S., & May, C. (2019). *State-Permeated Capitalism in Large Emerging Economies*. New York: Routledge.

Nunes de Alcântara, J., Paiva, C. M. P., Bruhn, N. C. P., de Carvalho, H. R., & Calegario, C. L. L. (2016). Brazilian OFDI Determinants. *Latin American Business Review, 17*(3), 177–205.

Resende, P., Almeida, A., & Ramsey, J. (2010). The Transnationalization of Brazilian Companies: Lessons from the Top Twenty Multinational Enterprises. In K. P. Sauvant, G. McAllister, & V. A. Maschek (Eds.), *Foreign Direct Investments from Emerging Markets: The Challenges Ahead* (pp. 97–111). Basingstoke: Palgrave Macmillan.

Ricz, J. (2017). *Brazilian Companies Going Global. Home Country Push Factors of Brazilian Multinational Enterprises' (BMNEs') Investments, General Characteristics and Tendencies of Their Investments in the European, Especially East Central European (ECE) Region*. Centre for Economic and Regional Studies has Institute of World Economics, Working Paper No. 232.

Santiso, J. (2013). *The Decade of Multilatinas*. Cambridge: Cambridge University Press.

Sauvant, K. P. (2006). Inward and Outward FDI and the BRICs. In S. C. Jain (Ed.), *Emerging Economies and the Transformation of International Business: Brazil, Russia, India and China (BRICs)* (pp. 313–409). Cheltenham: Edward Elgar.

Schneider, B. R. (2013). *Hierarchical Capitalism in Latin America. Business, Labor, and the Challenges of Equitable Development* (Cambridge Studies in Comparative Politics). New York: Cambridge University Press.

Sennes, R., & Mendes, C. R. (2009). Public Policies and Brazilian Multinationals. In J. Ramsey & A. Almeida (Eds.), *The Rise of Brazilian Multinationals: Making the Leap from Regional Heavyweights to True Multinationals* (pp. 157–174). Rio de Janeiro: Elsevier-Campus.

Sheng, H. H., & Carrera Jr., J. M. (2017). *The Top 20 Brazilian Multinationals: Divestment under Crises*. Emerging Market Global Players (EMGP) Project Report March 2017. Fundação Getulio Vargas (FGV), Brazil and Columbia Center on Sustainable Investment (CCSI), New York.

Sheng, H. H., & Carrera Jr., J. M. (2018). *The Top 20 Brazilian Multinationals: A Long Way Out of the Crises*. Emerging Market Global Players (EMGP) Project Report January 2016. Fundação Getulio Vargas (FGV), Brazil and Columbia Center on Sustainable Investment (CCSI), New York.

Szent-Iványi, B. (Ed.). (2017). *Foreign Direct Investment in Central and Eastern Europe. Post-crisis Perspectives*. Basingstoke: Palgrave Macmillan.

UNCTAD. (2004, December 7). Outward FDI from Brazil: Poised to Take Off? Occasional Note. Retrieved July 6, 2017, from http://unctad.org/en/docs/iteiia200416_en.pdf

UNCTAD. (2019). *UNCTAD FDI Statistics Database*. United Nations Conference on Trade and Development. Retrieved from http://unctad.org/en/Pages/DIAE/FDI%20Statistics/FDI-Statistics.aspx

Vondra, A. (2011, April 14). Aero Lands Major Contract for Brazilian Military Plane. Retrieved from http://ceskapozice.lidovky.cz/aero-lands-major-contract-for-brazilian-military-plane-p1y-/tema.aspx?c=A110414_164724_pozice_11793

CHAPTER 9

South Africa: A Re-emerging Player in Global Outward FDI and a New Investor in East Central Europe?

Judit Kiss

9.1 Introduction

Since 1994, South Africa has been successfully reintegrated into the world economy and has become a capital exporter country. The main carriers of outward FDI are South African multinationals, which are not newcomers in the international arena as they started to be internationalised earlier than other emerging markets' multinational enterprises (MNEs). Their investment decisions are mainly driven by home country push factors fuelled by the economic, social and political legacy of the apartheid regime, while market, efficiency and strategic asset-seeking strategies also play a role (Kiss 2017). Though the main destinations of FDI outflow are traditionally the European countries, especially the UK, the CEE region is a newly emerging destination for South African investors to where foreign capital is attracted by a wide range of political, macroeconomic and institutional pull factors.

J. Kiss (✉)
Institute of World Economics, Centre for Economic and Regional Studies, Budapest, Hungary

Á. Szunomár (ed.), *Emerging-market Multinational Enterprises in East Central Europe*, Studies in Economic Transition,
https://doi.org/10.1007/978-3-030-55165-0_9

In line with the above, this chapter tries to present the general characteristics, the magnitude, trends, the main forms, and the geographical and sectoral distribution of outward foreign direct investment (FDI) of South Africa. The chapter will also reveal the internationalisation strategies of South African MNEs and the main driving forces with special regard to the home country push factors. Besides mapping out the place of European countries and that of the CEE region in South Africa's outward FDI, we will also reveal the motivation of South African firms to invest in the East Central European countries, analysing pull factors that played a role in their location selection.

The study is based on secondary data collected from academic books, journals, government's documents and publications of international organisations. For quantitative analysis, FDI data have been collected mainly from the UNCTAD database, but in some cases IMF, OECD, UN, World Bank and national data also have been used. One of the limitations of the study is the lack of coherent and transparent data and the fluid status of South African MNEs due to frequent change of ownership. The other is the lack of data on the distribution of FDI by sources and destinations in the case of South Africa. Though with little success, an attempt was made to rectify this shortcoming by using the receiving countries' national statistics as mirror statistics.

The primary research was intended to be based on company data and in-depth interviews with a sample of firms active in ECE countries. Though we were granted access to the Amadeus database, it was almost useless in the case of South African enterprises. Data changed from one year to the other and the database was incomplete. Some companies in the database were not active anymore in the region, while those that actually have performing enterprises did not appear in the database. We also tried to approach all the South African embassies in the region, but the response rate was very low. As an alternative option, we compiled a list of South African companies from the grass roots level, based on anecdotal evidence and media news.

9.2 The Economic and Social Legacy of the Apartheid Era

After the demise of the apartheid regime South Africa emerged from political and economic isolation. International sanctions on trade and investment in the apartheid era, and the lack of access to foreign capital, resulted in an inward-looking, import-substituting, anti-export biased and protectionist economic strategy that reduced the growth potential and competitiveness of the country. The positive "side-effect" of this enforced self-sufficiency was the development of infrastructure (roads, ports, communication, electricity generation) and high-quality education for whites, and the emergence of a relatively highly developed, sophisticated and well-regulated financial sector (bond and equity market).

South Africa's transition to democracy, its reintegration into the world economy in 1994 and the re-assumption of its leading role in Africa led to increased trade and restored capital flows. Sound macroeconomic policies were expected to bring fiscal and monetary stability, foster economic growth and help alleviate poverty and reduce inequality via providing employment opportunities, redistributing income and wealth, and providing equal access to education and health (Manuel 2014). However, meeting these high expectations was made difficult by the economic and social legacy of the apartheid era. The successful reintegration of the South African economy into the world economy and the liberalisation of trade and capital flows required the increase of competitiveness and the restructuring of the resource-based, capital-intensive economy (Bhorat et al. 2014).

By now, the South African economy has changed significantly. Growth rates have increased to 5% between 2005 and 2007, though it decelerated to 1.8% between 2009 and 2014 as a consequence of the 2008 global financial crisis (De Beer 2015). The slowdown and fluctuation continued: real GDP growth rate was only 0.3% in 2016 (African Economic Outlook 2017), then increased to 1.4% in 2017 and decelerated to 0.8% in 2018 and further to 0.7% in 2019 (African Economic Outlook 2020). The growth rate expectations, 1.1% in 2020 and 1.8% in 2021, are far below the 5.4% target of the National Development Plan (The DTI 2019). Investments started to increase, investment rates are around 20%, though savings rates are still rather low, which makes it vital to attract foreign capital (De Beer 2015; Smit 2015). Macroeconomic stability is ensured due to public balance,[1] with declining public debt and relatively low inflation.[2] At the same time, South Africa has been downgraded from *moderately free* to

[1] Budget deficit was around 3% of the GDP in 2015 and 2016 (African Economic Outlook 2017), and then increased to above 4% in 2018 and 2019 (African Economic Outlook 2020).

[2] Government debt was 55.6% in 2019 (African Economic Outlook 2020), while the inflation rate was 4.4% in 2019 (African Economic Outlook 2020).

mostly unfree in 2019 according to the Heritage Foundation's 2019 Index of Economic Freedom (Economic Freedom of the World 2019).

Since 1994, the country's economic strategy has been formulated by different macroeconomic plans/programmes. For instance, the 1994 Reconstruction and Development Program (RDP) focused on meeting basic needs and attracting foreign investment to promote growth (Lundahl and Petersson 2013). The Growth, Employment and Redistribution program (GEAR)[3] in 1996–2000 aimed to transform South Africa into a competitive, outward-oriented economy with increased international credibility that may attract foreign capital (Manuel 2014). The Accelerated and Shared Growth Initiative of South Africa (ASGISA) in 2006–2012 focused on promoting growth, the diversification of the economy and reducing poverty and unemployment. The National Industrial Policy Framework (2007) and the Trade Policy and Strategy Framework (2010) concentrated on industry diversification and on a closer alignment between trade and industrial policies (Edwards 2014). The New Growth Path (2010) addressed job creation, poverty alleviation and labour absorption (Ashman et al. 2014). In 2012, the National Development Plan (NDP) was launched for the period 2012–2030.[4] Its main aims are to reduce inequality and poverty through wide-ranging reforms in government and in society, to improve education, to raise employment and to boost exports to generate resources for investment (Manuel 2014). NDP might promote inclusive growth alongside the transformation and restructuring of the economy.[5]

9.3 South Africa as a Capital Exporter

By now South Africa became a more open and globally integrated economy. One of the ways through which South Africa was reintegrated was by re-entry into global capital markets in the framework of revitalising international financial relations. After 1994, the South African government gradually implemented policy reforms to facilitate the inflow of foreign capital while also permitting capital outflow and outward investments

[3] For details see Aron et al. (2009).
[4] For more see National Development Plan 2030—our future.
[5] For a deeper analysis of the different development programmes see Ricz (2017).

(Leape and Thomas 2009). These reforms included trade liberalisation,[6] capital account liberalisation, elimination of restrictions on cross-border transactions, lifting controls on foreign investment, exchange control reform[7] and liberalisation of institutional investments. These regulations, which were accompanied by macroeconomic and financial stability, solid institutional framework for protecting investors, sound exchange rate policy and increasing trade openness, led to improved sovereign credit ratings, stronger external position and the acceleration of international capital flows, including FDI flows.

As South Africa is the most developed resource-rich country in Africa, it has become a capital exporter right after the collapse of the apartheid regime.[8] Recently, South Africa has become the largest African investor abroad. Of the 9.801 billion total outward FDI from Africa, 46.4% (USD 4.552 billion) came from South Africa (World Investment Report 2019). South Africa belongs to the third wave of outward foreign direct investors from the developing countries. This wave started in the 1990s, and the main players are the BRIC-countries plus Malaysia and Turkey (Verhoef 2016). Today, South Africa is among the top ten emerging market investors (Black 2014).

Outward FDI from South Africa has also fluctuated significantly (Fig. 9.1), reaching a peak in 2014 with a value of USD 7.6 billion. Capital outflow highly depends on commodity prices, exchange rates, domestic economic and political situation, legal regulations (like the exchange control and capital account reform regulations or the PIA of 2015),[9] the international demand for foreign assets and the strategy of the South African MNEs. Among external uncertainties one should mention slug-

[6] For details see Aron et al. (2009), Edwards et al. (2009), Lundahl and Petersson (2013), and Edwards (2014).

[7] For details see: Leape and Thomas (2009) and Lundahl and Petersson (2013).

[8] Under apartheid, South African corporations were not able to invest abroad due to international sanctions. (Manuel 2014) During the 1980s, over 200 US companies left the country (Black 2014).

[9] South African residents, including corporations, are still subject to exchange controls: the ceilings for taking capital abroad were progressively raised from USD 4.3 million in 1997 to USD 132.2 million in 2003, though approval was necessary for new investments. Since 2008, approval was required only for new investments above USD 7.75 million at the time and in 2009 the threshold was raised so approval was required only for new investments larger than USD 59.25 million. Companies investing abroad get no direct support from government, except for risk insurance (Gelb 2010). South African corporations are still limited in the quantity of money they can take out of the country (Manuel 2014).

Fig. 9.1 FDI outflow from South Africa, 1990–2018 (USD million). * "FDI financial transactions may be negative for three reasons. First, if there is disinvestment in assets—that is, the direct investor sells its interest in a direct investment enterprise to a third party or back to the direct investment enterprise. Second, if the parent borrowed money from its affiliate or if the affiliate paid off a loan from its direct investor. Third, if reinvested earnings are negative. Reinvested earnings are negative if the affiliate loses money or if the dividends paid out to the direct investor are greater than the income recorded in that period" (https://www.oecd.org/daf/inv/FDI-statistics-explanatory-notes.pdf). (Source: own compilation based on UNCTAD database)

gish global economic situation, the consequences of Brexit, as the UK is one of the largest economic partners of South Africa, and the change in US administration (African Economic Outlook 2017). In 2018, outward FDI equalled USD 4.5 billion, around 1.6% of the country's GDP.

Between 1990 and 2018, South Africa's outward FDI stock increased from USD 15 billion to USD 237.9 billion (Fig. 9.2), reaching almost 65% of the country's GDP with wide fluctuation. At the end of 1995, this

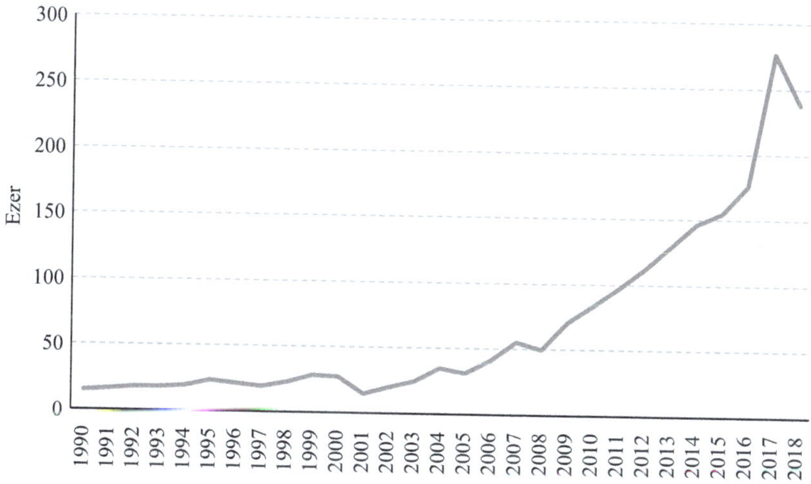

Fig. 9.2 FDI outward stock, 1990–2018 (USD million). (Source: own compilation based on UNCTAD database)

ratio was 16%; many companies left the country due to political instability and deteriorating economic situation. In the 1990s, some major South African corporations, especially in resource industries (like the Anglo American or De Beers), relocated their headquarters to the UK or the USA. This led to capital outflow, statistically defined as outward FDI (Gelb and Black 2004). The highest outward stock/GDP ratio was reached in 2000 with 59%, then it fell to 44% in 2006 (Leape and Thomas 2009, p. 28.), and reached its highest ratio (65%) in 2018. This improvement reflects the progress made by South African companies towards becoming significant foreign investors. Among developing countries, South Africa is the most internationalised through OFDI (Pereira and Stephenson 2018). As capital outflow is higher than capital inflow, South Africa can be considered a net capital exporter country with a 0.45% share of the world's capital exports.

In the case of South Africa, the main forms of FDI flow are greenfield investments[10] and mergers and acquisitions (M&A) (Figs. 9.3 and 9.4). In 2018, 0.5% of the world's greenfield investments were realised in South

[10] According to the UNCTAD, greenfield investment is a kind of FDI where a parent company starts a new venture in a foreign country.

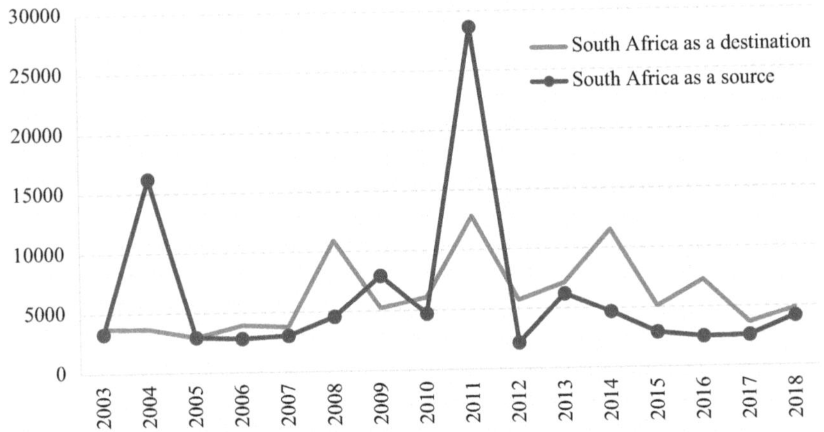

Fig. 9.3 Greenfield investment projects, 2003–2018 (USD million). (Source: own compilation based on UNCTAD database)

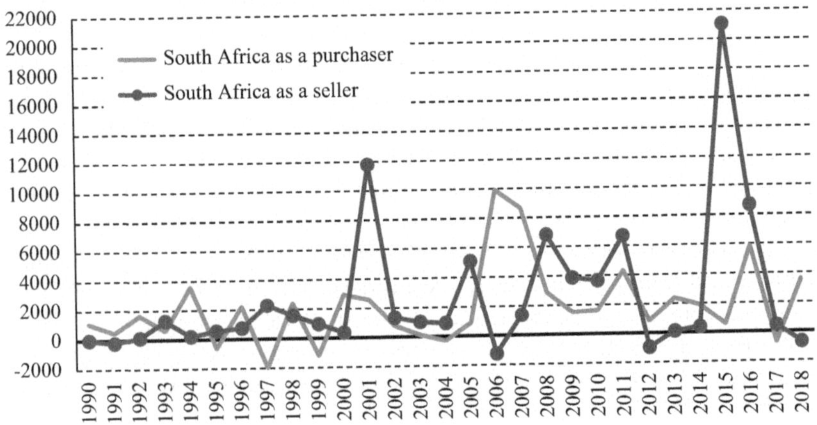

Fig. 9.4 Value of net cross border M&A, 1990–2018 (USD million). (Source: own compilation based on UNCTAD database)

Africa and 0.4% of the world's greenfield investments were implemented by South African firms and capital. The same figures for mergers and acquisitions are 0.065%, and 0.44%, respectively. While there were 150 greenfield projects in South Africa in 2015, this number decreased to 94 by 2018. In the same year, there were 110 South African greenfield projects and 136 M&A deals abroad.

The value of greenfield investments highly fluctuated in the case of outward projects (between USD 2.1 billion in 2012 and USD 28.6 billion in 2011), reflecting the high fluctuation of outward FDI. The value of inward greenfield investments varied between USD 2.9 billion in 2005 and USD 12.8 billion in 2011 (Fig. 9.3).

As it can be seen from Table 9.1, the largest outward M&A transaction in the period of 2013–2015 was executed by Aspen Pharmacare with its

Table 9.1 The top ten outward M&A transactions by South African companies, 2013–2015

	Purchaser's name	*Seller's name*	*Economic sector*	*Shares to be acquired (%)*	*Transaction value (USD million)*
1	Aspen Pharmacare	France's GlaxoSmithKline Plc's Arixtra & Fraxiparine Drug Brands	Chemicals	100	1153
2	Alaris	Antenna Research Associates (USA)	Machinery, equipment	100	1013
3	Mediclinic International	Remgro Jersey (UK)	Services	100	645
4	Nedbank	Ecobank Transnational (Togo)	Banking	20	493S
5	Foschini	Phase Eight (UK)	Wholesale and retail trade	100	361
6	Public Investment Corporation	Dangote Cement (Nigeria)	Chemicals	1.5	287
7	Goldfields	Barrick Gold Corporation (Australia)	Metals and metal products	100	270
8	Public Investment Corporation	Ecobank Transnational (Togo)	Banking	19.578	250
9	Distell	Burn Stewart Distillers (UK)	Food and beverages	100	246
10	Naspers	Flipkart Internet (India)	Services	unknown	210

Source: Author's own compilation based on data from Bezuidenhout and Rensburg (2016)

100% takeover of France's GlaxoSmithKline Plc's Arixtra & Fraxiparine Drug Brands. Of the ten largest South African multinationals, Goldfields was involved in a USD 270 million acquisition of the Australian gold mining company Barrick Gold. Naspers conducted three transactions: a USD 210 million acquisition of Flipkart Internet in India; a USD 130 million acquisition of a 70% stake in Dante International in Romania and lastly a USD 100 million merger and acquisition with Ambatana Incorporated in the USA (Bezuidenhout and Rensburg 2016). In 2018, the main target countries were the UK, Australia and the USA. Among African countries, Nigeria was the most popular target country, with transactions concentrated on manufacturing, resources, consumer products, services, financial and high-tech sectors (Evans 2019).

Compared to outward M&As, between 2013 and 2015 the main targets of the top 20 outward greenfield investments were African countries (17 out of 20), namely Mozambique, Ghana, Algeria, Egypt, DRC, Angola, Zimbabwe, Burkina Faso, Rwanda, Ethiopia, Zambia, Guinea Bissau and Botswana, showing the firm embeddedness of South African firms across the African continent. The main fields of investment were the extractive industry (coal, gas, oil), building and construction, real estate, chemicals, metals, transportation, communication and healthcare. The biggest greenfield investment was made by Beacon Hill Resources in the oil and gas sector of Mozambique with a value of USD 1.6 billion) (Bezuidenhout and Rensburg 2016, p. 10). It is interesting to note that outward greenfield investments were not conducted by the biggest South African multinationals.

9.4 The Internationalisation of South African MNEs

The main carriers of South African outward FDI are multinational enterprises. While no South African company can be found on the 2017 list of the world's top 100 non-financial MNEs ranked by foreign assets (World Investment Report 2019), two made it on the 2012 list: Anglo American Corporation Plc, which is no longer assigned to South Africa as a home country, and SABMiller, which also has UK domicile. However, Naspers emerged as the only South African company on the 2019 list, with a USD 102 billion market capitalisation. In 2017, 5 South African conglomerates made it to the list of top 100 non-financial MNEs in the developing and emerging markets category, a decrease from 2014, when 7 South African companies appeared in that list (Table 9.2).

Table 9.2 Leading South African non-financial MNEs in the top 100 non-financial MNEs from the developing countries, ranked by foreign assets (USD million 2017)

Ranking by foreign assets	*Corporation*	*Industry*	*Assets*		*Sales*		*Employment*		*TNI (%)*
			Foreign	*Total*	*Foreign*	*Total*	*Foreign*	*Total*	
17	Naspers Ltd.	Telecommunication	30,091	35,344	3115	6058	13,439	24,887	63.5
41	Sasol Ltd.	Chemicals and allied products	16,671	30,514	6647	12,675	4842	30,600	41.0
44	MTN Group Ltd.	Telecommunication	16,357	19,788	6790	9975	18,814	25,424	74.9
64	Steinhoff Int. Holdings Ltd..	Retail trade	11,199	20,667	15,118	20,761	90,189	120,000	67.4
88	Mediclinic International PLC	Healthcare services	8352	8933	2624	3803	15,777	31,504	70.9

Source: Based on UNCTAD database (WIR 2019)

TNI = Transnationality index, calculated as the average of the following three ratios: foreign assets to total assets, foreign sales to total sales and foreign employment to total employment

By the end of 2015, the top 20 ranked South African non-financial MNEs had nearly 50 billion USD in foreign assets, 49.0 billion USD in foreign sales and around 222,000 employees abroad. In terms of foreign assets, energy and chemical company Sasol is the largest with USD 9.1 billion, followed by retail-giant Steinhoff (8.7 billion USD) and mining company Goldfields (5.3 billion USD). The top five MNEs dominated the list, accounting for more than two-thirds of the foreign asset-share (Bezuidenhout and Rensburg 2016, p. 7). Sixteen out of the top 20 MNEs were partially publicly owned, with 22% state share in the Sasol being the highest. Four firms have no state involvement. All top 20 MNEs were listed on the Johannesburg Stock Exchange (JSE), with seven firms (like the three gold mining companies) also having a secondary listing on foreign stock exchanges (Frankfurt, London, New York, Swiss Stock Exchanges).

The vast majority of the top 20 MNEs' board members were South African nationals, with only four companies' (Sasol, Sappi, Datatec and Pick n Pay) CEO being foreign (British and Canadian) (Bezuidenhout and Rensburg 2016, p. 2). As far as the sectoral distribution of top 20 MNEs is concerned, mining is the largest contributor with 4 firms, followed by retail (4 firms) and energy and chemicals. Two firms are in the field of transport and logistics, while healthcare and pharmaceutical firms are also represented. In terms of foreign sales, MTN is the leader with a total of US$ 10.5 billion in foreign sales in 2015. Datatec is next with US$ 5.8 billion, followed closely by Naspers with US$ 5.7 billion. With regard to foreign employment, Bidvest is on the top with 27,975 foreign employees. Anglogold is second with 26,164 foreign employees, followed by Shoprite with 22,600 foreign employees (Bezuidenhout and Rensburg 2016, p. 7).

9.4.1 *Main Strategies and Motivations of South African Outward FDI*

Besides the traditional motivations for outward investment—such as market-, resource-, efficiency- or strategic asset-seeking—MNEs from emerging economies are driven to invest outside the mother country in order to avert constraints in the domestic market, to avoid domestic competition, financial constraints and reduce risks (Verhoef 2016). In the case of South Africa, these push factors are especially critical. The main constraints are the size of the domestic market (slow and fluctuating GDP growth), the stratified nature of the demand, the rigid labour market, lack of skilled labour force, inflexibility in factor market, unreliable electricity supply, compliance with the Black Economic Empowerment requirements, HIV/AIDS, brain drain and the need for risk aversion deriving from uncertain political climate in the country. A new push factor was added in 2015 in the form of the newly adopted Protection of Investment Act, which might lead to the further outflow of capital due to its compensation provision. These push factors lead to market- and efficiency-seeking strategies of South African MNEs, as operation outside of the country offers better opportunity to reduce costs and risks, and to increase productivity.

The internationalisation of South African firms occurred primarily by means of mergers and acquisitions, as market- and asset-seeking strategies could be primarily conducted through these means. New investments were relatively small, below US$ 1 million in most transactions, and were stimulated by the unbundling strategies of big conglomerates, as well as the privatisation policies of African governments after the early 1990s.

The big South African conglomerates, like the mining company *Anglo American Corporation* (AAC) and the South African Breweries (SABMiller), have already started their internationalisation in the mid-1960s, and their main strategy has been the diversification of the conglomerate structure. The companies belonging to the AAC group—such as De Beers, the famous diamond mining and distribution company—were operating in the mining of metals and minerals, finance, exploration, property development, administration of businesses, housing, industrial manufacturing, food production, engineering and so on (Verhoef 2016, p. 9). They were active in Australia, Canada, Indonesia, Malaysia and various African countries even before the political changes of the 1990s. After 1994, AAC unbundled its diversified holdings in non-mining sectors, moved the headquarters of De Beers to London and listed on the London Stock exchange as AAC Plc (Verhoef 2016, p. 9). The AAC group appointed a non–South African chairman in 2001 and an American CEO in 2004. This entrepreneurial orientation enhanced the market- and asset-seeking operations of the group and the international entrepreneurship of the new leadership intensified the evaluation and exploitation of opportunities outside the original home country (Verhoef 2016, p. 10). Currently, AAC is no longer seen as a South African MNE.

The success of *SABMiller's* globalisation was due to the management's global orientation, operational excellence, significant investment in training and skills development, the knowledge of the African market and the ability to integrate its knowledge of both developed and developing markets into a successful management and marketing strategy. Furthermore, SABMiller managed to capitalise on the isolation prior to 1994 as business was protected from foreign competition; the company could accumulate capital resources and diversify operation into different sectors.

The globalisation of South African companies was motivated by a range of factors. Firm-specific advantages in production sophistication, management and product innovation resulted in expansion beyond the boundaries of the domestic market. Market constraints before and after 1994 motivated MNEs to enhance efficiency. Their advanced production methods, new technologies and solutions were exported to new markets, mainly in Africa, as the cases of Gold Fields Limited, Sappi and Sasol show (Verhoef 2016). *Gold Fields*, for example, was one of the first gold mining companies in South Africa, established in 1887 in London (Verhoef 2016, p. 12), that used its superior managerial skills and technology in gold mining to expand into other gold mining operations, mainly in West Africa, but also in Peru and in the Philippines. By 2000, Gold Fields became the largest gold mining company in the world.

The role of leading technology in driving globalisation was also critical in the globalisation strategies of Sappi and Sasol (Verhoef 2016, p. 13). *Sappi* (the South African Paper and Pulp Industries) was established in 1936, and acquired an international footprint utilising its locally developed knowledge base. The company started paper exports to European markets towards the late 1980s. Sappi International was formed in 1986 to manage the sales and product distribution internationally. After 1991, Sappi embarked on M&As in the UK, Germany, Hong Kong and the USA. By 2000, it was the world leader in the manufacturing of coated wood-free paper (Verhoef 2016, p. 13). In 2004, the company expanded into the Chinese market by acquiring a 34% stake in a joint venture with Jiangxi Chenming. The reason for the joint venture was technology and expertise transfer. Similarly, *Sasol*, the South African chemical and energy company, was also using its advanced technology to drive its globalisation strategy. Sasol was a strategic industry for South Africa during the apartheid era and became competitive in the international chemical industry through innovative technology. After 2000 Sasol started global acquisitions and joint ventures (Nigeria, Qatar) partially due to the limitation of the domestic market (Verhoef 2016, pp. 14–15).

In the telecommunication industry, two South African MNEs became global players: Naspers and MTN. *Naspers* (Nasionale Pers), a global internet and entertainment group established in 1915 as a holding company in the print media, started its first pay television business M-net in 1985 and became a multimedia company in 1997. It made acquisitions in China, Brazil, in other Latin American countries, Russia and in some Eastern European countries (Poland—Allegropl, a leading online auction site; Romania—eMAG, a major e-commerce portal; Czech Republic—79% stake in Netretail), later on in Iran, Nigeria and India. These massive expansions made Naspers the leading emerging market electronic communication company that operates on all continents (more than 130 countries) in e-commerce. The main success factors are innovative leadership, strategic business repositioning, innovative solutions[11] and massive e-commerce acquisitions. *MTN* (Mobile Telephone Network), which is the highest-ranked emerging market non-financial company with a market share of around 40% in South Africa and the leading mobile operator in Africa, had expanded its services to Cameroon, Nigeria, Rwanda, Swaziland and Uganda through joint ventures and independent operations. A global brand logo was introduced, the "Y'ello". A new marketing concept was developed: *glocalisation*, meaning focussing on local needs and culture while keeping the global brand values (Verhoef 2016, p. 16). It pursued penetration through joint ventures with mobile operators and conducted greenfield investments to establish the necessary infrastructure. Its market expansion was driven by firm-specific advantages based on ownership advantages in management strategic vision, knowledge of and adaptation to the African market, the innovative application of brand marketing, use of leading technology and innovative solutions.

South African MNEs have emerged in the field of healthcare, too (Life Healthcare, Mediclinic Group, Netcare) and retail (Steinhoff International, SHL), which is an emerging sector as there are shortages in medical services in Africa, while the expanding middle class has effective demand for quality healthcare. All healthcare groups were established in the early 1980s and they penetrated markets in Namibia, the Middle East and the UK. Their expansion was driven by the firm-specific advantages of medical expertise and the advantage of proprietary knowledge in seeking new markets.

[11] Like its direct-to-home video entertainment reaching eight million customers in 37 African countries.

As it was revealed by the short case studies above, the internationalisation of the South African MNEs was motivated mainly by market-, asset- and efficiency-seeking strategies and less by resource-seeking motives.

The market-seeking strategy was fuelled by the limited size of the domestic market and political constraints, leading companies to seek for fast-growing markets, especially in other African countries in order to increase market share. This strategy was practised by MTN and Shoprite, whose competitive advantage and firm-specific advantages were embedded in their strategic managerial capabilities, knowledge of the African market (culture, consumption pattern, language) and smooth adaptation to the constraints caused by under-banking.

The asset-seeking strategies of some firms (like Sasol, AAC, Gold Fields, MTN, Netcare, Sappi) were based on the proprietary knowledge of locally developed technologies inserted into the African and Middle East markets and the integration of newly acquired technologies into the existing knowledge base. These technologies and innovative solutions provided a strategic tool to access new markets, to gain market share and handle growing constraints in the domestic market. Similarly, managerial and organisational capabilities, strategic leadership and management vision, change management skills, innovative managerial activity, international orientation of the management, extensive business networks outside the country, capability to manage political instability and social turmoil, as well as to take and manage risks are the key factors in the successful internationalisation of South African MNEs.

In the case of the mining companies (AAC, Gold Fields, AngloGold), the market-seeking strategy was coupled with asset- and resource-seeking strategies reflected by the extension and diversification of mining operations. Access to new mineral resources and new mining companies outside the home country reduced the risk associated with black empowerment policy, labour market rigidities and cost pressures.

As far as future trends are concerned, it is expected that efficiency-seeking motives will become stronger, leading to increasing international orientation, development of alliances and networks outside of the country, increasing the size and capabilities of the corporations to challenge competitors (Verhoef 2016). The market-seeking motives will be strengthened, especially in relation to other African countries. This attempt will be supported by the envisaged Trilateral Free Trade Agreement (TFTA) between the East African Community (EAC), the Common Market for Eastern and Southern Africa (COMESA) and SADC (Edwards 2014;

Wentworth et al. 2014), as this regional grouping will cover 26 countries with a population of 625 million, and with a combined GDP of around one trillion USD (African Economic Outlook 2015).

9.5 Geographical and Sectoral Distribution of South African Outward FDI

The most prominent pull factors for outward FDI are related to the state of institutions in the host market in providing stability, minimising market failures, reducing uncertainty and alleviating information complexity in economic exchanges (North 1990; Verhoef 2016). Especially those "written laws, regulations, policies, and enforcement measures are important, which prescribe the actions and behaviour of people, systems, and organizations" (Verhoef 2016, p. 7). However, in the era of globalisation not only host country conditions are essential but regional ones as well. Most of the MNEs think globally but act locally and regionally. This statement is valid in the case of South African investments both in Central European countries and in the neighbouring African countries. EU membership, free movement of goods, services and capital make Central European countries attractive. In the case of Africa, the different integrations, customs unions and free trade agreements should be kept in mind while making investment decisions. However, "small domestic markets, unsophisticated demand, institutional instability and physical infrastructure limitations mitigate against expansion into neighbouring and regional markets in Africa" (Verhoef 2016, p. 9).

Studying the geographical distribution of outflowing FDI on the basis of South Africa's outward FDI stock (see Table 9.3), it is interesting to note the decreasing share of the developed countries, from around 90% in 2001 to 53% in 2012, and consequently the increasing share of developing countries, from 10% to 45% in the same time period. South African FDI outflow is not as Europe-centric as it was at the turn of the century. The largest destinations in Europe are the UK, Luxemburg and the Netherlands. As both FDI inflow and outflow are still dominated by the UK, it is a big question how Brexit will modify the direction of FDI flow. The share of the USA is around 5%.

Within the developing world, South African FDI is almost equally divided between the African and the Asian regions, with 48% and 47% share of the total outward FDI stock in the developing countries. In Africa,

Table 9.3 Geographical distribution of outward FDI stock (USD million)

Country of destination	*2001*	*2005*	*2010*	*2011*	*2012*
Total	17,751	38,193	90,887	97,051	111,780
Developed economies	15,995	33,916	52,865	53,451	58,999
Europe	14,794	30,424	43,774	42,818	47,060
European Union	14,694	30,234	42,438	41,485	45,365
Czech Republic	–	3	3	–	14
France	43	110	142	784	752
Germany	5050	684	963	1734	1880
Hungary	–	–	2	15	14
Luxemburg	606	11,832	15,522	7810	9637
Netherlands	712	1129	2616	2376	4265
Poland	–	13	803	1106	1691
UK	4980	11,203	14,944	18,272	17,966
USA	832	2279	4325	4195	6027
Developing economies	1753	4253	37,929	41,118	49,344
Africa	1239	3100	18,524	22,789	23,579
Ghana	–	1	855	1376	1951
Mauritius	546	544	8051	9915	10,622
Mozambique	340	725	1158	2926	2175
Nigeria	–	789	3618	1775	2171
Asia	348	831	18,068	15,478	23,539
China	1	684	13,995	12,744	20,284
India	6	11	160	183	203
Latin America	166	322	1336	2850	2226
Brazil	6	22	128	569	718
Russia	–	–	67	2482	3434

Source: Own compilation based on data of WIR, UNCTAD various issues

the main destination is Mauritius due to the strategic role of this country. Asian investments of South Africa are dominated by the Chinese location. It is interesting to note that four times more capital is directed from South Africa to China than vice versa.[12] With the exception of China, none of the other BRIC-members are important FDI partners for South Africa.

As far as the Central European countries are concerned, Poland is the most important destination with some investment in the Czech Republic, Hungary and Romania.

The above geographical direction of South African outward FDI contradicts the so-called Uppsala model of internationalisation and the

[12] About the China-South Africa FDI links and some case studies see Gelb (2010).

investment strategy and practice of the first and second waves of developing countries' investors, focusing first on the neighbouring, ethnically similar countries and then moving farer, to the developed countries. In the case of South African MNEs, more than half of outward FDI was directed to the European and EU markets (56% in 2013), 17.5% to North and South American markets, 16.2% to the Asian markets and only 8.2% into the neighbouring African countries (Verhoef 2016). The similarity of developed markets in terms of demand, structure and operations explains the direction of South African MNEs' internationalisation strategy, its focus on the more developed countries of the world. They proved to be successful due to their advanced proprietary knowledge, technology and strategic management capabilities.

Though in the last few years cross-border business transactions in Africa increased due to regional economic integrations, the share of outward FDI from South Africa into other African countries remained below 10%. With this share, South Africa is the largest intra-regional investor in Africa, followed by Kenya. However, South Africa's investments to other African countries are gradually increasing, and in 2014 already 18% of the country's outward FDI was directed to the African continent. The main African destinations are Mauritius, Mozambique, Swaziland and Zimbabwe (Orosz 2017).

However, if we take into account the *number of foreign affiliates* instead of the amount of outward investment, the picture differs a bit as the top 20 ranked South African non-financial MNEs were primarily located in sub-Saharan Africa. Of the 1178 foreign affiliates 443 were in sub-Saharan Africa (37.6%), followed by Europe with 225 foreign affiliates (19%). Only Sappi and Harmony Gold do not have African affiliates. Bidvest and Aveng have a large footprint in EU countries, with 93 and 42 affiliates, respectively (Bezuidenhout and Rensburg 2016, p. 7). There were altogether 74 affiliates in Central Europe and Central Asia. Life Healthcare and Naspers have the most affiliates in this region, 33 and 13, respectively (Bezuidenhout and Rensburg 2016).

As far as the sectoral distribution of outward FDI is concerned, it is well illustrated in the breakdown of the top 20 South African MNEs' foreign assets (see Fig. 9.5). In 2015, mining (Goldfields, AngloGold, Impala Platinum, Harmony Gold) accounted for 23% of foreign assets, followed by retail (Steinhoff, Barloworld, Shoprite, Pick n Play) with 20%, and the energy and chemicals sector, represented solely by Sasol, with 18%. The only other sector represented was the transport and logistics industry

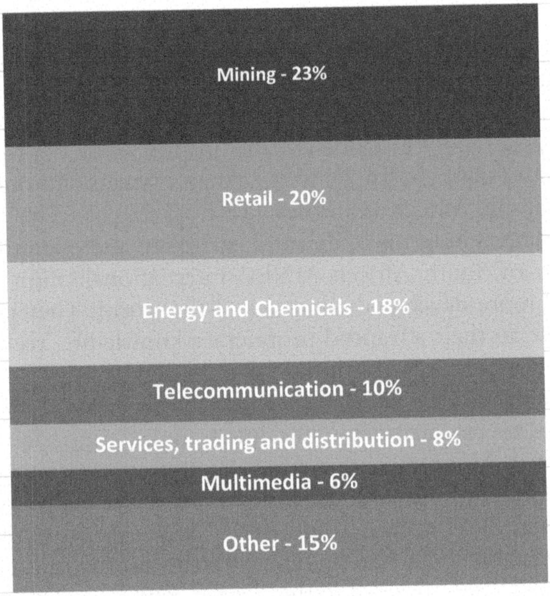

Fig. 9.5 The distribution of the foreign assets of the top 20 multinationals by main economic activity, 2015. (Source: Author's compilation based on data from Bezuidenhout and Rensburg [2016])

(Imperial, Supergroup), with 5% of total foreign assets resulting from South Africa's status as gateway to Africa. Other industries (like services, multimedia, information, technology, forestry and paper, food and beverages, healthcare) were represented solely by one firm (Bezuidenhout and Rensburg 2016).

9.6 South African OFDI in Central and Eastern Europe

South Africa has been reintegrated into the world economy, its capital movement has been revitalised and the European Union plays a dominant role in its economic relations. Central Europe is nevertheless still a marginal partner for South Africa. Trade relations are negligible compared to the total trade of the CEE countries, and existing trade balances are in favour of the CEEs (Kugiel 2016). At the same time, a significant part of the CEEs' trade with Africa is with South Africa. Many companies invest via third countries due to more favourable tax or regulatory treatment. Investment flows are hectic, showing high volatility depending on actual transactions. What is nonetheless clear is that South Africa invests more in the ECE region than the other way around.

As illustrated in Table 9.4, the most important destination of *South African outward FDI* in the ECE region is *Poland*, which hosts a considerable amount of South African FDI stock (1691 million USD in 2012). According to the data of the Polish National Bank, this stock amounted to USD 140.6 million at the end of 2013, while according to the OECD data (Table 9.4) it was above USD 2 billion in 2013. In 2017, around 2% of all Polish inward FDI arrived from South Africa. The "leading" role of Poland is due to the market size and the fact that this country was less affected by the financial and economic crisis of 2008.

Apart from Poland, there are some marginal investments in the Czech Republic, Hungary and Romania. South African FDI stocks were USD 14 million, 14 million and 7 million in these countries, respectively, for the year 2012. According to another source (Kugiel 2016), South Africa invested more than USD 200 million in Hungary. This is different from OECD data (Table 9.4), which exhibit a South African FDI stock value of around USD 20 million in Hungary. According to data of the National Bank of Hungary, FDI inflows from South Africa based on ultimate owner were as follows (USD millions): 14.2 in 2014, 22.5 in 2015, 45.9 in 2016

Table 9.4 South African FDI flow to ECEs, 2013–2017 (millions USD)

		2013	*2014*	*2015*	*2016*	*2017*
Czechia	Flow	-1.3	-2.7	-5.4	2.2	0.5
	Stock	176.8	87.3	168.7	c	c
Hungary	Flow	-17.2	0.2	7.2	-2.0	3.4
	Stock	–	17.3	24.9	21.4	–
Poland	Flow	-54.2	15.4	0.8	-2.4	-1.1
	Stock	2064.6	1530.8	133.3	1167.5	502.9
Slovakia	Flow	–	0.9	–	c	–
	Stock	-2.3	-2.6	-1.7	-9.8	–
Slovenia	Flow	-	0.1	0.0	-0.2	0.2
	Stock	–	–	–	–	–

Source: OECD International Direct Investment Statistics, 2008–2017, Paris, OECD, 2018

c = confidential

and 50.5 in 2017. This means that in general around 0.06% of total Hungarian FDI inflow arrived from South Africa.

As data available from international (UNCTAD, OECD), South African and CEE (national) sources are rather contradictory, not to mention the various calculation systems that make it extremely difficult to get a clear picture.

South African outward FDI to Europe, including Central Europe, is carried out mostly by the activity of *MNEs*. While the overall value of capital inflow is rather limited, the footprint of South African multinational companies can be found in the ECE region as South African MNEs took part in the privatisation process and in different mergers and acquisitions. The majority of the investments are done via mergers and acquisitions; there are very few, almost none, greenfield investments. The biggest South African MNEs (like SABMiller, Naspers, Mondi, Bidvest, Nowaco, Pepco, Life Healthcare, NEPI Rockcastle) are active in more than one ECEs, suggesting that South Africa considers the region as a single market. The next question to be answered: why South African investors select ECE countries as their location?

9.6.1 *The Main Motivations of South African Investors in ECE*

9.6.1.1 *Negative and Positive Push Factors*

In the previous chapters, we have already presented the main home country macroeconomic and political *push factors*, like unstable political and economic climate, social unrests, fluctuating exchange rate, volatile depreciating currency and requirements of empowerment legislation. These make the home country a risky place to invest and push South African investors to look for yield-enhancing foreign location (Rankin 2014). These factors are accompanied by the internationalisation of South African multinationals and their resource-, market-, efficiency- and asset-seeking strategies.

The above factors are highly supported by some South African public policies (like economic liberalisation, the exchange control policy that has been streamlined recently to facilitate legitimate cross-border investments[13]) and by those rules, regulations, legislations, institutions, diplo-

[13] Despite the relaxation of exchange control regulations, companies are allowed to transfer up to ZAR 1 billion (around USD 70 billion) per year for FDI purposes (Sulaiman and Abdullatief 2020).

macy, regional and international agreements, and organisations that stimulate and ease outward FDI via minimising risks and easing doing business (Manyuchi and Mugabe 2018). Bilateral Investment Treaties (BITs), Double Taxation Agreements (DTAs), Investment Protection and Promotion Acts, Memorandum of Understandings (MoUs), state-level visits, the activity of missions (embassies) and that of the TISA (= Trade and Investment South Africa, within the Department of Trade and Industry)[14] and DIRCO (Department of International Relations and Co-operation)[15] should be mentioned. These factors are catalysts for outward investments, so they might be interpreted as *positive push factors* in contrast to those home country push factors that are not unambiguously positive; hence, they can be called *negative push factors.*

9.6.1.2 Host Country's Pull Factors

Even if the above *positive and negative push factors* are in full drive, it does not mean that the South African investors would opt for CEE destinations. The recipient country/region's *pull factors* have a decisive role in attracting foreign capital. These factors can be grouped into three: (a) political, (b) structural macroeconomic and (c) institutional factors.

Political Pull Factors

Political factors, like political and institutional stability, social harmony, respect of human rights, lack of internal conflicts, rule of law, property rights security, low country risk and economic freedom, are essential for all investors. However, in the case of South African investors, they all have a special importance. In the case of ECE countries, all these "requirements" are mostly met and guaranteed by these countries' EU membership and their transition towards democracy and market-led economy. According to the *2019 Index of Economic Freedom* of the Heritage Foundation, the ECE countries, with the exception of the "mostly free" Czech Republic, are *moderately free*, outperforming the *mostly unfree* South Africa (Miller et al. 2020).

[14] TISA services include investment recruitment, providing investment information, facilitating domestic and outward investment, introducing South African MNEs abroad and supporting MNEs on project financing (Manyuchi and Mugabe 2018).

[15] DIRCO conducts foreign affairs and bi- and multilateral co-operation through missions, embassies and consulates, helping South African investors to easily invest in the very countries (Manyuchi and Mugabe 2018).

Structural Macroeconomic Pull Factors

Market. For ***market-seeking*** investors population size, purchasing power, steady economic growth[16] and market potential of the host countries are significant factors. In addition, market access, economic openness, low level of protection and competition are further attraction points. Though the ECE countries are not as populous as the African countries (Poland has the highest population with 38 million), the regional, less saturated market might expand due to increasing consumption fuelled by increasing per capita GDP, low unemployment rate, rise in the minimum wage level and lower level of inequality (especially compared to South Africa).

South African investors are—like most of any other foreign investors—thinking and investing "regionally"; that is, they intend to capture the market of the whole region. This was the intention of the *SABMiller* brewery, and this is the strategy of the Pepkor with its more than 1300 Pepco stores across the Visegrád countries with the headquarters and logistical centre in Poland.

Despite significant global FDI inflow into the ECE region, there are some market niches or some emerging fields in services, e-business and e-commerce. This was realised by those South African enterprises that invested in retail (*Pepkor*, *Bidvest*, *Nowaco*), in e-commerce (*Naspers*), in real estate (*NEPI Rockcastle*) or in healthcare (*Life Healthcare*) (Tarrósy 2014). In addition, investing in any of the ECE country implies free, unlimited access to the EU single market of 500 million people. That is why the ECE is seen by South African investors as a gateway to Western Europe.

Compared to highly developed countries, factor costs are lower in ECE countries, especially in the case of educated, skilled and highly qualified labour force, which might motivate enterprises with ***resource-seeking*** investment strategies. However, investors should consider the increasing shortage of skilled labour power and the wage pressure. Consequently, investing in labour-intensive industries is getting risky. So far, South African investors did not prefer manufacturing projects. The only exceptions were *SABMiller* in the brewery industry in the four Visegrád countries and *Mondi*, the paper packaging company in Hungary and Slovakia. A further pull factor is infrastructure: water and electricity supply is well developed and reliable compared to most of the African countries, including South Africa itself. Professional services are also available.

[16] Growth rates in the CEE region are more than double of the growth rate of South Africa.

When it comes to financing, ECE's capital markets and the banking systems are rather developed. The currencies are stabile especially in those countries where the euro had been introduced (Slovenia, Slovakia and the Baltic states). This is an especially attractive factor for South African investors facing huge currency volatility in their home country. Interest rates are low, there is easy access to cheap debt and, consequently, cost-benefit ratio is attractive.

Though privatisation is mostly over, there are opportunities for *asset-seeking* investors in the form of *acquisitions or mergers.* The asset-seeking strategy of the South African investors is reflected by the fact that the overwhelming majority of investments in the ECE region occurred via mergers and acquisitions and not by greenfield investments.[17] The other explanation might be that investors from South Africa are not planning for the long run due to geographical distance and the uncertainty concerning the home scene. Consequently, the overall investment activity is rather hectic, connected to one or two deals resulting in high volatility of FDI flow.

All in all, ECE countries provide a stable and predictable business environment, where South African investors "feel comfortable" according to one of the experts (Mundy 2018). According to the 2019 Global Competitiveness Index 4.0, the ECE countries' rankings out of 141 countries are as follows: Czech Republic—32, Slovenia—35, Poland—37, Slovakia—42 and Hungary 47, while South Africa is in the 60th place (Global Competitiveness report, 2019).

Institutional Pull Factors

Like in the case of the previously mentioned positive push factors, the home countries also have a wide range of institutional factors that encourage the inflow of foreign capital. They appear at two levels: national and international/regional levels.

One part of the *national-level institutional pull factors* is based on the *equal treatment* principle, valid for all kinds of investors. These are, for instance, the legal system, the public policies of the host countries' government, the rules and regulations, the competition law, privatisation and acquisition opportunities, investment screening, the tax system (especially

[17] The most notable was the acquisition of CEE breweries by SABMiller, or the acquisition of Hungary's Scitec Holding, leading sports nutrition producer, by SA Ascendis Health for EUR 170 million in 2016.

the corporate tax[18] or the tax burden of the labour force), direct investment promotion (like tax incentives or subsidies) and the establishment of special economic zones, that is, the whole business environment. According to the World Bank's latest *Doing Business* report, the ECE countries' economic rankings in 2019 were as follows: Slovenia (37), Poland (40), Czech Republic (41), Slovakia (45) and Hungary (52), while South Africa took the 84th place out of 190 countries. The higher the ranking, the more conducive is to start and operate a local firm in a particular country (Doing business 2020).

The other part of national-level institutional pull factors is "non-absolute". This means that these advantages are provided to selected investors for directing foreign capital to the earmarked sectors, regions via providing tax holidays, tax exemptions or signing strategic agreements with selected investors/companies as it has happened in the case of Hungary, where strategic agreements have been signed with many foreign companies, including non-European (e.g. Chinese) ones.

The *regional-/international-level institutional pull factors* are the different international and bilateral agreements, trade agreements, embassies, joint committees and investment promotion agencies (HIPA, IPA). All four Visegrád countries plus Bulgaria and Romania have embassies in South Africa, and Hungary, Poland, Slovakia plus Croatia and Estonia have consulates. Each Visegrád country established its separate joint economic commission with Southern African counterparts for developing and diversifying bilateral relations, facilitating market access, supporting trade and mutual investment.

In 2013, Poland signed an economic cooperation agreement during the Polish prime minister's visit to South Africa promoting bilateral trade and investment. Furthermore, two MoUs were signed with the Trade and Investment South Africa by the Polish Information and Foreign Investment Agency, and with the Industrial Development Corporation of South Africa by the Industrial Development Agency of Poland. In 2016, the Hungarian Chamber of Commerce and Industry signed a MoU with the Johannesburg Chamber of Commerce and Industry with the objective to establish cooperation channels for enterprises. Every second year a Budapest-Africa forum is organised,[19] where high-ranking government officials and busi-

[18] The lowest in the ECE region is in Hungary with 9%.

[19] The fourth one was planned to be held in May 2020 but had to be cancelled due to the coronavirus pandemic.

ness people from different African countries, including South Africa, have an opportunity to meet with the representatives of Hungarian companies and the Hungarian government.

In the case of the ECE region, membership in the EU and WTO is essential. In 2016, the EU and six members of the SADEC (Southern African Development Community), including South Africa, signed an Economic Partnership agreement (EPA), which might promote mutual investment flow once it comes into effect.

9.6.2 *The Sectoral Preference of South African Investors*

During the last decades South African companies—in contrast to Asian investors (Szunomár 2018)—were not so much keen on investing in manufacturing industries compared to the services sectors. Their main preference was the real estate, retail trade, consumer goods and healthcare sectors.

9.6.2.1 Real Estate

South Africa has a substantial and successful *real estate* sector with 24 real estate investment services (REIS) and 37 real estate investment trusts (REITs) with a market of around EUR 50 million. As the domestic market is becoming saturated due to oversupply and sluggish growth, real estate investors decided to diversify their portfolio and opt for offshore expansion. Their outward-looking strategy was fuelled by political uncertainty, currency weakness, stringent exchange control legislation, high cost of funding, the threat of a downgrade in sovereign bonds and increasing risks (Harper 2016; Jordaan 2017; "Spotlight" 2018).

Real estate companies in the framework of their internationalisation strategy are looking for yield enhancing assets abroad, including the ECE region. Of the 61 real estate companies listed on the JSE (Johannesburg Stock Exchange), 40% of them have assets abroad, half of which are in Central and Eastern Europe (CEE) (Shah 2019), for instance, NEPI Rockcastle, Redefine Properties, Atterbury Europe, Hyprop Investment, Prime Capital, Accelerate and Tower (Harper 2016). NEPI Rockcastle is the largest real estate firm in the ECE region ("Spotlight" 2018).

Among the advantages of the region experts (Harper 2016; Jordaan 2017; Mundy 2018; Sulaiman and Abdullatief 2020) mention: conducive business and economic environment, the safety of the EU regulatory structure, well-educated workforce, stable currencies, limited international and internal competition, growing online transaction level, low interest rates, low cost of borrowing, lower funding costs, high yields[20] and attractive risk-reward profile with high initial yield spreads.[21] Combined, these factors allow for meaningful investments that grow organically.[22] Their goal is not only to acquire properties but to build sustainable local business platforms. As the real estate market is less mature in the ECE region, South African investors find it very attractive and their investments are likely to increase in the foreseeable future until an inflection point driven by ECE yield compression is reached (Mundy 2018). However, South African investors face some challenges, too, in the ECE region (Hillis 2020), like having the right and trusted local partner that can ease transaction and speed execution.

Between 2008 and 2018, more than €5.4 billion has been invested into the broader Central and Eastern European region by South African real estate companies ("Spotlight" 2018). Around half of South African investment in the region has been in fast-maturing Poland. In March 2016, *Redefine* paid EUR 2 billion for control over Polish Echo Prime Properties, the largest property transaction in the CEE region and the largest offshore purchase of a South African property company (Foy 2016). The other half of South African real estate investment was directed to Croatia, the Czech Republic, Hungary, Macedonia, Montenegro, Romania, Slovakia, Serbia and Slovenia (Hillis 2020). In 2016, New Europe Property Investment bought stakes in Romania for EUR 1.5 billion and Tower Property made investments in Croatia (Foy 2016).

Retail assets in particular have proved popular. In 2015, REIT Hyprop entered Serbia and Montenegro as part of a joint venture with Homestead to acquire two Delta City shopping centres for a total of EUR 202.7 million (Harper 2016). In 2015, Redefine Properties made a record-breaking acquisition in Poland when it bought a 75% stake in a retail-based portfolio—the largest real estate transaction in the history of the Polish market (Harper 2016). During 2016 EUR 3 billion was invested in the Traditional Shopping Centre (TSC) segment in CEE (Jordaan 2017). The *NEPI*

[20] In 2018 the investment yields for offices of central Warsaw was 4.75% and for prime Polish shopping centres 4.9% (Mundy 2018).

[21] This is the gap between yield on investment and cost of debt.

[22] "Other than economic and political reasons for investing outside South Africa, international investment is a natural evolution and diversification of a growing sector looking for new markets and investment opportunities", says Len Van Niekerk, senior property analyst ("Spotlight" 2018).

Rockcastle bought the Arena Plaza shopping mall in Hungary for EUR 275 million in 2017, and bought the Mammut 1 and Mammut 2 shopping malls in Hungary for EUR 254 million in 2018.

According to experts (Jordaan 2017; Hillis 2020), there is great potential in the TSC segment as the market is expected to expand due to relatively high economic growth rates, low unemployment rates, increasing wages, increasing disposable incomes and emerging middle class and low consumer base. This optimistic scenario is backed by high rents, high occupancy rate and increasing waiting lists.

9.6.2.2 Retail Trade and e-Commerce

According to experts (Shah 2019) the retail sector is underdeveloped in the CEE region, while there is a huge potential due to highly educated population that is financially included and coming from a low consumer base. On the other hand, in South Africa retail has tended to outperform other asset classes and this preference is going to be translated into investors' strategies in CEE (Harper 2016).

One of the success stories in this field is the discount retailer *Pepco*, part of the Pepkor group. This non-food (discount clothing and household appliances) retail chain produced a rapid expansion in a short time. There are already 1300 Pep-type format stores in Poland, the Czech Republic, Romania, Hungary, Slovakia and Croatia, employing more than 12,000 people. The success is shown by the fact that for the three months to 31 December 2018, Pepco's revenue in Poland and Romania grew by 37% in constant currencies to 477 million euros (Shah 2019). Two new stores were opened in Bulgaria in 2019 and the company is planning to invest EUR 85 million in a logistics centre in Gyál, near the Hungarian capital.

Further investor in the retail sector is the *Bidvest Group,* which manages *Bidfood, Nowaco* and *Farutex*. *Bidfood* is an important player in food distribution and gastronomy in the Czech Republic and Slovakia, with a EUR 273 369 asset and 1218 employees in 2018. *Nowaco* works in the field of frozen food retail in the Czech Republic. *Farutex* is a wholesale of meat and meat products in Poland. Other actors in the retail and wholesale sectors are *Food and wine*, a retail of beverages in specialised shops in Poland; *Aspen Polska*, a wholesale of pharmaceutical goods; *Midex Ltd.*, a wholesale of solid liquid in Poland; *Westcon Group Poland*, a wholesale of electronic and telecommunications equipment. *Portland Steel International* and *English with Joy* are non-specified wholesalers in the Czech Republic.

In the field of e-commerce, *Naspers* is a significant player. It owns the Polish *Allegro Group Europe*, a leading e-commerce group in the ECE region that manages, among others, such Hungarian sites as the vatera.hu, the grando.hu and the arukereso.hu. It owns Mall.cz in the field of internet retail and Heureka.cz, the price comparison site in the Czech Republic. It is active in Poland via Allegro.pl, a leading online auction site, and bought a majority stake (79%) in the Slovakian Netretail, which operates online stores not only in Slovakia but also in Poland and the Czech Republic. Naspers focuses primarily on e-commerce (see the example of eMAG later), and has spread its full range of online services across Central and Eastern Europe.

One of the members of the above-mentioned *Allegro Group Europe* is the *eMAG*, a successful leading Romanian online web shop, a multinational company active in nine CEE countries.[23] The company's majority shares were bought up in 2012 by Naspers. In 2019, the *Extreme Digital*, a Hungarian leading online electronic retailer company,[24] decided to merge with the eMAG on a 48:52 ownership base in favour of eMAG, which belongs to the South African Naspers Group.[25] The headquarters of the new company will be in Hungary, all international expansion will be controlled from Hungary and both brands will be kept alive (Forbes 2019). It will be the largest player on the CEE e-commerce market: "With the market knowledge of Extreme Digital, the logistic capacity and professional web system of eMAG, and the financial backing of the South African Naspers parent company, we can become the decisive e-commerce company of the region"—told Balázs Várkonyi, head and co-founder of the company ("Extreme digital" 2019). With this fusion the company could offer better prices and higher-quality services to customers and enter the international arena.

[23] About the development of the company see: https://business-review.eu/business/emag-expands-to-9-countries-following-merger-with-hungarian-extreme-digital-reaches-eur-1-billion-in-turnover-at-group-level-201561

[24] It is present in 8 countries, has 16 shops and some 100,000 available products, and has a 10% market share in Hungarian e-commerce market (Extreme digital 2019).

[25] Previously South African Steinhoff had a share in Extreme Digital but the cooperation proved to be a failure, to tell the least (Forbes 2019).

9.6.2.3 Manufacturing

South African investment into manufacturing is represented in the brewing, paper processing, food-supplement industries and in quarrying.[26]

The *SABMiller* started its internationalisation in 1993 in Hungary when it bought up Hungary's leading Brewery, the Kőbányai Sörgyár (later Dreher Breweries), for USD 100 million and reached a market share of 30%. The experimental acquisition was followed by a series of deals: in the Czech Republic the company owned Pilsner Urquell and controlled half of the Czech beer market; it owned the majority of Topwar brewery in Slovakia and was active in Poland and Romania, too. The company's European regional operations were managed from its London headquarters. The job creation effect of the company was outstanding: the company created directly 3261 jobs in Poland, 2045 jobs in the Czech Republic and 1415 jobs in Romania, while the indirect job creation effect was even greater (24,000, 3500 and 5800, respectively) (Kurtagic 2019).

In 2016, Anheuser-Busch InBev, the leading multinational drink and brewing company based in Belgium, bought the Central Eastern European assets of SABMiller and a merger was concluded under the condition of the European Commission that SABMiller's all the CEE assets should be sold. It happened in 2017 when the Japanese Asahi Group Holdings bought up the Czech, Hungarian, Polish, Romanian and Slovakian factories, brands and export ventures for EUR 7.3 billion. The name of the new company from the 1st of April 2017 is Asahi Breweries Europe Ltd (ABEL), with its regional headquarters in Prague.

The above short story is not about the decreasing competitiveness and attractiveness of the CEE region, rather about SABMiller's changing company strategy. Its lucrative regional position has been sacrificed for further internationalisation and upgrading its global position.

The *Mondi Group (Mondi Flexibles)* is a global paper and package group originating from South Africa that operates manufacturing plants in the Czech Republic, Hungary, Poland and Slovakia with significant job creation effect (Kurtagic 2019) and offering full range of products.

The *Scitec Nutrition* originally was a Hungarian food supplement distributor for American products. In 2009, the Scitec manufacturing was established at Dunakeszi, near the Hungarian capital, producing sports food supplements. In 2012, the factory was bought by a financial investor, the Enterprise Investors, and was later sold to Ascendis Health, a South

[26] *Geograph Polska* is quarrying ornamental and building stone, limestone in Poland.

African company. The management is Hungarian; production, product development, research (Scitec Institute) and marketing are conducted in Hungary in close co-operation with the owner. The yearly revenue was HUF 22 billion in 2016/2018, the number of employees was above 500. The company exports its products to more than 90 countries and takes part in e-commerce via its newly opened web shop.

9.7 Summary

Since 1994, South Africa has successfully reintegrated into the world economy. By 2018, it has become the biggest African capital exporter with USD 4.5 billion outward FDI. Today, South Africa is among the top ten emerging investors.

The main carriers of outward FDI are South African multinationals that started their internationalisation earlier than other emerging markets' MNEs. Their investment decisions are mainly driven by home country push factors fuelled by the economic, social and political legacies of the apartheid regime. The main domestic constraints have to do with the size of the home market (slow and fluctuating GDP growth), the stratified nature of the demand, the rigid labour market, lack of skilled labour force, inflexibility in factor market, unreliable electricity supply, compliance with the Black Economic Empowerment requirements, HIV/AIDS, brain drain and the need for risk aversion deriving from uncertain economic and political climate in the country. These push factors lead to market- and efficiency-seeking strategies of South African MNEs, as operation outside of the country offers better opportunity to reduce costs and risks, and to increase productivity.

The geographical direction of South African outward FDI contradicts the so-called Uppsala model of internationalisation and the investment strategy and practice of the first and second waves of developing countries' investors, which tend to focus first on the neighbouring, ethnically similar countries and then moving further to more distant developed countries. By contrast, more than half of South African MNEs' outward FDI was directed to the European and EU markets (56% in 2013), 17.5% to North and South American markets, 16.2% to the Asian markets and only 8.2% into the neighbouring African countries.

South African investment decisions are affected by both push factors, negative and positive, and pull factors. The latter primarily concerns the recipient country's and/or region's political, structural macroeconomic, and national, regional and international institutional conditions. These factors provide a plethora of opportunities for market-, resource- and asset-seeking investors. South African outward FDI is carried out mostly by MNEs that participated in the privatisation wave of the 1990s. As the majority of investments is done via mergers and acquisitions, there are very few, almost none, greenfield investments. The biggest South African MNEs (like SABMiller, Naspers, Mondi, Bidvest, Nowaco, Pepco, Life Healthcare, NEPI Rockcastle) are active in more than one regional country, which suggests that South Africa considers the region as a single market. The most important destination is Poland, followed by the Czech Republic, Hungary and Romania.

As far as the sectoral preference of investors is concerned, South African companies clearly differ from Asian firms. While Asian investors show preference for manufacturing industries and the services sectors, South African companies target the real estate, retail trade, e-commerce, consumer goods and healthcare sectors.

To summarise, after the apartheid era ended and foreign sanctions no longer confined South African companies to the domestic market, they rapidly adapted and internationalised in the 1990s, especially because domestic markets are saturated, unreliable and deficient in key respects. As most of them are multinational companies, they fared better in this transition than others. Their successful pursuit of investment opportunities abroad has since been driven by a mixture of push and pull factors.

The CEE region is a newly emerging destination for South African investors. Investment flows are hectic, showing high volatility depending on actual transactions. This volatility is a function of South African investors' reluctance to plan for the long run due to geographical distance and the uncertainties in the home country. Many companies invest via third countries to take advantage of more favourable tax or regulatory treatment. Data from international (UNCTAD, OECD), South African and CEE (national) sources are rather contradictory and in most of the cases confidential. What is nonetheless clear is that South Africa invests more in the ECE region than the other way around.

References

Africa Investment Report 2017: Investing for Inclusive Growth. The Financial Times Ltd.

African Economic Outlook. (2015). AfDB, OECD, UNDP, Washington.

African Economic Outlook. (2017). Special Theme, Entrepreneurship and Industrialisation, 316 p. Retrieved from http://www.oecd-ilibrary.org/development/african-economic-outlook_19991029

African Economic Outlook. (2020). Retrieved from https://www.afdb.org/en/documents/african-economic-outlook-2020

Aron, J., Kahn, B., & Kingdon, G. (2009). South African Economic Policy under Democracy: Overview and Prospects. In J. Aron, B. Kahn, & G. Kingdon (Eds.), *South African Economic Policy under Democracy* (pp. 1–43). Oxford Scholarship Online.

Ashman, S., Fine, B., Padayachee, V., & Sender, J. (2014). The Political Economy of Restructuring in South Africa. In *The Oxford Companion to the Economics of South Africa*. Oxford Press Scholarship Online, Chap. 5.

Bezuidenhout, H., & Rensburg, J. V. (2016). *An Original Ranking of South Africa's Global Players for 2013–2015.* Potchefstroom and New York: School of Economics of the North West University and Columbia Center on Sustainable Investment, 35 p. Retrieved from http://ccsi.columbia.edu/files/2013/10/EMGP-South-Africa-Report-2016-FINAL.pdf

Bhorat, H., Hirsch, A., Kanbur, R., & Ncube, M. (2014). Economic Policy in South Africa—Past, Present and Future. In *The Oxford Companion to the Economics of South Africa* (pp. 1–36). Oxford Press Scholarship Online. Introduction.

Black, A. (2014). The Evolution and Impact of Foreign Direct Investment into South Africa Since 1994. In *The Oxford Companion to the Economics of South Africa*. Oxford Press Scholarship Online, Chap. 9.

De Beer, B. (2015). *South Africa's Experience with Capital Flows Since the Financial Crisis. From Measurement to Analysis.* Paper presented at the IFC Satellite Meeting during the 60th ISI conference, Rio de Janeiro.

Doing Business. (2020). Comparing Business Regulations in 190 Countries, World Bank Group, 2020, Washington, 149 p.

Economic Freedom of the World. (2019). Annual Report. Retrieved January 30, 2020, from https://www.fraserinstitute.org/studies/economic-freedom-of-the-world-2019-annual-report

Edwards, L. (2014). Trade Policy Reform in South Africa. In *The Oxford Companion to the Economics of South Africa*. Oxford Press Scholarship Online, Chap. 1.

Edwards, L., Cassim, R., & Seventer, D. v. (2009). Trade Policy in South Africa. In J. Aron, B. Kahn, & G. Kingdon (Eds.), *South African Economic Policy under Democracy* (pp. 1–53). Oxford Scholarship Online, Chap. 6.

Evans, M. (2019). M&A Deal Value Down in South Africa in 2018 but Improvement is Expected in 2019. Retrieved from https://www.bakermckenzie.com/en/newsroom/2019/01/south-africa-global-transactions-forecast

Extreme digital. (2019, March 21). eMAG to Merge. *Budapest Business Journal.*

Forbes. (2019). Óriási üzlet a magyar e-kereskedelemben: összeolvad az eMAG és az Extreme Digital. *Forbes*, 21 March.

Foy, H. (2016). Wave of Investors Hunts for Returns in Central and Eastern Europe. *Financial Times*, April 12.

Gelb, S. (2010). *Foreign Direct Investment Links between South Africa and China.* Johannesburg: The EDGE Institute, 63 p.

Gelb, S., & Black, A. (2004). Foreign Direct Investment in South Africa. In S. Estrin & K. E. Meyer (Eds.), *Investment Strategies in Emerging Markets* (pp. 177–212). Cheltenham, UK: Edgar Elgar.

Glass Half Full, The 2017 A. T. Kearney Foreign Direct Investment Confidence Index.

Global Competitiveness Report. (2019). World Economic Forum, 666 pp.

Harper, J. (2016). South African investors shift focus onto Central and Eastern Europe real estate, Financial Observer.eu.

Hillis, K. (2020). South African Capital Continues to Court Central and Eastern Europe. *CEE Legal Matters*, 20 January. Retrieved from https://ceelegalmatters.com/legal-markets/12331-south-african-capital-continues-to-court-central-and-eastern-europe

Investment Policy Monitor, UNCTAD, Various Issues.

Investment Trend Monitor, UNCTAD Various Issues.

Jordaan, J. (2017). Out of Africa. South African Capital in CEE, Mondaq. Retrieved from http://www.mondaq.com/southafrica/x/641238/Fund+Management+REITs/Out+of+Africa+South+African+capital+in+CEE

Kiss, J. (2017). *South Africa—A Re-emerging Player in Outward FDI.* IWE Working Papers 235. Institute for World Economics.

Kugiel, P. (Ed.). (2016). *V4 Goes Global: Exploring Opportunities and Obstacles in the Visegrad Countries' Co-operation with Brazil, India, China and South Africa.* The Polish Institute of International Affairs, Warsaw, 85 p.

Kurtagic, D. (2019). *Central and Eastern Europe and Sub-Saharan Africa. The Potential of Investment Partnership for Mutual Benefit.* Research Paper, Africa Programme, October 2019, Chatham House, The Royal Institute of International Affairs.

Leape, J., & Thomas, L. (2009). Capital Flows, Financial Markets, and the External Balance Sheet. In J. Aron, B. Kahn, & G. Kingdon (Eds.), *South*

African Economic Policy under Democracy (pp. 1–49). Oxford Scholarship Online, Chap. 5.

Lundahl, M., & Petersson, L. (2013). Post-apartheid South Africa: An Economic Success Story? In: A. K. Fosu (Ed.), *Achieving Development Success: Strategies and Lessons from the Developing World*. Oxford Scholarship Online, 1–32 pp.

Magyar portól izmosodik a világ (The world is muscled by Hungarian food supplement). Retrieved from https://index.hu/gazdasag/2020/01/07/taplalek_kiegeszitok_scitec_biotech_usa_protein_feherje_testepites_sport/

Manuel, T. (2014). Twenty Years of Economic Policymaking—Putting People First. In *The Oxford Companion to the Economics of South Africa*. Oxford press Scholarship Online, Chap. 1.

Manyuchi, A. E., & Mugabe, J. O. (2018). Public Policies and Institutions Influencing South Africa's Outward Foreign Direct Investment. *Politikon, 45*(2), 261–275.

Miller, T., Kim, A. B., & Roberts, J. M. (2020). *2019 Index of Economic Freedom* (25th Anniversary ed.). Washington: Heritage Foundation, 496 pp. Retrieved from https://www.heritage.org/index/pdf/2019/book/index_2019.pdf

Mundy, T. (2018). Where next for South African Investors? JLL Investor, 22 August, 2018. Retrieved January 2020, from https://www.theinvestor.jll/news/south-africa/others/where-next-for-south-african-investors/

National Development Plan 2030, Our future—make it work, Executive Summary, National Planning Commission, South Africa.

North, D. (1990). Institutions, Institutional Change and Economic Performance. Cambridge: Cambridge University Press.

OECD Economic Surveys, South Africa, July 2017, OECD. Retrieved from http://www.oecd.org/eco/surveys/economic-survey-south-africa.htm

OECD Foreign Direct Investment Statistics. Explanatory Notes. Retrieved January 2020, from https://www.oecd.org/daf/inv/FDI-statistics-explanatory-notes.pdf

Orosz, Á. (2017). A multinacionális vállalatok szerepe szubszaharai Afrikában. In Z. Biedermann & J. Kiss (Eds.), *Szubszaharai Afrika gazdasága a 21. században* (pp. 204–233). Budapest: Akadémiai Kiadó.

Pereira, J. R., & Stephenson, M. (2018). *Outward FDI from Developing Countries*. Global Competitiveness Report, 2017/2018, pp. 1–34.

Rankin, N. (2014). Investment Climate. In *The Oxford Companion to the Economics of South Africa*. Oxford Press Scholarship Online, Chap. 23.

Ricz, J. (2017). A dél-afrikai fejlesztő állam kudarca. In Z. Biedermann & J. Kiss (Eds.), *Szubszaharai Afrika gazdasága a 21. században* (pp. 273–289). Budapest: Akadémiai Kiadó.

SA, Poland Sign Co-operation Agreement. Retrieved from https://www.brandsouthafrica.com/investments-immigration/international-news/poland-181013b

Shah, S. (2019). South African Companies Look to emerging Europe for Growth. Retrieved from https://emerging-europe.com/business/south-african-companies-look-to-emerging-europe-for-growth/

Smit, B. (2015). Macroeconomic Scenarios for South Africa: 2013–2025. In *The Oxford Companion to the Economics of South Africa.* Oxford Press Scholarship Online, Chap. 3.

Spotlight on SA REITs and Global Real Estate Market. Retrieved January 2018 from https://www.fin24.com/Money/Property/spotlight-on-sa-reits-and-global-real-estate-market-20180312

Sulaiman, S., & Abdullatief, A. (2020). The Main Pull Factors for South African Investors in Central and Eastern Europe. *CEE Legal Matters Magazine*, 6 January. Retrieved January 2020, from https://ceelegalmatters.com/legal-markets/12333-the-main-pull-factors-for-south-african-investors-in-central-and-eastern-europe

Szunomár, Á. (2018). *Pull factors of Chinese FDI in East Central Europe, Institute of World Economics.* Centre for Economic and Regional Studies, Hungarian Academy of Sciences, 25 pp. IWE Working Papers, 249.

Tarrósy, I. (2014). South African brands find market in Central Europe. Retrieved from https://moguldom.com/65423/south-africa-invests-central-europe/

The DTI (Department of Trade and Industry) Annual Report 2018/2019. 2019. Republic of South Africa, 310 pp.

Verhoef, G. (2016). *Latecomer Challenge. African Multinationals from the Periphery.* ERSA (Economic Research Southern Africa) Working Paper 570, 29 p. Retrieved January 2020, from https://www.econrsa.org/system/files/publications/working_papers/working_paper_570.pdf

Wentworth, L., Schoeman, M., & Langalanga, A. (2014). Foreign Direct Investment and Inclusive Growth in Southern Africa. Economic Diplomacy Programme—SA Institute of International Affairs, Cape Town University, 18 p.

World Investment Report (WIR), 2019. UNCTAD, Various Issues.

CHAPTER 10

Final Reflections: Emerging Market Multinational Enterprises in East Central Europe

Ágnes Szunomár, Tamás Gerőcs, Judit Kiss, Tamás Peragovics, Judit Ricz, Miklós Szanyi, Tamás Szigetvári, Katalin Völgyi, and Csaba Weiner

Although the current status of East Central European (ECE) countries in the process and level of their integration into global business varies, a rather general phenomenon is the exhaustion of the foreign direct investment (FDI)-led development model, at least its dominant version of the

Á. Szunomár (✉) • J. Ricz
Institute of World Economics, Centre for Economic and Regional Studies, Budapest, Hungary

Institute of International, Political, and Regional Sciences, Corvinus University of Budapest, Budapest, Hungary
e-mail: szunomar.agnes@krtk.mta.hu

T. Gerőcs • J. Kiss • T. Peragovics • M. Szanyi • T. Szigetvári • K. Völgyi • C. Weiner
Institute of World Economics, Centre for Economic and Regional Studies, Budapest, Hungary
e-mail: szigetvari.tamas@krtk.mta.hu; volgyi.katalin@krtk.mta.hu; weiner.csaba@krtk.mta.hu

Á. Szunomár (ed.), *Emerging-market Multinational Enterprises in East Central Europe*, Studies in Economic Transition,
https://doi.org/10.1007/978-3-030-55165-0_10

1990s and early 2000s. On the one hand, this is a result of multinational affiliates' isolated and strongly integrated presence in a strictly designed international cooperation system with no physical contact with local firms to deliver spillovers. On the other hand, even those affiliates that are entangled in the development of local supplier networks deliver spillovers only to a limited level. As a consequence, they are not becoming primary players of innovative local business clusters, while the design of affiliates' activity range is usually specialized on low value-added segments of global value chains (GVC).

One can observe changes in the perception of multinational business in the ECE region as a result of the slowing down of economic progress based on the FDI-led economic model, increasing dependency on and the rather disadvantageous changes in the institutional frames of global business conduct. FDI attraction remained an important policy target; however, some governments applied investment incentives on selective basis and differentiated among "good" and "bad" investments. Hungary and Poland, for instance, continued the support of manufacturing investments but made efforts to limit the strong multinational influence in some sectors. The Hungarian government also signed strategic cooperation agreements with many of the largest and most important multinational companies and initiated an Eastern as well as a Southern opening policy to diversify its economic relations and to attract non-EU investors. As regards attraction policies, OECD's FDI Regulatory Restrictiveness indices show that advantageous investment conditions remained in place in the ECE countries.

It seems that the ECE region will continuously rely on the primary role of multinational business, but the governments will use investment attraction policies more selectively. There will be further efforts to strengthen the locally owned companies to access multinational companies' GVCs. Also, more intensive direct state intervention occurs in specific markets. The support of local big business and bourgeoisie will be another main target of economic policies. This should counterbalance the asymmetric dependence on global business and provide new impetus for economic progress.

When it comes to emerging market multinational enterprises (EMNEs), their role as a global investor has grown rapidly in recent decades. Although the majority of these companies target their neighbouring regions, mainly developing countries, their presence in the more developed regions, including Europe, became more visible in the past two decades. Although EMNEs' economic impact on ECE countries is still relatively small, it has accelerated significantly in the past two decades since ECE countries have become more open to new business opportunities, especially after the global economic and financial crisis of 2008, with the intention of decreasing their economic dependency on Western (European) markets. At the same time, as mentioned above, ECE's appetite for investment has not been saturated yet.

China has pursued both proactive and interventionist strategies at the same time to promote the international expansion of Chinese companies in various sectors. The prominent role of the state in initiating and intervening in corporate capital outflows seems to be a distinctive element in the behaviour of Chinese MNEs when compared to multinational corporations of developed countries. While based on Chinese as well as international statistics, Asia continues to be the largest recipient of total Chinese outward FDI, accounting for nearly three quarters; however, according to project-level analysis, 60 per cent of Chinese outward FDI is aimed at developed economies, including the EU.

Chinese investment in ECE countries constitutes a small share in China's total FDI stock, even if compared to Chinese total FDI stock in Europe, and is quite a new phenomenon. Nevertheless, Chinese FDI in the ECE region is on the rise and may increase further as a result of Chinese initiatives such as the 17+1 cooperation and the Belt and Road project. Chinese companies target telecommunication, electronics, chemical industry and transportation in the ECE region and often use intermediary countries and companies for their investments. The analysis of the motivations behind Chinese outward FDI in ECE shows that Chinese MNEs mostly search for markets. ECE countries' EU membership allows them to treat the region as a "back door" to the affluent EU markets; moreover, Chinese investors are attracted by the relatively low labour costs, skilled workforce and market potential. It is characteristic that their investment patterns in terms of country location resemble that of the world's total FDI in the region. However, macroeconomic or structural factors do not fully explain the decisions behind Chinese FDI in the ECE region. This indicates that institutional factors—supranational as well as national level—may be crucial for Chinese companies when deciding on investment locations. Moreover, a causal link seems to exist between the level of political relations and the amount of Chinese investment in ECE countries; that is, good political relations between the respective host country and China seem to play an important role in attracting investment from Chinese state-owned as well as private companies.

The driving force for Indian companies to internationalize is to improve their competitiveness by accessing advanced technologies which they can build into their home-based production systems. Consequently, about two-thirds of Indian outward FDI went to developed Western countries, mostly notably to the EU, including the ECE region, while only the remaining third was placed in developing countries. Indian outward FDI entering into ECE are indeed technology- and asset-seeking type of investments, as the ECE region is well embedded in German GVCs, hosting key manufacturing activities as lower-cost locations. The most important regional networks which Indian companies targeted are automotive, pharmaceutical, IT and BPO services. From these locations Indian multinationals are better able to access state of the art technologies which they can transfer back to their parent companies. ECE also serves as an entrance to the European Single Market. Many Indian companies relocate operations first here to gain experience, but when they obtained adequate knowledge and experience they might move forward to the core of the European market, using ECE as a gateway.

When it comes to the motivation of the other important Asian investors—South Korea, Taiwan, Malaysia, Thailand, Indonesia and Vietnam—in the ECE region, geographical distribution of outward FDI varies but is generally characterized by Asian orientation, which is often underpinned by governmental policy. Therefore, the EU—including ECE—is not among the primary regional destination for outward FDI. Despite the low shares of these countries in non-EU inward FDI in the EU, some of them—especially South Korea and Taiwan—are among the most important non-European FDI sources in the ECE region, while FDI from the four ASEAN countries are very small. Companies originated from the six Asian countries have been operating in several sectors of the ECE region, but the automotive and electronics industry are the most preferred ones. An analysis of the motivations and pull factors for the investments of those Asian companies (mainly South Korean and Taiwanese) operating in these two sectors shows that market- as well as efficiency-seeking motivations are most prominent. The main pull factors of the ECE countries are the access to the EU market, relatively low-cost production base, skilled labour, government incentives and relatively developed infrastructure. In addition, many components manufacturers of the six Asian countries have followed their customers investing in ECE; that is, the presence of large (South Korean or Taiwanese) manufacturing companies is also a significant pull factor.

Domestic push factors are also very important in driving Russian corporate decisions to invest abroad, including the state's role in directly promoting foreign expansion of both the largest Russian multinationals as well as private companies. Due to the specific features of Russian outward FDI—such as round-tripping and trans-shipping—and the lack of statistics referring to the ultimate host/investing country, the role of host countries is difficult to estimate. Nevertheless, Europe's leading role in Russian outward FDI remains unchallenged, though Europe's share has been falling. The five ECE countries are not among the main destinations, though Russian FDI in Czechia and Poland is far from being negligible. Nevertheless, company data demonstrate that the activities of Russian investors in ECE countries have been paved with failures. The low share of Russian investment in ECE countries may be referred to as business opportunities that the Russian parties have failed to exploit.

Russian investment in ECE countries is dominated by market-seeking and, to a lesser extent, efficiency-seeking projects carried out by state-owned and state-related private firms. Most Russian FDI has been done in hydrocarbons, iron, steel and machinery, but banking, software solutions, electronic production, real estate and even the light industry have also been targeted. When analysing the activities of Russian multinationals in ECE countries, we found only traces of acquiring competitive advantages or ownership advantages, while identified investment aiming at exploiting existing asset-based advantages. As for Russian firms' asset-based advantages, it is obvious that their access to domestic raw materials and related technical knowledge is very important for their investments in ECE countries, as investments in oil, gas and metals are predominant, while technology-based firms show characteristics similar to developed-country multinationals.

Turkey has also become one of the leading investors among emerging economies in its neighbouring regions in recent years. The rising presence of Turkish investments abroad is due to both economic and political reasons as the rapidly growing—and structurally changing—Turkish economy created a bunch of internationally competitive sectors and firms, while the changing Turkish foreign policy also promoted the active presence of Turkish companies in neighbouring countries. As statistics show, the majority of Turkish outward FDI went to European countries, but it is not concentrated solely in developed Western European countries, a lot of Turkish capital has flown to Eastern Europe and the Balkans.

When looking for the motivations of Turkish MNEs, one can find different reasons depending on the type of firms and the sectors they are active in. There are Turkish firms making resource-based investments, especially in Russia, in Central Asia and in the Middle East and North

African region but also in some ECE countries. Market-seeking is also a common motivation, and the Turkish MNEs are able to exploit their country-specific advantages: the experiences earned on the relatively competitive but institutionally underdeveloped Turkish domestic market. A continuously increasing motivation is brand-building and the upgrading of their technologies, in order to improve EU costumers' perceptions and attitudes towards their products and to be able to compete on more developed markets.

Brazilian outward FDI reveals a very concentrated pattern in terms of sectoral composition, mainly dominated by the extractive and commodities sectors, and also in terms of company size. There are, however, some outstanding examples in more technology-intensive sectors, such as the aviation industry and information technology. As regards push factors, government policies have actively—both directly and indirectly—influenced Brazilian companies' internationalization decisions, especially in the mid-2000s. Although the Brazilian going global policy was a more defensive and limited one compared to the Chinese strategy, when compared to some regional counterparts (such as Chile and Argentina), the proactivity of the Brazilian Development Bank stands out. When looking at host country determinants, the expansion of Brazilian firms seems still very much determined by geographical and cultural proximity and tax issues. Depending on the very specific cases and companies, the availability of natural resources, human capital and large host markets might play very different roles during the locational decisions. At the same time, due to their home country experiences, Brazilian firms tend to be highly resilient to macroeconomic or political instabilities and often less affected by institutional voids.

The ECE region does not represent any special emphasis in the internationalization strategies of Brazilian (or even Latin American) firms; on the contrary, there are only a few companies which are actively present in this region. Among the real driving forces of those few Brazilian companies which have successfully invested in the ECE region, diaspora, personal ties and/or informal relations, the relatively low labour costs, the presence of other Brazilian firms (agglomeration effect), the relatively high skilled labour force and a thriving local market can be mentioned. Even though the ECE region was by far not among the main destinations of the Brazilian outward investments, still some outstanding success stories can be found.

South African MNEs' internationalization had started earlier than other EMNEs. Their investment decisions are mainly driven by home country push factors fuelled by the economic, social and political legacies of the apartheid regime. The main domestic constraints have to do with—among others—the slow and fluctuating GDP growth, the stratified nature of the demand, the rigid labour market, lack of skilled labour force, inflexibility in factor market, brain drain and the need for risk aversion deriving from uncertain economic and political climate in the country. These push factors lead to market- and efficiency-seeking strategies of South African MNEs, as operation outside of the country offers better opportunity to reduce costs and risks and increase productivity. The geographical direction of South African outward FDI contradicts the so-called Uppsala model of internationalization that tends to focus on the neighbouring, ethnically similar, countries first and then moving further to more distant developed countries. By contrast, more than half of South African MNEs' outward FDI was directed towards the European markets.

Pull factors primarily concern the recipient country's political, macroeconomic and institutional conditions. These factors provide a plethora of opportunities for market-, resource- and asset-seeking companies. The ECE region is a newly emerging destination for South African investors, with the most important destinations being Poland, followed by the Czech Republic and Hungary. Investment flows are hectic, showing high volatility depending on actual transactions. This volatility is a function of South African investors' reluctance to plan for the long run due to geographical distance and the uncertainties in the home country. Many companies invest via third countries to take advantage of more favourable tax and regulatory treatment.

As presented in the pages above—as well as through the chapters of this volume—the rise of EMNEs is a new and dynamic process, while their approach towards their host economies are relatively unique compared either to the more developed MNEs or to each other. There are many differences in their internationalization strategies and major push and pull factors behind their localization decisions; however, one can also find several similarities, even when it comes to their presence in the ECE region.

As mentioned earlier, several types of push factors contribute to the internationalization of EMNEs. Among institutional push factors, both the home country diaspora and government policy seem to be important for the majority of EMNEs. Public policies to promote outward FDI came onto the development agenda for almost all emerging countries during the 1990s or the early 2000s. There are a number of public policy areas where the state can directly or indirectly influence the internationalization of EMNEs—labour policies, trade policies, privatization and taxation are just some of them. Nevertheless, when it comes to emerging markets, there are also explicit policy interventions that directly promote the international expansion of EMNEs. There is clear evidence for such direct intervention in the case of China, Russia, Brazil and Turkey in particular.

The ECE region is certainly not among the most important destinations of EMNEs' localization strategies but their outward FDI stock has increased in the past decades, particularly after 2004 and 2008: after the ECE countries' accession to the EU and the economic and financial crisis, respectively.

Majority of EMNEs are investing in ECE countries in order to enter new markets; thus market-seeking is the most prominent motivation for EMNEs. By entering ECE markets, EMNEs can not only avoid customs duties and non-tariff restrictions but also access the whole EU market as well as—through free trade agreements between the EU and third countries—even further markets throughout the world, in, for example, the Mediterranean, North America or the Commonwealth of Independent States. Efficiency-seeking motives, however, also play a role where the labour market is to be considered as one of the most important elements: a skilled labour force is available in sectors towards which most EMNEs' interest is growing, with labour costs being lower in ECE than the EU average. Agglomeration effect—when EMNEs from the same country increase their efficiency by locating close to each other—and demonstration effect—whereby EMNEs that have already invested in ECE send signals to new potential investors on the reliability and attractiveness of the host country—seem to be important, too. Corporate taxes and various tax incentives are among the further potential pull factors of ECE.

As far as the sectoral preference of EMNEs are concerned, majority of EMNEs show preference for manufacturing industries, especially in electronics, IT and automotive sector, while Russia (where investments in oil, gas and metals are predominant) and South Africa (where real estate, retail trade, e-commerce, consumer goods and healthcare sectors attract investors) seem to be exceptions.

In many cases EMNEs use firms located in other European countries—Luxembourg, the Netherlands, Switzerland, Cyprus, and so on—as the direct investor company. The reason for this can be tax optimization, the aim of decreasing bureaucratic burdens, the ability to hide their real origin or to nominate a regional headquarter. In some cases, EMNEs might use their investment strategy in other developing or transitional economies—that are located close to advanced markets—as a catch-up strategy to access technology, increase domestic capacity, upgrade production processes, boost competitiveness, augment managerial experience and access financial markets for their global aspirations. ECE may also serve as a springboard for EMNEs to the core EU markets. Through their presence in ECE, EMNEs can prove that they are capable of meeting EU standards, adapting to local regulations and competing with developed MNEs on developed markets.

As demonstrated in this volume, macroeconomic or structural factors do not entirely explain EMNEs' location decisions when investing in ECE: institutional factors—such as institutional stability, privatization opportunities, investment incentives and golden visas—also seem to be crucial for all of the analysed EMNEs. Moreover, personal connections and/or good political relations may also play a role.

When it comes to EMNEs' impact on the ECE region, it is difficult to evaluate the real effects as of now, since the phenomenon of EMNEs in ECE is rather new. However, so far it seems that EMNEs—especially those that are followed by their suppliers and service companies—do not contribute to the development of host country firms and do not generate, for example, locational advantages through their own activities. Majority of EMNEs indeed prefer to cooperate with companies from their home country. As a result, the chances for local enterprise development—for example, through linkages with suppliers—are little or at least limited. However, there are some exceptions, especially in the case of those companies that arrived several years ago. Consequently, there might be a potential for positive spillover effects after a certain period of time.

Annex

Questionnaire

For semi-structured interviews in the framework of the research project "Non-European emerging-market multinational enterprises in East Central Europe"

1. How and when was the company set up?
2. Has the company expanded in (ECE country) since then?
3. Why was this particular location in (ECE country) chosen?
4. Which factors influenced your company's investment decision? (e.g. market size, access to regional market, low-cost unskilled labour, availability and cost of skilled labour, strategic assets—e.g. brand, R+D capacity, EU membership)
5. Did government—or state-level relations—play a role in the company's investment decision?
6. Did the company use the services of the (ECE country)'s investment promotion agency before entering the (ECE country) market?
7. Do you have a strong link with Korean/Taiwanese/Thai/Malay/Indonesian/Vietnamese HQ (decision-making hierarchy)?
8. What is the main profile of the company?
9. Does the company carry on its different activities in-house or apply outsourcing?

Á. Szunomár (ed.), *Emerging-market Multinational Enterprises in East Central Europe*, Studies in Economic Transition,
https://doi.org/10.1007/978-3-030-55165-0

10. What kind of activities does the company outsource to other companies?
11. What kind of inputs does the company procure?
12. How many suppliers of inputs does the company have? Please identify some of them.
13. Where are your suppliers located (other ECE country or else)? How many of them are (ECE country) companies?
14. Is the company planning to increase the number of suppliers?
15. What kind of goods does the company produce?
16. Where does the company sell its final products (inland/abroad)?
17. How much percent of the final products are exported?
    Is the company planning to enter new markets?
18. How many employees does the company have?
19. Does the company recruit only local workers or organize recruitment in other parts of (ECE country) or abroad?
20. What percent of employees are from (ECE country)?
21. What is the extent to which company uses expatriate managers?
22. Does the company have any relations with (ECE country) higher education institutions?
23. Does the company organize local social events?
24. What is the company's annual sales?
25. How much tax does the company pay into the central budget and the local government's budget?
26. How important is the company for the local economy (tax revenue, employment, attraction of new investors)?

Index[1]

[1] Note: Page numbers followed by 'n' refer to notes

Á. Szunomár (ed.), *Emerging-market Multinational Enterprises in East Central Europe*, Studies in Economic Transition,
https://doi.org/10.1007/978-3-030-55165-0

The manufacturer's authorised representative in the EU is Springer Nature Customer Service Centre GmbH, Europaplatz 3, 69115 Heidelberg, Germany. If you have any concerns regarding our products, please contact ProductSafety@springernature.com

Printed and bound by CPI Group (UK) Ltd, Croydon, CR0 4YY
23/09/2026
02221528-0001